EARLY MODERN WOMEN'S MANUSCRIPT POETRY

Manchester University Press

Early modern women's manuscript poetry

edited by Jill Seal Millman and Gillian Wright
with contributing editors Victoria E. Burke and Marie-Louise Coolahan

with an introduction by Elizabeth Clarke and Jonathan Gibson

Manchester University Press

Copyright © Manchester University Press 2005

While copyright in the volume as a whole is vested in Manchester University Press, copyright in individual chapters belongs to their respective authors, and no chapter may be reproduced wholly or in part without the express permission in writing of both author and publisher.

Published by Manchester University Press
Oxford Road, Manchester M13 9NR, UK

www.manchesteruniversitypress.co.uk

British Library Cataloguing-in-Publication Data
A catalogue record for this book is available from the British Library

ISBN 0 7190 6916 5 *hardback*

ISBN 0 7190 6917 3 *paperback*

First published 2005

Designed in Adobe Garamond by Max Nettleton FCSD
Typeset by SNP Best-set Typesetter Ltd., Hong Kong

CONTENTS

List of plates—vii
Notes on contributors—viii
Acknowledgements—ix
Abbreviations—x

Introduction *Elizabeth Clarke and Jonathan Gibson*—1
Textual introduction *Jill Seal Millman and Gillian Wright*—11

1 Jane Seager's translations of the ten sibyls' prophecies of the birth of Christ
British Library Additional MS 10037
❧ 15 ❧

2 Mary Sidney's psalm paraphrases
British Library Additional MS 12047
❧ 21 ❧

3 Lady Mary Wroth, *Pamphilia to Amphilanthus*
Folger Shakespeare Library MS V.a.104
❧ 35 ❧

4 Anne Southwell's poetry
Folger Shakespeare Library MS V.b.198, British Library Lansdowne MS 740
❧ 57 ❧

5 Anna Ley's posthumously collected writings
William Andrews Clark Memorial Library MS L6815 M3 C734
❧ 77 ❧

6 Presentation volume of Jane Cavendish's poetry
Yale University, Beinecke Library Osborn MS b. 233
❧ 87 ❧

7 Lucy Hutchinson's 'Elegies'
Nottinghamshire Archives, DD/HU2
❧ 97 ❧

8 Hester Pulter's 'Poems Breathed forth By The Nobel Hadassas'
Leeds University Library, Brotherton Collection MS Lt q 32
❧ 111 ❧

9 Presentation volume of Katherine Philips's verse
National Library of Wales MS 776B
❧ 128 ❧

10 Mary Roper?'s 'The Sacred Historie'
Leeds University Library, Brotherton Collection MS Lt q 2
❦ 153 ❦

11 Julia Palmer's 'Centuries' of devotional verse
William Andrews Clark Memorial Library, MS P1745 M1 P744
1671–3 Bound
❦ 169 ❦

12 Mary Astell's presentation manuscript for Archbishop Sancroft
Bodleian Library MS Rawlinson poet. 154
❦ 182 ❦

13 Marie Burghope's country house poem, 'The Vision'
Huntington Library MS EL 35/B/62
❦ 194 ❦

14 Octavia Walsh's verse miscellany
Bodleian Library MS Eng. poet. e. 31
❦ 215 ❦

Interpretative notes—229
Select bibliography—269
Index of poetry titles and first lines—277

PLATES

PLATE 1—16
Jane Seager, British Library Additional MS 10037, fols 2v–3r
(reproduced by permission of the British Library)

PLATE 2—20
Mary Sidney, British Library Additional MS 12047, fol. 58v
(reproduced by permission of the British Library)

PLATE 3—58
Anne Southwell, British Library Lansdowne MS 740, fol. 158v
(reproduced by permission of the British Library)

PLATES 4 AND 5—78, 79
Anna Ley, William Andrews Clark Memorial Library
MS L6815 M3 C734, fols 92v and 139r
(reproduced by permission of the Clark Library)

PLATE 6—96
Lucy Hutchinson, Nottinghamshire Archives, DD/HU2, pp. xxii–xxiii
(reproduced by permission of Mrs Hugh Priestley and the Principal
Archivist of the Nottinghamshire Archives)

PLATE 7—110
Hester Pulter, Leeds University Library, Brotherton Collection
MS Lt q 32, fol. 100v
(reproduced with the permission of the Brotherton Collection
at Leeds University Library)

PLATE 8—154
Mary Roper?, Leeds University Library, Brotherton Collection
MS LT q 2, pp. 157–8
(reproduced with the permission of the Brotherton Collection
at Leeds University Library)

PLATE 9—214
Octavia Walsh, Bodleian Library MS Eng. poet. e.31, fol. 161v
(reproduced by permission of the Bodleian Library, University of Oxford)

NOTES ON CONTRIBUTORS

Victoria E. Burke is Associate Professor of English at the University of Ottawa. Her published articles on women and manuscript culture include those in *The Seventeenth Century*, *English Manuscript Studies*, *The Library* and *The Yearbook of English Studies*. She is the co-editor (with Elizabeth Clarke) of *The 'Centuries' of Julia Palmer* (Trent Editions, 2001).

Elizabeth Clarke is Reader in English at the University of Warwick, and the director of the Perdita Project. She is the author of *Theory and Theology in George Herbert's Poetry* (Oxford University Press, 1997) and co-editor with Danielle Clarke of *'This Double Voice': Gendered Writing in Early Modern England* (Macmillan, 2000).

Marie-Louise Coolahan is a lecturer at the English Department, National University of Ireland, Galway. She works with the Perdita Project (Nottingham Trent and Warwick Universities) on women's manuscripts in the sixteenth and seventeenth centuries. She is currently working on a study of women's writing practices in early modern Ireland.

Jonathan Gibson works at the English Subject Centre (Royal Holloway, University of London). He previously worked for the Perdita Project and has held lectureships at the Universities of Exeter and Durham and at Queen Mary, University of London. His publications include articles on Renaissance topics in *The Review of English Studies* and *The Seventeenth Century*. He has co-edited *Early Modern Women's Manuscript Writing: Selected Papers from the Trinity/Trent Colloquium* (Ashgate, 2004) with Victoria E. Burke.

Jill Seal Millman is a research fellow on the Perdita Project at the University of Warwick, having worked for the project at Nottingham Trent University. She has published articles on humanities computing, psalm translation and women's manuscript poetry, and is working on an edition of Alice Thornton's 'Book of Remembrances' for publication with Trent Editions.

Gillian Wright is a lecturer in English Literature at the University of Birmingham, and a former visiting research fellow at the Institute of English Studies, London. She has published articles on women's writing, Samuel Daniel and the history of translation, and is currently collaborating with Mary Morrissey of Nottingham Trent University on a study of early modern women's devotional manuscripts.

ACKNOWLEDGEMENTS

This book would not have been possible without the generosity of many people and institutions. For permission to reproduce texts and photographs we are grateful to the British Library, London; the Bodleian Library, University of Oxford; the Brotherton Collection at Leeds University Library; the National Library of Wales, Aberystwyth; the William Andrews Clark Memorial Library, Los Angeles; the Folger Shakespeare Library, Washington; the Huntington Library, San Marino, California; and the James M. and Marie-Louise Osborn Collection, Beinecke Rare Book and Manuscript Library, Yale University. Nottinghamshire Archives DD/HU2 (Lucy Hutchinson's Elegies) is the copyright of the Hutchinson family, for which Mrs Hugh Priestley and the Principal Archivist of Nottinghamshire Archives give permission to reproduce extracts. Marie Burghope's 'The Vision' is included by kind permission of His Grace the Duke of Sutherland.

Thanks are due to all the librarians who have answered our queries and facilitated our research in innumerable ways. We are especially grateful to Oliver Pickering of the Brotherton Library, for his help with the Roper manuscript, and to Frances Harris of the British Library, who has been a generous and knowledgeable adviser to us over several years.

Victoria Burke's edition of Julia Palmer's poetry in this volume adapts material which first appeared in *The 'Centuries' of Julia Palmer*, ed. Victoria E. Burke and Elizabeth Clarke, under the Trent Editions imprint in 2001. We are indebted to Professor R. J. Ellis on behalf of Trent Editions for permission to reproduce this material in slightly altered form. We are also deeply obliged to the Arts and Humanities Research Board, which has supported the Perdita Project since 1999.

Particular thanks are due to Martyn Bennett, for help with the Civil Wars background to the Roper and Hutchinson sections, and to David Norbrook for advice on Lucy Hutchinson. Robert Wilcher, Sarah Hutton and especially Jayne Archer provided essential information for glossing the political, scientific and alchemical allusions in Hester Pulter's poetry. Robert Cummings gave advice on Octavia Walsh's classical references.

The biographical note on Hester Pulter is adapted from Sarah Ross's unpublished doctoral thesis. We would like to thank Sarah for generously granting us permission to use this material.

Mary Morrissey has provided unobtrusive but vital support throughout the last few months of work on this anthology. Mike Millman's practical assistance has been invaluable. Kathleen Taylor valiantly proof-read the entire typescript of the anthology and has also been an unfailing source of advice and encouragement.

Finally, we would like to express our sincere gratitude to our editorial team at Manchester University Press. Their belief in our project, their understanding and patience through the process of completion, and their willingness to tolerate a dauntingly complex typescript are all deeply appreciated.

Any faults which remain are our own responsibility.

ABBREVIATIONS

b.	born
BL	British Library
CSPD	*Calendar of State Papers Domestic*
d.	died
DNB	*Dictionary of National Biography*
fol.	folio
fols	folios
n.	note
NLW	National Library of Wales, Aberystwyth
n.p.	no place of publication
OED	*Oxford English Dictionary* (second edition)
r	recto
rev.	reversed
sig.	signature
Summary Catalogue	*Summary Catalogue of Post-Medieval Western Manuscripts in the Bodleian Library, Oxford*
Tilley	Tilley, Morris Palmer (1950), *A Dictionary of the Proverbs in England in the Sixteenth and Seventeenth Centuries*
v	verso
VCH	*Victoria County History*

INTRODUCTION

This volume presents for scrutiny some intriguing examples of a literary phenomenon that has until recently been hidden from view—early modern women's manuscript poetry. The texts have been edited by six researchers connected to the Perdita Project, a research initiative which since 1997 has been compiling a catalogue of prose and verse manuscripts put together by sixteenth- and seventeenth-century women.[1] The project has been driven by the conviction that printed works by women between 1500 and 1700, on which most teaching, and attempts at early modern women's literary history, have tended to be based, represent the efforts of a minority of early modern women writers: a greater volume of writing activity took place in manuscript. Convinced that the gender ideology of the period inhibited the publication of women's writing in print, but not necessarily women's writing *per se*, the Perdita team set out to find, in manuscript, writing practices more fully representative of early modern women.

The importance of manuscript writing in the sixteenth and seventeenth centuries can hardly be over-emphasised. Many early modern writers of both sexes were reluctant to use print publication to distribute their work, preferring to write solely in manuscript, sometimes allowing or encouraging their work to circulate widely, sometimes drastically limiting its dissemination. Print publication by women in particular (especially of original non-religious works) was often held up to scorn—for example in the famous case of Margaret Cavendish, Duchess of Newcastle—manuscript circulation being considered more respectable.[2] In general, texts written in manuscript enjoyed at least as much and often far more prestige with their early modern readers than printed books.

For many years early modern manuscripts tended to be looked at by critics only when they contained texts by major authors. Since the mid-1980s, however, an exciting awakening of interest has developed, both in individual sixteenth- and seventeenth-century manuscripts and in the phenomenon of 'manuscript culture' as a whole. Articles in the journal *English Manuscript Studies 1100–1700* and books by Peter Beal (1980, 1998), Mary Hobbs (1992), Harold Love (1993), Arthur Marotti (1995), H.R. Woudhuysen (1996), Steven W. May (1991) and Margaret Ezell (1987, 1993, 1999) have vividly highlighted the important part played by manuscript culture in early modern England, especially among the elite. Ezell's work is particularly germane to the aims of this anthology, as it has conclusively shown that the failure of twentieth-century critics to treat manuscripts with the seriousness they deserve has fatally distorted our understanding of early modern women's writing: 'If all that is known is a list of women who published their works [in print]', Ezell argues, 'we do not really know who the women writers of the seventeenth century were or how and why they wrote' (Ezell 1987, 64). Our aim in this volume is to help carry out Ezell's programme by drawing attention to some of the ways in which early modern English women used poetry in their manuscript writing.[3]

Much recent criticism, whilst recognising the importance of the actions and choices of individual writers, nevertheless lays considerable stress on the complexly mediated nature of authorial 'agency'. This practice draws attention to the often very complicated roles both of the writer and of other people immediately implicated in the moment(s) of textual composition and construction: addressees, patrons, members of coteries, printers, scribes, editors and so on.[4] Reflecting this approach, our aim here has been to emphasise the importance of the manuscripts themselves—the material artefacts in which the poetry is present—at least as much as their absent authors. Thus the headnotes to each selection of poems supplement biographical information about the author with physical information about the manuscript and suggestions about its origin and readership.[5] Our texts are unmodernised, and textual notes—rather more detailed than in most other books of this type—register finicky details such as deletions, alterations, illegible words and differences from variant texts of the poems in other manuscripts or in printed books. The anthology has been put together in this unusual way to highlight and explore the complicated details of women's involvement in manuscript culture. Throughout, our aim has been to heighten readers' appreciation of the varied and complex functions of manuscript poetry in the period.

Verse by women appears scattered through many different types of early modern manuscript, popping up in all sorts of places—sprinkled throughout miscellanies, scribbled on the back of legal documents and so on. Much of this poetry is intriguing and well worth reading.[6] We have, though, made selections for this book only from manuscripts which contain a significant amount of verse by a single female author—manuscripts, that is, which present the reader with a relatively clear overview of the work of a single poet and which thus allow both the author herself and the contexts of her poetry to come into focus. All the women in this anthology have a known personal history of some sort, and for most of them there is some evidence outside the manuscripts represented here that indicates their practice as authors.

We have included substantial selections of each woman's poetry, in some cases because there is no reproduction of the texts in the public domain. For other poets, such as Katherine Philips, there are at present few anthologies which offer substantial selections. We hope that the resulting anthology, with its variety of writers from different social classes and religious and political affiliations, will appeal both to students and to seasoned academics, forming a useful staging-post for courses on early modern women's writing, courses on early modern manuscript culture and courses on early modern culture in general.

As well as introducing to a modern public the poems of some very little-known women, this anthology illustrates ways in which the study of well-known women authors can be deepened and made more valuable by consideration of the medium in which they primarily wrote. Thus, we have included texts of Mary Sidney's psalm translations from a manuscript transcription owned by Sir John Harington, a contemporary of hers who translated psalms himself. The section on Mary Wroth's poetry emphasises the striking differences between the familiar printed text of *Pamphilia to Amphilanthus* and the little-studied manuscript version, providing a new context for her poetry that has been largely ignored by critics and hidden from modern-day readers. Katherine Philips's poems, meanwhile, are given in texts taken from a manuscript put together after Philips's death as part of the contemporary drive to consolidate her reputation.

The relationship between print publication and manuscript circulation in the early modern period was complex, and it is significant that controversy and ambiguity currently surround the attitudes of Sidney, Wroth and Philips towards print publication. Wroth's long romance *Urania* was heavily criticised on its printing in 1621 by Sir Edward Denny, who attacked Wroth in letters and in a poem which Wroth answered in kind (Wroth 1992, 32–5). The assumption of most recent critics that Wroth withdrew the book as a result of Denny's complaints, is, it has recently been argued, wrong.[7] Instead, Rosalind Smith suggests, Wroth merely offered to withdraw *Urania*, but did not in fact do so (Smith 2000). Nevertheless, the second part of the *Urania* never appeared in print, and survives only in manuscript. In a poem included in this anthology, Katherine Philips, meanwhile, claims that the 1664 edition of her poems had been printed against her will, dragging her 'Muse' from its 'private shade' 'maliciously into the Light' ('To my Lord Arch-Bishop of Canterbury his Grace', lines 1, 8). Some critics, however, treat her complaint as disingenuous and argue that she deliberately orchestrated her move into print.[8] Mary Sidney arranged for the printing of some of her own works as well as the writings of her brother Philip. Yet she circulated her major work—the Sidney psalms—in manuscript only, an apparently anomalous state of affairs that has been recently analysed in articles by Margaret P. Hannay (2002) and by Debra Rienstra and Noel Kinnamon (2002).

Daily occupations—daily work—set the framework for the involvement of both women and men in manuscript writing. While many men's manuscripts were connected with their compilers' professional careers (two particularly important fields being the law and the church) and with political debate, most women's manuscripts formed part of their work as wives and mothers.[9] As part of their housewifely duties, women were encouraged to write account books, recipe books and letters. Associated by all denominations—both Catholic and Protestant—with intense piety, women were also encouraged to write devotional texts, such as notes on sermons, prayers, spiritual journals and collections of religious meditations in prose and verse.[10] Religious poetry, of many different kinds, was written by nearly all the women included in this anthology. Potentially sinful secular genres such as love poetry were often excoriated (by both men and women) as forms inappropriate for women writers. Despite this, women did write love poems, sometimes, alongside male courtiers, within the context of the royal court.[11]

Excluded from male grammar school education, with its heavy emphasis on Latin literary composition, a good number of early modern women nevertheless managed to gain a grounding in classical literature. A significant minority of sixteenth-century girls, including the future Queen Elizabeth I, became, through private tuition, highly educated humanists, a trend which faded out in the seventeenth century under pressure from increasingly dominant ideals of elegant, 'feminine' behaviour. The composition of original poetry in English was not a priority for sixteenth-century humanist women, whose manuscript texts consist mainly of translations of classical and patristic writings and of occasional verse in Latin and Greek. Seventeenth-century women wrote many more English poems—hence the marked bias of this anthology towards the seventeenth century.[12] Throughout the period covered in this anthology, literacy levels, among both men and women, rose dramatically, leading to the production of manuscript texts by women who would previously have not written anything at all.[13]

The texts in this anthology span more than a hundred years, a reflection of the continuing importance of manuscript culture throughout the seventeenth century.[14] The poetry in this book therefore belongs to many different cultural and political contexts, both 'conservative' and 'subversive'. Stylistically, it ranges from Julia Palmer's plainness through Mary Wroth's complex, backward-looking Jacobean Petrarchism (a throwback to the Elizabethan sonnet vogue) and Mary Sidney's eloquent psalm translations, to the elegantly witty late seventeenth- and early eighteenth-century writings of Octavia Walsh and Mary Astell. The political and religious contexts are equally varied. Jane Seager's manuscript was presented to Elizabeth I shortly after the defeat of the Spanish Armada. Mary Wroth's apparently apolitical *Pamphilia to Amphilanthus* has recently been read, by Rosalind Smith, as a militantly Protestant rebuke to James I, and the work of Wroth's godmother Mary Sidney is written from a similar politico-religious perspective. The manuscripts of Anne Southwell and Anna Ley both engage with the religious controversies of the early to mid-seventeenth century, at the height of the dispute between 'puritans' and Catholic-leaning 'Arminians'. Ley's texts support the monarchy's Arminianism, whilst Southwell's (which quote from the Calvinist Geneva Bible) belong to a far more 'puritan' context. The English Civil Wars cast a shadow across the poetry of many of the authors in this book. In two manuscripts, Jane Cavendish's and Hester Pulter's, female royalists use manuscript culture as a means of confronting defeat and despair in the 1640s and 1650s. Cavendish's poems constantly forge connections between people, pre-eminently between herself and her absent father, to build up a sort of fictive community, while Pulter uses an extraordinarily impressive array of literary devices to ponder her political and personal isolation. The poetry of the royalist Katherine Philips, much of it written during the Commonwealth period, conjures up (like Cavendish's) an idealised but biographically based paper community, constructed by Philips according to an elevated, neoplatonic view of friendship. Philips consolidated her large contemporary reputation in the early years of Charles II's reign, the period in which the republican writer Lucy Hutchinson wrote her elegies on the death in prison of her husband, John Hutchinson. Two religious manuscripts dating from the reign of Charles II belong to diametrically opposed religious contexts. Julia Palmer's poetry is the work of a nonconformist, whilst Mary Roper's manuscript, dedicated to Charles's Catholic Queen, Catherine de Braganza, contains royalist verse. Two manuscripts from the end of our period illustrate the conflict between Whigs (who favoured limiting the powers of the monarchy) and Tories (who believed in passive obedience to royal authority). Mary Astell's dedication of her poetry to Archbishop William Sancroft is the first documentary evidence of her lifelong commitment to Tory principles. Octavia Walsh, on the other hand, had family connections with the post-revolutionary Whig party.

The juxtaposition in this volume of well-known poets, such as Mary Wroth and Katherine Philips, with women who are currently largely unknown to the academic community throws up interesting areas of comparison: Philips can be compared with Hester Pulter, whose fate as an isolated royalist woman poet Philips should have shared; Wroth, meanwhile, can be compared with Anne, Lady

Southwell, who made very different choices in writing from the fringes of the Jacobean court. In many cases, of course, the imperative is not to relate one woman's writing to another's—geographical and period location is so disparate that it is hard to begin talking of a female tradition, and by definition most of this work never saw the dissemination that print allows—but to place it in the context of discourses circulating in that woman's place and time. Hester Pulter's royalist poetry, for example, is informed by much of the writing of the 1640s and early 1650s, possibly including Andrew Marvell's poems, which she would have had to see in manuscript. A consideration of the pamphlet gender debate of the early seventeenth century, in which both women and men participated, would be a very interesting context for the study of Anne Southwell's poetry (Clarke 2002).

The manuscripts included in this anthology are of a number of different types. Many are formal presentation manuscripts, written out fair in italic (sometimes by a scribe) and presented as gifts, by the author or by someone else, to a variety of people: important strangers, long-established patrons, senior family figures. As the texts included in this book by Seager, Southwell, Philips, Cavendish, Roper, Astell and Burghope show, presentation manuscripts could perform many different functions. Margaret Ezell has argued that the composition of manuscripts of this type implies a willingness to make writings public, and thus undercuts the longstanding assumption that early modern women's writing was predominantly a 'private' affair, composed for a very limited audience if any audience at all.[15] Presentation manuscripts lacking dedications either by design (in the case of a manuscript copied out for a friend) or by accident[16] are often practically impossible to distinguish from a category that might be called 'fair copy manuscripts', made either as records for the compiler's own files or for revision before recopying.[17] The poems included below by Wroth, Hutchinson, Pulter and Walsh appear in manuscripts of this type. Fair copy manuscripts, like presentation manuscripts, could be public texts, available for showing to friends and acquaintances of the poet, and a variety of things could happen to them in their later history, as the author/compiler and/or later owners added material. The two most physically complicated documents from which we have made selections are Anne Southwell's Folger manuscript and Anna Ley's Clark manuscript. Both of these manuscripts are 'miscellanies' (a very common category of manuscript in the early modern period) bringing together both original texts written by the compiler and 'secondary' material gleaned by the manuscript's compiler from printed and/or manuscript sources. Both texts seem to have been preserved by their compilers' husbands as memorials to their wives.

For all the writers included in this anthology, the encouragement and interest of other people—parents, siblings, friends, husbands—was crucial, not least in providing them with a ready-made readership. Unsurprisingly, many of the poets come from families of writers.[18] Jane Seager's manuscript echoes the interests of her brothers William and Francis. Two poets, Mary, Countess of Pembroke, and her god-daughter Mary Wroth (both of whom had the maiden name 'Mary Sidney') were born into the pre-eminent literary family of early modern England. Pembroke's psalm translations started as a continuation of work initiated by her brother Sir Philip Sidney, while Wroth's sonnets seem to have been written in part imitation both of her uncle Philip's *Astrophil and Stella* and of her father Sir Robert Sidney's manuscript love poetry. Wroth's lover and cousin, William Herbert (the

Countess of Pembroke's son) also wrote verses, and was, with his brother Philip Herbert, Earl of Montgomery (the husband of Susan, the dedicatee of Wroth's printed romance *Urania*), one of the dedicatees of the Shakespeare first folio. Anne Southwell's second husband took a keen interest in her writing, annotating some of her poems and writing verse in praise of his wife, as well as probably being responsible for the preservation of both of the manuscripts which contain her verse. Anna Ley's father and husband both had literary interests. Her own poetry is found in a manuscript interspersed with theological texts by her husband, Roger Ley. Jane Cavendish's writing was actively encouraged by her father, the important literary patron William Cavendish, first Duke of Newcastle, and two manuscripts of her poems were dedicated to him. Both of these manuscripts—transcribed by Newcastle's secretary—also contain drama co-authored with her sister, Elizabeth Brackley. Newcastle's second wife was the notorious print author Margaret Cavendish. Octavia Walsh's poems, meanwhile, have close connections with the poetry of her brother William, a prominent literary figure.

If we are interested in the study of gendered writing practices, and women's literary history, we have to establish that what we are looking at is indeed poetry authored by women, and not by what Jane Stevenson and Peter Davidson in their anthology of early modern women's poetry call 'infiltrators', men who for some reason are writing as women, or whose work is mistaken for women's writing.[19] Few anthologies of women's writing are exempt from such infiltration. Manuscript poetry is particularly vulnerable to such cross-gendering: one of the manuscripts originally designated for this anthology, Beinecke Library Osborn MS b. 4, was finally rejected because we could not prove that the verse in the manuscript signed by Elizabeth Newell was composed by her rather than merely transcribed by her. Bodleian MS Don. e.17, which has been assumed to include poetry composed by Elizabeth Middleton, whose name is prominent in the manuscript, has perhaps a more interesting history: it seems to have been one of a series of texts transcribed by John Bourchier who prepared gift manuscripts and was probably commissioned to do so by several women (Burke and Ross 2001).

While we believe that all the poems that follow were indeed written by women—they are accompanied in most cases by biographies that help to confirm their status as poets—it is very hard to claim that our selection is representative of early modern women as a whole. It may be representative of early modern women who wrote poetry, but that is impossible to tell at so many hundred years' distance. The selection of any kind of early modern women's writing practice as 'representative' is highly problematic. Manuscripts are vulnerable, and have a huge attrition rate: the survival of any piece of paper for three or four hundred years is by definition exceptional, and it means, unfortunately, that most of the women's manuscript writing we now have access to was preserved in family papers in stately homes, and valued because of those women's relationships to famous men. That is not true for all the manuscripts represented here. One is preserved because it was sent to Queen Elizabeth and was, perhaps, too beautiful to neglect; one was probably preserved because it was very important to a Dissenting community; one was an early attempt in a literary career that was to go in a rather different direction.

The woman who developed any kind of poetic facility was bound to be a rarity in the early modern period; the unevenness of women's education, even amongst the aristocracy, and the generally pervasive, if usually unspecific, discouragement from more literary writing, entailed that a more widespread women's writing practice was more likely to be found in non-poetic texts: recipe books, many of which survive from this period, or possibly sermon notes, the writing of which, Katherine Ranelagh noted in the middle of the century, had caused many a good woman in England to fall into spiritual pride.[20] As an example of that discouragement we can cite the Isham family of Lamport, in Northamptonshire, obsessive writers who believed in educating their daughters rather well. Amongst the desirable feminine qualities which Justinian Isham lists in a letter to his four daughters in 1642 are 'Modestie', 'Obedience' and 'Silence'.[21] This last is rather a disincentive to the composition of poetry, but it was obviously a relative silence, because in the same letter the wife of Lord Edward Montagu of Boughton is held up as a role model. Ann Montagu, *née* Crouch, was a poet, of sorts. Her moral advice to her children is framed in verse simply to make it more palatable, an 'excuse' for poetry widely used by women and men in the seventeenth century from George Herbert's 'Church-porch' onwards, and which explicitly distances the author from the self-display considered so destructive of a woman's reputation. This stanza ends 160 moralising verses:

> I willing was to put these noates
> in verse to please your minde
> & reade them ought practise them much
> in them trew joy yowle finde. [22]

This, the kind of writing practice implicitly approved of by the Isham patriarch, illustrates vividly the limits of the rhetorical horizons of many potential woman writers.

By the middle of the seventeenth century, when more godly women were writing poetry, a form for women's religious poetry may well have become established. Printed works by pious women, such as Dorothy Leigh's *A Mother's Legacie*, had invariably been written in prose, yet often there was an example of the author's poetry attached at the beginning or the end of the volume.[23] Several of these poems—Elizabeth Richardson's 'My owne Prayer in Meeter' attached to *A Ladies Legacie to her Daughters* (1645) and Frances Cooke's Psalm of thanksgiving, attached to an account of a shipwreck in the Irish Sea in 1650, *Mris. Cooke's Meditations*, are very similar in form to many of the poems in Julia Palmer's 'First Century', included here. An analysis of such poetry perhaps gives the twenty-first-century reader a sense of what the spiritual ideal of female-authored poetry was thought to be. All these poems are in a very simple metre, usually four-line ballad metre, which was reminiscent of the psalms sung in church: the connection with 'holy' poetry may have added to the sense that this was legitimate rhetorical endeavour. That there was an illegitimate poetics for the religious author is seen in, for example, the struggles of George Herbert to produce a poetry uncontaminated by rhetorical display and self-seeking.[24] It is safe to assume that this kind of restraint operated even more strongly for women. Even Isaac Watts, the hymn writer, felt that he should restrict the metre and tone down the metaphor of his religious lyrics (Watts 1728, ix).

A peculiarly gendered restriction on rhetorical sophistication is articulated, and demonstrated, in the manuscripts of Anne Southwell. Southwell is likely to have been the 'A.S.' whose contribution to 'Newes' games at court is recorded in an appendix to the 1614 edition of *A Wife, now the Widdow of Sir Thomas Overbury*, along with, apparently, the efforts of Thomas Overbury himself, John Donne, Sir Thomas Roe and Cicely Bulstrode. 'Rhetorical sophistication' is the point of these games: it appears that the contestants are given a subject on which to compose 'Newes', and have to respond with a witty and eloquent paragraph. If the entries attributed to 'A.S.' are hers, Anne Southwell in her youth was extremely rhetorically sophisticated. However, writing of this type was not seen as proper discursive practice for a woman. In a passage included in this volume, from British Library MS Lansdowne 740, Southwell comments on her own writing career in her defence of the 'sanguine woman'. Despite the superiority of the sanguine disposition in a man, 'a sanguine woman is of all accurst'. She cannot help making jokes, but it is at a high price: 'shee must bee merry though her neck were burst' ('Precept 4', lines 463, 465). Misogynist judgement condemns the merry woman as less than virtuous: 'it cannott bee / goodnes & mirth should hold a simpathye.' Elsewhere in the same manuscript, Southwell talks about her experience in witty, satirical discourse, her own practice of 'flouting', which is satirical, witty writing, the offspring of 'a sanguin witt'. This unbroken colt led her into trouble:

> when first I backed this jade hee dashed at princes
> & almost broke my neck from of his back.

This is a tantalising glimpse of a younger Anne Southwell who dared to make fun of royalty, but there is nothing in either of the surviving manuscripts that comes close to 'flouting', although there are flashes of a rather delicious wit. Southwell says that she has given up this kind of writing: 'flouting' is fit only for 'shallow wits' at court who play games. In contradistinction to the 'wild hott proud snorting Dromedarye' that is wit, Southwell perhaps rather ruefully characterises her present writing as 'a sluggish asse' (Southwell 1997, 138).

Readers of women's writing may occasionally regret the gendered prejudice which forced those who wished to conform to society's expectations into what can be a rather solemn mode. Poems such as the delicious satire of Sir William Davenant by Hester Pulter are rare. It is also true to say, of course, that, in the fevered religious climate of the seventeenth century, to identify a godly writing practice for women which was by definition not rhetorically sophisticated was implicitly to offer it as an opportunity for spiritually gifted but socially less advantaged women. The 'Centuries' of Julia Palmer is one such example of a woman finding a voice in an approved 'feminine' form: despite her spiritual bravado, she too is aware of the gendered prejudice that to write in verse is somehow to transgress the limits of female modesty. She renounces this 'modesty' as a sin, in the context of what she feels is an imperative from a higher authority to write: fortunately for her, and fortunately for us.

These cultural pressures on women poets—above all, the pressure on them to justify the decision to write at all—impinge on all the poems in this anthology, even when not openly confronted in the text. Thus, ironically, almost the only common thread linking the varied and stimulating pieces of writing which follow—composed for a very wide range of different purposes, with many different types of audience in mind—is indeed a gendered one, deep-seated cultural opposition to their very existence. Happily, readers of this anthology will find in the pages below many ways in which early modern women wrote their way around this baleful situation to produce texts that can be read with pleasure and advantage centuries later.

EC and JG

Notes

1 The project began at Nottingham Trent University with Elizabeth Clarke (now at the University of Warwick) as director and Victoria E. Burke (now at the University of Ottawa) as researcher. The other full-time researchers on the project have been Jonathan Gibson, Jill Seal Millman and Gillian Wright. Marie-Louise Coolahan, the sixth member of the editorial team for this volume, worked as a graduate student on the project before taking up her current post at the National University of Ireland, Galway. For much of its lifetime, the project has been supported by grant aid from the Arts and Humanities Research Board in the UK and the Social Sciences and Humanities Research Council of Canada. A prototype catalogue is available on the Perdita Project website at http://human.ntu.ac.uk/perdita.
2 Most famously, the letter-writer Dorothy Osborne wrote of Cavendish 'Sure the poore woman is a litle distracted, she could never be soe rediculous else as to venture at writeing book's and in verse too' (Osborne 1987, 75). In the later seventeenth century, anxiety about the amorality of women's involvement in print publication centred particularly on the controversial figure of Aphra Behn (see e.g. Medoff 1992).
3 A key text in the revival of interest in early modern women's manuscript writings is the influential anthology *Kissing the Rod* (Greer *et al.* 1988). Other anthologies of early modern women's writing containing manuscript material include Stevenson and Davidson (2001), Trill *et al.* (1997) and Crawford and Gowing (2000). There are a growing number of manuscript texts by early modern women available in modern editions, including Klene's edition of Anne Southwell's miscellany (Southwell 1997) and Travitsky's edition of the meditations of Elizabeth Cavendish Egerton (Egerton 1999). Three essay collections on early modern women and manuscript culture have recently been published: Justice and Tinker (2002), Beal and Ezell (2000) and Burke and Gibson (2004). Important work in progress includes David Norbrook's edition of Lucy Hutchinson's writings and Elizabeth Hageman's edition of the works of Katherine Philips.
4 This critical trend is a reaction against both the 'post-structuralist' attempt to expunge authors from literary studies and the post-Romantic idealisation of the inspired author, free of material constraints. For a penetrating analysis of critical developments in this area see Wheale (1999), 9–11. Ezell has recently argued against the frequently stated view that early modern print publication in effect created the category of author (Ezell 1999).
5 More detailed information on the physical states of the manuscripts is available in the Perdita Project's catalogue (see above, note 1).
6 For examples of this kind of verse see Stevenson and Davidson (2001) and Greer *et al.* (1988).
7 Smith (2000), 408–12.
8 For example, Greer in her introduction to *Kissing the Rod*, p. 7. For recent discussions of Philips's manuscripts see Beal (1998) chapter 5 and Barash (1996), chapter 2.
9 The universities and the inns of court (where lawyers were trained), exclusively male preserves, were major centres of manuscript activity, a lot of it in verse. Women do not seem

to have been much involved, either, in the very substantial manuscript circulation of political tracts and parliamentary proceedings.
10 For historical contexts see Crawford (1993). Religious groupings that came to the fore during the Civil Wars, such as the Quakers, proved particularly hospitable to women's writing.
11 For a bird's-eye view of the types of text written in manuscript by early modern women, see the selections in Crawford and Gowing (2000).
12 This 'feminising' approach to women's manuscript writing in the seventeenth century seems to have been in part a reaction against the increasing number of 'immoral' printed texts written by women authors such as Aphra Behn.
13 See Wheale (1999) for a stimulating treatment of this topic. The period also witnessed a considerable increase in the printing of texts by women.
14 The year 1660 (the date of the Restoration to the throne of Charles II), commonly used as a cut-off point in English literary history, makes little sense in relation to manuscript verse, as Harold Love has pointed out (1993, 8). For women's continuing involvement in manuscript culture during the late seventeenth century and the eighteenth century see Barash (1996) and Justice and Tinker (2002).
15 Ezell (1987, 68). The work of many writers, including Katherine Philips and Mary Sidney, circulated extremely widely in manuscript. For detailed studies of some of the mechanisms of this circulation see Love (1993) and Woudhuysen (1996), and for a stimulating reassessment of the nature of 'manuscript networks' Scott-Warren (2000).
16 A common feature: early modern manuscripts often lack a few opening leaves.
17 Sometimes manuscripts look as if they were started as presentation texts, then to have been revised so much that they appear to have served as a fair copy manuscript instead—kept for the record while a new presentation manuscript was prepared.
18 A similar point is made by Wynne-Davis (1998), xxi–xxiii.
19 Stevenson and Davidson (2001, xxxiii–xxxvi) list a number of interesting and valuable criteria for identifying 'infiltrators'.
20 Elizabeth Anne Taylor, 'Writing Women, Honour, and Ireland 1640–1715', unpublished PhD thesis, University College Dublin (1999), I: 285.
21 Northamptonshire Record Office, MS IC 3415.
22 Northamptonshire Record Office, Montagu of Boughton Correspondence vol. 3, p. 247.
23 Examples of this important prose genre, including the texts by Richardson and Leigh, are collected in Brown (1999). See also Ezell (2002).
24 See, for example, 'Jordan ii' and 'A true Hymne' in Herbert (1945, 102, 168).

TEXTUAL INTRODUCTION

There are as many opinions about editing as there are editors. No two scholars will produce identical editions of the same text. Similarly, no two texts present the same editorial challenges. These considerations are especially relevant in an anthology assembled through the collaboration of six academics with varying backgrounds, attempting to grapple with the editorial issues presented by fifteen very different manuscripts produced by numerous poets and scribes in various locations over a period of more than a century.

We have not attempted to introduce absolute uniformity into this anthology: this, given the requirements of our material, would have been impossible. However, the general principles adopted in the production and organisation of our introductory material, texts and notes are outlined below.

Structure

The work of fourteen women poets has been included in this anthology. Each has her own separate entry, prefaced by an introduction. In thirteen out of the fourteen entries (those poets for whom a single manuscript is included), this introduction is divided into two sections. The first section—the headnote—describes the manuscript which we have chosen to reproduce in our edition, providing information about its physical structure, its contents and anything that is known about the circumstances in which it was produced. The second section—the biographical note—summarises what is known about the woman poet herself. In the case of Anne Southwell, where we have chosen to reproduce material from both major extant manuscripts of her poetry, the introduction includes two headnotes.

Editorial responsibility for specific sections is denoted by initials at the end of each of the introductions. Victoria Burke has prepared the Palmer and Burghope entries; Elizabeth Clarke, Pulter; Marie-Louise Coolahan, Ley, Cavendish and Philips; Jonathan Gibson, Seager, Wroth and Southwell; Jill Seal Millman, Sidney, Hutchinson and Roper; and Gillian Wright, Astell and Walsh.

Textual notes on individual poems immediately follow the poems themselves. Interpretative notes are provided in a separate section at the back of the anthology.

Transcription conventions

All texts reproduced in this anthology have been edited afresh from original manuscripts, and checked by at least one person other than the named editor.

Original spelling has been reproduced in all entries. However, contractions commonly used in early modern manuscripts—such as 'wth' for 'with' (e.g. plate 1, 'Samia' line 8) or 'y^e' for 'the' (e.g. plate 2, Psalm 122 line 9)—have been silently expanded. Early modern manuscripts also commonly use the tilde (~) over 'm' and 'n' to denote a doubled consonant, or over 'c' to represent 'ci'; such contractions have similarly been silently expanded.

The use of i/j and u/v has been modernised. The symbol '=', used in many manuscripts at the end of lines, has been replaced in this edition by its modern equivalent, the hyphen. A few obvious transcription errors have been corrected; this is noted in the textual apparatus. In many manuscripts, it is difficult to distinguish the upper- and lower-case forms of certain letters, such as 'c', 's' and 'w'. In such cases, the choice of upper- or lower-case in our transcriptions is editorial.

Punctuation is original unless otherwise stated. Flourishes (e.g. at the end of poems) have not normally been reproduced. Line numbering is editorial. The foliation or pagination of manuscripts has usually been inserted by later owners (often libraries), for ease of reference; where foliation or pagination is original, this is mentioned in the introductory headnote. Square brackets have been used within the text of poems to denote words which have been supplied editorially; their use is explained in each case in the textual apparatus. Omissions from Mary Wroth's crown of sonnets, Anne Southwell's 'Precept 4' and Mary Roper's biblical and political poems are indicated by [. . .].

We have tried as far as possible to reproduce the original layout of poems in the manuscripts. However, we have not normally noted the exact location of page divisions within poems. No attempt has been made to reproduce the original lineation of prose in the dedicatory letters. However, line numbers have been added to prose texts to facilitate the identification of textual and interpretative notes. Salutations have been routinely printed on a separate line, and are not counted in the line numbering.

Textual apparatus

The unusually detailed textual apparatus (or textual notes) in this edition serves several purposes. Most importantly, it notes corrections and revisions in the manuscript copy-text, as well as the few occasions where the editors have modified the original text of prose or poems. Where appropriate, it also registers substantive differences between extant manuscripts of the same poem (e.g. Southwell, Cavendish), and/or between the manuscript copy-text and a contemporary printed text (e.g. Wroth). In the comparatively few instances where our reading of manuscripts differs significantly (i.e. on matters more substantive than spelling or punctuation) from that of previous editors, these differences are also registered in the textual notes.

Devising conventions for registering the often complex layers of correction and revision in our copy-texts has been one of our most difficult tasks in preparing this anthology. Since every early modern manuscript is unique, it is, ultimately, impossible to invent conventions which do justice to the range of idiosyncrasies in all manuscripts, while being practical and intelligible to the reader. Many of the manuscripts reproduced in this anthology are extremely complex, with numerous corrections by the poet herself and/or her scribe(s). Some presentation manuscripts, however, are almost impeccably clear and straightforward, with no corrections or blotches permitted to mar a text intended for a valued patron.

Scribal habits and textual problems particular to a specific manuscript are typically discussed in the headnote to the manuscript itself, while especially complicated corrections or revisions are described in prose notes within the textual apparatus. Otherwise, the following conventions have been used:

- In the textual notes, quotations from the original manuscript are in roman, editorial comments in italics.
- Text above the line is described as 'inserted'. For example, one of the most common types of textual correction can be seen in line 1 of the Octavia Walsh poem reproduced in plate 9. Here the original 'Since' has been deleted, and replaced above the line by 'Can'. This is represented in the textual apparatus as:

1. Can] *inserted, replacing* Since *deleted*

- Text added above the line with no deletion is simply registered as 'inserted'. For example, in Anna Ley's 'Upon the death of King James' (plate 4), the supralinear 'i' in line 6 is recorded in the notes as:

6. waine] i *inserted*

- However, where text has been inserted above the line simply for reasons of space— i.e. because the scribe has run out of page at the end of a line—this is not regarded as a correction, and is not registered in the notes.
- Text which has been added to a first draft within or along the original line (i.e. not above or below) is described as 'added'.
- Where text within a line has been deleted, without any corresponding supralinear insertion, this is registered in the notes as 'replacing'. For example, in the Octavia Walsh poem 'An enquiry into the cause of the miserys of Mankind', line 237, the original draft 'little' has been deleted, and is immediately followed by 'Narrow':

Within the compass of a ~~little~~ Narrow State

This correction is represented in the textual apparatus as:

237. Narrow] *replacing* little *deleted*

This use of 'replacing' refers to the disposition of text on the page; it does not necessarily reflect the intentions of the scribe.

- Where the current version of a word or letter(s) has been written on top of a previous version, this is registered as 'superimposed on'. Where possible, we have attempted to read and record the text beneath the superimposition. In a few cases, when it is not clear which version of the text is the more recent, this is indicated by 'or vice versa'.
- Editorial uncertainty is indicated by (?)

References and bibliography

To simplify references to printed books in a volume already dense with notes of various sorts, we have opted to use the author-date system. Printed sources are cited within the text of headnotes, biographical notes and interpretative notes. A 'Bibliography' section at the end of the introduction to each manuscript summarises the printed sources which have been consulted in the preparation of the headnote and biographical note. Manuscripts mentioned in the introductory sections are not separately detailed in these individual bibliographies. However, all manuscripts listed in the Select bibliography at the end of the volume are identified according to the section of the anthology in which they are cited.

All manuscripts and secondary printed sources alluded to in this volume are included in the Select bibliography. Primary printed sources, however, have been omitted if they fall into one of two categories:

(1) Classic books with a (relatively) stable text. By this criterion, references to Milton's *Paradise Lost* are not keyed to a specific edition. However, since modern editions of Shakespeare differ so greatly, line references to Shakespeare's plays in this anthology are keyed to the Oxford Shakespeare.

(2) Books have also been omitted from the Select bibliography if they are fully cited where they appear in the headnote, biographical note or interpretative notes, and if either they are not explicitly quoted or they are not significant sources for biographical or contextual material. Examples of texts excluded by this criterion are John Harington's translation of *Orlando Furioso* (cited but not quoted in the interpretative notes to Hester Pulter's 'To Sir Wm. D.') and Mary Astell's published treatises, mentioned but not quoted in the biographical note on Astell.

All quotations from the Bible are from the King James or Authorised Version, unless otherwise stated.

Miscellaneous

Many of the women mentioned in this anthology married at least once, and thus were known by more than one name during their lifetimes. The fourteen poets whose work is reproduced here are each generally referred to by the name which she used in her writing, regardless of marital status. (Mary Sidney, who published as 'the Countess of Pembroke', is a partial exception to this policy.) Otherwise, married women are typically referred to by both unmarried and married surnames: e.g. Alice Egerton Vaughan; Elizabeth Basset Howard.

The date of the new year in Britain during the period of our anthology was officially 25 March ('Old Style'), but 1 January (the Gregorian or 'New Style' new year) was also recognised. Where dates fall between these points, we give both years (e.g. 1634/5).

JSM and GW

I

Jane Seager's translations of the ten sibyls' prophecies of the birth of Christ

British Library Additional MS 10037

Jane Seager's only known writing appears in this twelve-leaf vellum presentation manuscript, dedicated by her to Queen Elizabeth I in 1589. The manuscript contains a dedicatory epistle and eleven ten-line poems. Ten poems predicting the birth of Christ, each in the voice of a different sibyl, are followed by an eleventh poem prophesying future happiness for Elizabeth. The manuscript, ruled in gilt and with gilt capital letters, is written in a calligraphic italic script, accompanied by facing-page transcriptions into 'charactery', the shorthand system invented the previous year by Timothy Bright (Bright 1588; Westby-Gibson 1888; Kraner 1931; Brewerton 2002; see plate 1). Seager, apparently both scribe and translator, was probably also responsible for the paintings—putti, caryatids, strapwork, the royal motto in charactery and the date 1589—on the manuscript's sumptuous glass binding (cover illustration). As in other books presented to Elizabeth, the binding is trimmed with red velvet. A complete text of the manuscript has been printed (Kraner 1931).

The sibyls were pre-Christian prophetesses, thought to have predicted the birth of Christ. Short texts of sibylline prophecies, belonging to a long and complex tradition (de Clercq 1978–79; 1981), were often accompanied in the Renaissance by visual images of the sibyls themselves—in illustrated manuscripts and printed books, as well as in wall-paintings and in stained glass. Seager's use of charactery in her manuscript bears witness to the widespread classical and Renaissance interest in the manner in which the sibyls' prophecies were originally delivered and recorded—whether on leaves, orally, and/or in hieroglyphic inscriptions. She produced her book at a time when, following the apparently accurate prophecies of the defeat of the Spanish Armada in 'the wonderful year' 1588, there was great interest in prophetic literature.

Jane Seager was the sister of William Segar, a prominent herald, portrait painter and author. Her manuscript echoes her brother's work in its interest in the relationship between textual meaning, the visual appearance of text and unusual types of visual signifiers. Trained as a scrivener, William Segar wrote a sequence of books on heraldry and chivalry in which symbolic images play an important role. The presentation of Jane's manuscript to Queen Elizabeth may be connected, perhaps as a New Year's gift, with William's promotion to Somerset Herald on 4 January 1588/9 and with the preferment of Timothy Bright, previously a physician, to a lucrative clerical appointment in 1590.

Samia.

Behold the cheerfull daye shall shortly come,
Which shall remoue the worldes obscuritye:
Unfoulding all the Prophets prophecies
And knotty volumes of the Iewish race:
So as the people more declare in verse
How this great King shall touched be of men:
And how a virgine most inviolate
Shall beare, and nourish hym in humane brest,
The Heauens of this happynes dreames;
And glistring starrs foreshew it by N^w Signes

An: Mundj 2720

Along with his brother Francis, William was one of the leading portrait painters in Elizabethan England (Piper 1957). Jane's manuscript shows that she too painted. Intriguingly, the painted decoration on the glass binding of Additional MS 10037 shares stylistic elements with a far more sophisticated manuscript book cover, a portrait of John Colet, currently at Mercers' Hall, for which 'Segar' (no first name given) was recorded as having been paid in 1585/6 (Grossmann 1950, 211–12). Jane Seager's handwriting in the sibyls manuscript is very similar to handwriting in manuscripts written by her brother William (Woudhuysen 1996, 74).

Though the manuscript was clearly intended as a presentation text for Elizabeth, there is no evidence that it ever reached her. It was bought from an unknown vendor for the British Museum library (now the British Library) in 1836.

BIOGRAPHICAL NOTE

Jane Seager was the daughter of Francis Segar and his wife Anne, *née* Sherrard. Her date of birth is unknown, and little information about her life is extant (see BL Additional MS 6409, fol. 5r–v; Bodleian MS Eng. misc. c. 19, fols 182v–5r). She married Lionel Plumtree, a Russia merchant—presumably after 1589, when she described herself, in the dedicatory epistle printed below, as a 'Mayden' (line 8). Plumtree was perhaps a member of a prominent Nottingham merchant family—if he is the 'Leonellus Plumptre' listed in a nineteenth-century genealogy (Berry 1830, 89). The date of Seager's death is not known.

Bibliography:
Bright (1588), Segar (1587)
Berry (1830), Brewerton (2002), de Clercq (1978–79; 1981), Grossmann (1950), Kraner (1931), Piper (1957), Westby-Gibson (1888), Woudhuysen (1996)

JG

To the Queenes most Excellent Majesty

Sacred Majesty

Maye yt please those most gracious eyen (acquaynted with all perfections, and above others most Excellent) to vouchsafe to make worthy of their princely view, the handy-worke of a Mayden your Majesties most faithfull Subject. It conteyneth (Renomed Sovereigne) the divine prophesies of the ten Sibills (virgyns) upon the birthe of our Saviour Christ, by a most blessed virgyn; Of 5
which most holy faith, your Majesty being cheife Defendress, and a virgyn also, yt is a thinge (as yt weare) preordeyned of god, that this Treatis, wrytten by a Mayden your Subject, should be only devoted unto your most sacred selfe. The which, albeit I have graced both with my pen and pencell, and late practize in that rare Arte of Charactery, invented by Dr. Bright, yet accompt- 10
ing yt to lack all grace withoute your Majesties most gracious acceptaunce, I humbly presente the same, with harty prayers for your Majesty.

Jane Seager.
[fol. 1r]

Samia.

Behold the cheerfull daye shall shortly come,
  Which shall remove the worldes obscurity:
  Unfoulding all the Prophets prophecies
  And knotty volumes of the Jewish race:
  So as the people maye declare in verse   5
  How this great King shall touched be of men:
  And how a virgine most inviolate
  Shall beare, and nourish hym with humane brest.
  The Heavens of this happynes divines;
  And glistring starrs, foreshew it by their signes.   10

      Anno Mundi. 2720.

                              [fol. 2v]

Cimmeria.

In tender yeares a sacred virgine myld,
  Of beauty rare and perfect excellence:
  Shall nourishe with the milke of her chast brest,
  The Lord of hosts, and everlasting King
  By whom all thinges in Heaven and in Earth   5
  Shall hartely rejoyce, and clap their hands.
  A wondrous starr shall from the eastern coste
  Appeare, and lead the wisemen to the child;
  And bringing guyfts, when hym they shall behold,
  They shall present mirhe, frankensence, and gold.   10

      Anno Mundi. 3380.

                              [fol. 4v]

Tyburtina.

The most true god hath gyven mee the power
  That I am able to declare in verse,
  How that a mayden shall conceave a child
  Within the borders of poore Nazareth.
  That god (I saye) which Bethlem countrey shall   5
  Behold, and see, in habytt of our flesh:
  Whose mother by an Angell shall receave
  Grace from above, as blest of women all
  Oh happy mother worthy heaven bright,
  That shall gyve sucke to such a sonne of light.   10

      Anno Mundi. 3890.

                              [fol. 9v]

'Lo thus in breife (most sacred Majestye)'

Lo thus in breife (most sacred Majestye)
I have sett downe whence all theis Sibells weare:
What they foretold, or saw, wee see, and heare,
And profett reape by all their prophesy.
Would God I weare a Sibell to divine	5
In worthy vearse your lasting happynes:
Then only I should be Characteres
Of that, which worlds with wounder might defyne
But what need I to wish, when you are such,
Of whose perfections none can write to much.	10

       Anno Domini. 1589.

[fol. 11v]

But where Dauids howse of spring heaunly beloved
shall both iudge sitt, & raigne kinge throned in honnor
pray then peace to Salim, to hir frend & all happy spee-
with to her walls all rest to her forts all blessed abonndant
this with cause J do praie, since from these / blissed, a blessing
my brother & kinsman, my frend & country, Doe vothe
this J doe with & moue, of most good will to bee wished
for o: god heer buildeth him an house allmightie Jehoua

Idem.
Psal: 122. Lætatus sum

O what a liuelie delight o what a iollitie
this news vnto mee brought, newly deliuered
that gods howse ruined should bee reedified
and that shortly wee should coiñ man enter yt
Now thy galleries lovely Jerusalem
thy gates shal bee my rest: now not vnordered
now rudly scattred ab east: But very titty like
all conioyned in one, shall be Jerusalem,
Now there conuenient place to ye Company
gods hand hath gathered, shall be allotted her
his passed benefitts ioyntly to testifye
and so praise him as ence praised him I will

None

Mary Sidney's
psalm paraphrases

British Library Additional MS 12047

The selection of poems in this section is based on rather different criteria from the others in the volume. Begun by Sir Philip Sidney, completed by his sister Mary, Countess of Pembroke, and reworked by the Countess several times, the Sidney Psalms exist in at least eighteen manuscript versions. For descriptions of these manuscripts see Herbert (1998) (henceforth referred to in this section as *Works*), and Alexander (2000). (The manuscript described by Alexander has now been catalogued as British Library Egerton MS 3789.)

The following poems are taken from the Countess's Psalms as they exist in an eclectic manuscript from the late sixteenth century, owned by Sir John Harington (1560–1612), and copied by an anonymous scribe, with a few corrections in another hand (possibly Harington's). Harington was very interested in the Sidney Psalms. He owned two manuscript versions (the other is British Library Additional MS 46372), and also produced his own version of the psalter (extant in two copies: Ohio State University Library MS Eng. 16, and Bodleian MS Douce 361), drawing heavily on the Countess's poetry in some cases. In this manuscript, after the first twenty-six psalms, there is a selection of eighty-eight psalm versions (from eighty-five different psalms), some roughly in chronological order, some not. *Works* refers to the collection as an 'anthology' and a 'miscellany', and points out that it 'can have no serious claim to authority' as a copy-text (II: 342, 356). The text is quite uneven, probably copied from various sources at different times, written in a secretary hand, with titles and marginal notes in italic. There are fair transcriptions of some psalms and very poor texts of others, with lines overrunning, lines inserted between other lines, and occasional blotches, alterations, cancellations and insertions throughout.

Despite its faults, this manuscript is a fascinating example of an unusual contemporary approach to the Sidney Psalms, viewing them as individual poems rather than as fixed parts of a sacred whole. One of its most notable features is its treatment of variant versions, perhaps demonstrating a poet's interest in the variety of possible verse renderings of the psalms. It records two versions of each of Psalms 75, 89 (where the variant is unique to this manuscript) and 122; see plate 2. These have been included in this edition, along with a psalm presented in a unique version, Psalm 113. To distinguish between the versions, I have added *[ii]* to the variants; this is an editorial intervention, not present in the manuscript itself. As a later annotator of the manuscript (a British Museum librarian?) points out,

Psalms 75 *[ii]*, 89 *[ii]*, 113 and 122 *[ii]* were printed from this manuscript in *Sidneiana* (Butler 1837).

Titles have been standardised. Catchwords have not been noted; these appear on most pages. Major variant readings from the edited text in *Works* (which uses the Penshurst MS as its copy-text, except where otherwise stated) have been noted, but I have not attempted to compare variants from other manuscripts. For a fuller description of the manuscripts and their variants see *Works*.

BIOGRAPHICAL NOTE

Mary Sidney Herbert, Countess of Pembroke (1561–1621), was the daughter of Sir Henry Sidney and Mary Dudley. Her aunts and uncles included Catherine Dudley Hastings, Countess of Huntingdon, who was very close to Mary, and Robert Dudley, Earl of Leicester, the Queen's long-standing favourite. She had three sisters, all of whom died young, and three brothers, the eldest of whom was Sir Philip Sidney (1554–86). She became the third wife of Henry Herbert, second Earl of Pembroke, in 1577, at the age of fifteen. This arranged marriage further cemented relations between the powerful Protestant families of Dudley, Sidney and Herbert. The Countess had two sons, William (1580–1630) and Philip (1584–1650), and two daughters, Katherine, who died in 1584 aged three, and Anne (1583–c.1606). In 1586, her father and mother died, and she became dangerously ill. In the same year, Philip Sidney died in the Netherlands fighting against Spanish forces. It was largely after his death, as his successor as patron, editor of his works, and translator and poet, that she found literary fame.

Mary began to publish Philip's works in 1593 with *The Countess of Pembroke's Arcadia*. In 1598 she authorised another edition which also included his 'Defence of Poesy', 'Astrophil and Stella', and the 'Lady of May'—in effect, an edition of Sidney's works. She had already published works of her own in 1592: a blank verse translation of Robert Garnier's neo-Senecan tragedy *Marc Antoine*, entitled *Antonius*, and a prose translation of Philippe de Mornay's *Excellent discours de la Vie et de la Mort* which she styled *A Discours of Life and Death* (apparently Philip had begun translating de Mornay's *De la verite de la religion chrestienne*, later completed by Arthur Golding and published in 1587). An elegy on her brother, possibly her work (though often considered to be by Spenser), was published as 'The Doleful Lay of Clorinda' with Spenser's *Astrophel* in 1595. 'A Dialogue between Two Shepherds', a poem in praise of Elizabeth, was published in 1602 in Francis Davison's *Poetical Rhapsody*. The largest part of the Countess's work, however, the translation of Psalms 44 to 150, completing Philip's work, was circulated purely in manuscript. She may have begun working on the Psalms as early as 1586, possibly continuing to revise them until 1611. She also translated Petrarch's 'Triumph of Death' (Inner Temple Library, MS Petyt 538, vol. 43) and it may be that this text, unique in manuscript, is only a part of a longer, otherwise lost, translation from the *Triumphs*.

As well as assuming Sidney's poetic mantle, the Countess took on the patronage of poets such as Breton, Fraunce and Daniel, and became a major patron to those allied to the Dudley, Sidney and Herbert families, especially after Leicester died in 1588. With the death of her husband in 1601, however, she was required to take more responsibility for their estates and business, and for the positions of their

sons William and Philip at court. The Countess's importance as a literary patron then declined, as poets looked instead to her sons William (the new Earl of Pembroke) and Philip (created Earl of Montgomery by James I in 1605).
Bibliography:
Butler (1837), Herbert (1998), Rathmell (1963), Sidney (1962)
Alexander (2000), Brennan (1988), Hannay (1990), Seal (1997), Waller (1979)

JSM

Psalm 75 Confitebimur

Thee god, o thee, we sing we celebrate
thy acts with wonders, who but doth relate
   so kindly nigh thy name our need attendeth
sure I, when once this chardge I undergoe
of this assembly will not faill to show 5
   my judgments such as justest rule commendeth

The peeple loose, the land I shaken find
this will I firmly prop, that straightly bind
   and then denownce my uncontrolled pleasure
Brag not you braggers you your sawcy horne 10
lift not lewd mates; no more with heavens scorne
   glance on in words your old repining measure

Wheare sonne first shews or last enchardgde his light
devides the day or pricks the mids of night
Seek not the fountanes whence preferment springs 15
   gods only fixed course that all doth sway
   limmits dishonors night and honors day
the king his crowne the slave his fetters brings

A troubled cup is in Jehovaes hand
weare wine & winy lees compounded stand 20
   which frankly fild as frankly he bestoweth
yet for theire draught ungodly men doth give
gives all not one except that lewdly live
   only what from the dregs by wringing floweth

So I secure shall spend my happy times 25
in my though lowly never dying rimes
   singing with praise the *God* that Jacob loveth
my princly cares shall drop ill doers lowe
in glory plant to make with glory growe
   who right approves or doth what right approveth 30

[fol. 37r–v]

Title (marginal note). Deleted text morninge prayer 15 Day.
2. wonders] *Works* wonder
3. nigh] *MS* migh

4. once] *superimposed on* I
this] *Works* the
10–17. Brag not . . . honors day] *inserted, replacing lines 43–50 of Psalm 71 (copied out in error and deleted. Psalm 71 directly precedes this psalm in MS)*
10. braggers] *Works* braggardes
12. glance] *Works* dance
13. enchardgde] *Works* enshades
14. mids] *Works* midst
15. fountanes] *Works* fountayne
springs] *Works* springeth
16. fixed course] *replacing* councell *deleted*
18. brings] *Works* bringeth
21. frankly he] *Works* freely he
25. So] *Works* And
28. cares] *Works* care
drop] *Works* crop
29. to] *Works* and
30. or] *Works* and

Psalm 89 Miserecordias

Eveninge
prayer
17 Day.

    The constant promises, the loving graces
        that cause our debt, eternall Lord to thee
till ages shall fill up their endles spaces
    my thankfull songs unaltred theame shall bee
        for of thy bownty thus my thoughts decree.   5
It shall bee fully built, as fairly fownded,
    and of thy truth attesting heavns shall see
the bowndless periods though theirs bee bownded

Lo I have leagud (thow saist) with my elected,
    and thus have to my servant *David* sworn   10
thy ofspring kings, thy throne in state erected
    by my support all threats of tyme shall scorn
    and Lord, as running skies, with wheels unworn
seace not to lend this wonder their Commending
    so with one mynd & praise no less adorn   15
this truth the holy troops, thy coart attending

For who with thee among the clowds compareth
    what angell there, thy paragon doth raign
whose Majestie, whose peerless force Declareth
    the trembling awe of thine immortall fame   20
    Lord god whom hosts redoubt, who can maintain
with thee in powerfullnes a rivalls quarrell?
    strongist art thow, and must to end remain
whome complete faith doth armor like apparrell

Thie lordly check, the seas proud courage quailed   25
    and highly swelling, lowly made reside

to crush stout *Pharao*, thy arme prevailed
 what one, thie foe, did undisperst abide,
 the heaven the earth, & all in bosome wide
this huge rownd engin clipps, to thee pertayneth   30
 which firmly based, not to shake, to slide
the unseene hindge, of north & south sustayneth

For north & south were both by thee created
 and those cross points our bounding hills beehold
Thabor and *Hermon* in whose joy related   35
 thy glorious grace, to east & west is told
 thy arme all pow'r all puisance doth enfold
thy lifted hand a might of wonder showeth
 justice & judgment doe thy throne uphold
before thy presence, truthe with mercy goeth   40

Happie the people who with hastie running
 poste to thie court, when trumpets triumphs blow
on paths enlighted, by thie faces sunning
 their steps Jehova unoffended goe
 thie name makes them glad & holds them soe,   45
high thoughts in to their harts thie justice powreth
 the worship of their strength from thee doth flow
and in thy love their springing empire flowreth

For by Jehovahs sheild, stand wee protected,
 and thow gavst Israell their sacred king,   50
what tyme in vision, thus thie word directed
 thy loved prophet, ayd I will yow bring
 against that violence, your state doth wring
from one among my folke, by choice appoyntet
 David my servant, him to act the thing   55
have I with holy oyle, my selfe, annoynted;

My hand shall bide his never failling piller
 and from myne arme shall hee derive his might
not closlie undermind by cursed willer
 nor overthrown by foe in open fight   60
 for I will quaill his vexers in his sight
all that him hate by mee shalbe mischanced
 my truth my clemency on him shall light
and in my name, his head shall bee advanced;

Advanced so that twixt the watry borders   65
 of seas & flouds this noble land desine,
all shall obay subjected to the orders
 which his imperious hand for laws shall singne
 hee unto mee shall say thow father mine

Thow art my god, the fort of my salvation 70
   and I my first born roome will him assigne
more highly thrond, then king of greatest nation

While circling time, still ending & beegining
   shall runn the race, where stop nor start apperes
my bownty towards him not ever lining 75
   I will conserve, nor writ my league in yeers
   nay more his sonns whome fathers love endeers
shall fynd like bliss, for legaci bequeathd,
   a stedfast throne I say till heav'ly peers
shall faint in course, where yet they never breathed 80

Now, if his children doe my laws abandon
   and other paths, then, my plain judgments chuse
break my beheasts, & plainly walk at randon
   and what I bid, with froward hart refuse
   I meane indeed, on their revolt to use 85
correcting rodd, their sinn with whips to chasten
   not in their fault my loves deefect excuse
nor loose the promise, once my faith did fasten,

My league shall hold, my word persist unchanged
   once sworn I have & sworn in holynes 90
never shall I from David bee estranged
   his seed shall ever bide, his seat no less
   the daies bright guide, the nights pale governess,
shall claime no longer lease of their induring
   whome I behold as heavnly witnesses 95
in termlesse turns my termlesse truth assuring.

And yet o now by thee abjected scorned
   scorcht with thy wrath is thy anoynted me
Hated his leagues, the crown him late adorned
   puld from his head by thee augments his mone 100
   raz'd are his forts, his walls to ruyn gone.
Not symplest passenger, but on him prayeth
   his neighbours laugh of all his haters none
but boasts his wrack, & at his sorrow playeth

Takes hee his weapon? thow the edg rebatest 105
   coms to the feeld to fight? thow makst him fly
would march with kingly pomp? thow him understand
   ascend his throne? yt overthrown doth ly,
   his ages spring, and tyme of jolity
winter of woe before the day Defineth 110
   for praise reprouch, for honor infamy
hee overloaden bears, and bearing pineth

H[ow] long o lord, what still in dark displeasure
   wilt thow thee hide and shall thy angry thought
still flame? o think how shall our ages measure   115
   think if wee all created were for nought?
   for who is hee whome birth to life hath brought?
But life to death and death to grave subjecteth
   from this necessity, (let all bee sought)
no privileedge exempteth; no aid protecteth,   120

Kind lord where is the kindnes once thow swareth
   swarest in truth, thy Davids stock [should find]
thow lord, yet show thow for thy servant carest
   holding those shames in unforgetting mind
   which wee imbosomd beare of many a king   125
but all at thee, and at thy Christ Directed
   to endles whome bee endles praise assignd
bee this again I say bee this effected;

                                               [fols 42r–44v]

Title. Miserecordias] *Latin* Misericordias
1–2 *(marginal note).* Eveninge prayer 17 Day.] *in right margin*
2. our debt] *gap (obliterated text) between these words*
3. endles] *Works* still void
14. Commending] *MS* Commeding
15. mynd & praise] *Works* minded praise
17. with thee among the clowds] *Works* among the cloudes with thee
among] *MS* a mong
19. peerless force] *MS* peerles forc
20. fame] *Works* traine
22. powerfullnes] *first* e *inserted*
29. heaven] *last* e *inserted*
30. huge] *MS* hug
rownd] *MS* rowd
31. to slide] *Works* or slide
36. to east & west] *Works* from West to East
42. triumphs] *Works* tryumph
45. name makes] *Works* name both makes
makes] *MS* nakes
47. flow] *altered from* floweth; eth *deleted*
48. flowreth] r *inserted*
54. among] *MS* omong
61. his sight] *MS* h sight
64. advanced] *MS* adavnced
65. borders] *MS* borderd
66. desine] *Works* define
68. singne] *altered from* singue; n *superimposed on* u
71. first born] *Works* first-bornes
79. heav'ly] *Works* heavn'ly
peers] *preceded by a vertical pen stroke*
83. & plainly] *Works* prophanely
84. hart] *MS* hard
98. me] *Works* one

99. leagues] *Works* league
100. augments] *MS* ougments
107. march] *MS* marth
understand] *Works* unstatest
109. tyme] *Works* prime
113. H[ow]] *Works;* ow *illegible in MS because of a hole in the page*
115. shall] *Works* short
117. for who . . . hath brought?] *this line is inserted above line 118 on a new page*
hee] *altered from* thee *(?);* t *deleted (?)*
120. exempteth] *Works* exemptes
aid] *Works* age
121. swareth] *Works* swarest
122. [should find]] *Works; omitted in MS*
123. thow lord] *Works* Show lord
125. king] *Works* kind
127. praise] r *inserted*

Psalm 89 Miserecordias [ii]

idem.
    Gods boundles bownties gods promise ever abyding
    shall bee my songs eternall theme still gladly recording
    of fowloing ages, while ranged in absolute order
    gold armed squadrons of stares shall muster in heaven
    yea this soaner I think that stares best ordered order   5
    shall to disorder fall, confusd in contrary courses
    then that league be reverst, that sacred treatye pealed
    thus by thy selfe sometime confirmd, thus sworn to thy David
    while earth, while waters, while palace of heev'n abideth
    stablish I will thy elected seed & loftily seated   10
    on throne will hold them, till endles eternities ending
    O father highe heavens at thee most worthily wonder
    O father earth Dwellers, whose hearts al on god bee reposed
    Bend to thy thruthe their praise, when so their company meteth
    who is above that may compare with mighty Jehova?   15
    who can among th'exalted train of gloriows angells
    like to Jehova be fownd? all him with an awfull obeisance
    terrible acknowledge, and flock affrighted abowt him,
    thow comander of hosts, indeed most mighty Jehova
    seest not a match in powr in verity knowst not an equall   20
    Thow of foaming seas, dost still the tumultuows outcries
    thow their high swelling, dost coole with lowly residing
    prowd Phæroa hath felt thee: all enemies all thy resisters
    felt thy revendging hand, disperst & bloudily wounded
    thow thow only the fownder of earth, and former of heaven   25
    framer of all this vawted rownd, which hanged on hindges
    north & south sustain thie benignity, Thabor and hermon
    that where sunn falleth, this where his charret ariseth
    testify with praises: thee, thee, all only belongeth

all powre, all puisance, makes earth with wonder amazed
thow sitte on justice and suply severyty throned
yet so these holding as truth and mercy beholding;
what shall I say? o blest thrice blest, who hastily hy them
unto thy joyfull feasts, with trumpets harmony rowzed
who lighted by thy wholsome face, kept glad by thy gladnes
rising from thy renowned name, advanc'd by thy justice
frankly receave from thee great lord strength Dignity empire
lastly a king, as a sheild, strenght empire Dignity guarding
These things in visions to thy prophets plainly revealed
thus were uttred againe, on a man: very mighty reputed
one exalted, I have, Devoted, wholly to serve mee
David I meane, whose head hath streamd by my sacred anointing
force & strength from me, shall mightily ever uphold him
no manifest violence no cloaked villany hurt him
his cruel oppressors prickt on by malicious envie
prostrat in his presence will I lay past hope of rissing
never shall hee my kindnes want my fidelity never
raisd to that haight of rule that from seas watery border
unto the streames Eufrates rolls, all lands shall obey him
His father his fortress, his gracious god shall he call mee
& him againe I my first born sonn will grace to bee called
placed above all earthly monarchs by my mercy for ever
and constant covenant in state most happy remayning
yea such bliss to his heirs as a legacy shall be bequeathed
They shall sitt kings loftily thrond, & loftily throned
their thrones continuance a paragon to the ages of heeven
yf so my laws they leave & bend not their steps to my judgments
yf they breake my beheasts what I bidde perversly relinquish
their misdemeanors, their sinns, with a whipe with a scourging
visit I will indeed; yett as unto my Dearly beloved
kind will I ever abide, in truth & mercy for ever
holding firmlye my league not a jot my tru promises altring
Once this I sware this I holily sware, nor can be remedied
David I will not faill his progeny shall bee eternall
his seate mayntaine while sunns most glorious ardor
guilds the rejoicing Day: while night in unaltred order
Hides the repining day, with moons pale silver adorned
which of this covenant, still shines a true witnes in heaven
Yet now alas: thie annointed king thow angry rejectest
pulst of his Diadem, his alliance wholy refusest
his bulwarks raisest, ruinest his mighty defences
left for a pray to the passengers of a scorn to the neighbours
victory crowns his foes proud joy possesseth his haters
his sword quite blunted, from feld with filthie Dishoner
chased hee flies, his throne thrown down his glory defaced

spring of his age is winter grown disgraced hee pineth
How long ever alas? wilt thow most mighty be hidden
shall once kindled fire, still flame in furiows ardor
Thinke o think yet again how short our earthly residing
think whether all to bee speedily slayn, were rashly created   80
who is he now living, but death prepareth his harbor
in toombs cold bosome whither hevy nesessity sends him
Lord wher is old kindnes in verity sworn to thy David
our foule disgraces, sweet lord in mercy remember
whose laps are filled with words of many reproches   85
lighted on us but bent to thee & at thine anoyntet
But thow mighty Jehova eternall eternities author
blessed eternally bide and yeeld these blisses a blessing

[fols 44v–46r]

Works uses this MS version as the copy-text for this psalm
Title. Misercordias] *Latin* Misericordias
1 *(marginal note).* A later hand has written Pr.ᵈ in Sidneiana *in the left margin in pencil*
2. theme] *MS* them
5. think] *MS* thing
6. contrary] *preceded by a vertical pen stroke*
7. pealed] *altered from* repealed; re *deleted*
10. loftily] *preceded by a vertical pen stroke*
12. O father . . . wonder] *this line is inserted (i.e. squeezed in) between lines 11 and 13*
highe] *MS* hight
13. hearts] *MS* heares
al] *Works; MS unclear because of a hole in the page*
god] *altered from* gog; d *superimposed on* g
reposed] *MS* repose
16. who] *replacing* like *deleted*
17. be] *MS* he
23. Phæroa] *the capital* P *is much larger than normal and is dotted in the loop*
28. charret] e *superimposed on* i (?)
29. only] *MS* oly
31. suply] *inserted, replacing* justice *deleted*
33. o blest] *altered from* ablest; o *inserted,* a *deleted*
hy] *MS* by
39. to] *inserted, replacing* th *deleted*
40. thus were . . . reputed] *this line inserted above line 41 on a new page*
42. sacred] *conjectural reading; MS unclear*
43. him] *preceding this word is a heart or W shaped mark*
47. hee] *altered from* bee; h *superimposed on* b
50. gracious] *MS* gricious
54. yea] *MS* yee
55. They] *replacing* and *deleted*
56. thrones] *MS* thones
a] *conjectural reading; MS unclear*
57. steps] *MS* steeps
61. ever abide] *MS* everabade
62. tru] *altered from* tre; u *superimposed on* e; *Works* true
63. holily] i *inserted*

64. eternall] *MS* eterall
65. mayntaine] *Works* myntaind
sunns] *altered from* sonns; u *superimposed on* o
ardor] *MS* ador
67. day,] *Works omits comma*
70. refusest] *altered from* refuseth; st *superimposed on* th
71. defences] *first* e *inserted*
74. feld] *Works* field *(corrected from* flld*)*
78. once] *MS* onc
82. hevy nesessity] *MS* hevynes ssity
84. lord] *replacing* k *deleted*
86–7. lighted . . . author] *The scribe seems to have written the first word of line 86 (*lighted*) followed by the rest of line 87 (*thow mighty . . .*) on line 86; he then wrote the first word of line 87 (*But*), realised his mistake, left the rest of line 87 blank and squeezed the rest of line 86 (*on us . . .*) above* thow mighty . . .
86. to] *altered from* at; a *deleted*
88. bide] *altered from* bibe; d *superimposed on* b
blisses] *Works* blissed *(corrected from* blisses*)*

Psalm 122 Letatus sum

O fame most joyfull, o joy most lively Delightfull
lo I doe heare, gods temple as erst, so againe be frequented
and wee within thy porches agayn, glad wonted abiding
lovely Salem shall find thow cittie rebuilt as a citty
late disperst but now united in absolute order   5
now there shall be the place for gods holy people apointed
first to behold his pledge, there sing all mightie Jehova
now there shall be the seat, where not to be justiced only
all shall freely resort whome strife, hate, injury vexeth
But where Davids howse & ofspring heav'nly beloved   10
shall both judges sitt, & raigne kings throned in honnor
pray then peace to *Salem*, to hir frend & all happy proceeding
wish to her walls all rest to her forts all blessed abonndance
this with cawse I do praie, since from these blisses, a blessing
my brother & kinsman, my freind & country Deriveth   15
this I doe wish & more, if more good rest to bee wished
sinc our god heer builds him an house allmightie *Jehova*

[fol. 58r–v]

Title. Letatus] *Latin* Laetatus
5. disperst] *MS* dsperst
6. place for gods] *inserted, replacing* seat, wher *deleted*
7. there] *Works* then
8. only] *MS* oly
10. ofspring] *MS* of spring
12. *Salem*] *MS* Salm
frend & all] *Works* frends all
13. blessed] *altered from* blesses; d *superimposed on* s
abonndance] *MS* abonndanc

14. since] *MS* sinc
blisses] *preceded by a vertical pen stroke*
16. if] *altered from* of; i *superimposed on* o

Idem
Psalm 122 Letatus sum *[ii]*

O what livelie delight o what a jollitie
this news unto mee brought, newly delivered
that gods howse ruined should bee reedified
and that shortly wee showld ev'ry man enter yt

O now thy galleries lovely Jerusalem 5
thy gates shal bee my rest: now not unordered
nor wiyde scattred as east: but very city like
all conjoyned in one, shall be Jerusalem,

Now there convenient place to the Company
gods hand hath gathered, shall be allotted her 10
his passed benefitts, joyntly to testify
and so praise him as once praised him Israell

Now there shall bee the seat where to bee justiced
all shall freely resort weary of injuries
Seat, whose loftie receipt, loftily may receave 15
Davids posterity royally honored,

Pray then pray wee I say peace to Jerusalem;
to yow prosperity frends to Jerusalem
thy walls thy joyfull fortifications
peace & plenty betide, never abandoning 20

with good reason I wish thee now all happines
whose bliss is generall unto my contry men
with good cause shall I pray dayly thy bettering
where gods mansion is now to bee edified

[fols 58v–59r]

Spacing after lines 4, 8 and 12 is conjectural
Title. Letatus] *Latin* Laetatus
1 (marginal note). *A later hand has written* Pr.^d in Sidneiana *in the left margin in pencil*
1. O] *the capital* O *is much larger than normal and is dotted inside the loop*
3. reedified] *MS* reedifield
6. thy] *altered from* this (?); y *superimposed on* is (?)
7. east] *Works* erst
9. Company] *the* C *is formed like an* O *with a cross inside the loop*
10. her] *added in another hand; Works* out
12. Israell] *MS* Isarell
14. all] *MS* and
17. Pray] *the capital* P *is much larger than normal and is dotted inside the loop*
21. wish thee now] *Works* now wish thee

Psalm 75 Confitebimur *[ii]*

   wee o god to thee doe sing
   wee to thee doe praises bring
for thie name is nygh,
   when our cause assistance needs,
us with succour to supply 5
   therefor saved wondrowsly
     wee recount thie wondrous deeds

   As for mee whenso they shall,
   under my directions fall,
who to mee pertayn, 10
   righteous doo we shall bannish wrong,
Thise loose land I will again
into sownder site restrain,
   I will make hir pillers strong

   I will say to bragards then 15
   bragg no more, to wicked men;
sett not upp your horne,
   set not up your horn on high
be no more perversly born
onward with rebellious scorn 20
     to speake repiningly

   East whence clining sunn ascends
   west where sliding sunn descends
   [South his standing tide]
   can to no man honor bring 25
only god who all doth guide
makes men clime, or stand, or slide
   makes the caitife & the king;

   Then not mee, god yow withstand
   him whose ever right right hand 30
holds a filled cupp
   not of wine but winy lees,
   of the which thow all shall supp
   supp said I? nay suck yt upp
   whome unjust his justice sees 35

   So then I will spend my Daies
   in recording still his praise
still my song shall flow,
   from the land of Jacobs god
I will cropp ill doers low 40
I will make well doers grow
   spreading branches farr abroad;

[fols 75r–76r]

Title (marginal note). A later hand has written Pr.^{d} in Sidneiana *in the right margin in pencil*
8. they] *Works* thy
9. directions] *Works* direction
11. doo] *second* o *inserted (possibly making it one word with* we, *i.e.* doowe*)*
   doo we] *Works* dome
15. bragards] *altered (?);* ards *superimposed on illegible letters (?)*
21. to] *Works* Thus to
22. clining] Works climing
24. [South his standing tide]] *Works; omitted in MS*
27. slide] *MS* slid
33. thow] *MS* thew
42. spreading] *MS* speading

Psalm 113 Laudate dominum

Yow that the life of servants doe professe
Jehova's name in worthie praise expresse
Jehova's name to blesse wee must indever
from this age to the next, both now & ever
Jehova's name to praise our thought Devises   5
from whence it sets, to where the sunn arises
high is Jehova over all the nations
yea high above all heavnly habitations
with our Jehova who can bee compared
our lord whose dwelling is in height prepared   10
yet doth vouchsafe to make himselfe so low
things done in heav'n things done on earth to know
that lifts the weake, that lay in dust dejected
and ev'n from dongue the poore man hath erected
to make him with the greatest peers to sitt   15
to sway the state, with courage & with witt
by him the barren womb hath beene so blest
to bee of many babes a joyfull nest
To father sonn & spryte of both proceeding
there was & is & shalbe praise exceeding   20

[fol. 94r–v]

Works uses this MS version as the copy-text for this psalm
Title. Laudate dominum] *Latin* laudate servi Dominum
(marginal note). A later hand has written Pr.^{d} in Sidneiana *in the right margin in pencil*
5. Devises] *Works* devises

3

Lady Mary Wroth
Pamphilia to Amphilanthus

Folger Shakespeare Library MS V.a.104

Two early texts survive of Lady Mary Wroth's innovative, female-voiced Petrarchan sonnet sequence *Pamphilia to Amphilanthus*: a manuscript copy in Wroth's formal italic hand, with authorial corrections (Folger MS V.a.104) and a later printed version tacked on to the end of Wroth's romance *The Countess of Montgomery's Urania* (1621). The printed text has been frequently reprinted and anthologised, and is the version on which most Wroth criticism has been based. The selection of poems which follows is the first to give modern readers the chance to read *Pamphilia to Amphilanthus* in the form found in the Folger manuscript. The introduction and notes have been designed to clarify for readers the differences between the two versions of the sequence.

The later, printed text incorporates some of the corrections Wroth made in the manuscript. There is no clue as to how long before 1621 the manuscript text (written on late sixteenth-century paper) was composed. The earliest date at which Wroth is known to have been writing poetry is 1613, one year before the death of her husband, Sir Robert Wroth (Wroth 1992, 18–19).

The sequence's title refers to two characters from the *Urania*: Pamphilia ('all-loving'), the female speaker of the poems, and Amphilanthus ('lover of two'), Pamphilia's faithless lover. The relationship between Pamphilia and Amphilanthus seems to have been partly modelled on the long-term extra-marital affair between Wroth and her cousin William Herbert, himself a poet. Petrarchan commonplaces (Venus, Cupid, love's agonies) dominate the sequence, though with comparatively little emphasis on the appearance of the beloved and a concomitant stress on Pamphilia's 'constancy', a quality with which she is strongly associated in *Urania*. Wroth's imagery is often dark and involved and the poetry is frequently cryptic. Her view of love veers between the earthly and the spiritual. Pre-echoes of some of Wroth's imagery in the poetry of William Herbert, Wroth's famous uncle Philip Sidney and her father Robert Sidney are listed by Roberts (Wroth 1992), Pritchard (Wroth 1996a) and Wynne-Davies (1998).

As the manuscript lacks dedicatory and prefatory material, it seems likely that it was intended as a fair reference copy for Wroth's own use, though this is by no means certain. Wroth's sonnets are not known to have circulated beyond this manuscript before their publication in 1621. The terms for much recent criticism of the sequence have been set by Masten's suggestion that the poetry's preoccupation with darkness and enclosure dramatises 'a withdrawal from circulation' and 'a woman's . . . unwillingness to circulate among men' (Masten 1991, 69). Smith finds these features politically significant, arguing that Wroth 'uses the discourses of withdrawal and banishment to express a disenfranchisement from Jacobean rule' (2000, 417).

Wroth's work is not, like other English examples of the genre, a single numbered sequence of sonnets. Instead, following French models, it is a collection of several sequences of numbered and unnumbered love sonnets and love poems (or 'songs') in other metres. The structure of the Folger manuscript may be broken down as follows:

Section 1: forty-eight numbered sonnets interspersed with seven numbered songs (fols 1r–29r).

Section 2: one unnumbered sonnet, eight unnumbered songs and a verse dialogue (fols 30r–34v).

Section 3: ten numbered sonnets, five unnumbered songs (fols 35r–42v).

Section 4: fourteen numbered sonnets in 'corona' (or 'crown') form, the last line of each sonnet being repeated as the first line of the next and the opening line of the sequence reappearing at the very end ('A crowne of Sonetts dedicated to Love'; fols 43r–46v).

Section 5: one unnumbered sonnet, four numbered songs interspersed with one unnumbered song, followed by eight numbered sonnets and one unnumbered sonnet (fols 47v–54v).

Section 6: One unnumbered song, two unnumbered sonnets (fols 55r–56r).

Section 7: One long unnumbered song, two unnumbered sonnets, one unnumbered song (fols 57r–64r).

As Alexander (1996–97) has shown, Wroth uses a number of devices to mark out this structure in the manuscript: blank pages, titles, catchwords, rules, a slashed S symbol or '*s fermé*' ($) used by Wroth's aunt Mary Sidney, and the signature 'Pamphilia'.

The arrangement of the poems in the 1621 printed book differs markedly from that in the manuscript. One poem is added, six are cut, sixteen shifted about between different sections of the sequence and nine embedded in the text of the *Urania*. The extent to which Wroth authorised the printing of the *Urania* is uncertain, though critics generally agree with Wroth's editor Josephine A. Roberts that she is responsible for the many, frequently very significant, revisions found in its text of *Pamphilia to Amphilanthus*. The 1621 structure can be summarised as follows:

Section 1 (P1–P55 in the numbering of Roberts's edition): forty-eight numbered sonnets interspersed with seven numbered songs.

Section 2 (P56–P62): one unnumbered sonnet, six unnumbered songs.

Section 3 (P63–P76): ten numbered sonnets, three unnumbered songs.

Section 4 (P77–P90): fourteen numbered sonnets ('A crowne of Sonetts dedicated to Love').

Section 5 (P91–P94): four numbered songs.

Section 6 (P95–P103): nine numbered sonnets.

One of the aims of the following selection of poems is to give readers an impression of the structure of the Folger manuscript. Although, as Alexander has pointed out, the Folger manuscript 'is in some ways a finished product' (Alexander 1996–97, 15, n. 9), no printed text of the poems in the manuscript order has ever appeared. Roberts's edition, the standard modern text, prints *Pamphilia to Amphilanthus* in the order found in the printed book. (She incorporates the major revisions of the 1621 edition whilst following the spelling and punctuation practice of the manuscript.) Roberts's choice of copy-text, in itself thoroughly justifiable and well-argued, has had the unhappy side-effect of obscuring the nature of the manuscript sequence. In particular, it has meant that intriguing links between the Folger *Pamphilia and Amphilanthus* (c.1613, or possibly earlier) and Shakespeare's *Sonnets* (1609) have escaped notice (Gibson 2004). Like Shakespeare's much better known work, Wroth's Folger text is an anomalously late English sonnet sequence containing love poems addressed to a fickle young man. In both cases, the fickle young man is likely to have been William Herbert, a prime candidate for the addressee of Shakespeare's first 126 sonnets as well as the probable model for 'Amphilanthus'. Both sequences are followed by a long poem in the genre of the lover's complaint—Shakespeare's *A Lover's Complaint*, Wroth's 'A sheapherd who noe care did take'—in which a betrayed lady mourns the fickleness of her lover in conversation with a third party. Wroth—a musical woman who dressed up as an Ethiopian nymph in two Jacobean masques—would seem to be a contender for the role of 'Shakespeare's Dark Lady', the subject of his sonnets 127–52.

The Folger manuscript, which contains no indication of authorship, is written in the same hand as several autograph Wroth manuscripts (Wroth 1992, 61–2). The manuscript is ruled in pink; punctuation marks are often difficult to decipher. The $ symbol used in the manuscript, and reproduced in the texts below, does not appear in the printed text.

BIOGRAPHICAL NOTE

Lady Mary Wroth (1587–c.1653) was the eldest child of Sir Robert Sidney, first Earl of Leicester, and Barbara Gamage. In 1604, she married Sir Robert Wroth, a favourite of James I, a match that appears to have been unhappy. She had one child, a son, by Wroth. Following the death of her husband in 1614, she withdrew from court and bore two illegitimate children by her first cousin William Herbert, third Earl of Pembroke. Her liaison with Pembroke may have predated Sir Robert's death.

Among early modern English women writers, Wroth was unusual in her concentration on non-religious genres. Her major work was the long prose romance, *The Countess of Montgomery's Urania*, the first part of which was printed in 1621. The *Urania*'s apparent references to scandals at the Jacobean court caused controversy on its publication (see Introduction). The second part, known today only from a manuscript held in the Newberry Library in Chicago, was unpublished in Wroth's lifetime (Wroth 1999). Wroth also wrote a sonnet sequence, *Pamphilia to Amphilanthus* (from which the selections printed here are taken) and a pastoral play, *Love's Victory* (extant in two manuscripts). Wroth came from an extremely literary family. *Urania* is heavily influenced by *The Countess of Pembroke's Arcadia*, the romance written by her uncle Sir Philip Sidney, whilst *Pamphilia to Amphilanthus* has links both to Philip's *Astrophil and Stella* and to her father's poetry. Mary

Sidney, Countess of Pembroke (whose translations of the psalms are excerpted elsewhere in this volume) was Wroth's aunt and godmother. Wroth's writings were praised by contemporary authors who sought her patronage, including Ben Jonson (whom she seems to have known particularly well), George Chapman and Joshua Sylvester.

NOTE ON TRANSCRIPTION

Textual notes record differences in sequence position and wording between the manuscript (*MS*) and the printed book (*1621*) as well as alterations made by Wroth both in the text of the Folger manuscript and in her own personal copy of the printed *Urania*, currently privately owned and recently printed in facsimile (Wroth 1996b). The texts are keyed to poem numbers in Roberts's 1992 edition of Wroth's poetry (*Roberts*), to page numbers in Roberts's edition of the *Urania* (*1995*) and to two independent page numberings (one for the romance, one for *Pamphilia to Amphilanthus*) in the facsimile edition of the 1621 printed text (Wroth 1996b).
Bibliography:
Wroth (1992, 1995, 1996a, 1996b, 1999), Wynne-Davies (1998)
Alexander (1996–97), Gibson (2004), Masten (1991), Parker (1998), Smith (2000)

JG

From Section 1 of the Folger manuscript.

$ Pamphilia to Amphilanthus $

.1.

When nights black mantle could most darknes prove,
    and sleepe deaths Image did my senses hiere
    from knowledg of my self, then thoughts did move
    swifter then those most swiftnes need require:

In sleepe, a Chariot drawne by wing'd desire   5
    I sawe: wher sate bright Venus Queene of love,
    and att her feete her sonne, still adding fire
    to burning hearts which she did hold above

Butt one hart flaming more then all the rest
    the goddess held, and putt itt to my brest   10
    deare sonne, now shute sayd she: thus must wee winn

Hee her obay'd, and martir'd my poore hart,
    I, waking hop'd as dreames itt would depart
    yett since: O mee: a lover have I binn $

[fol. 1r]

Roberts P1; *1621*, [section 1], 1, sonnet 1
2. senses] *1621*; *MS* senceses
11. shute] *1621* shut
14. have I] *1621* I have

.16.

My paine, still smother'd in my grieved brest,
   seekes for some ease, yett cannott passage finde
   to bee discharg'd of this unwellcome ghest;
   when most I strive, more fast his burdens bind,

Like to a ship, on Goodwines cast by wind
   the more she strives, more deepe in sand is prest
   till she bee lost; so am I, in this kind
   sunk, and devour'd, and swallow'd by unrest,

Lost, shipwrackt, spoyl'd, debar'd of smallest hope
   nothing of pleasure left; save thought's have scope,
   which wander may: Goe then, my thoughts, and cry

Hope's perish'd; Love tempest-beaten; Joy lost
   killing dispaire hath all thes blessings crost
   yett faith still cries, Love will nott falsefy. $

[fol. 10r]

Roberts P68; *1621*, [section 3], 31–2, sonnet 6
6. strives] *1621* strive
9. smallest] *MS* swallest
13. blessings] *1621*; *MS* blessing

.19.

Come darkest night, beecoming sorrow best;
   light; leave thy light; fitt for a lightsome soule;
   darknes doth truly sute with mee oprest
   whom absence power doth from mirthe controle:

The very trees with hanging heads condole
   sweet sommers parting, and of leaves distrest
   in dying coulers make a griefe-full role;
   soe much (alas) to sorrow are they prest

Thus of dead leaves her farewell carpett's made;
   theyr fall, theyr branches, all theyr mournings prove;
   with leavles, naked bodies, whose huese vade
   from hopefull greene, to wither in theyr love,

If trees, and leaves for absence, mourners bee
Noe mervaile that I grieve, who like want see $

[fol. 12r]

Roberts P22; *1621*, [section 1], 10–11, sonnet 19
For absence *written by Wroth opposite this poem in her copy of 1621*

23.

When every one to pleasing pastime hies
    some hunt, some hauke, some play, while some delight
    in sweet discourse, and musique showes joys might
    yett I my thoughts doe farr above thes prise

The joy which I take, is that free from eyes   5
    I sitt, and wunder att this daylike night
    soe to dispose them-selves, as voyd of right;
    and leave true pleasure for poore vanities:

When others hunt, my thoughts I have in chase;
    if hauke, my minde att wished end doth fly,   10
    discourse, I with my spiritt tauke, and cry
    while others, musique is theyr greatest grace

O God, say I, can thes fond pleasures move?
Or musique bee butt in deere thoughts of love? $

                                                                 [fol. 14r]

Roberts P26; *1621*, [section 1], 12, sonnet 23
4. doe] *altered from* did; oe *superimposed on* id
6. this] *MS* thiss, *first s dotted*
12. is theyr] *1621* choose as
14. deere] *1621* sweet

31.

After long trouble in a tædious way
    of loves unrest, lay'd downe to ease my paine
    hopeing for rest, new torments I did gaine
    possessing mee as if I ought t'obay:

When Fortune came, though blinded, yett did stay,   5
    and in her blessed armes did mee inchaine;
    I, colde with griefe, thought noe warmth to obtaine
    or to dissolve that ice of joyes decay;

Till, 'rise sayd she, Venus to thee doth send
    by mee the servante of true lovers, joy   10
    bannish all clowds of doubt, all feares destroy,
    and now on fortune, and on Love depend

I, her obay'd, and rising felt that love
Indeed was best, when I did least itt move $.

                                                                 [fol. 19r]

Roberts P36; *1621*, [section 1], 16–17, sonnet 31
9. Venus] *1621* Reward

36.

Juno still jealouse of her husband Jove
   desended from above, on earth to try
   whether she ther could find his chosen love
which made him from the heaven so often fly;

Close by the place, wher I for shade did ly
   she chafeing came; butt when she saw mee move
   have you nott seene this way sayd shee to hy
one, in whom vertue never ground did prove,

Hee, in whom love doth breed to stirr more hate,
   courting a wanton Nimph for his delight
   his name is Jupiter, my Lord by fate
who, for her leaves mee, heav'n, his throne, and light,

I sawe nott him, sayd I, although heere are
Many in whose harts love hath made like warr $

[fol. 21v]

Roberts P97; *1621*, [section 6], 45, sonnet 3
4. heaven] *1621* Heav'ns
6. chafeing] *Roberts* chaseing; *the f is clear in both MS and 1621*
13. nott him] *1621* him not

48.

How like a fire doth love increase in mee,
   the longer that itt lasts, the stronger still,
   the greater purer, brighter, and doth fill
noe eye with wunder more, then hopes still bee

bred in my brest, wher fires of love are free
   to use that part to theyr best pleasing will,
   and now impossible itt is to kill
the heat soe great wher Love his strength doth see.

Mine eyes can scarce sustaine the flames my hart
   doth trust in them my longings to impart,
   and languishingly strive to show my love;

My breath nott able is to breathe least part
   of that increasing fuell of my smart;
   Yett love I will till I butt ashes prove $

$
$ Pamphilia $
$

[fol. 29r]

Roberts P55; *1621*, [section 1], 25 (the second page to be so numbered), sonnet 48
1. mee,] *1621* mee?
5. wher] *1621* when
7. impossible] *1621* unpossible
10. longings] *1621* passions
12. to breathe] *1621* to breath
1621 also ends with Pamphilia's signature, closing section 1.

From Section 3 of the manuscript.

10.

Like to the Indians, scorched with the sunne,
   the sunn which they doe as theyr God adore
   soe ame I us'd by love, for ever more
I worship him, less favor have I wunn,

Better are they who thus to blacknes runn,   5
   and soe can only whitenes want deplore
   then I who pale, and white ame with griefs store,
nor can have hope, butt to see hopes undunn;

Beesids theyr sacrifies receavd's in sight
   of theyr chose sainte: Mine hid as worthles rite;   10
   grant mee to see wher I my offrings give,

Then lett mee weare the marke of Cupids might
   in hart as they in skin doe Phœbus light
   Nott ceasing offrings to love while I Live $
                $

                              [fol. 39v]

Roberts P25; *1621*, [section 1], 12, sonnet 22
4. favor] *1621* favours
9. receavd's] *1621* receiv'd
10. chose] o *probably superimposed on* i
13. doe] *1621* of

From Section 4 of the manuscript.

A crowne of Sonetts
dedicated to Love $

In this strang labourinth how shall I turne?
   wayes are on all sids while the way I miss:
   if to the right hand, ther, in love I burne;
   lett mee goe forward, therin danger is;
If to the left, suspition hinders bliss,   5
   lett mee turne back, shame cries I ought returne

nor fainte though crosses with my fortunes kiss;
   stand still is harder, allthough sure to mourne;
Thus lett mee take the right, or left hand way;
   goe forward, or stand still, or back retire;   10
   I must thes doubts indure without allay
   or help, butt traveile find for my best hire;
Yett that which most my troubled sence doth move
is to leave all, and take the thread of love,

2.

Is to leave all, and take the thread of love
   which line straite leads unto the soules content
   wher choyce delights with pleasures wings doe move,
   and idle phant'sie never roome had lent,
When chaste thoughts guide us then owr minds ar bent   5
   to take that good which ills from us remove,
   light of true love, brings fruite which none repent
   butt constant lovers seeke, and wish to prove;
Love is the shining starr of blessings light;
   the fervent fire of zeale, the roote of peace,   10
   that lasting lampe fed with the oyle of right;
   Image of fayth, and wombe for joyes increase
Love is true vertu, and his ends delight
his flames ar joyes, his bands true lovers might.

[. . .]

8.

Hee that shunns love doth love him self the less
   and cursed hee whos spiritt nott admires
   the worth of love, wher endles blessednes
   raines, and commands, maintaind by heavnly fires
made of vertu, join'de by truth, blowne by desires   5
   strengthned by worth, renued by carefullnes
   flaming in never changing thoughts, briers
   of jelousie shall heere miss wellcomnes;
nor coldly pass in the pursuites of love
   like one longe frozen in a sea of ise,   10
   and yett butt chastly lett your passions move
   noe thought from vertuouse love your minds intise
Never to other ends your phant'sies place
butt wher they may returne with honors grace,

[. . .]

13

Free from all fogs butt shining faire, and cleere
   wise in all good, and innocent in ill
   wher holly friendship is esteemed deere
   with truth in love, and justice in our will,
In love thes titles only have theyr fill   5
   of happy lyfe maintainer, and the meere
   defence of right, the punisher of skill,
   and fraude; from whence directnes doth apeere,
to thee then Lord commander of all harts
   ruller of owr affections kinde, and just   10
   great King of Love, my soule from fained smarts
   or thought of change I offer to your trust
This crowne, my self and all that I have more
except my hart which you beestow'd beefore;

14.

Except my hart which you beestow'd before,
   and for a signe of conquest gave away
   as worthles to bee kept in your choyse store
   yett one more spotles with you doth nott stay
The tribute which my hart doth truly pay   5
   faith untouch'd is, pure thoughts discharge the score
   of debts for mee, wher constancy bears sway
   and rules as Lord, unharm'd by envyes sore,
Yett other mischiefs faile nott to attend,
   as enimies to you, my foes must bee;   10
   curst jealousie doth all her forces bend
   to my undoing; thus my harmes I see
Soe though in Love I fervently doe burne,
In this strange labourinth how shall I turne?
                $ $

                    [fols 43r–46v]

Roberts P77–8, P84, P89–90; *1621*, [section 4], 36–41, sonnets 1, 2, 8, 13, 14

[1]
2. on] *inserted*

2
2. line] *inserted, replacing* path *deleted*
3. with] *superimposed on illegible letters, possibly* do *or* on
11. that] *superimposed on* the; *1621* The

8.
13. phant'sies] *altered from* phant'sis

13.
8. directnes] *1621* directions
11. soule] *superimposed on* sence

14
2–4. and for . . . nott stay] *MS* lines not indented
6. faith untouch'd is] *1621* Is faith untouch'd

From Section 5 of the manuscript.

1.

Faulce hope which feeds butt to destroy, and spill
   what itt first breeds; unaturall to the birth
   of thine owne wombe; conceaving butt to kill,
   and plenty gives to make the greater dearth,
Soe Tirants doe who faulsly ruling earth   5
   outwardly grace them, and with profitts fill
   advance those who appointed are to death
   to make the greater falle to please theyr will.
Thus shadow they theyr wicked vile intent
   coulering evill with the mask of good   10
   while in faire showes theyr malice soe is spent
   hope kills the hart, and tirants shed the blood
For hope deluding brings us to the pride
   of our desires the farder downe to slide, $
                      $

                                                            [fol. 50v]

Roberts P40; *1621*, [section 1], 20, sonnet 35
Sonnet numbers in this section of the manuscript are positioned above the top horizontal rule
8. the] *1621* their
10. the mask] *1621* a show

'My muse now hapy, lay thy self to rest'

My muse now hapy, lay thy self to rest
   sleepe in the quiett of a faithfull love,
   write you noe more, butt lett thes phant'sies move
   some other harts, wake nott to new unrest,
Butt if you study, bee those thoughts adrest   5
   to truth, which shall eternall goodnes prove;
   injoying of true joye, the most and best,
   the endles gaine which never will remove;
Leave the discource of Venus, and her sun
   to young beeginers, and theyr brains inspire   10
   with storys of great love, and from that fire
   gett heat to write the fortunes they have wunn,

And thus leave of, what's past showes you can love,
Now lett your constancy your honor prove, $
                                    $
                              $ Pamphilia $.
                                    $

[fol. 54v]

Final poem of section 5 in manuscript; final poem of whole sequence in 1621
Roberts P103; *1621,* [section 6], 47–8, sonnet 9
9. sun] *1621* sonne
Pamphilia] *not in 1621*

From Section 7 of the manuscript.

'A sheapherd who noe care did take'

.1.

A sheapherd who noe care did take
  of aught butt of his flock
whose thoughts noe pride cowld higher make
  then to maintaine his stock,
Whose sheepe his love was, and his care   5
  theyr good his best delight,
the lambs his joye, theyr sport his fare,
  his pleasure was theyr sight,

2.

Till love, an envier of mans blis
  did turne this merry lyfe   10
to cares, to wishes which ne're miss
  incombrances with strife,
for wheras hee was best content
  with looking on his sheepe
his time in woes must now bee spent,   15
  and broken is his sleepe;

3.

Thus first his woefull chang began
  a lambe hee chanc'd to miss
which to find out about hee ran
  yett finds nott wher itt is,   20
Butt as hee past O! fate unkind
  his ill lead him that way
wheras a willow tree behind
  a faire young mayden lay;

4.

Her bed was on the humble ground   25
  her hed upon her hand

While sighs did show her hart was bound,
   in lov's fast tying band,
clear tears her cleerest eyes lett fall
   upon her love borne face 30
which heavnly drops did sorrow call
   prowd wittnes of disgrace;

5.

The sheapherd stay'd and fed his eyes
   nor furder might hee pas
but ther his freedome to sight ties 35
   his bondage his joye was,
His lambe hee deems nott haulf soe faire
   though itt were very white,
and liberty hee thinks a care
   nor breathes butt in her sight; 40

6.

His former lyfe is alterd quite
   his sheep feed in her eyes
her face his field is of delight,
   and flocks hee doth dispise;
The rule of them hee leaves to none 45
   his scrip hee threw away,
and many hee forsakes for one
   one hee must now obay:

7.

Unhapy man whose loosing found
   what better had bin lost 50
whose gaine doth spring from such a grownd
   wherby hee must bee crost,
The worldly cares hee now neglects
   for Cupids service ties
care only to his fond respects 55
   wher wavelike treasure lies,

8.

As this lost man still gazing stood
   amased att such light
immagining noe heavnly food
   to feed on butt her sight 60
wishing her bright beams to behold
   yett grievd hee for her griefe
when mournfully she did unfolde
   her woes without reliefe

9.
His new sun rose, and rising sayd
   farwell faire willow tree
The triumph of my state decayd
   the fruit for haples mee,
What though thy branch a signe be made
   of labor lost in love
Thy beauty doth noe sooner vade
   then those best fortunes move;

10.
My songs shall end with willow still
   thy branches I will weare
thou wilt accompany my ill,
   and with mee sorrow beare,
true freind sayd she, then sigh'd, and turn'd
   leaving that restles place,
and sheapheard who in passion burn'd
   lamenting his sad case;

11.
The mayd thus gon, alone he left,
   still on her steps he gaz'd,
and hartles growne by love bereft
   of mirth, in spiritt raysd,
to satisfy his toyling thought
   hee after her will hy,
his ruin to bee surer bought,
   and sooner harme to try,

12.
Then thus his latest leave hee tooke
   my sheepe sayd hee farwell,
lett som new sheapherd to you looke
   whose care may mine excell,
I leave you to your freedome now
   loves lawes soe fast mee bind
as noe time I can you allow;
   Or goe poore flock, and find

13
The mayd whom I soe deerly love
   say itt was her deere sight
which from your keepe doth me remove,
   and kills my first delight,
goe you my dog who carefull were
   to guard my flock from harme,

looke to them still noe care forbear
   though love my sences charme;

14.
Butt you my pipe that musique gave,   105
   and pleasd my silent rest
of you I company will crave
   our states now suteth best
for if that faire noe pitty give
   my dying breath shall cry   110
through thee the paines wherin I live
   wherby I breathe to dy;

15.
Madly hee ran from ease to paine
   nott sick butt far from well
hart rob'd by tow faire eyes, his gaine   115
   must prove his earthly hell,
After his hart hee fast doth hy,
   his hart to her did fly,
and for a byding place did cry,
   within her brest to ly;   120

16.
She that refus'd: when hee her spide
   her whom hee held most deere
ly weeping by a river side
   beholding papers neere
Her ruling eyes yett must bee dimd   125
   while pearlike tears she shed
like shadowes on a picture limd,
   att last thes words she read

17.
When I unconstant am to thee
   or faulse doe ever prove   130
lett hapines bee banisht mee
   nor have least taste of love:
Butt this too soone alas cride she
   is (ô) by thee forgott
my hopes, and joys now murderd bee,   135
   and faulshood is my lott;

18.
Too late I find what t'is to trust
   to words, or othes, or tears,
since they that use them prove unjust,
   and couler butt owr fears   140

poore fooles ordain'd to bee deceav'd;
   and trust to bee betraide,
scornd when owr harts ar us bereav'd
   sought to, awhile delay'd;

19.

Yett though that thou soe faulse have bin
   I still will faithfull bee
and though thou think'st to chang, noe sin
   I'le make my loyalty
to shine soe cleere as thy foule fault
   to all men shalbee knowne
thy chang to thy changd hart bee brought
   my faith abroad bee blowne

20.

This having sayd againe she rose
   the papers putting by,
and once againe a new way chose
   striving from griefe to fly,
Butt as she going was along
   that pleasant runing streame
she saw the sallow trees amonge
   the sheapherd Aradeame.

21.

for soe this woefull lad was call'de,
   but when she him beheld,
What wichcraft hath thee now inthralld,
   and brought thee to this field?
What can the cause or reason bee
   that thou art hether come
wher all must taste of misery,
   and mirth with griefe intombe;

22.

Iff mirthe must heere intombed bee
   faire sheapherdes sayd hee
this place the fittest is for mee
   if you use crueltie,
For know I hether com to see
   thy self, wherin now lies
my lyfe, whose absence martirs mee
   whose sight my powre tyes

23.

Give mee butt leave to live with you
   itt is the lyfe I crave

to you I bound am to bee true
   my self to you I gave,
When first I did behold you ly
   in shade of willow tree
that time, my soule did to you ty,
   those eyes did conquer mee,

24.

Is this the reason; ah cride she
   the more I waile thy cace
who thus partaker needs will bee
   in griefe, and in disgrace,
I pitty thee, butt can nott ayde
   thee, nor redress thy ill
since joy, and paine together payd
   scarce satisfies the will;

25.

Iff I doe ty you I release
   the band wherin you are
your freedome shall nott finde decrease
   nor you accuse my care,
The paine I have is all mine owne
   non of itt can beare part
sorrow my strength hath overthrowne
   disdaine hath kil'd my hart.

26.

And sheapherd if that thou dost love
   this counsell take of mee
this humour fond, in time remove
   which can butt torture bee,
take itt from her who too too well
   can wittnes itt is soe
whose hope seem'd heav'n, yett prov'd a hell,
   and comfort chang'd to woe

27.

For I was lov'd, or soe I thought,
   and for itt lov'd againe
but soone those thoughts my ruin brought,
   and nourisht all my paine,
they gave the milk that fed beliefe
   till wean'd they proved dry,
theyr latter nourishment was griefe
   soe famished I must dy;

28.
Then see your chance; I can nott chang
　　nor my affection turne
disdaine, which others move to rang
　　makes mee more constant burne;   220
My sighs I'me sure can nott you please
　　my griefe noe musique prove
my flowing teares your passions ease
　　nor woes delight your love.

29.
Iff my sight have your freedome wunn   225
　　receave itt back againe
soe much I find my self undun
　　by guifts which prove noe gaine
as I lament with them that love
　　soe true in love I ame,   230
and liberty wish all to prove
　　whose harts waste in this flame,

30.
Yett give mee leave (sigh'd hee with tears)
　　to live butt wher you are
my woes shall waite upon your fears   235
　　my sighs attend your care,
I'le weepe when you shall ever waile
　　if you sigh I will cry
when you complaine, I'le never faile
　　to plaine my misery,   240

31.
I will you guard, and safely keepe
　　from danger, and from feare,
still will I wach when you doe sleep;
　　and for both sorrows beare,
make mee nott free I bondage crave   245
　　nor seek els butt to serve,
this freedom will procure my grave,
　　thes bands my lyfe preserve

32.
For lyfe, and joye, and ease, and all
　　alas lies in your hands   250
then doe nott cause my only fall,
　　I tyde ame in such bands
part hence I can nott, nor love leave
　　butt heer must ever byde

then pitty lett my paine receave 255
  doe nott from mercy slide;

33.
Iff that sayd she you constant are
  unto your coming ill
I'le leave this place yett lett all care
  accompany mee still; 260
And sheapherd live, and hapy bee
  lett judgment rule thy will,
seeke one whose hart from love is free,
  and who thy joye may fill;

34.
For I lov's bondslave ame, and tyde 265
  in fetters of disdaine
my hopes ar frozen, my spring dri'de
  my autume drownd with paine;
I lov'd, and wurse, I sayd I lov'd
  free truth my ruin brought, 270
and soe your state the like hath mov'd,
  and loss for gaining bought,

35
With that away she hasted fast
  left him his cares to hold
who now to sorrow makes all hast, 275
  woes drive his hopes to fold,
now hee can see, and weeping say
  his fortune blind hee finds
a hart to harbour his decay,
  a state which mischief binds 280

36.
This now hee feels and woefully
  his birth, and lyfe hee blames,
yett passion rules when reasons ly
  in dark, or quenched flames;
That place hee first beheld her in 285
  his biding hee doth make;
The tree his liberty did win
  hee calls his martir stake;

37.
And pleasingly doth take his fall,
  his griefe accounts delight, 290
freedome, and joye his bitter thrall,
  his food her absent sight,

> In contraries his pleasures bee
>   while mourning gives him ease,
> his tomb must bee that haples tree 295
>   wher sorrows did him seaze
>
>   38.
> And thus did live, though dayly dide
>   The sheapherd Aradeame
> whose ceasles tears which never drid
>   were turn'd into a streame, 300
> him self the hed, his eyes the springs
>   which fed that river cleere,
> that unto lovers this good brings
>   when they aproach itt neere,
>
>   39.
> And drinke of itt to banish quite 305
>   all ficle thought of chang
> butt still in one choyce to delight,
>   and never think to rang;
> Of this sweet water I did drink
>   which did such faith infuse 310
> as since to change I cannott think
>   Love will death sooner chuse; $

[fols 57r–63r]

First unnumbered song in Section 7 of the manuscript
Roberts U52; *1621*, 520–9 *(embedded in the text of the romance); 1995, 614–23*
11. cares] *1621* teares
28. fast tying] *1621* untying
34. nor furder] *1621* no farther, *corrected by Wroth in her copy of 1621 to* nor farther
40. in] *1621* by
53. cares] *1621* care
58. light] *1621* a sight
61. her bright] *1621* but her
63. she] *1621* he
67. triumph of my state] *1621* roote of my estate
72. move] *1621* prove
79. passion] *1621* passions
81. thus] *1621* now
82. steps he] *1621* footsteps
85. toyling] *1621* restlesse
87. surer bought] *1621* sooner brought
102. flock] *1621* Sheepe
114. butt] *1621* yet
116. earthly] *1621* worldly
123. river] *1621* Rivers
125. yett must] *1621* must yet
133. too soone alas] *1621* alas too soone
145. have] *1621* hast

147. chang] *1621* leave
174. thy] *1621* Your
175. martirs] *1621* martir'd
180. self] *1621* life
184. conquer] *1621* murther
186, 190. thy] *1621* your
189, 190. thee] *1621* you
194. band] *1621* bond
197. mine] *1621* my
198. non of itt can] *1621* None can of it
201. thou dost] *1621* you doe
204. bee] *1621* thee
208. comfort] c *written over illegible letter*
219. move] *1621* moves
227. I find my self] *1621* my selfe I finde
237. when you shall ever] *1621* whenever you shall
240. plaine] *1621* waile
248. bands] *1621* bonds
262, 264. thy] *1621* your
268. autume] *1621* Sommer
271. state] *1621* speech
275. makes] *1621* make
283. passion] *1621* passions
291. his] *1621* this, *corrected by Wroth in her copy of 1621 back to MS reading*
295. must] *1621* shall
296. sorrows] *1621* sorow
298. Aradeame] *1621* Arideame, *corrected by Wroth in her copy of 1621 back to MS reading*
299. ceasles] *1621* causlesse, *corrected by Wroth in her copy of 1621 to* ceaslesse
301. springs] *1621* spring
303. that] *superimposed on* and?; *1621* Which, *corrected by Wroth in her copy of 1621 to* and unto lovers . . . brings] *1621* to true harts . . . doth bring
306. thought] *1621* thoughts

'I, who doe feele the highest part of griefe'

I, who doe feele the highest part of griefe
   shall I bee left without reliefe:
I, who for you my torments patient beare
   now doe nott leave mee in my feare;
O comfort never could more wellcom bee   5
   then in this needfull time to mee,
One drop of pitty will bee higher priz'd
   then seas of joye, if once dispisd;
Turne nott the tortures which for you I try
   upon my hart to make mee dy;   10
Have I offended? t'was att your desire
   when by your words, you felt lov's fire;
Iff I did ill, itt was to please your will,
   can you gett, and the ofspring kill?
The fault which I in this committed have   15
   was, you did ask, I freely gave,

    show yett som pitty, then lett torments hy,
        give butt one sigh, I blest shall dy:
    Butt o you can nott, I have you displeasd,
        and change, from mee your hart hath seaz'd;   20
    Now lett noe fauning hope of fained skill
        seeke any joye, butt joyes to kill;
    Lett all conspire to breed my wrack, and end,
        yett nott enough my days to spend;
    My state I see, and you your ends have gain'd   25
        I'me lost, since you have mee obtain'd,
    Yett though I can nott please your first desire
        I yett may joye in scorners fire
    As Salimanders in the fire doe live
        soe shall love flames my living give,   30
    And though against your minde I bee, and move
        forsaken creatures feede on love;
    Doe you proceed, you one day may confess
        you wrong'd my care, when I care less;

                                          [fols 64v–65r]

Second unnumbered song in Section 7. The final poem in the manuscript
Roberts U24; *1621 (embedded in the text of the romance), 271–2; 1995, 326–7*
3. my torments patient beare] *1621* doe cruell torments beare
4. *1621* will you alasse leave me in feare?
5. O] *1621* Know
7. pitty] *1621* comfort
8. joye] *1621* joyes
12. words] *1621* vowes
13. Iff I did ill, itt] *1621* What I did erre in,
15. *1621* The greatest fault, which I committed have
16. was] *1621* is
17. *1621* Kindly relent, let causlesse curstnes flye,
19. you] *1621* much
20. *1621* striving to gaine, I losse have seaz'd
21–4. not in *1621*
27. Yett though] *1621* And since
28. *1621* I'le blow, and nourish scorners fire
30. love] *1621* those
    living] *1621* being
31. minde] *1621* will
    bee] *1621* live
32. feede on] *1621* live and
33. proceed . . . confess] *1621* proceed, and you may well confesse
34. when I care] *1621* while I can, *corrected by Wroth in her copy of 1621 back to MS reading*

4

Anne Southwell's poetry

Folger Shakespeare Library, MS V.b.198
British Library Lansdowne MS 740

1 Folger Shakespeare Library, MS V.b.198

Poetry by Anne Southwell, a strongly Calvinist writer, appears in two extant manuscripts. It is possible that they were both assembled under the supervision of Southwell herself and/or her second husband Henry Sibthorpe.

As well as secular and religious poetry by Southwell, the Folger manuscript contains a wide range of miscellaneous material: verse from songbooks and poems by Henry King, Arthur Gorges and Walter Ralegh (none attributed correctly), prose texts by Southwell and others and memoranda of various kinds, including 'A List of my Bookes' (Cavanaugh 1967). The manuscript is written in many different hands—including Southwell's own, an angular, informal italic—and on several different types of paper. The manuscript was in the library of the Southwells, the family of Lady Anne's first husband, when it was offered for sale by a bookseller in 1834. Having belonged to two other collectors, it was purchased by the founder of the Folger Shakespeare Library in 1927. A complete edition of the manuscript has recently been published (Southwell 1997).

The manuscript, a large folio, was first used in the 1580s by John Sibthorpe—presumably a relative of Henry's—to transcribe financial military records. John left most leaves blank and it has been conjectured that Henry may have presented Southwell with the book, for her own use, on the occasion of their marriage in 1626 (Cavanaugh 1967, 244). The first page is headed, in a scribe's hand, 'The workes of the Lady Ann Sothwell: Decemb 2° 1626'. Texts were written in the book in many different hands, most of them apparently those of Southwell/Sibthorpe amanuenses, with sporadic corrections and additions by Southwell herself. Most of this copying took place in the last years of Southwell's life, from 1631 to 1636, starting at both ends of the manuscript: by and large, poetry was written at the front of the volume, prose at the end. Bits of paper containing other miscellaneous texts linked to Southwell were inserted later (or 'tipped in') at an unknown date or dates. The book now contains 74 leaves. The most notable tipped-in addition is a collection of long verse meditations by Southwell on the decalogue (the Ten Commandments): scribally copied poems corrected by the author together with related rough drafts in her own hand (Southwell's only extensive writing in the manuscript). Decalogue meditations are also found in the Lansdowne manuscript (for which see below). Those tipped into the Folger miscellany (poems on the first, second, third, fourth, fifth, seventh and eighth command-

22. The sixt day all the beastes & beastly natures
of Turke & Pope & other brutish factions
at Euen the Lord & soueraigne of those creatures
gods image comes to keepe them in subiection
when all the heresyes must fade away
& then drawes on the holy sabbath day.

23. Yett first god calles his Image to the barre
those that of the forbidden tree haue eaten
a fierye sword from Paradise doth scarre
& from the tree of life theyr boldnes threaten
Thus goeing hand in hand wth the creation
it pointes out the worldes end, mans perturbation.

24. & now me thinkes I heare some wizzard say
how dares this foolish woman bee soe bold
ask Jahells ---- ^that Siseraes head did stay
& Judiths sword that made a hott loue cold
Hee that enabled them, enables mee
yf thou seeke knowledge hee'll enable thee.

25. How cloudye is that soule that will not seeke
to know as farre as finite dust may knowe
who made him & the world & both doth keepe
Angells & men & the darke hell belowe
in whose breath all things bee & liue & moue
whose prouidence doth gouerne all wth loue.

26. mans mind a mirror is of heauenly formes
& though created, yett hee can create
his polisht thoughts the quill & booke adornes
wch clouds of ignorance doth captiuate

yf thou ff thou
A All the

ments) seem to have been written in James I's reign (1603–25), well before the compilation of the bulk of the manuscript. The final two leaves in the manuscript contain, on tipped-in leaves, material which must postdate Southwell's death: two versions of an epitaph on her (composed and possibly written out by Henry Sibthorpe) together with verse eulogies by Sibthorpe and Roger Cox, curate of Acton.

Roger Cox is one of many associates of Southwell's mentioned in the Folger miscellany. He was clearly an important contact, for one of Southwell's poems praises his *Hebdomada Sacra* (1630), a book of verse meditations on nativity week, and two of his sermons were copied into the manuscript. Southwell also refers to Cox's superior, Daniel Featley, the absentee rector of Acton and a prominent author of religious works. Other patrons and associates include the poet Francis Quarles (Dove 1998), Cicely, Lady Ridgway (for whom Southwell wrote a prose defence of poetry (Cavanaugh 1984), a mock elegy and an epitaph, all of them included in the Folger manuscript), Viscount Falkland, and Bernard Adam, Bishop of Limerick.

Burke and Klene argue that the manuscript—both the original book and the insertions—was assembled by Henry Sibthorpe as a kind of posthumous testament to his wife's poetic skills (Burke 2002, 112–13; Southwell 1997; Klene 2000). Burke suggests that the inclusion in the manuscript of poems not by Southwell herself 'may be her husband's attempt to make her more prolific than she was' (Burke 2002, 95). Longfellow proposes that Sibthorpe presented the manuscript to the Southwells, a wealthy family, in an attempt 'to curry favour with his wife's in-laws' (Longfellow 2004).

All the poems included in this selection are from the main volume of the manuscript (i.e. not the tipped-in leaves). In many cases, it is difficult to tell one hand from another, and the hand classification made by Southwell's modern-day editor, Jean Klene (Southwell 1997, 117–23)—broadly followed here—should not be regarded as definitive.

2 British Library, Lansdowne MS 740, fols 142r–167v

The most substantial verse written by Southwell is her incomplete sequence of long meditative poems on the Ten Commandments. Southwell's decalogue poetry occurs in both the Folger miscellany (described above) and in one section of British Library Lansdowne MS 740 (a collection of seventeenth-century literary manuscripts bundled together at a later period). The Lansdowne volume was sold to the British Museum library (now the British Library) in 1807 by the first Marquess of Lansdowne, having at some earlier stage been in the collection of the antiquary Ralph Thoresby (1658–1725) (Klene 2000, 183). Its earlier history is unknown and its current binding nineteenth-century.

Each of Southwell's decalogue poems takes its starting point from a commandment, but rapidly digresses, taking in material apparently very remote from the commandment in question. A major influence on the poetry is Du Bartas's *Divine Weeks and Works* in Joshuah Sylvester's popular translation (1592–1608). A nineteenth-century bookseller's catalogue lists a manuscript (now lost) as 'Lectures on the Commandments and Moral Ethics, the Collections of Lady Anne Southwell' (Burke 2002, 97). Perhaps this manuscript contained a complete sequence of decalogue poetry by Southwell. Alternatively, it may have contained prose texts by Southwell and/or others on the commandments—the raw material for Southwell's decalogue poetry.

The Lansdowne manuscript, a scribal fair copy, opens with a verse dedication by Southwell to 'the kinges most excellent Majestye', followed by meditations on the third commandment ('Thou shalt not take the name of the Lord thy God in vain') and the fourth commandment ('Remember the Sabbath day to keepe it holy'). Meditations on the same commandments in the Folger manuscript are radically different and, Klene (2000) and Burke (2002) think, earlier. The Lansdowne manuscript concludes with a fragmentary poem in praise of Southwell's writings by 'H', presumably Southwell's second husband Henry Sibthorpe. The roughness of the manuscript suggests that it was not intended as a presentation copy. Though Southwell's own handwriting does not occur in the Lansdowne manuscript, the phrasing of the dedication and of the poem at the end imply that she was alive at the time when it was put together.

As passages praising James I in the Folger version of Southwell's poem on the fourth commandment are omitted in the Lansdowne text, it has been argued that this manuscript was intended for Charles I rather than for his father (Southwell 1997, xxxii; Burke 2002, 106; Longfellow 2004, n. 16). There are, however, other references to James in the Lansdowne text, and it is possible that the absence of the passages in praise of him simply expresses a growing disenchantment with James's religious attitudes.

The Sabbath was an explosive topic in the seventeenth century. Southwell's insistence in 'Precept 4' below on the importance of keeping the Sabbath echoes the sabbatarian concerns of those puritans who opposed the laxity of James I's 'Book of Sports' (1618). This controversial book sanctioned the practice of traditional sports and recreations on Sundays, and was thus opposed by puritans, who believed that the whole day ought to be reserved for devotional activities. Southwell's acquaintance Daniel Featley got into trouble with the King in 1625 for licensing books which advocated sabbatarianism (Featley 1629). The controversy over Sunday observance flared up again in 1633 when Charles I reissued the 'Book of Sports' at the insistence of Archbishop Laud.

The scribe of this manuscript also copied the text of Southwell's prose letter to Lady Ridgway in defence of poetry in the Folger manuscript (fols 3r–v; Southwell 1997, 4–5). The textual notes in this edition tentatively distinguish between revisions in two hands: 'scribe' (the scribe's neat mixed hand, in two different inks) and 'revising' (a different mixed hand, working after the scribe's work was complete, speculatively identified by Burke (2002, 96) and Klene (2000, 181–2) as Henry Sibthorpe's). Both hands make significant alterations to the text (see, for example, the lines excised from the dedication to the King, and the alterations at lines 139–50 of 'Precept 4'—see plate 3). The 'revising' hand also frequently intervenes simply to modernise Southwell's language and the scribe's spelling. Stanza numbering in 'Precept 4' is original.

BIOGRAPHICAL NOTE

The daughter of Sir Thomas Harris, a lawyer and MP, and Elizabeth Pomeroy, Anne Southwell was born in Devon in 1574. She married her first husband,

Thomas (later Sir Thomas) Southwell (a nephew of the Jesuit poet Robert Southwell) in 1594 and moved with him to Poulnalong Castle in Ireland shortly after 1603. They had two children, Elizabeth and Frances. It has been suggested that Anne Southwell wrote three witty prose pieces published in the 1614 and 1615 editions of the popular anthology *Sir Thomas Overbury's Wife* and there attributed to 'the Lady Southwell' and 'A.S.' (Overbury *et al.* 2003, 298–300; 301–2, 304–5), though this has recently been disputed (Burke 2002, 109–12; Southwell 1997, xxviii–xxxi; Schleiner 1994, 107–10, 114–22; Considine 2000, 69; Ross 2000, 42–6; Overbury *et al.* 2003, 388–9, 391; Longfellow 2004, 130, n. 5).

Shortly after Sir Thomas Southwell's death in 1626, Southwell married Captain Henry Sibthorpe, a soldier and administrator in Ireland, retaining her title from her first marriage. Some time after 1627, Southwell and Sibthorpe left Ireland to live in Clerkenwell, London, moving to Acton in 1631. Anne Southwell died in Acton in 1636.

Bibliography:
Cavanaugh (1984), Featley (1629), Overbury *et al.* (2003), Southwell (1997)
Burke (2002), Cavanaugh (1967), Considine (2000), Dove (1998), Klene (2000), Longfellow (2004), Ross (2000), Schleiner (1994).

JG

Folger Library, V.b.198.

Sonnett

Beauty, Honor, yeouth, and fortune
   I importune
None of yow to be my freind
   Theise Gambols end.
And I have gaynd a Rosy bed.   5
   Uppon your head
Trod out of thornes and cruell Cares
   And now your wares
Semes noysome trumpery to my thoughts
   Things good for noughts   10
O happy state that dying lives
   And reason gives
A just accompt of her disdayning
   By her lost Gayning:

[fol. 9r]

Copied in a hand hesitantly attributed by Klene to John Bowker
  Title. Sonnett] *The title, as in other poems copied by this scribe, is to the left of and slightly above the first line*
  11. dying] *MS* diiing

Sonnett

O how happy were I dearest
Far above all tonges Expressing

If thow wert as thow appearest
Never Queene had such a blessing
In the Pride of Fortunes dressing   5

Thow hast sworne might I beleeve the
Ill do I deme my suspition
And to say so much, Doth greive me
That I see thy bad Condition
And my faults are thy Addition.   10

[fol. 9v]

Copied in the same hand as the preceding poem
Title. Sonnett] *See note on preceding poem*

'All.maried.men.desire.to.have good wifes'

All.maried.men.desire.to.have good wifes:
but.few.give good example.by thir lives
They are owr head they wodd have us thir heles.
this makes the good wife kick the good man reles.
When god brought Eve to Adam for a bride   5
the text sayes she was taene from out mans side
A.simbole of that side, whose sacred bloud.
flowed for his spowse, the Churches savinge good.
This is a.misterie, perhaps too deepe.
for blockish Adam that was falen a sleepe   10

[fol. 16r]

Copied by an unidentified scribe. This short poem, transcribed in a small hand, occupies one whole folio page
1–2, 7, 9. *The puzzling use of stops in these lines is unique in the manuscript*

British Library Lansdowne MS 740.

To the kinges most excellent Majestye

Darest thou my muse present thy Battlike winge,
before the eyes of Brittanes mighty kinge.
Hee that all other states exceedes as farre
as doth the sunne a litle glimmering starre
To whose blest birth the Cherubins did tender   5
all the endowments for a princely splendor
You lines, excuse my boldnes in this matter
& tell the truth; my hart's to bigg to flatter.
Yf in the search of this world I could find
one to exceed the vertues of thy minde   10

the height of my ambition would aspire
to offer up these sparckles to that fire.
since all fall shorte of thy soules qualitye
more short then of thy states abilitye.
Tis thy attractuve goodnes gives mee scope   15
to come (dread Soveraigne) on the knees of hope
& offer up this tribute to thy meritt
this sacrifice to thy devinest spiritt.
I know in God there doth no ill abide
nor in his true Epitome, no pride.   20
Thou art the nursing father of all pietye,
the mightye champion for the Deitye.
Tis of the high Jehovah I doe singe
to whome doth this belonge but to the kinge.
Great God of heaven, thankes for thy gracious favours,   25
great king on earth, accept the poore endeavors

    of your majestyes most humble
     & faythfull subject.

    Anne Southwell.

        [fol. 142r]

This dedicatory poem occupies the whole of the first page of Southwell's original manuscript. This page is very dirty and smudged, having been used at one stage as an outer cover. Throughout the manuscript it is difficult to distinguish between accidental ink marks and deliberate punctuation

 4–5. *Deleted text between these lines (scribe):*
  The only touchstone of great natures storye
  in whome all artes reside, & hold theyr glorye.
 6–7. *Deleted text between these lines (scribe):*
  whose sacred lippes doe never part asunder
  as the Heralds of all grace & wonder
 14. short] *altered from* shorte *(revising);* e *deleted*
 19, 20. no] *altered from* noe *(revising);* e *deleted*
 Anne Southwell] *copied in the scribe's italic hand, not Southwell's autograph*
 On the back of the opening page (fol. 142v) is the following stanza, written upside down in pencil in a hand different from any other in the Lansdowne manuscript. Another version of this poem, in the same hand, thought by Klene to be Samuel Rowson's, is found in the Folger manuscript (fol. 28v), variants for which are given below

  with feet of clay to enter the most hollye
  or watrye balles to stare against the Sunne
  alas it is but blinde presumptuous follie
  a parchase sought, by which wee are undonne
   if off thy court I am, there will I rest   5
   leave secret councell to thy sacred brest

 5. if . . . there] *Folger* lett me be of thy Court, there; thy *inserted*
 6. leave secret] *replacing* thy sacred
 leave . . . brest] *Folger* leaving thy secrets, to thy sacred brest

Precept 4

Remember the Sabbath day to keepe it holy, six
dayes shalt thou labour & doe all thy worke,
but the seventh day is the sabaoth of the
lorde thy god, in it, thou shalt not doe
any worke, thou nor thy sonne, nor thy
daughter, thy manservant nor thy
mayd, nor thy beast, nor thy stran-
ger that is within thy gates.
for in six dayes the Lord made the heavens & the earth
the sea & all that in them is, & rested the seventh
day; therefore the Lord blessed the Sabbath day &
hallowed it.

1. In six dayes God made this admired ball,
   this verdant couch with lillyes overspred
   engrayl'd it with a liquid christall wall,
   & hunge a double vallence over head
      of fire & ayre, fring'd round with starrye lights   5
      under whose fabrick walke all living wights.

2. There this immortall mortall prince hee plac'd
   who had free will & high commaund of all.
   thus all compleat & with all graces grac'd
   the voyce of voyces to his type doth call   10
      Labour six dayes, but keepe the seventh day holy
      when hee biddes rest, all labour is but folly.

3. In this day summon up thy weekes expence
   that from thy lord thou mayst acquittance have
   & heape not up offence uppon offence   15
   ingrave thy sinnes before they thee engrave
      Mercy is for the living not the dead
      when life is gone, Justice in power doth spredd.

4. In this day rest from all thy worldly paynes,
   take out the harrow from the plowmans handes   20
   refresh his faynting limmes & tired braynes
   & from thy oxen take theyr yoaked bandes
      tis six to one, then having soe much oddes,
      twere badly done to steale that day that's gods.

[. . .]

6. Six dayes thou art to labour sayth the Lord,
   heer's Adams curse chaynd to necessitye
   but then thy labours plentye shall affoord

which doth agayne sweeten calamitye.
    All thyne owne worke in six dayes thou mayst doe   35
    though not soe much as sinne invites thee to.

7. for yf thy worke in those six dayes bee bad
or left undon, the seventh is defaced,
for worldly cares will make thy visage sad
& guilt of ill will in thy harte bee placed   40
    Then to keepe holy this high day of rest
    thou must worke faithfully in all the rest.

8. Nor art thou bid to sleepe out this high day
to singe, daunce, game or guzzell out thy time
but in gods vineyard thou art willed to stay   45
& cutt downe thornes that overtoppe his vine
    for thou must never rest whilest thou art heere
    yett in this day thy future rests appeare.

9. Nor art thou bidd to labour heere alone
but thou art bound to bring thy familye   50
thy wife & thee, two loving hartes make one
Christ & his church explane that simpathye
    thy children & thy servants are exprest
    by thee & them gods vineyard must bee drest.

10. Besides the honor due to the creator   55
how beneficiall is this time to all
where wee may learne to knowe both god & nature
& what by sinne or grace to us doth fall
    & by our knowledge like to mortall gods
    resolve & reconcile what is at ods.   60

11. Where yf there were noe time given us by grace
but still like swine to grovell in the mire
how should the soule her facultyes deface
or how would man to higher state aspire.
    O gratious god thou forcest us to this   65
    not soe much for thy glorye as our blisse.

12. Thou hast noe need of us to fill thy skyes
for Cherubines & Thrones adorne that place;
where all doe stand with loving watchfull eyes
& joy to see the glorye of thy face   70
    still singing Halelujahs to thy name
    & with due reverence aye extoll the same.

13. Thou hast noe need of us to fill thine earth
    or to dresse up thine altars with perfumes

>   Thou canst replenish it with Angells birth 75
>   whose heavenly formes noe humane stuffe assumes.
>   where noe rebellious thoughts, or heedlesse sloth
>   shall rowse thy justice or provoke thy wroth
>
> 14.   Only thy love mov'd in those sacred springes
>   then darke, now cleere & blessed element, 80
>   the very soule & nurse of growing thinges
>   with whome thy gratious spiritt did frequent
>   & moving there, sett all the world in order
>   & made her flowing armes earthes fruitfull border.
>
> 15.   & from the light the darke did seperate 85
>   deviding cold & moyst the hott & drye,
>   yett ech with others to participate
>   & propagate by a sweete simpathye.
>   Soe that, not men, but Angells, starres & spheares
>   ech one the elementall livery weares. 90
>
> 16.   Gods first weekes worke doth as a symbole stand
>   of all the time that is to come & past
>   by milliarious yeeres, prophetick handes
>   hath drawen earthes longitude, times reckoning cast.
>   A thousand yeeres are one day with the Lord 95
>   six dayes of worke, the seventh did rest affoord.
>
> 17.   The first day voyd & emptye doth present
>   Adams apostasye, voyd of all grace.
>   raigning a thousand yeeres in Cains descent
>   in Seth the promised seed, the light takes place 100
>   God seperates the darkenes from the light
>   good men are day, the wicked men are night.
>
> 18.   The second day god made the firmament
>   & partes the moist deepe counsells of the proud
>   Babells confusion with the deluge went 105
>   the blessed seede & spouse an ark doth shrowd
>   & her fresh springes a christaline doe make
>   the rest theyr place in sulpharous channell take.
>
> 19.   The third day when the waters were devided
>   the virgin earth presents all store of treasure, 110
>   Abraham & moses by gods word now ayded
>   in a Satrapick dance keepe sacred measures
>   as fruitfull solid ground, in them god graves
>   his drad commandes, the rest are giddye waves.
>
> 20.   The fourth day god did make the sunne & moone 115
>   In the fourth thousand yeere came Christ that sonne

   his church the moone, Apostles starlike shone
   lightening the gentiles with cloudes overrunne
    Thou Alpha & omega, thou blest light
    thy sacred beames be ever in our sight.   120

21. The fift dayes worke was fish & fowle that flyes
   & now those monstrous Hydraes did crall
   the Dragons & the Locustes did arise
   that on heavens childing wombe throwe seas of gall
    who to the wildernes afrighted runnes   125
    to ease her throes, & beare her groning sonnes.

22. The sixt day all the beastes & beastly natures
   of Turks & Pope & other brutish factions
   at even the Lord & soveraigne of those creatures
   gods image commes to keepe them in subjection   130
    when all the heresyes must fade away
    & then drawes on the holy Sabbath day.

23. Yett first god calles his Image to the barre
   those that of the forbidden tree have eaten
   a fierye sword from Paradise doth scare   135
   & from the tree of life theyr boldnes threaten
    Thus goeing hand in hand with the creation
    it pointes the worldes end out, mans perturbation.

[24. & now mee thinkes I heare some wizzard say
   how dares this foolish woman bee soe bold?   140
   ask Jahells nayle that Siseraes head did stay
   & Judiths sword that made her hott love cold
    Hee that enabled them, enables mee.
    yf thou seeke knowledge hee'l enable thee.

25. How cloudye is that soule that will not seeke   145
   to know as farre as finite dust may knowe
   who made him & the world, & both doth keepe,
   Angells & men & the darke hell belowe
    in whose breath all thinges bee & live & move
    whose providence doth governe all with love.] 150

26. The life & soule of soules is contemplation
   It makes a man to differ from a beast
   & bringes him to the god of his creation
   & shewes, how first hee tumbled from his nest
    & by his fall how both his winges fell lame   155
    & how hee may impe fethers to the same

27. Unto that god of order & of time
   wee owe the time that his word hath sett downe

Religion is the stayre by which wee clime
the gole wee seeke is an immortall crowne.   160
All worldly pleasures are expired by death
that hanges in the incertaynty of breath.

28. & who, to play a kinges parte for a day
would spend these pretious minutes in attiring,
who are more traytors to theyr state then they   165
that peacocklike stand still themselves admiring
who can enjoy themselves or what they have
that seeke not god till they have found theyr grave.

29. Seven hundred twenty names the Rabbines found
to expresse god to theyr capacityes   170
who sayles to farre, may sett his shipp on ground
& gazing on the sunne, dazell his eyes
for what hee is, noe man hath ever told
nor none shall knowe whilst hee is wrap'd in mold

[. . .]

33. Hee knowes god best that first himself doth knowe
to bee but wretched, poore, though proud & vayne.
how like a shadowe hee doth come & goe,   195
that all his labours heere are greefe & payne
that all his sences beare deathes fearefull skarres
& all his thoughts are still at civill warres.

34. & when poore wretched man beholdes his weakenes
who cannott make a flye with all his skill   200
hee may behold the all creators greatnes
& stand the more obedient to his will
beyond his chayne poore ape hee cannott skipp
yett naught can tame this bedlame but a whipp.

35. Spend not your time in cobwebbes like a spinner   205
but with the publicane confesse & say
O god bee mercifull to mee a sinner
to come to god there is noe other way
for faythfull prayers pierce the christall skyes
& is the best accepted sacrifice.   210

[. . .]

47. To lay fayre colours on a wrinckled hide
or smooth up vice with eloquent discource
who writes for pence, be he soe turpified
& lett those nine Chima'raes bee his nurse.   280
to teach him crawle the Heliconian hill
& in Pernassus dipp his ivorye quill.

48. for mee, I write but to my self & mee
    what gods good grace doth in my soule imprint
    I bought it not for pelf, none buyes of thee   285
    nor will I lett it at soe base a rent
        as wealth or fame, which is but drosse & vapor
        & scarce deserves the blotting of a paper.

49. Nor am I soe affected unto rime
    but as it is a help to memorye   290
    because it doth commaund a larger time
    to wrapp up sence in measures quantitye
        nor marres it truth, but gives wittes fire more fuell
        & from an Ingott formes a curious Jewell.

50. & though some amorous Idiotts doe disgrace it   295
    in making verse the packhorse of theyr passion
    such cloudes may dimme the sunne but not deface it
    nor marvell I that love doth love this fashion
        To speak in verse, yf sweet & smoothly carryed
        to true proportions love is ever maryed   300

51. Tis love hath wove this rugged twine of mine
    quickening my harte with such a sprightly flame
    that frozen death can never make it pine
    nor sad affliction hath the power to lame.
        for love & fire ech other best resemble   305
        both hott & bright, both vigilant & nimble.

52. Away base world, hence shadowes, hence away.
    You shalbee noe corrivalls to my love.
    for hee is fresh as is the flourye may
    & truly constant as the turtle dove.   310
        his breth like beddes of roses cheere the morne,
        his hayres reflex the sunne beames doth adorne.

53. From his fayre eyes, the world hath all her light
    & till hee look'd on her, shee lay as dead
    she'd eyes before, but those eyes had noe sight   315
    They now are in her soule, then in her head
        shee spake before, but knew not what shee sayd
        like pratling babes, or doting age decayed.

54. Some few could see & speake with triple sence
    & what were these, but harolds of thy comming   320
    thou gavest theyr eyes, the point of future tense
    Coles from thine altar tipp'd theyr tongues with cunning
        to tell great Davids ofspring they should see
        a new Jerusalem raysed up in thee

[. . .]

57. & now my Love with hope doth gather winge
    leaving this dunghill & her bed of clay,
    & with the mounting larke beginnes to singe
    in joy & honour of this Halcion day.
        when men & Angells all at once shall move
        rays'd by the flame of sweete bright fervent love.

[. . .]

60. Can love bee barren, noe, it cannott bee
    the active sunne may sooner loose his heate,
    & passive earth well labourd, yeeld noe fee
    & mortalls live that have but stones to eate.
        Tis male & female, & both sex is full
        absence inflames, & neerenes cannot dull.

61. Hence Lothsame ground baytes, I am sick with love;
    & growen to queasye for such fussome dyett,
    on payne of curses doe not seeke to move
    my thoughts awry that now are all at quiett
        & fill'd with admiration of his beautye
        to whome all true perfection oweth dutye.

62. Mine eares bee deafe against the clamorous world
    & yee mine eyes see not her fluttering pride
    lightening & thunder that abroad is hurld
    with which my hart to longe was stupifyed.
        yett now I see twas but a dunghill smoke,
        the more wee pudder in't, wee sooner choke.

63. You witty wantons, leave your foolish loves,
    though pearle & currall overspredd your skinne
    making you looke like swannes & silver doves
    & love that love which makes you fayre within.
        Colour's an accident that will decay.
        a superficies spred but over clay.

64. To boast of it I could as well as you
    to whome kind nature hath noe stepdame bene,
    but sinnes infection makes them more to rue
    that beare a leprous soule in a fayr skinne.
        To him that built us wee doe give abuse
        & turne best mettaill to the basest use.

65. But bee as loving Dames as you are Lovely,
    not to your flattering servants, formes or glasses,
    to place or trappings; these thinges are but follye
    & will approve the lovers of them asses.
        Your loves soe layed doe make men thinke you moles
        fayre soft & wittye but devoyd of soules

66. Are you denyed soules then, you shelles of men,
    are they but hatched in you & flye away
    noe marvell though theyr wisedomes doe contemne
    your sex, since you are only formall clay.
       but trust them not that would perswade you soe   395
       such serpents but advise you to more woe.

67. Goe search the sacred writt, where you shall find
    what your creation was & to what end
    Lett not theyr envious folly make you blind
    who pittyes him that is not his owne frend.   400
       Adam did sleepe whilst god built your fayre frame:
       & hee still sleepes that would have you thus lame.

[. . .]

73. Rayse you the superciliums of your eyes
    though but to see theyr fellow spheare, the sunne,
    they say from thence a shower of arrowes flyes   435
    to wound theyr hartes by which they are undonne.
       Natures free dowrye they call sett temptation
       to quitt theyr faultes they'l challenge great creation

74. Dare you but write, you are Minervaes bird
    the owle at which these battes & crowes must wonder,   440
    they'l crittickize uppon the smallest word
    this wanteth number case, that tense & gender
       then must you frame a pittifull epistle
       to pray him bee a rose was borne a thistle.

75. Could you, as did those Sybells, prophecye   445
    men will but count you witches for your skill
    or bee endowed with any qualitye
    they'l poyson it with some depraving ill
       Envye is barren & yeeldes nought but weedes
       & feares least better ground have better seedes.   450

76. Nay should a wise & honest harted man
    commend a virtuous woman for her life
    would they not say the worst of him they can
    & cutt his good names throat with envyes knife.
       call him your bedesman, parasite or minion   455
       what sanctitye can scape from bad opinion

77. & where lives hee dares row against this tide
    noe not while that admired virgin Queene
    who sometimes raignd & your sex stellifyed
    who like stout Debora, did skorne the teene   460
       of Romes proud bulles whose ever watchfull eye
       the church and state did truely fortifie.

78. A sanguine woman is of all accurst
    although that constitution bee the best,
    shee must bee merry though her neck were burst   465
    & mirth setts all these spanniells up in quest.
        to hunt on drye foot, for it cannott bee
        goodnes & mirth should hold a simpathye.

79. A melancholly woman that is sadd
    although her deedes bee good & thoughts bee holy   470
    yett shall shee beare the censure to bee mad,
    & all her actions must bee skornd as folly
        yf shee bee great in place, her gravitye
        must bee the nurse of some foule prodegye

80. But what neede I speake further of complexion   475
    on which none but your sophist spend theyr dotes
    the landskip witt can find a fitt detection
    for all your gestures wordes, & for your coates
        But good men will not doe thus that are wise
        for they will tender you as theyr owne eyes.   480

81. Then for theyr sakes pardon the others errors
    lett not theyr evill harden you in evill
    but chuse the wise for fathers frends & mirrors
    & knowe hell was not made but for a Devill
        The wise will stay you yf your weakenes fall   485
        & rayse you without envye pride or gall.

82. Bee wise as serpents, innocent as Doves
    you are borne subjects & you must obey
    that death, which all you feare all clogges removes
    tis god you honour in it lett them bray   490
        hee will reward you; at theyr bountyes spurne
        naked they came, & naked shall returne.

83. & when you both are stript out of this clay
    there will not bee a difference in your sex
    you have one Judge & must goe both one way   495
    the good with good & bad with bad soules mix
        twill bee to late when you in hell shall grone
        to curse those soules that taught you, you had none.

84. Virgines bee wise, & keepe your lampes still burning
    wives to your head bee full of constant truth,   500
    widowes rejoyce in him that cheeres all mourning
    turnes black to white & wrinckled age to youth
        gives you new names, new honours, hyer places
        whose pompe Queene Sabaes silver throne disgraces.

85. And would you hold this state, enjoy these joyes 505
   then in the mire lett not your spiritts fall
   reject not god, nor count his judgments toyes
   nor with the foole, say, ther's noe god at all
      but that there is a god you must consent
      then are you bound to keepe his testament. 510

[. . .]

96. To what an angle is the true church driven
   for pittye sake, looke downe Lord on her cares
   & send forth faithfull laborers from heaven
   to gleane thy wheate & cast away the tares
      Least sectes & schismes & fowlest heresyes 575
      choake up thy seed with sad calamityes

97. Thou bread of life, yf shee want thee shee starves
   thou living water, yf thou fayle shee dyes
   nought but the sacred flesh & bloud will serve
   to please the judge, or cleere our clouded eyes 580
      In thee wee only live & move & be
      & our dead soules are all revived in thee.

[. . .]

109. Hee gives not up a lively sacrifice
    that stayes till withered age hath made him dead 650
    who letts the sunne sett ere hee doe arise
    hee were almost as good still keepe his bedd
       O come & learne at great Jehovaes schoole
       a sabaoth breaker is a busye foole.

[fols 156r–167r]

A very different version of this meditation occurs in the Folger manuscript, in an unidentified scribal italic (fols 37r–44r; Southwell 1997, 60–72). Variants are recorded only for lines 1–72 of the Folger text, as the rest of the Folger poem has no textual relationship with the Lansdowne version edited here

  Title. Remember . . . hallowed it] *Folger* Thou shalt keepe holy the saboth daye
  6. walke] *altered from* walkes; s *deleted (scribe)*
  7. plac'd] *altered from* please (?) *(revising?); first* e *deleted,* c *superimposed on* s, *second* e *deleted,* ' *inserted*
  8. high commaund] *Folger* free commande
  9. thus] *Folger* this
  11. day] *inserted (scribe)*
  12. labour is] *Folger* labours ar
  Folger inverts stanzas 3 and 4
  18. power] *Folger* her power *inserted, replacing* his power *deleted*
  20. handes] *Folger* hande
  21. faynting . . . braynes] *Folger* wearyed limmes and faynting braynes
  22. & . . . bandes] *Folger* and free thy oxen from theyre yoaked band
  24. that day] *Folger* the day

31. *Before this stanza, Folger inserts three stanzas attacking the Jews' use of the Sabbath*
31. Six . . . labour] *Folger* full six dayes thou shalt labor
32. heer's] *Folger* heere is
33. but then thy] *Folger* and these thy
37. for yf] *Folger* But if
those] *Folger* these
42. faithfully] *Folger* faithfull
44. singe . . . guzzell] *Folger* sing game dance or goosell
45. art willed] *Folger* arte bid
46. & cutt] *Folger* to cut
overtoppe] *altered from* overtoppes; s *deleted (scribe)*
48. thy future rests appeare] *Folger* thy rest doth most
52. explane that] *Folger* explaynes this
65. thou] *altered from* that; ou *superimposed on* at *(scribe?)*
68. adorne] n *inserted (scribe)*
74. dresse up] *inserted, replacing* adresse *deleted (revising)*
79. mov'd] *altered from* moved; ' *inserted,* e *deleted (scribe?)*
93. by] *superimposed on illegible word (scribe)*
yeeres] *inserted (scribe)*
101. seperates] *inserted, replacing* seperateh *deleted (revising)*
106. the . . . ark] *The scribe left a gap between* the *and* ark, *which s/he later filled in with* blessed seede & spouse an. *There is an illegible deletion following* an
111. now] *inserted, replacing* were *deleted (scribe)*
113. fruitfull] *inserted, replacing* true fields *deleted (scribe)*
117. the] *altered from* ther; r *deleted (scribe)*
118. lightening] *inserted, replacing* souccoring *deleted (scribe)*
120. be] *altered from* bee; *second* e *deleted (revising?)*
122. monstrous] *altered from* monster *(scribe);* rous *superimposed on* er
Hydraes] *inserted, replacing* Heresyes *deleted (scribe)*
124. wombe] *altered from* woman *(scribe);* be *superimposed on* an
throwe seas of] *altered from* throwes out *(scribe);* seas of *inserted, replacing* s out *deleted*
126. sonnes] s *added (scribe)*
135. scare] *altered from* scarre; *second* r *deleted*
138. pointes . . . out] *altered from* pointes out the worldes end; out *inserted,* out *deleted (scribe)*
Stanzas 24–5 and a fragmentary first draft of stanza 26 are deleted in the manuscript, 24 and 25 by revising hand, 26 by scribe
139. wizzard] *inserted, replacing* gazeling *deleted (revising);* gazeling *inserted in a previous stage of revision, replacing* gallant *deleted (scribe)*
140. ?] *superimposed on full stop (scribe)*
141. ask] k *added (scribe)*
that] *superimposed on* in *(scribe)*
Siseraes] S *superimposed on illegible letter, perhaps* s *miswritten*
142. that] *inserted, replacing* soone *deleted (scribe)*
her] *inserted, replacing* a *deleted (scribe)*
144. hee'l] *inserted, replacing* will *deleted (scribe)*
145. soule that] *inserted (scribe)*
147. made] *replacing deleted letter part (scribe)*
The scribe deleted the following first, fragmentary attempt at a twenty-sixth stanza, transcribing a new stanza 26 on the next leaf:

26. Mans mind a mirror is of heavenly formes
   & though created, yett hee can create.
   his polish'd thoughts the quill & booke adornes
   which clouds of ignorance doth captivate.

Yf thou   If thou   [155]
A   All the
[155–6]. Yf thou *and* A *smudged out*
154. shewes,] , *added*
155. how both] *inserted (scribe)*
lame] *replacing* all soe *deleted (scribe)*
156. & how . . . impe] *inserted, replacing* noe *deleted*
to the same] *replacing* can bee imped in *deleted*
159. Religion is] *altered from* Religion's *(scribe);* i *superimposed on* s, ' *deleted,* s *added*
stayre] *inserted, replacing* Cedar *deleted (scribe)*
203. skipp] *altered from* skape *(scribe);* i *superimposed on* a, *second* p *superimposed on* e
279. be he] *altered from* bee hee *(scribe?); second* e . . . e *deleted*
309. flourye] u *inserted (revising)*
315. she'd eyes before] *A two-stage revision: (1)* It had an eye *deleted,* shee had eyes before *inserted (scribe); (2)* shee *altered to* she'd (e *deleted,* ' *inserted),* had *deleted (revising)*
those] *altered from* that *(scribe);* o *superimposed on* a, se *inserted,* t *deleted*
316. They] *inserted, replacing* which *deleted (scribe)*
321. theyr] *altered from* them *(scribe);* yr *superimposed on* em
point] *inserted, replacing* payne *deleted (scribe)*
322. Coles] *inserted, replacing* bowles *deleted*
tipp'd] *altered from* tipped *(revising);* ' *inserted,* e *deleted*
338. clay,] *comma added (revising)*
361. Lothsame] *altered from* Lothsome *(scribe);* a *superimposed on* o
363. on] *altered from* in *(scribe);* o *superimposed on* i
365. fill'd] *altered from* filled *(revising);* ' *inserted,* e *deleted*
367. bee] *inserted, replacing* are *deleted (scribe)*
368. yee] *inserted, replacing* though *deleted (scribe)*
372. in't] *altered from* in *(revising?);* 't *added*
381. sinnes] *replacing* may not *underlined and deleted (scribe)*
389. doe] *inserted (scribe)*
men] *replacing* wise *underlined and deleted (scribe)*
390. wittye, but devoyd of soules] *The scribe originally wrote* fayre soft & wittye, blind for want of soules. *S/he then inserted* smooth but *above* wittye, blind *(presumably intending the text to read* fayre soft & smooth but blind for want of soules*), underlining but not deleting* wittye. *(See notes to lines 381 and 389, above, for instances of underlining by the scribe in this section of the manuscript, possibly as a preliminary to deletion.) S/he subsequently deleted* smooth. *The scribe also deleted* blind for want, *inserting above it* meere voyd *(line thus reading:* fayre soft & wittye, but meere voyd of soules*). Finally the revising hand inserted* de *over* meere, *bringing the line to its current state*
394–5. *Deleted text* Goe search the sacred writt, where you shall find *(i.e. line 397) between these lines (scribe)*
401. god] *inserted, replacing* hee *deleted (scribe)*
437. sett] *inserted, replacing* a *deleted (scribe)*
441. crittickize] *altered from* crettickize *(revising?);* i *superimposed on* e
442. wanteth] *altered from* wandeth *(scribe);* t *superimposed on* d
447. qualitye] *replacing* facultye *deleted*
449. nought] *altered from* naught (?); o *superimposed on* a (?) *(scribe)*
459. who sometimes raignd] *inserted, replacing* that lately raigned *deleted (revising)*
461. whose] *inserted, replacing* her *deleted (scribe)*
eye] *altered from* eyes *(revising?);* s *deleted*
462. and . . . truely] *inserted, followed by* be (?) *deleted, replacing* like cannon strongly *(revising)*
fortifie] *altered from* fortifies; s *deleted*
463. sanguine] *altered from* sanguin (?); e *added* (?) *(revising?)*
466. spanniells] i *added (revising?)*

476. sophist] *altered from* sophies *(revising);* st *superimposed on* es
dotes] *inserted, replacing* mouthes *deleted (scribe)*
478. coates] *inserted, replacing* clothes *deleted (scribe)*
481. theyr] *altered from* theyrs *(scribe?);* s *deleted*
489. that] *inserted, replacing* till *deleted (scribe)*
you] *altered from* yours *(revising?);* rs *deleted*
feare] *altered from* feares *(scribe);* s *deleted*
all] all *inserted, replacing* & *deleted (scribe)*
490. lett them bray] *inserted, replacing* & not they *deleted (scribe)*
491. at] *replacing* in it *deleted (scribe)*
498. soules] u *inserted* (scribe)
500. head] *altered from* heads *(scribe?);* s *deleted*
575. fowlest] *replacing* fowll *deleted (revising);* fowll *previously altered from* fowell, e *deleted (scribe)*
578–9. *Deleted text* they still repine although they still increase *(i.e. line 585) between these lines*
579. nought] *replacing* the *deleted (scribe)*
the] *altered from* thy; e *superimposed on* y *(revising)*
581. be] *altered from* bee *(revising?);* e *deleted*
582. revived] *altered from* received *(revising?);* v *superimposed on* c, e *deleted,* v *rewritten*

Anna Ley's posthumously collected writings

William Andrews Clark Memorial Library MS L6815 M3 C734

This manuscript is a compilation of the writings of Anna Ley and her husband, Roger. It comprises a number of different sections: Anna Ley's commonplace book (which is largely extracted from the popular printed *Meditations* by Bishop Joseph Hall); her poems; her letters; her will, funeral sermon and epitaph; two of Roger Ley's theological treatises; his elegy cycle, 'Albion in blacke or Happie England growne miserable'; his prose celebration of the Restoration; a funeral sermon on Joan Winship; and further extracts from Hall. The size of the gatherings varies greatly, which suggests that it may initially have been incorrectly bound. The manuscript is in three hands—two italic, one secretarial forms. Given that the commonplace book and initial poetry section are in one italic (Hand A), and the letters attributed to Anna Ley and the remainder of the manuscript—some of which was certainly composed after her death—are in Hands B and C (see plate 5), the supposition is that Hand A corresponds to Anna Ley and Hands B and C to her husband. However, the titles to her poems, and a number of emendations to them, are provided by Hand B (see plate 4), suggesting Roger Ley may have been engaged in a retrospective (re)ordering of his wife's writings. The extent to which he may also have manipulated them is a matter worth consideration. The manuscript was certainly constructed as a testament to both Anna and Roger Ley, to their royalist and conformist beliefs and social circle.

It is a fair copy, with a number of corrections. The later provision of titles for the first poetry section, the transcription of the letters in Hand B, and the transcription of Roger Ley's treatises suggest that it was compiled from a number of now lost copy-texts. The earliest datable piece is Anna Ley's poem commemorating a sermon of 1623, while Roger Ley's elegy cycle was composed during the interregnum and right up to the Restoration. Composition of the texts, therefore, dates from c.1623 to the 1660s.

The manuscript was acquired in 1825 by Joseph Hunter, who received it from the antiquarian Benjamin Heywood Bright. It later became Phillipps MS 17400, and the Clark Library purchased it from Peter Murray Hill (probably as a result of a recent Phillipps sale) in 1952. It is a quarto of 262 folios, with a number of short blank sections, bound in brown calf, repaired and rebacked at an unknown, although much later, date. This text follows the librarian's foliation (1–262) of 1991.

17.

Upon the death of king James.

5

Our Sunne departed yet no night appeard,
the cause obscure was by Urania cleard,
who heard this hymne sung in the Ionian groue.
Phœbus must leaue his orbe, and shine with Ioue.
And in the moment when this thing is donne,
must Charles his wane be Englands glorious Sunne.

Then ride on Charles keepe Sols olde tracked wayes,
and may thy radiant beames equall his rayes.
Heauens grant thy steeds may nere bee out of winde
till thou quite through the vniuerse hast shinde
And that our ophere admitt no other Carre,
till thou our Planet beest a fixed starre.

Upon the great plague following the death
of king James.

6

Afflicted England how thine ills increase,
and seemes to threaten thine approching fall,
And to bereaue thee of that happie peace
for which all nations doe thee blessed call.

The dreadfull pestilence doth now begin
to shed its venoum in thy cheifest seat,
Denouncing iudgment for thy hanyous sin
except repentance mercy doe intreat,

And lest this punishment should seeme too small,
behold another stroke doth wound thy head,
Renowned James that was admird of all
for learned skill thy king of peace is dead,

PLATE 4 Anna Ley, William Andrews Clark Memorial Library MS L6815 M3 C734, fol. 92v. This plate reproduces Anna Ley's 'Upon the death of King James' and the first three stanzas of 'Upon the great plague following the death of King James'. Titles are in the secretarial forms of Hand B, poetry in the italic Hand A

Antichriste shall come upon the fall of the Empire, 54
and it is confest by Protestants, who observe the 139
Pope advanced upon the Emperours ruine. It is
granted by Papists themselves, but onely to defend
their Pope from Antichristianisme, they are forced
to shift, and save themselves under the Emperour
of Germany, as if the Empire continued in him,
who hath but a shaddow and title, no jurisdiction
at all in Rome, for indeede his holiness is veall
king of the Romans. This second beast rising
after the first persecution of 42 monethes, is
ceased, cometh out of the earth, as the former
came out of the sea. The former out of an In-
quiett variable Common weale, the second out
of wordly ends, and desire of earthlie honour.
This beast hath the hornes of the Lambe, Usur-
peth the power of Christe, but by his doctrine
of devils, and false and proud brags speaketh
as a dragon.

And he exerciseth all the power of the   Rev.
first beast before him, and causeth   13.12
the earth, and them that dwell
therein to worship the first beast,
whose deadly wound was healed.
The Pope shall continue the like tyrannie
which the Emperour did before him & exer-
cise against Gods people, and shall make
the world admire Rome still, after the grie-
vous wound given by the Goths &c. is cured,
and Rome lifted up by this new government.

And he doth great wonders, so that he   35
maketh fire to come downe from hea-   Rev.
ven, on the earth, in the sight of   13.13
men.
The Pope and his party are great miracle-
mungers, and with wonderfull deceit,

(150)

PLATE 5 Anna Ley, William Andrews Clark Memorial Library MS L6815 M3 C734, fol. 139r. This plate reproduces a page from the later section of the Clark MS, which consists of writing by Roger Ley, Anna's husband. The main text here is transcribed in secretarial forms (Hand B), with italic (Hand C) used for the quotations from Revelation. Hand C differs in several respects from Hand A (see plate 4), thus strengthening the likelihood that Hand A represents a different scribe

BIOGRAPHICAL NOTE

Anna Norman Ley's date of birth is unknown. She married Roger Ley, curate of St Leonard's, Shoreditch, at St Botolph's Church, Bishopsgate, on 25 February 1621/2. According to John Squire's funeral sermon, the couple had fallen in love, but owing to the fact that 'their portions were onelie virtue; and that virtue would buy neither foode nor raiment', they waited seven years before getting married. The couple ran a school in the parish to supplement their income, Anna learning Latin and Greek for the purpose (Clark MS L6815 M3 C734—henceforward 'Clark MS'—fol 108r–v). Her letters to two young scholars—one about to attend university, the other currently reading for a degree—witness her continued investment in the further education of pupils who presumably attended their school (Clark MS, fols 102v–104v).

The writing of both wife and husband emerges from conformist familial, university and London ecclesiastical literary networks. Anna Ley's verse on contemporary religious issues, and her husband's involvement in theological controversy with his Cambridge contemporary Paul Best and commemoration of Cambridge-educated divines in his elegy cycle, witness their participation in the clerical strand of university tradition. A letter from Anna Ley to her father Thomas Norman, while she was in residence in the country, laments her exile from London, figuring herself as Ulysses. This self-figuration is further explicated in another letter to her father which delights in and encourages his literary activities, expressing a keen sense of participation in contemporary London literary culture: 'I am glad to heare you are so merilie disposed, as to enter into that veine of poetrie or else it may be, these times wherein our London is changed to Arcadia' (Clark MS, fols 98v–99r).

Anna Ley apparently anticipated her death as early as 1636, when she wrote a will (also transcribed in the manuscript). She appears to have suffered from a lengthy but unspecified illness, and was buried in St Leonard's on 22 October 1641.

M-LC

A Christmasse Caroll: or verses on the Nativitie of Christe

Most blessed time wherein we celebrate,
his happie birth which was both God and man,
Whoe came to save us from eternall hate,
Such length and depth of mercie none may scan.
We being dead and doomd to live in hell, 5
by Adams sinne of which we all pertake:
the promised seed that sentence did expell,
Being given us atonment for to make.
But after such a manner it was done,
as men and Angles could not comprehend, 10
that our offended God should send his Sonne
which was true God by death our fault to mend.
Whose birth was rare, conception most divine.

borne of a virgin pure of whome he tooke,
his humane part which sprung from Ishais line,   15
as we find writen in the Sacred Booke.
For such great love O let us then constraine,
our sloathfull harts some kindnesse backe to send,
for such a sea of mercie we obtaine,
since God and man is come to be our friend.   20
then let us prayses sing with one accorde,
and endlesse thankes to this our loveing Lord.
[fol. 91r]

Title. Hand B
7. sentence] *second* e *inserted, replacing* a *deleted*
8. Being] *inserted, replacing* and *deleted*
9. manner] *second* n *inserted*

Upon a sermon preached in S Paules Church upon the Second Commandement by Mr Squire Januarie 6. 1623

In this blest labour may each papist see
Out of sound proofes Roomes grosse idolatrie
How they with leaves their nakednesse would hide
Nor can their reasones touch of truth abide

Sweete are the streames which from this fountaine flow   5
Quickening those droopeing soules which hoodwinckt goe,
Use well this Antidote and you shall finde
It hath rare vertue to inrich the minde
Read with an humble hart 'tis worth your paine
Each sentance hath its weight, no word in vaine.   10
[fol. 92r]

Title. Hand B
2. Out] t *superimposed*
grosse idolatrie] *second* s *and second* i *superimposed*
3. nakednesse] *second* e *inserted,* sse *superimposed*
7. this] *inserted*
8. to] *inserted*

Upon the death of King James

Our Sunne departed yet no night appeard,
the cause obscure was by urania cleard,
Who heard this hymne sung in the Aonian grove,
Pheebus must leave his orbe, and shine with Jove.
And in the moment when this thing is donne,   5
must Charles his waine be Englands glorious Sunne.

Then ride on Charles keepe Sols olde tracked wayes,
and may thy radiant beames equall his rayes,
Heavens grant thy steeds may nere bee out of winde
till thou quite through the universe hast Shinde   10
And that our Spheare admitt no other Carre,
till thou our Planet beest a fixed Starre.

[fol. 92v]

Title. Hand B
6. waine] i *inserted*

Upon the great plague following the death of King James

Afflicted England how thine ills increase,
and seemes to threaten thine approching fall,
And to bereave thee of that happie peace
for which all nations doe thee blessed call.

The dreadfull pestilence doth now begin   5
to shed its vennoum in thy cheifest seat,
Denouncing judgment for thy hanyous sin
except repentance mercy doe intreat,

And lest this punishment should seeme too small,
behold another stroake doth wound thy head,   10
Renowned James that was admird of all
for learned skill thy king of peace is dead,

Whose gentle nature though it did decline
the sad aspect of wars most direfull looke,
In future ages shall his valour shine,   15
for one brave combat which he undertooke,

His pen the weapon was, the truth the cause,
His foe proude Rome the murderer of kings,
whose worthy worke deserving high applause,
hath left the Romanists a deadly sting.   20

And we are left in sorrow to lament
this heavie losse with feare what will ensue
But he which us this great affliction sent
in deepest woes his mercie did renew,

Our Sun no sooner set and dolefull night   25
seemed to threaten some disaster strange,
A glorious Star with splendour shineing bright
expeld those feares our greefe to mirth did change.

[fols 92v–93r]

Title. Hand B
5. pestilence] i *superimposed*
10. stroake] a *inserted*
14. direfull] *MS* driefull
22. ensue] e *deleted between* s *and* u
24. deepest] *second* e *inserted*
25. no sooner] *MS* nosooner
27. splendour] u *inserted*

An answer to Mercuries message anno 1641

A replie to a letter indited by him that did delight in bloud from the beginning, and is still an accuser of the Brethren, which letter seemeth to have been inspired by him at a late Conventicle, into his deere sonne Mercurie, a man made of the accursed dust of the olde Martines. Whose names yet Stinke in the nosthrils of all that doe love the Church of England,

> Whie how now Martin what's the newes from hell,
> Nay blush not man it is the better name,
> Mercury is heathenish, and fits not well,
> A holy brother come from Amsterdam,
> How fares old Satan there, and all the rest 5
> Of those Marprelates, now in this Strange time,
> When such as raile at goverment speede best,
> And on the Churches ruines hope to climbe,
> But Stay lets se, what news the carrier brings,
> His packet's open, let us cast a looke, 10
> Furies come forth in rime, the Pope he sings,
> Who hopes to gaine by this mad namles booke,
> For first he railes with most inhumane spite,
> Against a sad delinquent in disgrace,
> Spurning at him because he cannot bite, 15
> Whose title yet beares honour in the face,
> A Bishops name mauger the frothie wit,
> Of some mouth'd Schemer, the beginning way,
> Clearely produce out of the sacred writ,
> As cleare as sunne shines in the midst of day. 20
> And not the name alone but office too,
> The same authority may justly claime,
> As many learned Prelates have and doe
> Plainly demonstrate, were you not past shame.
> But what if 2 or 3 have gonne awry, 25
> To curbe those that the great disturbers were,
> As you, and such as doe with you complie,
> Whose insolence was such as they did feare,
> Had it not hindred beene, would soone oretop,
> Lawfull authority, and to prevent 30

A further growth some spurious boughs they lop,
Which by perswasion could no way be bent,
But bending too much backe this crooked Sticke,
It brake, and splinters flie into their face,
A scittish horse spurd hard begins to kicke,   35
And throws the rider, so doe you disgrace
Our Churches happie goverment, so long,
Inviolably kept, which first was made,
By those which for the truth were pillers Strong,
And for the same at length their lives downe laid.   40
These factious sectaries ere since the reigne,
Of Queene Elizabeth have still disturbd
Our true religion, and will prove the baine
Of Church and state, if soone they be not curbd,
Your predecessour Martine and that crew   45
Of barkeing libellers proceeded far,
To crush religion then reformd a new
Had they not hindred beene by that bright Star
Whitgift, the glorie of our Church, a man
In whome all vertue shin'd, to make him fit,   50
To prosecute a worke he then began,
And by divine assistance finnisht it.
Who like a skilfull pilot safely brought
The Church into the harbour, which so long
Against her feirce and mortall foes had fought,   55
The Papist and the Puritan so strong,
But now what Strange disorders have we seene
In courts and Churches by that bedlam route,
Of unconformists, who have alwaies beene,
Hatching of ill, but since the power went out,   60
Of Bishops who did keepe them still in awe,
They spurne at all authoritie, and dare,
Abuse Gods howse as if there were no law
And from his ministers their garments teare
Also the railes which decently did stand   65
About the holy boarde must also feele
The furie of each sacrilegious hand,
Because the Zelots would by no meanes kneele.
Let innovations justly be reform'd,
Which gave occasion of offence to those   70
Who though they say our Church must be adorn'd
With decent ceremonies; yet are foes
To altar boweings, and to that vaine hope
Of meeteing Rome halfe way, and thereby gaine
Some proselites, and to suppresse the Pope.   75
Which were the fancies of an active braine,

This project failing se what ill successe
Befalls himselfe, the Church and her best friends,
By this mad faction, seekeing to redresse,
His errours, but in truth far more offends,   80
Must all the other Bishops holy men
Whom you now call the droopeing hierarchie,
Be scornd and scandalized by thie pen,
Who skilfull are untruthes to multiplie,
Downe went you say all painfull teaching   85
The service booke more usefull was then preaching
A most noxious lie, had we not store,
Of learned pastours who did still discharge,
Their weekely labours, and besides them more,
Of lecturers this worke for to enlarge,   90
But some two houres will preach & thrice a weeke,
Which you like best, who with invention poore,
In sudden praiers are forc'd for words to seeke,
And wanting substance Strive to speak the more.
And as for matter that they prize not much   95
Because by sad experience it is found,
The manie headed people dote on such
Whose emptie vessels give the loudest sound
As for our service booke at first compilde
By some that martyrs were and holy men,   100
We finde it scorn'd by many and revilde
Now woe is me whence is this phrensie then?
Comes it not from the enemie of peace?
The prince of darkenes, whose inveterate hate
Like youres, against the Church will never cease,   105
To stir up instruments of such debate.
Next like a Jew or Pagan he doth rave
At those which at the name of Jesus bow,
Though Church commands, and we the scripture have
To save us harmlesse, and the act allow,   110
Sure he forgets that his unsavery jeere
Reflects on him that ownes that blessed name,
O let no Infidell nor Atheist heare
This man abuse religion to our shame,
Our harmlesse ceremonies much offend,   115
Your queasie stomach overcharg'd before
With sacriledge, rebellion, and to end
All in a word, though there be manie more
Linkes in this chaine, yet there is one besides,
Your want of charity, which bindes you fast,   120
Breathd from impostumed lungs, where you deride
The Bishops all at once, in that foule blast,

Now if great Belzebub himselfe be scard
Needes must the inferiour devils be affeard
Now wipe thie mouth foule hypocrite for shame,   125
Are these fit words for holie learned men,
Whose pious labours to their endles fame
Shall call them blessed, speake their praises, when
Thie name shall not, but be abhord of all.
Who love the churches welfare, and respect   130
Their ministers, who if they chance to fall,
Had rather cover errours then detect
And spread them with so foule and rude a hand.
Some charged are with faults, others are freed.
Where crimes augmented yet uncensur'd stand.   135
While spite and want of truth dissention breed.

[fols 95r–111r]

Title. Hand B
5. rest] *replacing* er *deleted*
8. on] *inserted*
11. sings] *followed by deleted letter*
14. disgrace] i *superimposed*
15. Spurning] *MS* Spurninig
18. Schemer] *MS* Shemer
beginning] *MS* beginnig
22. authority] y *superimposed*
claime] i *inserted*
40. their] *altered from* theire; e *deleted*
41. ere since] *replacing* if some *deleted*
44. they be] *inserted in Hand B*
46. proceeded] *altered from* proceeding; ing *deleted*, ed *inserted in Hand B*
55. feirce] i *superimposed*
63. there] *altered from* theire; i *deleted*
63–4. were no law . . . garments teare] *added in right margin in Hand B, replacing* garments teare *deleted*
66. boarde] a *inserted*
69. reform'd] ' *inserted, replacing* e *deleted*
73. altar] *altered from* alter; er *deleted,* ar *inserted in Hand B*
77. se] *replacing* this *deleted*
83. scandalized] *inserted in right margin in Hand B, replacing* stand alized *deleted between* and *and* by
85. teaching] *added in right margin in Hand B, replacing* teachers *deleted*
91. houres] re *superimposed*
97. manie] *conjectural reading; MS unclear*
headed] a *inserted*
98. give the] *inserted*
99. compilde] *inserted in right margin in Hand B, replacing* complide *deleted*
111. unsavery] *MS* vsauery
112. ownes] *MS* owes
123. *Following this line (at the end of fol. 96v), Hand B writes* The rest at the end after the Epitaph, *(i.e. the epitaph on Anna Ley transcribed on fol. 110v). The remainder of the poem is transcribed on fol. 111r by Hand B, under the heading* A supply to the end of the answer to Mercuries message

6

Presentation volume of Jane Cavendish's poetry

Yale University, Beinecke Library Osborn MS b. 233

The royalist Cavendish family of Welbeck, Nottinghamshire, was at the centre of a vibrant literary culture in the 1630s. William Cavendish (1592–1676), grandson of the Elizabethan courtier and property magnate Bess of Hardwick, was created Earl of Newcastle in 1628, and was raised to the rank of Marquis (the title by which he is named in this manuscript) in 1643. He became the first Duke of Newcastle at the Restoration in recognition of his services as the commander of royalist forces in the North during the first Civil War (until his defeat at Marston Moor and consequent exile in July 1644). Newcastle constructed and maintained a prolific and encouraging literary environment both for his literary clients (who included Ben Jonson, James Shirley, William Davenant, Richard Flecknoe, Alexander Brome and Robert Stapleton) and for his family. His second wife, Margaret Lucas Cavendish (1623–73), was an avid participant in print culture, publishing twelve different works between 1653 and 1668. Her stepdaughters, Jane and Elizabeth, however, writing in the mid-1640s, composed and circulated their poetry and plays in the manuscript tradition presented to them by their father's earlier literary environment.

Beinecke Osborn MS b. 233 and Bodleian MS Rawlinson poet. 16 are presentation copies of the verse of Jane Cavendish and the drama she co-authored with her sister Elizabeth. Both volumes are transcribed by their father's secretary, John Rolleston, whose hand is also to be found in Newcastle's manuscripts, and they date from the 1640s. Preserving eighty-one poems and a pastoral play in common, these manuscripts differ in that the Beinecke volume contains two dedications not found in the Bodleian manuscript, while the latter contains eight additional poems and the collaborative play, *The Concealed Fansyes* (see Starr 1931 and Cerasano and Wynne-Davies 1996; cf. Ezell 1988). The Beinecke copy's two dedications reveal that Jane is the sole author of the poetry collected in both volumes; the manuscript opens on a dedicatory epistle to her father signed by Jane (see below), and closes on a poem entitled 'Upon the right honourable the Lady Jane Cavendish her booke of verses'—unattributed, but probably composed by the scribe. The poetry spans a period encompassing events from 1635 up to at least 1648, although the quantity of poems concerned with Newcastle's exile and 'Sister Brackley' (Jane's sister Elizabeth married John Egerton, Lord Brackley, in July 1641) locate the volume predominantly within the mid-1640s.

The manuscript itself is comprised of two blank flyleaves at the beginning, eighty-nine folios, and five flyleaves at the back. It is paginated consecutively, 1–77, with the page numbers taking no account of the numerous blank leaves in the manuscript: i.e. fols 22, 30, 41–68 (between the pastoral and the final dedicatory verses) and 69v–89v (between the dedicatory verses and the end of the volume). It is a scribal copy, with very few emendations or deletions (for a rare example see 'On her sacred Majestie', below). Each page is extensively ruled: double ruled lines run parallel to each side of the page, and each title is then enclosed in a further rectangle of double ruled lines. It is, therefore, clearly intended as a presentation compilation of literary activity, although the large quantity of blank pages suggests that the scribe never completed the compilation as first planned. Perhaps the scribe had originally intended to transcribe *The Concealed Fansyes* in the lengthy gap between the pastoral play and the dedicatory verses.

BIOGRAPHICAL NOTE

Jane Cavendish (1621–69), eldest child of Elizabeth Basset Howard (1599–1643) and William Cavendish, had a reputation in her family as a writer from a young age. Her father's couplets to his children, encouraging them to write, foreground his eldest daughter: 'Sweet Jane. / I knowe you are a rare Inditer.—/ Ande hath the Pen off a moste redye writer' (Hallward Library, University of Nottingham, Portland MS PwV 25, fol. 21r). This familial context for her literary activity is further emphasised in an important manuscript collection of poetry and drama compiled for her father, known as the Newcastle Manuscript, which includes a poem addressed to Jane Cavendish when a child, dated 14 August 1629 (British Library Harleian MS 4955, fols 86v–87r). Upon her father's and brothers' exile in July 1644, Jane was left in charge of the family estates at Welbeck and Bolsover in Derbyshire. Welbeck was besieged and taken by parliamentary forces in August 1644, retaken by the royalists in July 1645, and finally ceded to Parliament in November 1645, by which point, at the latest, Jane and her sister Frances (d. 1678) must have decamped to Bolsover. (The date of Elizabeth's departure for her husband's estate, Ashridge in Hertfordshire, is uncertain.) Their attempts to maintain the Cavendish estate and its goods are indicated by an inventory of plate hidden at Welbeck in 1645, which was to be restored to Jane and Frances Cavendish (Portland MS Pw1 367–368).

Jane married Charles Cheyne, later Viscount Newhaven (1624?–98) in 1654, and moved to Chelsea. William Davenant's 'Upon the Marriage of the Lady Jane Cavendish with Mr Cheney' commemorates the event. Her brothers returned to England in the 1650s, and letters exchanged between the siblings reveal the strength of the family bond beyond the period in which these manuscripts were compiled (see Portland MSS Pw1 69, Pw1 86–90, Pw1 118–20, for examples). She had three children: Elizabeth (b. 1656), William (b. 1657) and Catherine (b. 1658). While the survival of her verse in these volumes might at first glance suggest that she wrote only in a time of political crisis and in her father's absence, the survival of her elegy on her sister Elizabeth (1626–63) and anecdotal evidence suggest that she continued to write well beyond the 1640s. Thomas Lawrence, in his manuscript elegy on Jane Cavendish, presents her as an accomplished poet: 'Oh that I could Inheritt / Some Portion of her great Poetick spiritt . . . An Art she knew and Practised so well' (Portland MS PwV 19, p. 3). Adam Littleton's funeral sermon makes much of her literary activities, suggesting that she continued to write throughout her life:

'She took, when Young, special delight in her Father's Excellent Composures. And she hath left in Writing a considerable Stock of Excellent ones of Her own, ever spending the time that best pleased Her with her Pen' (Littleton 1669, sig. F3r).

In the texts below, page and folio references are to the Osborn manuscript of Cavendish's poetry, which is the copy-text for this edition and is referred to as *MS* in the textual notes. *Rawl.* refers to the page references of the equivalent texts in the Rawlinson manuscript. Textual variations between the two manuscripts are recorded in the notes.

Bibliography:
Cerasano and Wynne-Davies (1996), Littleton (1669), Starr (1931), Ezell (1988)

M-LC

[Jane Cavendish's dedicatory prose epistle to her father]

My Lord,

As nature ownes my creation from you, & my selfe my Education; soe deuty invites mee to dedicate my workes to you, as the onely Patterne of Judgement, that can make mee happy, if these fanceys may owne sense they wayte upon your Lordship as the Center of witt, I humbly thanke your Lordship; & if a distinction of Judgement, God reward your Lordship. For in a word, what I have of good, is wholly derived from you, as the soule of bounty and this booke desires noe other purchas, then a smyle from your Lordship or a word of like, which will glorifie your creature; That is affectionately 5

Your Lordships most obliged
obedient
Daughter
Jane Cavendysshe

[p. 1 / fol. 1r]

---

3. owne sense they] *inserted, replacing illegible deleted word*

Passions Contemplation

    Ther's nothing more afflicts my greived soule
    But that I cannot greive without controll
    And soe least others should interprett more
    Thoughts Centryes keepes out teares in each Eyes doore.
    O! how sorrow swells mee when it must rave,   5
    To wash it selfe with teares, then begg a grave
    Soe in contemplate thoughts I wishe to bee
    Teares Statue for sadder soules to drop to mee
    I am indeede a congeal'd peece of greife
    And without sight of you haue noe releife   10
    In every place where I have seene you in

Now's horrid to mee as a deadly sinn
What makes a Hell I'm sure Devines doe say
The presence of God's light deprived away
Our heavenly father then our earthly may   15
Make Hell on Earth to his Children the same way,
Then Hell I am in, since noe content can have
Yett I doe hope your presence will mee save.

                                       [p. 5 / fol. 3r; *Rawl.* p. 3]

---

1. afflicts] li *superimposed*
my] *inserted, replacing* a *deleted*
3. soe] *Rawl. inserted*
5. O!] *Rawl. deleted*
must rave] *Rawl.* must not rave; not *inserted*
14. presence] *inserted, replacing* beauty *deleted*
15. father] *inserted*
our] *inserted, replacing illegible deleted word*
17. I am] *Rawl.* I'm

On her Sacred Majestie

Your lookes are Courage, mixt with such sweetenes,
Which makes all Creatures, justly to witnes;
Themselves your Vassalls & noe longer stay;
Till you comand, and then their Tributes pay
Unto your quinticence of natures day,   5
Our honoured name then us obedience call
For other name what ever would bee thrall.

                                   [p. 14 / fol. 7v; *Rawl.* p. 12]

Rawl. main text headed Madam
4–7. and then . . . thrall] *alteration, replacing deleted first draft of lines 4b–6 (i.e. there is no line 7 in first draft). Lines 6–7 of the corrected version* ('Our honoured name . . . ever would be thrall') *have been squeezed between the deletion and the double rule enclosing the title of the subsequent poem. The legible first draft of lines 5–6 reads:* [. . .] at your Sacred feete / Soe cheerefully your [.], World may see't

The Quinticens of Cordiall.

Sister
Wer't not for you, I knew not how to live,
For what content I have, you doe mee give.
In this my sadd mortification life,
I deifyeinge you make good that strife
Soe your presence is Balsum to my braine,   5
And Gilberts water, if then soe but name,
My Lord's retorn'd, & add here, you'l retayne

                                   [p. 14 / fol. 7v; *Rawl.* p. 12]

---

6. Gilberts] *replacing deleted word* (Gilberts *miswritten*)

An answeare to the Verses Mr Carey made to the Lady Carlile

What doe your thoughts begin in love to stray
Soe you by Argument, your selfe betray
I would not bee a meare ridiculous foole,
But yet in love I would bee very coole;
I'de understand that Language, just to bee,   5
Onely a Summons to gaine love of mee;
If soe, I doe assure, hee should not come,
For I'le forbid possession, or a roome
I doe not hold a stoutnes 'tis att all
In parleinge, to lett my Honour fall;   10
Yett ne'r will forbid my selfe to say,
I'le looke on all, with a free modest way;
For I'le mistrust my selfe noe more then shee,
Let his designes then speake not love to mee
Greate Early plotts, I then may justly see,   15
Soe ignorantly, shall not smother'd bee;
Thus knowledge gives mee victoryes, as due,
And I my selfe to vertue, keepe most true.
For I'm resolv'd that none shall hope to fynd,
Mee, for to stile, a lady for his mind.   20

[p. 16 / fol. 8v; *Rawl.* p. 14]

Title. Carey] y *superimposed*
14. designes] *Rawl.*; MS desinges

On a Chamber-mayde

Thou lovely Bess, that art soe plumpe and young,
Therefore the only Theame, that our just Tongue;
Should singe of, and in our language thee first speak,
Or els wee ought to bee condemned for weake;
Then soe to you, our severall Poems send,   5
And if soe lik'd, wee thinke them then well pend.

[p. 18 / fol. 9v; *Rawl.* p. 16]

---

6. if] *inserted*

On my deare Brothers and Sister.

Fowre brothers and a sister such I had
Who was not fitt to sufferr with the bad
For Angles upon earth they were soe good
Their transformation could not bee withstood
With our loved pastions care, & every Eye   5
Did begg of God, they might them save though dye

But our teares was rejected, for God knew
They were most his, soe sav'd amongst the few
                    [p. 31 / fol. 16r; *Rawl.* p. 31]

---

3. Angles] *Rawl.* Angells
5. pastions] *Rawl.* passions

On my honourable Grandmother Elizabeth Countess of Shrewsbury

Madam
You weare the very Magazine of rich
With spirit such & wisdome which did reach
All that oppos'd you, for your wealth did teach
Our Englands law, soe Lawyers durst not peach
Soe was your golden actions, this is true   5
As ever will you live in perfect veiw
Your beauty great, & you the very life
And onely patterne of a wise, good, wife;
But this your wisdome, was too short to see,
Of your three sonns to tell who great should bee   10
Your eldest sonn your riches had for life
'Caus Henry wenches loved more then his wife
Your second children had, soe you did thinke
On him your great ambition fast to linke
Soe William you did make before your Charles to goe   15
Yet Charles his actions hath beene soe
Before your Williams sonn doth goe before
Thus your great howse is now become the lower
And I doe hope, the world shall ever see
The howse of Charles before your Williams bee   20
For Charles his William hath it thus soe chang'd
As William Conquerer hee may well bee named
And it is true his sword hath made him great
Thus his wise acts will ever him full speak
                    [p. 35 / fol. 18r; *Rawl.* p. 35]

---

3. oppos'd] *Rawl.* opprest
16. hath] *Rawl.* have

To heaven, or a confession to God

I doe confesse great God my sinns are great
Therefore thy mercy I doe humbly treat
As one whose sinns, may weepeinge begg thy love
For onely may the Trinity above
Mee make anew and soe mee save   5

And this I praying hartily so crave
That so forgiven, I may truely bee
Since I thy holy Supper doe not see
This Christmas; the reason is I'am loth
To receave thee, where nought but sloth   10
Thy table doth adorne by a rude way
And soe thy passions might they make a day
Of all deformityes, this is too true
Soe I will never crucefie a new
Thy sacred selfe, but begg that by thy birth   15
I may bee thine, & saved by thy death.
                    [p. 36 / fol. 18v; *Rawl.* p. 36]

6–7. so . . . so] *MS* to . . . to
9. I'am] *Rawl.* I'm

On the .30.th of June, to God

This day I will my thankes sure now declare
By Sermons, Bounties of each harty prayer
To thee great God who gave thy bounty large
Saveing my Father from the Enemies charge
Not onely soe, but made him victour leade   5
Chargeinge his Enemies, with linckes of lead
To let them now thy workes plaine see
Sayeinge my little flock shall Conquerers bee
And it was true Fairfax was then more great
But yet Newcastle made him sure retreat   10
Therefore I'le keepe this thy victoryes day
If not in publique, by some private way
In spite of Rebells, who thy Lawes deface
And blott the footsteps of thy sonns blood trace
Thus will my soules devotion to thee send   15
And all my life in thankes a votery spend.
                    [p. 38 / fol. 19v; *Rawl.* p. 38]

---

16. a] *inserted*

Hopes preparation.

Now I'm prepared against my Lord doth come
With serious face my reall totall summe
Of vizard, For I'le carry truely soe
My gravity, that each shall hardly know
That I am, I soe none shall angrye make   5
Leaven for a suspitious jealous Cake

Your comeinge is a Sacrament to mee
And when thy Lre my sinnes forgiven bee
Thus doth my soule even waiteinge say
Lord I'm ready call mee then away.   10
Now lord I begg of thee before I pray
Prepare mee for thee as a Holly day
Against I now receave thy blessed bread
Unite mee godly my sinn reccon dead
O lord & wilt thou truely prove soe good   15
To make a sinner now thy onely food
Then God lett mee confession fully make
And soe thy mercy begg for thy sonn sake
Whose bloody wounds my faythles soule will heale
For in a word my sinns a storme of Hale   20
Which should mee scourge noe drownd nay then mee dam
Wert not for thy deare sonn sweete holly lambe
Great Trinity I begg thy holly light
That is Christs blood to bath mee purely white

When I in prayer, pray God looke on mee   25
As one whose teares durst not appeale to thee
But as my teares doe my sad cheekes true clayme
Soe let Christs blood my soule cleare wash from shame
I have now received thy Sacrament, soe fynd
The differrence 'twixt my soule, and bodies mind   30
My soule that hath spoke guilty yet 'tis sav'd
And yet my bodies mind, that still doth rave
And as I'm clearely wash'd from all my sinn
Yet doe my mind still harsh dispare, suck in
Not that I have committed any deed of shame   35
But am as cleare as the first earths new frame
Yet will my mind my soule, true trouble make
In absence of my earthly Fathers sake
For though my Heavenly Father hath now sayd
Thy sinns forgiven bee, as thou art made   40
Yet I desire hee would say to mee
Thy Fathers landed safe, hath sent for thee.

I cannot speake, nor looke, nor nothinge say
But still your landinge here's my Bywords pray,
And if a custome gett none can mee disallowe   45
For if you will not come I'le make a Hermets vow.
              [pp. 39–41 / fols 20r–21r; *Rawl.* pp. 39–41]

---

34. doe] *Rawl.* doth
44. here's] *MS* here's; *Rawl* here's,

'My lord it is your absence makes each see'

J.C. My lord it is your absence makes each see
      For want of you what I'm reduc'd to bee
      Captive or sheppardesses life
      Gives envey leave to make noe striffe
      Soe what becomes me better then   5
      But to bee your daughter in your Penn
      If you'r now pleased I care not what
      Becomes of mee or what's my lott
      Now if you like I then doe knowe
      I am a witt, but then pray whisper't low.   10
                        [p. 76 / fol. 40v; *Rawl.* p. 84]

---

1. is] *altered from* 'tis; 't *deleted*

'My lord your absence makes I cannot owne'

E.B. My lord your absence makes I cannot owne
      My selfe, to thinke I am alone
      Yet sheppardesses can see to read
      And soe upon your stock of wit I feede
      Soe begs your blessing to like this   5
      Then am I crown'd with hight of blis.
                        [p. 76 / fol. 40v; *Rawl.* p. 84]

7

Lucy Hutchinson's
'Elegies'

Nottinghamshire Archives DD/HU2

The manuscript of the 'Elegies' is a fair copy of twenty-four poems, mostly numbered and carrying title phrases. The hand (see plate 6) is not Lucy Hutchinson's. All of the poems are unique to this manuscript and relate to the death of her husband Colonel John Hutchinson in 1664. The only exception is a single poem copied in later by Julius Hutchinson (see below), who states that it was written during the Colonel's imprisonment in the Tower of London in 1664. (However, that poem is in fact Eve's lament from canto five of Hutchinson's epic poem, *Order and Disorder* (Hutchinson 2001, 77–9).) Norbrook connects the composition of the 'Elegies' with that of the author's *Life of Colonel Hutchinson*, which she had finished by 1671 (Norbrook 1997, 470). One poem, 'On the Spring 1668', has a clear originating date. However, the exact date of transcription of the manuscript and the identity of its scribe are not known.

The manuscript contains twenty-six leaves (180 by 120 mm), stitched, with no cover. It was once owned by Julius Hutchinson (1678–1738), grandson of John Hutchinson's father by a second marriage. In 1891 it belonged to F. E. Hutchinson, at which time it was attached to Lucy's commonplace book (now DD/HU1); in 1921 he died and it passed to his nephew Charles Alleyre Hutchinson. It was deposited (with DD/HU1 and DD/HU3) by C. P. Hutchinson with the Nottingham City Library Archive Department on 26 September 1953, and transferred to Nottinghamshire Archives in 1974. The complete text of the 'Elegies' has been edited by David Norbrook (Norbrook 1997).

Insertions are above the line, usually with a caret, and deletions are struck through. As Norbrook acknowledges, particularly with regard to 'c', 's' and 't', it is almost impossible to distinguish between upper and lower case (Norbrook 1997, 486). I have capitalised at the beginning of lines; otherwise, I have aimed to capitalise as little as possible. Punctuation is almost entirely absent in the text. Poem numbers, which are provided in the main text in the manuscript, are recorded in the textual notes in this edition.

BIOGRAPHICAL NOTE

Lucy Hutchinson (1620–81) was the daughter of Sir Allen Apsley, lieutenant of the Tower of London, and Lucy St John (his third wife). Hutchinson had an extensive education, learning French, Latin, Greek and Hebrew as well as the more traditional feminine subjects of music, dancing and needlework. As a young woman she translated Lucretius's *De rerum natura* in verse (British Library Additional MS 19333; Hutchinson 1996). She married John Hutchinson (1615–64) on 3 July 1638 and they moved to his estate at Owthorpe, Nottinghamshire, in 1641. At the outbreak of the Civil Wars he took the parliamentary side, and became a lieutenant-colonel under Francis Pierrepont (d. 1659). Between 1643 and 1644 John took a commission from Thomas Fairfax (1612–71), the commander of the parliamentary army, to become governor of the castle and then the town of Nottingham. The town was frequently besieged in the next few years and its position was not strong; internal factions on the parliamentary side did not help the situation. John was sympathetic to radical Protestantism, and Hutchinson records (Hutchinson 2000, 210–11) how, as she became convinced that infant baptism was not scriptural, he accepted her position and did not have their newborn child baptised. He became MP for Nottinghamshire in 1646, and in 1648 agreed to bring Charles I to trial. He was one of the signatories of the death sentence against the King. Later, he opposed the Protectorate of Oliver Cromwell and was forced out of public life for a while. At the Restoration he was expelled from Parliament. Hutchinson called on her royalist links to save his life, even writing to the Speaker of the House of Commons in John's name (Hutchinson 2000, 281), a ploy which greatly displeased her husband. In 1663, accused of involvement in the Derwentdale Plot (Greaves 1986, 165ff), he was imprisoned, first in the Tower and then in Sandown Castle in Kent, where he died of a fever.

The Hutchinsons probably had ten children. Those for whom dates are known are twins, Thomas and Edward, born in 1639; Lucius, born in 1640; John, who died at the age of six (1641–47); and a girl who lived four years (1642–46). The remaining five were another John, Barbara (who married Andrew Orgill and moved to Jamaica), Lucy, Margaret and Adeliza (names listed on a tablet at Owthorpe Church: Hutchinson 1973, opposite 227).

Lucy Hutchinson was a prolific writer. Between 1664 and 1671 she wrote her *Life of Colonel Hutchinson* (extant in Nottinghamshire Archives DD/HU4), including a detailed, dramatic and partial account of the Civil Wars in Nottinghamshire and its wider context, based on an earlier diary she had kept (British Library Additional MS 25901 and fragments Additional MSS 39779 and 46172N). She probably wrote her 'Elegies' at about the same time. Other extant writings include two commonplace books (Nottinghamshire Archives DD/HU1 and DD/HU3); a religious treatise for her daughter Barbara Orgill, 'On the principles of the Christian religion' (Northamptonshire Record Office, Fitzwilliam Collection Misc. vol. 793); and the recently attributed religious epic poem on Genesis, partly published as *Order and Disorder* (1679; Beinecke Library, Osborn Collection, MS fb. 100; Hutchinson 2001). An article in *Notes and Queries* (Race 1938, 39) points to the burial of a Mrs Hutchinson at Owthorpe in 1681.

Bibliography:
Hutchinson (1973, 1996, 2000, 2001)
Greaves (1986), Norbrook (1997), Race (1938)

JSM

Elegies

'Leave of yee pittying freinds; leave of in vaine'

Leave of yee pittying freinds; leave of in vaine
Doe you perswade the dead to live againe
In vaine to me your comforts are applied
For, 'twas not he; twas only I that died
In that Cold Grave which his deare reliques keeps   5
My light is quite extinct where he but Sleepes
My substance into the darke vault was laide
And now I am my owne pale Empty Shade
If this your mirth or admiration moove
Know tis but the least meracle of Love   10
The effect of humane passion shuch as mine
Which ends in woe & death; But Love devine
Whose Sacred flame did his pure bosome fire
With more Stupendious working doth aspire
Untill it life & Victory Compleates   15
Fixing transformed men in blessed seates
This holy fire refind his happy Soule
And first did naturs Strong Impulse Controwl
Brought the wild passions Under Servitude
The haughty flesh & rebell Sence Subdued   20
Maide Carnall reason freely to lay downe
At the lords feete her Scepture & her Crowne
When this pure flame had burnt away the drosse
It maide him rich by universall Losse
Out of the Pile a Pheanix did arise   25
Enlightned with quick penetrating Eies
Which distant heaven into the mind did draw
And the disgiuzd world in its owne forme saw
At the emission of their powerfull Ray
Th' old Sorcerers Strong enchants fled away   30
The Groves the Pallaces the pleasant Pooles
Arbours sweetes musick beauties feast that fooles
Charmd by the mighty witch reale Esteeme
Appeard a loathsome dunghill unto him
Whoe through their deformd vizards too   35
And the darke mantle Sine about them threw
In prisons exile Sollitude disgrace
And death itselfe beheld a lovely face
On God alone he fixt his steadfast looke
Till God into himselfe his Creature tooke   40
Who all things elce with God like eies now viewd
And seeing them in God Saw they were good

Thus was delighted in the Creature Streames
While they were guilt with the Creators beames
But when that heavenly Sun withdrew no more 45
Did he the Inreflecting glasse adore
Nor in the Shadow Stayd but wheresoere
The glorious substance pleasd next to appeare
Thither did his attending heart remoove
And Sollacd theire his Chaste his Constant love 50
Love which alone best rellishes its sweetes
Where it least of the worlds disturbance meetes
By whose Greate power he free in prison remand
And in the *Bloody Tower* with triumph reignd
Dispising his oppressors rage while they 55
By lusts enslavd in sadder Thralldome lay
This Conqured the assaults of wrath greife feare
This did his head above the wild waves reare
This Painted dismall rocks & barrin Sands
With beauties equall to the fruitefull Lands 60
This gave Calamity a lovely face
And put on honours Crowne upon disgrace
This did the feavers force & fire abate
His Soule in her last conflicts recreate
His perfect Sence from feeling paine did keepe 65
And gave him rest without the ayd of Sleepe
This sweetely carried of expiring Breath
And brought him new life in approaching death
Which Could not fix its horrors in his face
That Pale & Cold reteind a Smiling grace 70

[pp. i–iii]

---

32. Arbours] u *superimposed on* a
50. Chaste] *MS* Cheast
56. Thralldome] *MS* Tharlldome

Another on the Sun Shine

Heavens glorious Eie which all the world surveyes
This morning through my window shot his rayes
Where with his hatefull & unwellcome beames
He guilt the Surface of aflictions Streames
In anger at their bold intrusion I 5
Did yet into a darker Covert fly
But they like impudent Suters brisk & rude
Me even to my thickest Shade persude
Whome when I Saw that I could no where Shun
I thus began to chide th'immodest Sun 10
How Gawdy Masker darst thou looke on me

Whose Sable Coverings thy reproaches be
Thou to our murtherers thy taper bearst
Th'oppressive race of men thou warmst & Chearst
The blood which thou hast Seene pollutes thy light   15
And renders it more hatefull than the Night
All good men loath thee growne a common bawd
The Brave that Leadst Impieties abroad
Who Smiling doest on lust & rapine shine
Nor Shrinkst thy head in at disgorgd wine   20
Which Sinners durst not let thee see before
Now thy conniving lookes they dred no more
Because thou makst their pleasant gardins growe
And Chearishest the fruitefull seeds they sowe
In feilds which unto them descended not   25
By Violence briberry & oppression gott
Thou sawst the league of God himselfe dissolvd
Which a whole Nation in one curse Involvd
Thou sawst a Thankelesse people slaughtring those
Whose noble blood redeemd them from their foes   30
Thy staind beams into the Prison came
But lost their boasts outshind with vertues flame
Thou Sawst the Innocent to exile Led
And for all this veildest not thy radiant head
But comst as a gay courtier to deride   35
Reuines we would in Silent Shadowes hide
Since then thou wilt thrust into this darke room
By thyne owne light read thy most certeine doom
Darkenesse shall shortly quench thy impure light
And thou Shalt Sett in Everlasting Night   40
Those whome thou flattriest shall se thee expire
And have no light but their own funerall fire
Theire Shall they in a dreadfull wild amaze
At once see all their glorious Idolls blaze
Thy Sister the pale Empris of the Night   45
Shall never more reflect thy borrowd light
Into black blood Shall her darke body turne
While your polluted Spheres about yow burne
And the Elementall heaven like melting lead
Drops downe Upon the impious rebells head   50
Then Shall our King his Shining host display
At whose approach our mists shall fly away
And wee Illuminated by his Sight
No more shall neede thy everquenched Light

[pp. ix–xi]

17, 21, 41. thee] *MS* y^e
19. rapine] *MS* rampine

21. not] *MS* no
23. Because] *MS* Becas
34. veildest] *first* e *inserted*
37. thrust] *MS* thurst
42. own] *MS* one

Upon two pictures one a Gallant man drest up in Armour the other the same Honorable Person looking through a Prison Greate & leaneing on a Bible

The table you here See presents
A true-borne Princes Lyneaments
No Vulgar hands sett on his Crowne
Nor could they cast his Empire downe
Whose soule stooped not to servile things 5
But triumpht over foyld Kings
Shuch Armes he had but his defence
Firme Courage was and Innocence
Shuch killing weapons too he wore
Not to destroy but to restore 10
Which done he threw the Sword away
Embraceing those who prostrate Lay
But O ungratefull treacherous Age
Those whome he Saved from tyrants rage
To tyrants rage abandond him 15
That did their Libertyes Redeeme
The foes he to protection tooke
Him when he needed itt forsooke
And basely hunted to the grave
Whose cryme was that he them did save 20
But lest your weake soule be dismaid
At vertue hunted and betraid
See him in Prison ne're so greate
As when his false aydes did retreate
His Courage then most brightly shone 25
When it was left to Conquer all alone
Whoe Chrusht his foes by his brave fall
And tryumphd in his funerall

[pp. xvii–xviii]

5. stooped] *MS* stoope
21. lest] *MS* least
23. ne're] *MS* nere

To the Gardin att O:

Poore desolate Gardin Smile no more on me
To whome glad lookes rude entertainments be

While thou & I for thy deare Master mourne
Thats best becoming that doth least adorne
Shall wee for any meaner Eies be drest 5
Whoe had the Glorie once to please the best
Or Shall wee prostitute those Joys againe
Which once did his noble Soule entertaine
Forbid it honour & Just Gratitude
Tis now our best grace to be wild & rude 10
He that empaled thee from the comon Ground
Whoe all thy walls with Shining frute trees Crownd
Me alsoe above vulgar Girles did rayse
And planted in me all that yelded prayse
He that with various beauties dect thy face 15
Gave my youth lustre & becoming grace
But he is gone & these gone with him too
Let now thy flowers rise Chargd with weeping dew
And missing him shrink back into their beds
Soe my poore virgins hang their drooping heads 20
And missing the deare object of their Sight
Close upe their Eies in Sorrows Gloomy Night
Let thy young trees which Sade & fading stand
Dried upe Since they lost his refreshing hand
Tell me too Sadely how your noblest Plant 25
Degenerates if it usuall Culture want
There spreading weeds which while his watchfull eies
Checkt their pernitious growth durst never rise
Let them orerun all the sweete fragrant bankes
And hide what growes in better ordered rankes 30
Too much alas this Parallill I find
In the disordred passions of my mind
But thy late lovelinesse is only hid
Mine like the Shadow with its Substance fled
Annother Gardiner & another Spring 35
May into the new grace & new lustre bring
While beauties seedes doe yet remaine alive
But ah my Glories never can revive
No more than new leaves or new Smiling fruite
Can reinvest that tree thats dead at roote. 40
When to his worthy memory thou then
Hast offerd one yeares fruite thou mayst again
In gawdy dresses to thy next lord Shine
And Shew weake Semblance of his grace in thine
For all thats generous healthfull sweete & fair 45
Imperfect emblimes of his vertue are
But Could I call back hasty flying time
The vanisht glories that once dect my Prime

> To me that resurrection would be vaine
> And like ungathred flowers would die againe
> In vaine would doting time which can no more
> Give shuch a lover Lovelinesse restore

50

[pp. xxi–xxii]

Title. Numbered 7th *in MS*
8. Soule] *MS* Sould
9. Just] *MS* Jus
11. thee] *MS* y^e
18. Chargd] *superimposed on* with
28. pernitious] *replacing* penetrating *deleted*
30. hide] *MS* hid
48. once dect] *replacing* dect once; *first* dect *deleted*

The Night

> Heavens Glorie was wrapt up in Shrowds
>   Earth which no more derivd from thence
>   A warme & chereing Influence
> Lay could beneath the weeping Clowds
>
> An artificiall heate and light
>   Vanquisht the shades in other roomes
>   But sade Orenas like the tombs
> The receptacles were of Night
>
> Night th'emblame both of death & hell
>   Not only heavens glorie stained
>   And over all the low world reignd
> But alsoe in her soule did dwell
>
> Woes sault floods quencht her inward light
>   Ore all her heaven darkenesse spread
>   Fretting remorce & guilty dread
> Added a horror to her Night
>
> Ah She Sayd why am I yet tost
>   Why live I yet to prolong my woe
>   Since life can no new Comforts shew
> Nor bring those back which I have lost
>
> Where is that love that once soe pleasd
>   Warming his kind and constant breast
>   On which I did my faint head rest
> And all my anxious Cares were Easd
>
> Where is that hand that dried my teares
>   Those lipps that did my sorrows Charme
>   Where is that kind Ensircling arme
> That held mee upe amidst all feares

5

10

15

20

25

Where is that Soft powerfull breath
   That kept alive my active fire 30
   And noble Courage did inspire
Against the worst assaults of Death

Those lipps & hands long since were Could
   And with them all the Noble frame
   Resoulved to dust from whence they came 35
But that is all the grave can hold

His Sperritt which from heaven was sent
   To Sojorne in the brittle Clay
   When that house fell into decay
Back to its Native pallace went 40

His truth faith love & Constancy
   His soaring wings to heaven were
   And are his Crowne of glorie their
Nor doe in the cold ashes Lie

What is Assended upe on high 45
   Why seeke wee then amoung the dead
   And fruitelesse teares on Cold graves shed
Bewayling that which cannot die

O could I rayse my Soule above
   This earthly low perplexing Sence 50
   I might through pure Intelligence
Againe communicate his Love

Our streames in their first head would mix
   Their constant course would them refine
   His & my long extended line 55
Would both in one Just centure fix
                           [pp. xxiii–xxiv]

Title. Numbered 8th *in MS*
7. Orenas] *MS* Orenats
10. stained] *MS* stand

The Recovery

My love life Crowne peace treasure Joys were lost
And seeking them Long was my fraile Barke tost
On Sorrowes raging flood where Stormes prevaild
And the Poore Leaking Vessell every way assaild
The Cordage Crackt the Shrowds & maine mast tore 5
Vane Skill and Industry could helpe no more
Then helplesse in these extreames at Last

Loves Rocke appeard & their we ancher cast
But thrice blessed Storme thus was I brought
Where I could only find the Things I sought
This rock is both worlds Centre all thats sweete
Greate beautious pleasant in this fixt poynt meete
Here heavens bright glorie to fraile earth descends
Here earth advanct to heaven its frailty ends
For the pure Nature taking in the Crosse
By its powerfull Touch to Gold converts the Drosse
And as it through the fleshly medium Shines
That body transubstantiates and refines
In this rocke is truthes Christiall healing Spring
Which shews the perfect forme of every thing
Strengthens the weake and doth the sick eies Cure
That they the radiant merror may endure
Here saw I the dear object of my love
Wearing the Martirs Crowne enthroned above
In Shuch Glorie that I could noe more
His exaltation as my losse deplore
But here I seast t'admire one single ray
Where the Unclosed Sun did all display
My love his Love & Lovelinesse were all
Recovered here in Their Originall
Here they concentred & refind were
At once both lost & found in the first faire
Whose powerfull attractions Charme us soe
Wee can noe more Consider things below
And as they draw & fix our greedy sight
Soe draw wee from them life & full delight
The bright reflections made me a new Crowne
While death & Sorrow Could no more cast downe
Sweete peace from Thence Into my Soule distilld
And Joys that left not one desier unfilld
Now my late Ignorant wishes I disdane
Discernd The Cheate of Joys that after paynd
Here viued the Luster Mortalls soe admire
Are gloomy Slime & nights misleading fire
Created beauties which blind Soules adore
Here sease to be their Idolls any more
For here their seene but darke declining streams
Guilt as they pas with lights reflected beames
The celebrated workes of vane mens hands
Are paper frames erected on the Sands
Which loosened & disperst with every wind
No memory no empression leave behind
That fixt world where I sought to fix before

Here lookt on was a Cheating flying Shore
Which while with Strong contest we strive to gaine   55
Engages more in the tempestious maine
But Sullen foggs & thick mists vanisht here
The tumult of the waves which did appeare
So horred late unto the now Cleard Sence
Seemd the well measurd dance of Providence   60
Th'awaking Thunders whose lowd dreadfull sound
No lesse mens trembling harts than rent Clowds wound
Heard in This Rock are the harmonus noyse
Of love & wisdomes Sweete according voyce
O rocke of life O quickning power of love   65
Here lett me fix; nor hence againe remoove
My wandring Eies to gaze on transeant Things
That glitter borne along on times Swift wings
But still in motion are least we Should See
What Lyes & Cousenage in their faire shewes be   70
Lett my Recoverd Soule for ever more
Rejoyse in what I lately did deplore
That wreck which cast me upon thee; I who
Till I did things in thy Cleare merror viue
Mistooke Th'appearance of ill & good   75
And nothing in its true forme understood
                    [pp. xxvii–xxviii, xliii, xiii]

The leaves containing this poem are disordered. Lines 45–76 follow a later poem in the manuscript, 'The Consecrated Attoms Sleeping here'. See Norbrook (1997), 506 (n.)
 1. were] *inserted*
 11. Centre all] *MS* Centriall
 23. object] *MS* objet
 24. enthroned] *MS* enthornd
 38. cast] *MS* cas
 51. wind] *MS* mind
 65. quickning] *MS* quckning
 66. hence againe] *replacing* from hence; from *deleted*, againe *inserted*

On The Spring 1668

As The Triumphant Sounds & Shewes
   Of Conquerors to their Captives be
Shuch is The Glory that now Growes
   On the restored world to me

The Shining rays that guild the Skeyes   5
   And glad all other mortalls Sight
Add but more payne to my bleard Eies
   And drive me from the torturing light

The Lately buried Corne is Seene
   Smiling againe in its new birth   10
All mantled in its gawdy Greene
   But my Joyes Lie still hid in earth

I heare The Chastly Amarous Dove
   Answerd againe by her kind mate
But what I say to my Dead Love   15
   Only the Rocks Reverberate

As mourners who their blacks Cast by
   New flowers the bankes & trees adorne
But Still greifes Sable Levery
   In my Sad heart & Eies is worne   20

You comely Daughters of The Spring
   Rayse not your heads with Soe much Pride
For Time That Changes every Thing
   Forbids your Triumphs to abide

That Sun that now so flatters you   25
   And in your Virgins bosomes playes
Will shortly change your pleasant hiew
   And scorch you with his burning rayes

That ayre whose wanton breath doth now
   Respire your Sweetes in Every place   30
Lik false men soone will Stormy growe
   And Scatter you in your disgrace

Blest mates whome love & Life unites
   Death alsoe must your Joyes Conclude
You must like me loose your delights   35
   And waste your age in Sollitude

And you faire Skies growne Calme & bright
   Againe your clowdy veiles must weare
And weepe black showers for your lost Light
   When battles in your bowells are   40

If naturall Glories have no stay
   Lesse Steddy are mens tottering States
Either by slowe time stolen away
   Or rudely throwne from their proud heights

Why Should it payne me then to See   45
   Others The precipices Climbe
Mines past their ruines futuer be
   Who Lies low falls no Second time

                                   [pp. xxxvii–xxxviii]

Title. Numbered xiv *in MS*
44. throwne] w *inserted*

'Here a greate Patriot lies if what the Grave'

Here a greate Patriot lies if what the Grave
Reteines right to Th'illustrious Title have
Of noble blood & vertuous parentage
The Shame & Glory of a Thankelesse age
Of Sons of fathers of freinds the best   5
That any of those deare Relations blest
Religious Honorable good wise Just
Yet all rakd up in Consecrated Dust
He once greate name in Armes & Councells bore
In glorious Sufferings advanced more   10
In death it selfe to fullist height did rise
When his fraile body fell a Sacrifice
For his Greate Kings Supreame pure perfect Laws
And his ungreatefull Cuntries righteous Cause
Engagd to these in life & death most true   15
Whome neither feare nor flatterry Could subdue
Till full of faith & heavenly hope he died
This weeping Stone doth his deare reliques hide
Waiting the blessed day when our Great King
Shall new Life to his Martiers Cold dust bring   20

[p. xli]

Title. Numbered xvi *in MS*

'Ye Sons of England whose unquenched flame'

Ye Sons of England whose unquenched flame
Of Pious love may yet that Title Clayme
Let not your rash feete on that Marble tread
Before you have its Sade Inscription read
Beholde it weepes doe not these tears presage   5
Decending Showers on this prodigious age
Where only Rocks for Innocent blood shed mourne
While humane hearts to flintie quarries turne
Now read this Stone doth Close up the darke Cave
Where Liberty Sleepes in her Champions grave   10

[p. xlvi]

Title. Numbered xx *in MS*

15 The Cruel Tiger Swiftly on doth Pass
Scorning Pursuers, till a Cristall Glass
Layed purposely, at which shee stands at gaze
Her self lov'd beuty, makes her in a Maze
Soe is the Early Riseing Lark a Lass
Onely infnar'd with looking in a Glass
Pride makes the flying fish display her Wings
Then hungrie Hawks her little neck offwrings
These are noe wonders Sacred Stories Show
That Pride the greatest Monarchs did ore throw
Brave Amazia gallant things did doe

*2 booke of kings Untill the Thistle did the Ceder Woo
cha the fourteen
vers the 8
*sam the first Book Saul and *Uzzia might have worn ye Crown
chap the 13 th
verse the 5 th
*2 Boock of Chrono Till catching at the Miter both fell down
chap the 27 th
° vers the 16 th
  2 Boock of kings Pride made good Hezechia to disclose
20 chap vers the 13
° Those Secret Treasures wch his Sons did lose

The Assyrrian King forgot his God, at least
Twas Pride that did Transceform him to a Beast
Herod that would not give to God the Glory
An Angell Struck, and Worms did end his story
Pride made our Parents know both good & evill
And Pride did turn an Angell to a Devill
Then by these stories you may See at least
That Pride destroys both, Angel, Man, & Beast.

PLATE 7 Hester Pulter, Leeds University Library, Brotherton Collection MS Lt q 32, fol. 100v
(poem not included in this edition)

8

Hester Pulter's 'Poems Breathed forth By The Nobel Hadassas'

Leeds University Library, Brotherton Collection MS Lt q 32

Hester Pulter's handsomely bound manuscript, MS Lt q 32, came to light in the mid-1990s, when it was discovered by Mark Robson, mis-catalogued, in the Brotherton Library at Leeds University. The manuscript is entitled 'Poems Breathed forth By The Nobel Hadassas'. Hadassas, Hester Pulter's pen name, is another name for the biblical Esther and she probably took it from Francis Quarles's 1621 work, *Hadassa: or The history of Queene Ester with meditations thereupon, divine and moral*. In fact only the first 130 folios are taken up with poetry: the final thirty folios of the manuscript consist of the transcription of an unfinished romance, 'The Unfortunate Florinda', written in from the back of the manuscript and inverted. The transcription of the romance seems to have begun in 1660: dating of the poems and watermarks suggest a transcription date in the mid 1650s for the main body of the poetry, although some of the titles include dates from the 1640s. Folios 90r–130v are designated a separate 'Booke of Emblemes': fifty-three poems, which, although they have no accompanying illustrations, follow the fable-like narrative and moralising tone characteristic of the seventeenth-century emblem.

Most of the manuscript is in a scribal hand, although there are corrections in a hand which is probably Hester Pulter's own (see plate 7). 'Hadassas Chast Fances' on the bound volume's second title page, and a description on the emblems' title page, 'The sighes of a sad soule Emblematically breath'd forth by the noble Hadassah', are both inscribed in this hand, as are three of the later poems, two dated January 1665 (fols 84v, 87r and 88v). A hand which appears throughout the manuscript in an annotating capacity seems to be that of an eighteenth-century antiquary who took an interest in the manuscript, transcribing what remains of the second book of 'The Unfortunate Florinda', adding a Pulter family tree and, probably, submitting the manuscript for binding. This hand has been tentatively identified by Sarah Ross as that of Angel Chauncy, grandson of the antiquarian Sir Henry Chauncy (Ross 2000, 162). Henry Chauncy gives a great deal of biographical information on the Pulters in his two-volume work *The Historical Antiquities of Hertfordshire* (Chauncy 1700, I: 141–7).

Hester Pulter's poems are in various genres. Several refer to events of her life: pregnancy, illness, deaths of her children. A concern for her children is one of the two preoccupations of this volume: the other is her royalism. Several of the poems are addressed to Charles I, and one is to the royalist leaders shot at Colchester in 1648. Several of her emblems carry a royalist message. A few of the poems are religious lyrics in a familiar strain of seventeenth-century piety. However, many of the poems show a more wide-ranging intellectual interest. She seems to have been familiar with the latest developments in alchemy, and astronomy (perhaps through the poetry of Henry More). Her wide reading is apparent throughout the volume: her emblems are often taken from translations of Plutarch or Pliny, and she is clearly familiar with much contemporary poetry. One of her emblems employs the story of the Pied Piper, which had recently been included by James Howell in his *Familiar Letters* (Howell 1645), although she cites the first work in which the story came to England, Richard Verstegan's *A restitution of decayed intelligence* (1605). One long poem entitled 'The Garden' is a philosophical poem, composed, she says, at the request of her daughter Anne.

Despite the literary and intellectual range of her work, Pulter represents her authorial activity as a harmless way of occupying her time (fol. 104r). The only obvious audience for this volume is her children, for whom several of the poems are written: she represents herself as 'shut up in A Countrey Grange' (fol. 79r) and there is no evidence that her poems circulated. Despite this, she clearly felt knowledgeable enough about royalist literary culture of the interregnum to write a satirical poem to Sir William Davenant on the loss of his nose from syphilis (fol. 83r).

The few marginal notes provided in the manuscript have been recorded in the textual notes.

BIOGRAPHICAL NOTE (ADAPTED FROM ROSS 2000)

Hester Pulter was born in the 1590s or the first decade of the 1600s, the daughter of James Ley, later Sir James Ley, the first Earl of Marlborough, and his first wife, Mary, née Petty, of Stoke Talmage in Oxfordshire. James Ley (1550–1629) was descended from the Ley family of Teffont Evias in Wiltshire. Hester was one of eleven surviving children.

There is some uncertainty about Hester's date of birth. No record of her birth or baptism is known to survive, and the poetry itself appears to give conflicting testimony on this point. A poem on fol. 88v of her manuscript is entitled 'Made when my spirits were sunk very low with sickness & sorrow. May 1667 I being seventy one years old', thus suggesting a birth-date of 1596. However, another poem in Pulter's manuscript dates her birth to 1607: 'Made when I was sick 1647' describes her soul's 'forty years acquaintance' with her flesh. A statement in the poem 'Alitheas Pearl', 'Thus have I liv'd a sad and weary life / Thirteen a Mayd, and Thirtie three a Wife' (fol. 51r), fits best with the probable chronology of Pulter's poems if a birth-date of 1607 is assumed. She represents herself in two poems as having been pregnant with her fifteenth child in 1648 (fols 10v, 67r). It is most likely that Hester Pulter was born in 1607, and that perhaps the scribe mistook the date in the title of 'Made when my spirits were sunk very low'. If the date 1607 is correct, then Hester Pulter was almost certainly born in Dublin, where James Ley was resident following his appointment as Chief Justice of the King's Bench in Ireland in December 1604. He was permanently recalled to England in 1608.

Hester's sister Margaret is the addressee of Milton's Sonnet X, 'To the Lady Margaret Ley'. Edward Phillips asserts that Milton spent time in the company of Ley and her husband in the autumn and winter of 1643–44, after the departure of his wife, Mary Powell. Phillips describes Lady Margaret as 'a woman of great wit and ingenuity', who 'had a particular honour for [Milton], and took much delight in his company; as likewise her husband, Captain Hobson, a very accomplished gentleman' (Masson 1871–94, III: 56–7). Margaret and Hester Ley allied themselves to opposing political factions in the 1640s and 1650s.

Hester Ley married Arthur Pulter, of the manor of Broadfield in Hertfordshire. If Hester was born in 1607 and married at the age of thirteen, the wedding would have occurred in 1620. The christening of Hester and Arthur's daughter Jane is recorded in the parish register of Cottered, Hertfordshire, on 1 May 1625 and another daughter, Mary, may have been born before Jane. Ten of the Pulters' children's names appear in the Cottered and Great Wymondley parish registers: Jane (1625), James (1627), Margaret (1629), Hester (1630), Penelope (1633), William (1634), Ann (1635), Arthur (1636), Edward (1638) and Elizabeth (1641). There is evidence of the birth of three other children to the Pulters: a second daughter Mary; Charles, whose burial is recorded in Cottered parish register in January 1640; and John, with whom Pulter describes herself as being confined in 1648 (fol. 67r).

Arthur Pulter inherited Broadfield from his grandfather, Edward, at some time after 1620. Arthur was a Justice of the Peace, a Captain of the Militia and, in 1641, a Sheriff of the county. Chauncy explains that 'shortly after the breaking forth of the late civil War, [Arthur Pulter] declin'd all publick Imployment, liv'd a retired life, and thro' the Importunity of his Wife, began to build a very fair House of Brick upon this Mannor' (Chauncy 1700, I: 145). Chauncy gives no intimation of the reason for his pejorative description of Hester Pulter's character, but the house to which he refers is Broadfield, whose garden features prominently in her writing. Chauncy implies that Arthur Pulter spent the 1640s and 1650s in rural retirement at Broadfield with Hester. Hester's poetry, written at Broadfield between the early 1640s and 1665, makes it clear that she, at least, was based there during these years (she appears to have remained resident there until her death). Arthur resigned the sheriffdom 'because of the Wars'. Whichever side he supported (and perhaps the resignation suggests he wished to stay neutral), Hester Pulter's occasional verses show that she was extremely royalist.

The earliest poem that can be dated has Pulter composing poetry before 1645. Much of her work seems to have been composed in the 1640s and 1650s, although a few poems are dated in the 1660s. The Cottered register contains the information that she was buried on 9 April 1678, having outlived all but two of her children.

Bibliography:
Chauncy (1700, I)
Masson (1871–94, III), Ross (2000)

EC

**Poems
Breathed forth By
the Nobel
Hadassas**

On the Same

Tell mee noe more, her haire was lovly brown
Nor that it did in Curious curles hang down
Or that it did her snowey shoulders shrowed
Like shineing Cinthia in A Sable Clowd
Tell mee noe more of her black Diamond eyes 5
Whose cheerfull looke made all my sorrowes fly
Like Glittring Phebus Influence and light
After a Northern Winters halfe years Night
Tell mee noe more her cheeks exceld the Rose
Though Lilly leaves did sweetly interpose 10
Like Ruddy Aurora riseing from her bed
Her snowey hand shadeing her Orient he'd
Tell mee noe more, of her white even Nose
Nor that her Ruby Lipps when they disclose
Did soe revive this drooping heart of mine 15
Like Golden Aples on A Silver Shrine
Tell mee noe more, her brests were heaps of Snow
White as the swans, where Cristall Thams doth flow
Chast as Diana was her virgin Bre'st
Her Noble Mind can never bee exprest 20
This but the Casket was of her rich soule
Which now doth shine above the highest pole
Tell mee noe more of her perfection
Because it doth increase my hearts dejection
Nor tell mee, that Shee past her happy dayes 25
In singing Heavenly and the Museses layes
Nor like the swans on Cristall Poe
Shee Sung her Dirges ere shee hence did goe
Nor never more tell my sad soule of Mirth
With her I lost most of my Joyes on earth 30
Nor can I ever raise my drooping spirit
Untill with her those Joyes I shall inherit
Those Glories which our finite thoughts transcend
Where wee Shall praises sing World without end
To him that made both her and mee of Earth 35
And gave us spirits of Celestiall Birth
Tell mee noe more, of her Unblemished fame
Which doth Immortalize her virgin Name
Like fragrant odours Aromatick Fumes

Which all succeeding Ages still perfumes 40
Nor why I mourn for her aske mee noe more
For all my life I shall her loss deplore
Till infinite power her dust and mine shall raise
To sing in Heaven his everlasting praise.
                                                          [fols 17v–18v]

---

2. curles] r *superimposed on* l
21. was] *inserted*
28. Dirges] i *superimposed on* e
29. Nor never] *the scribe began the line with* Never *and has altered it to* Nor
33. Glories] *written in Pulter's hand above scribal version which has overwritten another word and is not clear*
   thoughts] *inserted, replacing* doth *deleted*
   transcend] n *inserted*
36. Celestiall] *MS* Celetiall
39. Fumes] s *inserted above a blot*
42. all] *inserted above a blot*

The Circle

Those that the hidden Chimick Art profess
And vizet Nature in her Morning dress
To Mercurie and sulpher filterys give
That they consum'd with Love may live
In their Posterytie and in them shine   5
Though they their beeing unto them resign
Glorying to shine in Silver and in Gold
Which Fretting vermill poyson doth infold
Forgetting quite that they were once refin'd
By time and Fate to dust are all Calcind   10
lying obliviated in their Urn
Till they to their great Ancesters return
Soe Man the Universe's chiefest Glory
His primitive's Dust (Alas) doth end his story.
                                                          [fol. 40v]

---

1. the] the *inserted*
3. filterys] y *altered from* i
7. in Silver] in *inserted in Hester's hand, replacing* In *deleted*
13. Universe's] i *superimposed on* n

The perfection of Patience and knowledg

My soul, in strugling thou dost Ill,
The Chicken in the Shell lies still:
Soe doth the Embryon in the Womb,
Soe doth the Corps, within the Tomb,

Soe doth the Flower, Sleep in its Cause,　　　　　5
Obedient all to Natures Laws.
But tho'art still striving to bee free,
As if none were in Bonds but thee.
Though for A time thourt cloath'd with earth:
Er'e long thoult have a happy Birth.　　　　　10
The Chirping Bird will Break its Shell,
The Infant Leave it's Loathed Cell;
The Sleeping Dust will rise and speake,
And will her Marble prison Break:
The Flower her beuty will display;　　　　　15
then my infranchised soul, away
Beyond the Skie, will take her flieght,
And rest above the spheirs of Night;
In everlasting Life And Light.
Scorning this Dunghill Globe of earth:　　　　　20
Shee'l goe from whence shee had her Birth.
But (O my Soul) once more, return:
And call mee in my Silent Urn.
But if a Sleep I then am found,
Jog mee, and say the Trump doth Sound　　　　　25
Then will I rise and fly away,
With thee to everlasting Day:
Then shall our griefe and past annoys,
Bee swallowed up of infinite Joys;
Then beeing perfect and sublim'd,　　　　　30
Wee shall discern this Globe Calcin'd:
Then shall wee know these Orbs of Wonder,
Which in a maze wee now live under.
And why Sad Saturns heavie eye,
Frowns on mee with Malignancie.　　　　　35
And why Conjunctions should foreshew,
Som mighty Monarchies overthrow.
And by what (swift and infinite) Power,
Sol runs Three Hundred Miles an Hower.
And Why pale Cinthia, doth soe change　　　　　40
Her Lovly face, as shee doth range
All Night, a Hunting in the Shade,
And how fair Venus, can bee made
Hesperus, in the Orient:
And Vesperus, in the Occident.　　　　　45
Or whether Etheriall Fier doth Burn,
Or that this Terren Globe doth turn,
The Sun beeing Center Unto all,
And that hee ne're doth rise or fall,
Or whether they have a treble Motion,　　　　　50

Of which wee have soe smale A Notion.
All this (and more) wee then shall know,
Which are such wonders here below.
But which will most increase our Joys,
(Compard with which, these will prove toys)   55
Our unknown freinds wee then shall know,
Even those (aye mee) wee lost below.
Nay wee shall know (without which all is none)
The eternall essence, even as wee are known.
                                                        [fols 57r–58r]

---

1. strugling] u *inserted in Pulter's hand, replacing* a *deleted*
dost] *MS* do t
3. Embryon] y *superimposed on* i
15. beuty] *MS* beuly
16. then] *inserted in Pulter's hand, replacing* And *deleted*
24. if] *added between* But *and* a

This was written 1648, when I Lay Inn, with my Son John, beeing my 15 Child, I beeing soe weak, that in Ten dayes and Nights I never moved my Head one Jot from my Pillow, out of which great weaknes, my gracious God restored me, that I still Live to magnifie his Mercie. 1655

Sad, Sick, and Lame, as in my Bed I lay
Least Pain and Passion should bear all the sway
My thoughts beeing free I bid them take their flieght
Above the Gloomey Shades of Death and Night
They overjoyed with such a Large Commission   5
Flew instantly without all intermission
Up to that Spheir where Nights Pale Queen doth run
Round the Circumference of the Illustrious Sun
Her Globious Body Spacious was and Bright
That Half alone that from Sols Beams had Light   10
The other was imured in shades of Night
Nor did shee seem to mee as Poets fain
Guiding her Chariot with A silver Rein
Attir'd like som fair Nimph or Virgin Queen
With naked Neck and Arms and Robes of Green   15
Love sick EnDimion oft hath thus her seen
But as my thoughts about her Orb was Hurld
I did perceive Shee was another World
Thus beeing in my Fancie raisd soe fare
This World apear'd to mee another star   20
And as the Moon a Shadow Casts and Light
Soe is our earth the Empres of their Night
Next Venus, Usher to the Night and Day

Her ful Faced Beuty to mee did Display
Some time shee Waned then again increase 25
Which in our humours caus or Warr or Peace
My fancie next to Mercury would Run
But craftily hee popt behind the Sun
A wonder t'is the medium beeing Soe Bright
His Splendencie Should bee obscur'd by Night 30
Nor could I Sols refulgent Orb discrie
His raidient Beames dazled my tender eye
And now my Wonder is again renewed
That hee enlightening all could not bee vewed
Yet to my Reason this apeard the Best 35
That hee the Center was of all the rest
The Planets all like Bowlls still trundling round
The vast Circumference of his Glorious Mound
Hee resting quickens all with Heat and Light
And by the Earths motion makes our Day or Night 40
Next Jupiter that Mild Auspicious Starr
I did perceive about his Blazing Carr
Four bright Attendents alwayes hurrid Round
Next Flagrant Mars where noe such Moons are found
Then Saturn (whose Aspects Soe Sads my Soul) 45
About whose Orb two Sickly Cinthias rowl
Then on the Fixed stars I would have Gazed
But their vast Brightnes Soe my Mind Amazed
That my afrighted Fancie Downward Flew
Just as the Howers Auroras Curtain Drew 50
At which the Uglie Wife of Accharon
Bid drive and slashed her Drousey Monsters on
With Her there went her first born Brat old Errour
And Fierce Eumenedes poor Mortals terrour
Who with their snakes, and whips, and Brands, were hurld 55
To strike Amazement to the Lower World
Beeing scard themselves at the aproach of Light
To our Antipodes they took their Flieght
Sinnss Cursed ofspring with their Dam did Trace
That most Prodigious incestious Race 60
Pale Gastly, Shudring, Horrour, lost despair
And Sobbing Sorrow, tearing of her Hair
These of her sable Womb were born and Bred
And from the Light with her now frighted fled
And then my Mayds my Window Curtains Drew 65
And as my Pain soe Comforts did renew
Unto the God of truth, Light Life, and Love
Il'e such Layes Here begin shall end Above.

[fols 67r–68v]

Title. John] followed by Pulter *deleted*
1655] *altered from* 1665; 5 *superimposed on* 6. *A later hand has added* 1655 *as clarification*
7. that] *altered from* th; a *superimposed on* e *and* t *added before* Spheir
16. EnDimion] *altered from* in Dimion; *first* i *is partially erased,* E *superimposed on next* n, *and another* n *added between* E *and* D
26. or Warr] o *superimposed on* a
37. Bowlls] *altered from* Bowels; l *superimposed on* e
59. Sinnss] *altered from* Since; ss *superimposed on* ce
68. Above] A *superimposed on* in

The Larke

See how Arachne doth her Howres Pass
In weaving Tincile on the verdent Grass
Look how it glitters, now the sun doth Rise
The Bane of Harmles sheep, and death of flyes
And over it the slow and Unctious Snayl   5
In winding knots doth draw a slimey Trayl
The cheerfull Lark as in the Ayr shee Flyes
And on this Gossomeire casts down her eyes
Takes it for Merrours Laid by Rurall swains
And therefore fears to Light upon the plains   10
But with alacrity aloft shee Flyes
And early Sings her Morning sacrifice
And in her Language magnifies his Name
From whose imensity all creatures came
Doe thou my soul sing too, let none on earth   15
Or Ayr beyond thee goe, think on thy Birth
For though my Body's dust, thou art a Spark
Celestiall, For shame out sing the Lark
Shee hath but one life that shee spends in praise
Tho hast and shallt have two, yet wat's thy dayes   20
In Bleeding sighs, and Fruitless briney tears
In Melancholly thoughts vain causles Fears
Learn thou of this sweet Ayry Chorister
Doe thou her cheerfull Actions Register
For I have seen Walking one summers day   25
To take the Ayr when Flora did display
Her youthfull Pride as shee did smileing Pass
Shee threw her Flowered Mantle on the Grass
Which strait allured a Sunburnt Rurall Clown
To come and Mow thes Fadeing Beuties Down   30
Unbracet, unblest hee doth with hast repair
This valley to deflower, then Temp' more faire
Thus stew'd in sweet this Gripple hide bound slave
Cuts nere the Ground the greater Crop to have
Greedy of gain and sweltring him hee high'd   35

Mowing by chance neare where a spring did Glide
That in her Purling Language seemd to chide
Because hee Rob'd her of her chiefest pride
But hee Regardles of her murmering Woe
Still nearer to the Rill did stradling Goe 40
In this sweet place the Lark tooke such delight
Because it shadey was and out of sight
By this cool Rivolet shee took such Pleasure
That here shee placed her Young, even all her treasure
Was here inclosed, in one round little nest 45
Which this indulgent Bird warm'd with her brest
And by the Eccho of this Bubling Spring
Shee meant to teach her Ayry Young to sing
But in a Moment all her Joys were Quasht
In twinckling of an eye her hopes were Dasht 50
For this bold scoundrill without Fear or wit
Her Pritty Globe like Nest in Sunder split
Some are in Middle Cut, Some of their Head
Thus all her Young are either Maimd or Dead
One not quite kild doth weakly Fly about 55
Which soon perceived is by this Rude Lowt
Who Throws his Syth away to it doth run
Meaning to carry it to his little Son
Which having caught and it ins Pocket put
Withs swetty Glove hee doth't in prison shut 60
Next day hee Gives it to his crying squale
Who in a thred this pretty Bird doth Hale
Hither and thither, as his fond desire
Him Leads but ear't bee Night it doth expire
The poor old Dam seeing this sad Massacker 65
With heavie Heart to her light Wings betakes her
Yet Hovering below in hope to find
Some of her Brood according to their kind
To Follow her, but seeing at Last's ther's none
That doth survive shee sadly makes her moan 70
Yet mounts, and sings, Though in a sadder Tone
Thus as thou art afflicted here below
My troubled soul, still nearer Heaven goe
Let every troublesome Heart breaking Cross
Like Surly Billowes to thy Haven thee Toss 75
And As thy Friends And Lovly Children Die
Soe thou my soul to Heaven for Comfort Fly
There doe thou place thy whole and sole delight
There There are Joys nere seen by Mortall sight
Bee thou Possest my soul with those true Joys 80
And thou shalt Find worldly delights meer toys

Fix thou thy mind where those true pleasures dwell
Thou shalt noe leasure have to feare a Hell
And when Death ceaseth on thy Mortall Part
Thou mayest indure it with a constant Heart   85
And when thy Last Friends close thy Roleing Eye
Then chang thy place but not thy company.

[fols 68v–70v]

---

10. Light] *inserted, replacing* Like *deleted*
20. shallt] t *added in another hand*
22. Melancholly] *MS* Melaniholly
30. thes] s *added in another hand*
36. neare] *altered from* nere; ar *superimposed on* re, e *added*
37. seemd] *MS* seend
44. even] *first* e *inserted in Pulter's hand*
49. her] *inserted in Pulter's hand*
58. little] *inserted in Pulter's hand. The original reading* young *was deleted and replaced by* litle, *which was then deleted and replaced by* little *in Pulter's hand*
66. betakes] *conjectural reading;* s *may be* r *deleted*
86. Eye] *altered from* Eyes; s *deleted*

To Sir Wm. D. Upon the unspeakable Loss of the most conspicuous and chief Ornament of his Frontispiece

Sir:
    Extreamly I deplore your loss
    You'r like Cheapside without a Cross
    Or like a Diall and noe Gnoman.
    In pitty (trust mee) I think noe man
    But would his Leg or Arm expose   5
    To cut you out another Nose
    Nor of the Female Sex thers none
    But'ld bee one Flesh though not one Bone
    I though unknown would sleight the pain
    That you might have soe great a gain   10
    Nay Any Fool did hee know itt
    Would give his Nose to have your Wit
    And I my Self would doe the same
    Did I not fear t'wold Blur my Fame
    I as once said a Gallant Dame   15
    My Nose would venture not my Fame
    For who but that Bright eye above
    Would know twere Charity not Love
    Then Sir your Pardon I must Beg
    Excuse my Nose accept my Leg   20
    But yet besure both night and Day
    For mee as for your Self you pray
    For if I First should chance to goe

To visit those sad shades below
As my Frail Flesh there putrifies 25
Your Nose noe doubt will Sympathize
But this I fear least that blind Boy
Which Fate defend (yet such a Toy
May take the Chit) should shoot again
Then the Next loss would bee your Brain 30
Some Coy young Lass you Might Adore
Which would prefer some base Medore
And all your Witt and Titles sleight
Imbrace a Page before a Knight
Then should some Nobleminded Friend 35
Astolpho like to Heaven ascend
And having search'd neare and Farr
And found your most capacious Jarr
Then beeing with Joy returnd again
You could not then snuf up your Brain 40
Though all your strenght you should expose
You want the Organe cal'd a Nose
Prodigious the knight remains
Without or Nose, or Fame, or Brains.
Then A bold ordinance strook the Title of 45
Thus the proud Parces sit and at us scofe
What now remains the Man at Least
Noe surely nothing left but Beast
Then Royall Favour glu'd it on again
And now the Knight is Bon-di'de and in grain 50
Then Trample not that Honour in the Dust
In beeing a Slave to those are Slaves to Lust.

[fols 83r–84r]

---

3. and noe Gnoman] and noe *inserted in Pulter's hand, replacing* Gnoman *deleted*, Gnoman *added in Pulter's hand at the end of the line*
21. both] *MS* bot
28. defend] *MS* descend
34. Knight] *altered from* Kn^t; *superscript* t *remains above* ni, ght *added*
44. Without] *MS* Withous
50. Bon-di'de] *conjectural reading; MS unclear*

'Dear God from thy high Throne look down'

Dear God from thy high Throne look down
And lett my Suff'rings have their Crown
     I thee Implore
Tho' greif calcine my Flesh to Dust
Yett in thy Mercy still I Trust 5
     and thee Adore

Should I to Tears dissolved be
Yett will I still depend on thee
    for Evermore
Or should I sigh away to Air   10
Tho Rarify'd, I'd not Despair
    but in thee trust
Tho' I to Atoms am dispers'd,
I in their dances am unvers'd,
    yett shall no Dust   15
of my old Carcase e're be lost
tho' in a thousand Figures tost,
    for thou art Just.
What Mortal can or dares to look
into thy Glorious Blessed Book,   20
    Where written be
of mee, poor wretched mee, each part
E'en all my soul My thoughts My Heart.
    Thou plain may'st see
That I my Gracious God do love   25
a thousand thousand worlds above,
    and still praise thee.
             [fol. 86r]

In a later hand

The sighes of a sad soule Emblematically breath'd forth by the noble Hadassah:

Emblemes

             [fol. 90r]

Title page to subsequent poems
Emblematically] e *superimposed on* i
breath'd] *replacing* blea *deleted*

'When God (who is to Mercie most inclin'd)'

When God (who is to Mercie most inclin'd)
To punish or to trie hath once design'd
A People, each Reptell or insect
Or basest Animal will not neglect
But will their Habitation soe Annoy   5
Without a Countermand they'l all destroy
Thus Spain by Rabbits, Moles made Thesaly
Locusts made Affrica a Desert lye

France Frogs, Amycle Serpents, did destroy
Flyes, Lice, and Frogs, all Egypt did Annoy   10
Gyaros Rats, and too too many more
Their Sufferings (though not Sins) did then deplore
This made the Town of Hamell stand in Doubt
Cause of those vermine they had such a Rowt
They tri'de all waies, as poysons, Traps, and Catts.   15
Yett still their Houses pesterd were with Rats
At last a Piper chance'd to come that way
With whom they bargaind for a Certain pay
Their Town of this base Loathsom Beasts to free
The Fruits of Cursed Avarice now See   20
This Fellow pipeing went to Weasers brim
And all the Rats ran danceing after him
   Then instantly they skipt into the stream
Though some may thinkt a Fiction or A dream
Yet true it is for drowning was their Fate   25
But how t'was don noe story doth relate.
For whether a Telesma hee did take
Five such of Gold The Philistin's did make
Or what hee did I think noe man can say
But when hee came and asked for his pay   30
The Burgers in their Gravitie refus'd
To pay the Summe, the Piper thus abus'd
did vow Reveng, they bid him doe his worst
Now see how Breach of Promise is Accurst
The Fellow Pipeing went away againe   35
A Hundred and Thirty Children in his Train
Into a hill hee led these pretty Boys
And thus their Parents lost their hopes, and Joys
Which with Sad hearts they now too late deplore
For they nor hee were ever heard of more   40
By these their grievous Suff'rings you may see
that breach of Promise punished sure will bee
Then keep your word for better or for wors
Lest with these Saxons you pertake like Curs

                                      [fols 101v–102r]

Emblem numbered 17 *in MS*
13. Hamell] *second* l *superimposed on* e
15. waies, as] *inserted*
21. Weasers] W *superimposed on* w
21–2 *(marginal note).* See the story of this Pied Piper at Larg in Verstegan Folio 85
   23. First line on fol. *102r, preceded by number 18 deleted. The emblems were presumably numbered subsequent to transcription, and the indent at the top of the page misled the scribe into numbering the new page as a new emblem. Thereafter the emblems are numbered incorrectly*

31. Burgers] *altered from* Burges; r *superimposed on* s, s *added*
38. their] *superimposed on* those

'Who can but pitty this poor Turtle Dove'

Who can but pitty this poor Turtle Dove
Which was Soe kind and constant to her Love
And since his Death his loss shee doth Deplore
For his dear sake shee'l never Couple more
When others Wanton blood doth Nimbly Flow 5
Warm'd with the spring, hers then runs cool and slow
Nor Vallentine though t'is A Tempting Tide
Can make her lay her Chast resolv's aside
Not like that Wanton and Licentious Bird
Who loosing one a second and A Third 10
Like that Prodigious, Bedlam, Belgick, Beast,
Who had a score of Husbands at the least
A bitter Thraldome shee deserves to have
Who beeing Freed soe Oft, would bee A slave
Shame of her Sex! oh let her Loathed Name 15
Bee ne're inroled in the Booke of Fame.
But let Alcestis, and Artimitius, story
Bee still Remembred to her endles Glory
Some Deboras, and Annas, Sure have been
But in this Age of ours few Such are Seen 20
Then Ladyes immitate this Turtle Dove
And Constant bee unto one onely Love
Then if your Husbands rant it high and Game
Besure you Double not their Guilt and shame
Leave of Hide Park, Hanes, Oxford Johns, and kates 25
Spring, Mulbery Garden, let them have a Date
Buy not these Follyes at soe dear A Rate
These Places I know onely by their names
But t'is these places which doe blast your Fames
Who would with their dear reputation part 30
To eat a scurvey Cheescak or A Tart
For such poor follyes who Abroad would Roame
Have wee not better every day at home
They say to plays and Taverns some doe goe
I say noe Modest Ladyes will doe soe 35
Though Countis, Dutchis, or Protectors Daughter,
Those Places haunt, their Follyes run not after
Bee Modest then and follow mine advice
You'l find that Vertue's Pleasanter then Vice
Yet Anchorites I would not have you turn 40
Nor Halcions, nor bee your Husbands Urn

> But Chastly live and rather spend your dayes
> In setting Forth your great Creator's praise
> And for diversion pass your Idle times
> As I doe now in writeing harmles Rimes 45
> Then for your Honnours, and your fair souls sake,
> Both my example, and my Councell take,
> Infine love God, the fountain of all good
> Next those ahe'd by Mariage, Grace, and blood,
> Soe lets live here in Chast and vertuous love 50
> As wee'le goe on Eternally above
> Then o my God Assist mee with thy Grace
> That when I die I may but chang my place.
>
> [fols 103v–104r]

Emblem numbered 20 *in MS*
9. Not] *altered from* Nor; t *superimposed on* r
10–13 *(marginal note)*. This Monster liv'd within 2 Miles of Amsterdam, shee survivd 24 Husbands My Unckle Edw. P. did know her
14–20 *(marginal note)*. St: Jerom remembers (with a holy scorn) that hee saw a couple Maried in Room the Man had had 20 Wives the Woman 22 Husbands It was in the days of Pope Damascus. Doct: Duns sermon on easter day fol: 217
23. Husbands] *altered from* Husband; s *added*
50. Soe] MS Toe

'When royall Fergus Line did rule this Realm'

> When royall Fergus Line did rule this Realm
> My Father had the Third place at the Helme
> Out of the Privie Kitchin came his Meat
> Of sixteen Dishes hee might dayly Eat
> All things that were in season out were sought 5
> Amongst the rest they Welfleet Oysters Brought
> Which being set ready till my Father Comes
> A Mous leaps on the Table for the Crumbs
> Then Skipping up and down her Tayl did Glide
> By chance betwixt the shels, T'was then full Tide 10
> The Oyster Feeling one within her Hous
> Clapt close her doors, and thus shee Catch'd the Mous
> Oh that I now could speak the Mecian Tongues
> Or Frogian Language but I want such Lungs
> As hee that writ the dismale bloody Fights 15
> Betwixt the Frogian and the Mecian Knights
> Surely noe Weomen and I think few Men
> Can dance soe well as hee with feet and Pen
> But hee those Tongu's as I have heard did seek
> Before hee Learnd the Latin or the Greek 20
> But now the Captive Mous her dubious Fate

In my own Mother Tongue I must relate
As her imprisonment came by A Flow
Soe the next happy Tide did let her goe
O wonderfull who would have ever thought   25
That from the Deliane Twins help should bee brought
Then let us learn while Flesh doth here immure
Our Sinfull Souls, not think our Selves Secure
As this dul Fish was Torn up from A Rock
This spritely Mous in Prison thus to Lock   30
Soe from A vulgar one may rise to Raign
That many a Noble Spirit may restrain
This is too true, Yet let them patient bee
For Tide, or Time, or Death, will set them free.
Then trust in God, Extoll him Day, and Night: 35
For Sun, and Moon, and Stars, shall for thee Fight.

[fols 124v–125r]

Emblem numbered 48 *in MS*
14. Lungs] *altered from* Langs; u *superimposed on* a
16. Knights] *MS* Lnights
20. Latin] *altered from* Latine; e *deleted*

9

Presentation volume of Katherine Philips's verse

National Library of Wales MS 776B

Aside from the pirate edition of her *Poems* advertised by Richard Marriott on 14 January 1663/4, and withdrawn four days later, Katherine Philips's poetry was circulated predominantly through the medium of manuscript during her lifetime. The sole manuscript presentation copy of her works known to survive is National Library of Wales MS 776B. This manuscript was compiled after her death, between 1664 and 1667, by a scribe who signs himself 'Polexander' in his dedicatory epistle to her lifelong friend, Mary Aubrey Montagu, the 'Rosania' of Philips's poems. The manuscript itself is a 404-page quarto with a black morocco binding. All its poems are transcribed in the same italic hand as the dedicatory epistle, with the exception of 'Rosania's private Marriage' (included below). The manuscript opens with Philips's translation of Corneille's *Pompée*, acclaimed on its performance by John Ogilby's company at the Smock Alley Theatre in Dublin in February 1662/3. The texts of five verse translations follow, and these in turn are followed by her unfinished translation of Corneille's *Horace*, completed after her death by Sir John Denham, and performed at Whitehall in February 1667/8. The remainder of the volume comprises ninety-one original poems.

This manuscript bears little relation to the other key identified copy-texts of Philips's work. Philips's own autograph manuscript, compiled in the 1650s and now known as the Tutin Manuscript, is closely related to the Dering Manuscript (compiled by Philips's friend, Sir Edward Dering, 'Silvander'), the Clarke Manuscript (compiled by Sir George Clarke, whose father, Sir William, gave evidence at Philips's husband's trial in 1661) and the unauthorised 1664 print edition. (These manuscripts are: National Library of Wales MS 775B; University of Texas at Austin, Humanities Research Center, Misc* HRC 151 Philips MS 14,937; Worcester College, Oxford MS 6. 13, respectively.) The Rosania Manuscript (as NLW MS 776B is called) is copied from a variety of different sources. As Greer notes, twenty of the ninety-one original poems have had couplets excised, an editorial process which she argues is deliberate on the scribe's part (Greer 1996, 166–7). See also the comments of Philips's most recent editor, Patrick Thomas, in Philips (1990–93, I: 46), henceforth referred to in this section as *Works*. Furthermore, ten poems occurring in the Rosania Manuscript are known to occur only here prior to the publication of the posthumous *Poems* (1667).

This presentation volume, then, encompasses the majority of Philips's works to stand as her posthumous memorial for one of her closest friends. The prevalence of occasions and persons in Philips's poetry encourages the reading of biographical narratives in her work. However, this manuscript eschews such readings, presenting the events of her poetry achronologically, without fitting into any externally imposed cohesive life narrative. Indeed, the manuscript contexts for her verse belie such linear narratives (cf. Coolahan 2003). Moreover, new manuscript witnesses to her poetry are still being located. A new edition which will take such discoveries into account is currently being prepared by Elizabeth Hageman (cf. Hageman and Sununu 1994). The present standard edition (*Works*), edited by Patrick Thomas, Germaine Greer and Roger Little, varies in its use of copy-texts. Rather than recording minor variants, our edition records only readings which differ in the sense of the text where Thomas *et al.* have used the Rosania Manuscript as their copy-text.

The following selection of poems has been chosen in order to represent the range of genres and subject-areas encompassed in Philips's verse. Epitaphs and religious poetry are included, as well as examples of the political and friendship poems for which Philips is now best known. In following a manuscript rather than a printed copy-text, this anthology differs from almost all other selections of Philips's verse currently available. Certain poems demonstrate vividly the interplay of texts which was characteristic of manuscript culture ('To Antenor . . .', 'On the double murther . . .', 'To Palaemon . . .', and '[God]'), while others witness the complexity of her interactions with print culture ('To my Lord Arch-Bishop of Canterbury' and 'In Memory of Mr Cartwright').

BIOGRAPHICAL NOTE

Katherine Philips was without doubt the most widely read and acclaimed female poet of the seventeenth century. She was born in London on 1 January 1631/2, the daughter of John and Katherine Fowler. Both sides of her family had strong puritan inclinations. After John Fowler's death in 1642, his widow remarried, but her second husband died within a few years (*Works* I: 4). When, in 1646, she married Sir Richard Phillips of Pembrokeshire, her daughter moved with her to Wales. In August 1648, the young Katherine Fowler married James Philips (1594–1675), thirty-eight years her senior. Philips was a Cromwellian, and prospered during the Commonwealth, despite his wife's active and vocal royalist sympathies. The public threat posed to their delicate matrimonial balance of political sympathies is apparent in two of Philips's poems: one answering a poem by the Fifth Monarchist Vavasour Powell, the other, addressed to her husband, defending her royalist position and her right to express it (see 'On the double murther of the King' and 'To Antenor On a Paper of mine' below).

Philips's interregnum poetry is largely concerned with the joys of country life (a common topic in royalist verse of the period) and with sustaining her 'Society of Friendship'. Taking its inspiration from the French *précieuse* model of female friendship, adapted for the English court by Queen Henrietta Maria and Lucy Hay, Countess of Carlisle, and Platonic ideas about friendship, Philips's Society comprises her London, Wales and Dublin circles. In her poetry, she recasts herself as 'Orinda', and alludes to her friends via sobriquets largely derived from plays of the period. Her doctrine of friendship celebrates the harmonious and Platonic union of souls and notably forges a space for female friendship.

At the Restoration, Philips's political affiliations were to stand her and her family in good stead. Her husband's sequestration of royalist estates during the Commonwealth was subject to repeal on the Restoration, and he underwent trial for his role as member of the High Court of Justice. Katherine Philips lauded the returning monarch and his family, cultivating a close friendship with the reinstated royal Master of Ceremonies, Sir Charles Cotterell ('Poliarchus'), who was to prove a strong ally at court. Philips's close friend Anne Owen ('Lucasia') married the Irishman Colonel Marcus Trevor in 1662, and Philips accompanied them to Ireland, where she made the acquaintance of the court in Dublin. There, the politician, poet and dramatist Roger Boyle, Lord Orrery, instigated Philips's translation of Corneille's *Pompée*, which proved a great success, and trumped a rival group in England—led by Edmund Waller—who were also engaged in translating *Pompée*.

In July 1663, Philips returned to Cardigan, where she capitalised on her growing reputation, beginning her second Corneille translation (*Horace*). Select poems by Philips appeared in print within specifically royalist contexts during her lifetime; however, by far the majority of her verse was not officially authorised for print publication. The continuing scholarly controversy over the extent to which her work was intended to enter the sphere of print—focused on the question of her involvement in Marriott's publication of *Poems* in 1664—points to Philips as the perfect case study for the blurring of 'private' and 'public' boundaries in seventeenth-century women's manuscript writing (see Greer 1996, 156–64; Beal 1998, 161–5). Philips died from smallpox at the height of her fame and powers on 22 June 1664. Her fame grew after her death, most particularly after the publication of 121 poems and both plays in Herringman's folio edition of 1667 (reprinted in 1669 and 1678; octavo 1710).

Bibliography:
Philips (1664, 1667, 1990–93)
Beal (1998), Coolahan (2003), Greer (1996), Hageman and Sununu (1994), Souers (1931)

M-LC

To the Excellent Rosania

Madame

Orinda, though withdraw'n, is not from you; In lines so full of Spirit sure she lives; And to be with you, is that only spell can share her with the bright Abodes; your Eyes, her heaven on Earth; your Noble Heart her Center. Admit, that Lethe washes cares away; yet there's no Passage to Elisium debarr'd her Joyes. And the sweet intercourse your souls maintain'd, was of a Nature so   5
refined; Of the fruits of Paradise; a Taste of those above; and so entirely seized of Orinda's soul, no more to be devested with Mortality. Cease then, Adorable Rosania, to afflict your beauteous Mind, for that privation, which being hers, is your advantage; And freely sympathize in her beatitude. So her enlarged knowledg view's your Graces; & with un-dazzeld Opticks, in you beholds that   10
Fullness, whose but imperfect discovery, was so much her Wonder; and now

displayed, both justify's, & entertain's her admiration. Nor can she feele your absence, whose pure thoughts, she see's already, so familiar in those Glorious Mansions, & your candid breast, so fit, and lov'd a receptacle for her own. Here is a beatiffick converse! Angels, thus, are still ascending, & descending. It was this, Orinda's matchless Pen aspired; And having bequeath'd you these clear streams, you see how soon she thither took her flight, whence the rich veine derived. To appear in Print, how un:inclined she was? (I confess, an Edition, now, would gratify her Admirers, and 'twere but a just remeriting that value, which (in hers, & their own Right) was the Universall consent.) You, whose passionate concern so frankely exposed your admirable Beauty to that spitefull Disease, (whence all our grief,) led by the generous dictates of as inimitable Friendship; You, whose solicitous devoirs; whose bleeding anguish, shewed how readily you would have been her Ransom! You, in whose pious memory she shines, next to her lustre amongst the Stars! You alone; were her Ambition, as her Love. Enjoy these dear Remains, no more as a sad Monument; nor to remind her past, but present State. Thus, will her Raptures be to your harmonious Soul, a Jacobs-Staff, to levell at her Gloryes. Nor can these Charming Poems, so absolute over our affections, be themselves utterly insensible how Soveraign a bliss its to be yours,

  Madame
  Your Ladyships
      Most humble, & most
      devoted Servant
      Polexander

[pp. 5–7]

To Antenor
On a Paper of mine, which an unworthy Adversary of his, threatned to publish, to pregiudice him, in Cromwels time.

  Must then my folly's, be thy scandall too?
  Why sure the Devill hath not much to doe.
  My Love, & life, I must confess, are thine,
  But not my errours, they are only mine.
  And if my faults should be for thine allow'd,
  It will be hard to dissipate the cloud.
  But, Eves rebellion, did not Adam blast,
  Untill himself forbidden fruit did tast.
  But if those lines, a punishment could call,
  Lasting, & great, as this dark-Lantherns gall,
  Alone, I'de court the torments, with content,
  To testify, that thou art Innocent.
  So if my Ink, through malice prov'd a stain,
  My blood should justly wash it off again.
  But, since the Mint of Slander, could invent
  To make that triviall Rime his instrument,

Verse should reveng the quarrell, but hee's worse
Then wishes, & below a Poets curse.
And more then this, wit know's not how to give,
Let him be still himself, & let him live.   20

[p. 265]

On the double murther of the King.
(In answer to a libellous paper written by V: Powell, at my house)
These verses were those mention'd in the precedent coppy.

I think not on the State, nor am concern'd,
Which way soever that great Helm is turn'd.
But as that Son, whose Fathers danger nigh
Did force his native dumbness, & unty
The fetterd Organs, so this is a cause   5
That will excuse the breach of Nature's laws,
Silence were criminall, nay, passion now
Wise men themselves, for merit will allow.
What humane Ey could see, & careless pass,
The dying Lyon kick'd by every Ass.   10
Hath Charles so broke Gods Laws he must not have
A quiet Scepter, nor a quiet Grave.
Tombs have been Sanctuary's, Thieves ly there,
Secure from all their penalty, & feare.
Great Charles his double misery was this,   15
Unfaithfull friends, ignoble Enemy's.
Had any Heathen been this Princes foe.
He would have wept to see him Injurd soe.
His tytle was his crime, they'd reason good,
To quarrell at a right they had withstood.   20
He broke Gods law's, & therfore he must dy,
And what shall then become of you, & I?
Slander must follow Treason, but yet, stay,
Take not our Judgment with our King away,
Though you have seiz'd upon all our defence,   25
Yet doe not sequester our common-sence,
But I admire not at this new supply,
No bounds will hold those who at Scepters fly.
Christ will be King, but I ne're understood
His subjects built his Kingdome up with blood.   30
Except their own, nor that he would dispence
With his commands, though for his defence.
O! to what height of horrour are they come,
Who dare pull down a Crown, tear up a Tomb.

[pp. 266–7]

To Palæmon
on his discourse of friendship

We had been still undone, wrapt in disguise,
Secure, not happy, cunning but not wise,
War had been our design, Intrest our Trade,
We had not dwelt in safety, but in shade.
Had you not hung out light, more welcom far, 5
Then wandring Seamen, think the Northern Star.
To shew, least we our happiness should miss,
'Tis plac'd in friendship, mens, & Angells bliss.
Friendship, which had a scorn, or mask been made.
And still, had been derided, or betray'd. 10
At which the Politician still had laugh'd,
The souldier stormed, & the Gallant scoff'd.
Or worne not as a passion, but a Plot.
At first pretended, or at last forgot.
Had you not been her great Deliverer, 15
At first discover'd, & then rescu'd her.
And raising what rude malice had flung down,
Unveyl'd her face, & then restor'd her crown.
By that transcendent action, to convince
'Tis better to support, then be a Prince. 20
O! for a voice, as big as Thunder were
That all Mankind, these conquering truths might heare.
Sure the Litigious, as amaz'd, would stand,
As Fairy Knights touch'd by Cambina's wand.
Nations, & People, would let fall their arms, 25
Draw'n by your softer, & yet stronger charms.
But whilst great friendship, you have coppy'd out,
Y'have drawn your self so well, that we may doubt,
Which most appears, your candour, or your Art,
Or we ow more, unto your brain or heart. 30
But this we know, without your own consent,
Y'have rais'd your self a glorious Monument.
And that so solid as all fate forbid's,
And will outlast Egyptian Pyramids.
Temples, & Statues, Time will eat away, 35
And Tombs (like their inhabitants decay.
But here Palæmon lives, & so he must
When Marbles crumble to forgotten dust.

[pp. 280–2]

To the Queen's Majesty
on her late sickness, & recovery.

The publicke gladness is to us restor'd,
For your escape from what we so deplor'd.
Will want as well resemblance, as beleife,
Unless our Joy be measur'd by our greife.
When in your feaver we with terrour saw 5
At once our hopes & happiness withdraw
And every Crisis, did with Jealous feare
Enquire the newes, we scarce durst stay to heare.
Some dying Princes have their servants slain,
That after death they might not want a train. 10
Such cruelty, were heere a needless sin,
For had our fatal feares propheticke been,
Sorrow alone that service would have done,
And you by nations had been waited on.
Your danger was in every visage seen, 15
And only yours was quiet and Serene.
But all our Zealous greife had been in vain,
Had not great Charles's call'd you back again.
Who did your sufferings with such pain discern
He lost three Kingdom's once with less concern. 20
Labouring your Safety, he neglected his,
Nor fear'd he death in any shape but this.
His Genius did the bold distemper tame,
And his rich tears, quentch'd the rebellious flame.
As once the Thracian Heroe Lov'd, & greiv'd 25
Till he his lost felicity retreivd,
And with the moving accents of his woe,
His spouse recovered from the shades below.
So the Kings greife, your threaten'd loss withstood,
Who mourn'd with the same fortune as he woo'd, 30
And to his happy passion, we have been
Now twice oblig'd for so ador'd a Queen.
But how severe a choice had you to make,
When you must heav'n delay, or him forsake.
Yet since those Joyes you made such hast to find, 35
Had scarce been so, if he were left behind,
How well did fate decide your inward strife,
By making him a present of your life.
Which rescu'd blessing he must long enjoy,
Since our offences could it not destroy. 40
For none but death durst rivall him in you,
And Death himself was baffled in it too.

[pp. 285–6]

Arion on a Dolphin, beholding his Majesty, in his Passage to England

   Whom does this stately Navy bring?
O! 'tis Great Brittains Glorious King;
Convey him then, yee winds, & Seas,
Swift as desire, & calme as Peace.
In your respect, let him survey 5
What all his other Subjects pay,
And prophesy to them again
The splendid smoothness of his reign.
Charles & his mighty hopes you beare,
A greater now then Cesar's here, 10
Whose veins, a richer purple boast,
Then ever Hero's yet engross'd,
Sprang from a Father Great, & Just,
Who triumph's in his very dust.
In him two miracles we view, 15
His vertue, & his safety too,
For when compell'd by Traytors crimes
To breath & bow in forreigne climes,
Expos'd to all the rigid Fate
Which does on wither'd Greatness wait, 20
Had plots for life, & conscience layd,
By Foes pursu'd, by Friends betray'd.
Then Heav'n his secret, Potent Friend,
Did him from drugs, & stabs defend,
And, whats more yet, kept him upright, 25
Midst flattring hope, & bloody fright,
Cromwell his whole right never gain'd,
Defender of the Faith remain'd,
For which his Predecessours fought,
And writt, but none, so dearly bought. 30
Never was Prince so much besieg'd,
At home provok'd, abroad obliegd.
Nor ever Man resisted thus,
No not Great Athanasius.
No help of friends could, or foes spight, 35
To fierce invasion him invite,
Reveng to him no pleasure is,
He spar'd their blood who gasp'd for his,
Blush'd any hands the English Crown
Should fasten on him but their own. 40
As Peace & freedome with him went,
With him they come from banishment.

That he might his dominions win,
He with himself did first begin,
And that best victory obtain'd,
His Kingdoms quickly he regain'd.   45
Th'Illustrious sufferings of this Prince
Did all reduce, & all convince,
He only liv'd with such success,
That the whole world would fight with less.   50
Assistant Kings could but subdue,
Those Foes which he can pardon too,
He think's no slaughter-Trophy's good,
Nor Lawrell's dipt in Subjects blood,
But with a sweet resistless Art,   55
Disarm's the hand, & win's the Heart,
And like a God, does rescue those
Who did themselves & him oppose.
   Goe wondrous Prince, adorn the Throne,
Which birth & merit make your owne,   60
And in your mercy brighter shine
Then in the glorys of your line,
Find Love at home, & abroad feare,
And veneration every where.
Th'united World will you allow   65
Their Chief, to whom the English bow,
And Monarch's shall to yours resort,
As Shebah's Queen to Judahs Court,
Returning thence constrained more
To wonder, envy, & adore.   70
Discover'd Rome will hate your Crown,
But she shall tremble at your frown,
For England shall, rul'd & restor'd by you,
The suppliant World protect, or else subdue.

[pp. 291–4]

To the Queen-Mother
At her leaving England January 1st 1660/1

You justly may forsake a land which you
Have found so Guilty, & so fatall too,
Fortune injurious to your innocence
Shot all her arrows either here, or hence,
'Twas here bold Rebells once your life pursu'd   5
To whome 'twas Treason, only to be rude.
Till you were forc'd by their unweary'd spight
O! Glorious Criminall! to take your flight,
Whence after you, all that was humane fled.

For here, O! here, the Royall Martyr bled, 10
Whose cause, & heart, must be divine, & high,
That having you, could be content to dy.
Here they purloyn'd what we to you did ow,
And paid you in variety of woe,
Yet all these Billows in your breast did meet 15
A heart so firm, so Royall, & so sweet,
That over them you greater conquest made
Then your Immortall Father ever had.
(For we may read in storie of some few
Who fought like him, none that endur'd like you;) 20
Till fortune blush'd, to act what Traytors meant,
And Providence it self did first relent
But as our active, so our passive Ill
Hath made your share to be the Sufferers still,
As from our mischiefs all your troubles grew, 25
'Tis your sad right to suffer for them too.
Els our Great Charles had not been hence so long
Nor the Illustrious Gloucester dy'd so young.
Nor had we lost a Princess all confess'd
To be the greatest, wisest, & the best, 30
Who leaving colder parts, but less unkind,
For it was here she set, & there she shin'd.
Did to a most ingratefull Climate come
To make a visit, & to find a Tomb.
So that we might as well your smile despaire 35
As of your stay in this unpurged ayre.
But that your mercy does exceed our crimes,
As much as your example former times,
And can forgive our offerings, though the flame
Does tremble still betwixt regret & shame, 40
For we have Justly suffer'd more than you,
By the sad guilt of all your sufferings too.
   You, who the Great Idea have been seen
Of either Fortune, & in both a Queen.
Live still triumphant in the noblest war's 45
And justify your reconciled Stars
See your offendours for your mercy bow,
And your try'd vertue all mankind allow.
Whilst you to such a race have given birth
As are contended for by Heav'n & Earth. 50

[pp. 298–9]

19–20. *Parentheses probably added later: they occur outside the text block*
28. young] u *inserted*

**In memory of my Deare F:P:
who dy'd the 24.° of May. 1660;
at: 12:yeares & a half old**

If I could ever write a lasting verse
It should be laid (Deare Saint) upon thy Herse.
But sorrow is no Muse, & does confess
That it least can, what most it would express.
Yet, that I may some bounds to grief allow   5
I'le try if I can weep in numbers now.
   Ah! beauteous blossome, too untimely dead:
Whither? ah whither is thy sweetness fled?
Where are the charmes that always did arise
From the prevailing language of thy eyes?   10
Where is thy modest ayre, & lovely meene?
Where all the wonders that in thee were seene?
Alas! in vain! in vain on thee I rave!
There is no pitty in the stupid Grave.
But so the banckrupt, sitting on the brim   15
Of those fierce billows that had ruin'd him,
Beg's for his lost Estate, & does complain
To the inexorable floods, in vain.
As well we may enquire, when Roses dy,
To what retirement doe their odours fly.   20
Whither their vertues, & their blushes hast.
When the short triumph of their life is past,
Or call their perish'd beauty's backe with tears,
As add one moment to thy finish'd years.
No, no, th'art gone, & thy presaging mind   25
So thriftily thy early houres design'd,
That hasty Death was baffled in his Pride,
Since nothing of thee but thy body dy'd.
Thy Soul was up betimes, & so concern'd,
To grasp all excellence that could be learn'd. 30
That finding nothing fill her thirsting here,
To the Spring head she flew, to quench it there.
And so prepar'd that being free'd from Sin
She quickly might become a Cherubin.
Thou wert all Soul, & through thy eyes it shin'd 35
Asham'd, & angry to be so confin'd.
It long'd to be uncag'd, & thither flown,
Where it might know as clearly as 'twas known.
In these vast hopes, we might thy change have found,
But that Heav'n blinds, whom it decrees to wound. 40
For parts so soon, at so sublime a pitch,
A Judgement so mature, fancy so rich,
Never appeares unto unthankfull men,

But as a Vision, to be hid agen.
So glorious Scenes in Masques, Spectatours view
With the short pleasure of an houre or two,
But that once past, the Ornaments are gone,
The lights extinguish'd, & the curtains drawn.
But all these gifts, were thy less noble Part,
Nor was thy head, so worthy as thy heart.
Where the divine impression shin'd so cleare,
To snatch thee hence, & yet endeare thee here.
For what in thee did most command our love,
Was both the cause & sign of thy remove.
Such fooles are we so fatally we choose,
That what we most would keep, we soonest loose.
The humble Greatness of thy pious thought
Sweetness unforc'd, & bashfulness untaught,
The native candour of thy open breast,
And all the beams wherein thy worth was drest,
Might have foretold thou wert not so compleat,
But that our joy might be as short as Great.
T'is so, & all our cares, & hopes of thee
Fled, like a vanish'd dream, or wither'd Tree.
So the poor Swain, beholds his ripening corn
By the feirce wind, without a Sickle shorne.
Never! ah never, let poore Parents guess
At one remove, of future happiness!
But reckon children 'mong those passing Joy's
Which one houre gives them, & the next destroy's.
Alass! we were secure of our content
But find, too late, that it was only lent.
To be a mirrour wherein we might see
How fraile we are, how spotless we should be.
But if to thy blest soul my grief appears,
Forgive & pitty these injurious tears.
Impute them to affections sad excess
Too much oppressing Natures tenderness.
Since 'twas through dearest ty's, & highest trust,
Continu'd from thy cradle, to thy dust,
And so rewarded, & confirm'd by thine,
That (wo is me!) I thought thee too much mine.
But I'le resign, & follow thee as fast
As my unhappy minutes will make hast.
Till when, the fresh remembrances of thee
Shall be my Emblems of mortallity
For such a loss as thine, bright Soul, is not
Ever to be repaired or forgot.

[pp. 306–9]

Ode upon Retirement

No, No, unfaithfull World, thou hast
Too long my easy heart betray'd,
And me too long thy Football made,
But I am wiser grown, at last,
And will improve by all that I have past,
I know 'twas Just, I should be practis'd on.
    For I was told before
And told in sober, & instructive lore,
How little, all that trusted thee have won.
And yet I would make hast to be undone.
But by my sufferings, I am better taught.
And shall no more comitt that stupid fault.
    Go get some other Foole,
    Whom thou mayst next cajole,
On me thy frowns thou dost in vain bestow,
    For I know how
To be as Coy, and as reserv'd as Thou.

2

    In my remote, & humble Seat,
    Now I'me again possess'd,
    Of that late fugitive my breast
From all thy Tumult, & from all thy heat.
I'le find a quiet, & a coole Retreat.
    And on the fetters I have worne
Look with experienc'd & revengfull scorne.
    In this my Soveraign-Privacy,
    'Tis true I can not govern Thee,
    But yet my self I can subdue,
And that's the Nobler Empire of the two.
    If every passion had got leave
    It's Satisfaction to receive
Yet I would it a higher pleasure call,
To conquer One, then to indulge them all.

3

    For thy Inconstant Sea, no more
I'le leave that safe & Solid shore,
    No, though to prosper in the Cheat,
    Thou should'st my Destiny defeat.
And make me be belov'd, or Rich, or Great.
    Nor from my self, shouldst me reclaim,
With all the noyse, & all the Pomp of Fame.
    Judiciously I'le these despise,
Too small the bargain, & too dear the price,
    For them to cozen twice.

At length this secret I have learn'd,
Who will be happy, must be unconcern'd,
Must all their comfort in their bosom wear, 45
And seek their power, & their Treasure there.

4

No other wealth will I desire
But that of Nature to admire,
Nor envy on a Lawrell will bestow
Whilst I have any in my Garden grow. 50
    And when I would be Great
    'Tis but ascending to a Seat
Which Nature in a lofty Rock has built,
A Throne as free from trouble as from Guilt.
    Where when my soul her wings does raise 55
    Above what worldlings feare or praise,
With Innocent, & quiet pride, I'le sit
And see the humble waves pay Tribute to my feet.
O! Life Divine! when free from Joys diseas'd,
Not always merry, but 'tis always pleas'd. 60

5

    A Heart, which is too great a thing
    To be a present for a Persian King,
Which God himself would have to be his Court.
Where Angells would officiously resort
    From its own height would much decline 65
    If this converse it should resign,
      Ill natur'd World for Thine.
Thy unwise rigour hath thy Empire lost,
    It hath not only set me free,
    But it has let me see, 70
They only can of thy possession boast,
Who doe enjoy thee least, & understand thee most,
For loe the Man whom all mankind admir'd,
By every Grace adorn'd, & every Muse inspir'd
    Is now Triumphantly retir'd 75
    The Mighty Cowley this has done,
And over thee, a Parthian Conquest won,
    Which future ages shall adore
    And which in this subdues thee more
Then either Greek or Roman, ever could before. 80

                                  [pp. 311–12]

Title. upon Retirement] *smaller writing, possibly added later*
44. will] that *inserted above* will, *but with no deletion*
55. when] *inserted*
[pp. 311–12] *This includes two unpaginated pages:* 311, [unp.], [unp.], 312

A Retird friendship
To Ardelia 1651.

Come my Ardelia to this Bowre,
    Where kindly mingling thoughts awhile,
Lets innocently spend an houre,
    And at serious folly's smile.

Here is no quarrelling for Crowns,   5
    Nor feare of changes in our fate,
No trembling at the Great ones frowne,
    Nor any slavery of State.

Heere's no disguise, nor treachery,
    Nor any deep conceald design,   10
From bloody Plotts this place is free
    And calm as are those looks of thine

Heere let us sit, & bless our Starrs
    Who did such happy quiet give,
As that remov'd from noyse of wars,   15
    In one anothers hearts we live.

Why should we entertain a feare,
    Love cares not how the World is turn'd,
If crouds of dangers should appear.
    Our harmless Souls are unconcernd.   20

We weare about us such a charm
    No horrour can give us offence
Mischief it self can doe no harm
    To friendship, & to Innocence.

Lets marke how soon Apollo's beams   25
    Command the flocks to quit their meat,
And not entreat the Neighbour streams
    To quench their thirst, but cool their heat.

In such a scorching Age as this
    Who ever would not seek a shade   30
Deserve their happiness to miss,
    As having their own peace betray'd.

But we, (of one anothers mind
    Assur'd,) the boystrous world disdain,
And here can quiet be, & kind,   35
    Which Princes wish, but wish in vain.

[pp. 316–17]

21. weare] a *inserted*

Inconstancy
in Friendship

   Lovely Apostate! what was my offence?
Or am I punish'd for Obedience?
Must thy strange rigours find as strange a time?
The Act, & Season, are an equall crime.
Of what thy most ingenious Scorn can doe
Must I be subject, & Spectatour too!
Or were the sufferings, & sins too few
To be sustain'd by me, perform'd by you!
Unless with Nero, your uncurb'd desire
Be to survey the Rome, you set on fire.
While wounded for, & by your power I
At once your Martyr, & your prospect dy.
This is my doom, & such a ridling fate,
As all impossibles does complicate.
For obligation heere is injury,
Constancy crime, friendship a heresy.
And you appear so much on ruine bent,
Your owne destruction gives you new content.
For our two spirits did so long agree,
You must undoe your self to ruine me.
And like some frantick Goddess, be enclin'd
To raze the Temple, where you were enshrin'd.
And to be furious to the last degree,
Kill that which gave you Immortallity.
For glorious Friendship, whence your honour springs,
Ly's gasping, in the croud of common things.
And I'm so odious, that for being kind,
Doubled, & study'd Murthers are design'd.
Thy sin's all Paradox! for shouldst thou be
Thy self again, 'twould be severe to me.
For thy repentance, coming now so late,
Would only change, & not relieve the fate.
So dangerous is the consequence of ill,
Thy least of crimes, is to be cruell still.
For of thy smiles I should yet more complain,
If I should live to be betray'd again.
Go then (fayr Tyrant,) & securely be
Both from my kindness, & my anger free.
While I, who to the Swains had sung your fame,
And taught each Eccho to repeat your name,
Will now my privat sorrow's entertain.
To Rocks, & Rivers, not to you complain.
And though before, our Union cherish'd me,

'Tis now my Pleasure, that we disagree.
For from my Passion, your last rigours grew,   45
And you slight me, because I courted you
But my worst vow's shall be your happiness,
And ne're to be disturb'd by my distress.
And though it would my sacred flame pollute,
To make my heart a scorned prostitute,   50
Yet I'le respect the Author of my death,
And kiss the hand that rob's me of my breath.

[pp. 318–19]

To my Excellent Lucasia
on our mutuall friendship promis'd.
17. July 1651

I did not live, untill this time
   Crown'd my felicity,
When I could say without a crime
   I am not thine, but thee.
This Carcass breath'd, & walk'd, & slept,   5
   So that the World beleiv'd
There was a Soul, the motions kept,
   But they were all deceiv'd.
For as a watch, by art is wound
   To motion, such was mine,   10
But never had Orinda found
   A soul, till she found thine.
Which now inspire's, cure's, & supply's,
   And guides my darkned brest,
For thou art all that I can prize,   15
   My Joy, my life, my rest.
No Bridegroom's, nor crown'd Conquerours mirth,
   To mine compar'd can be,
They have but peeces of this Earth,
   I've all the World in thee.   20
Then let our flame still light, & shine,
   And no damp fear controule
As innocent as our design,
   Immortall as our Soul.

[p. 320]

---

24. Immortall] *superimposed on* As

Wiston Vault

   And why this vault & Tomb? alike we must
Put off distinction, & put on our Dust.

Nor can the stately'st fabrick help to save
From the corruptions of a common grave
Nor for the resurection more prepare   5
Then if the dust were Scatter'd in the ayre.
What then? th'ambition's Just, say some, that we
May thus perpetuate our memory.
Ah! false vain task of Art, Ah! poor weak man,
Whose Monument does more then's merit can,   10
Who's by his friends best care, & love abus'd,
And in his very Epitaph's accus'd.
For did they not suspect his name would fall
There would not need an Epitaph at all.
But after death too, I would be alive,   15
And shall, if my Lucasia doe survive.
I quit this pomp of Death, & am content
Having her heart, to be my Monument.
Though ne're stone to me. 'twill stone for me prove.
By the peculiar miracle of Love.   20
There I'le inscription have, which no Tomb gives,
Not here Orinda ly's, but here she lives.

[pp. 326–7]

---

19. ne're] *MS* ne^re

EPITAPH
ON HECTOR PHILLIPS. at St. Sith's Church

What on Earth deserves our Trust?
Youth, & Beauty both are dust.
Long we gathering are with pain,
What one Moment call's again.
Seaven years childless Marriage past,   5
A Son, A Son, is born at last;
So exactly limm'd, & Fair,
Full of good Spirits, Meen, & Aire;
As a long life promised;
Yet, in less then six week's dead.   10
Too promising, too great a Mind,
In so small room to be confind.
Therfore fit in Heav'n to dwell,
Quickly broke the Prison shell.
So the Subtle Alchymist,   15
Can't with Hermes-seal resist
The Powerfull spirits subtler flight,
But 'twill bid him long good night.

So the Sun, if it arise
Half so Glorious as his Ey's,   20
Like this Infant, takes a shroud,
Bury'd in a morning Cloud.

[p. 344]

Title. ON HECTOR PHILLIPS] *in smaller capitals*
14. Quickly broke] *Works* He Quickly broke

To my Lord Arch-Bishop of Canterbury his Grace 1664.

That private shade, wherein my Muse was bred,
She alwayes hop'd might hide her humble head,
Believing the retirement she had chose,
Might yield her if not pardon, yet repose.
Nor other repetitions did expect,   5
Then what our Eccho's from the Rocks reflect,
But hurry'd from her Cave with wild affright,
And dragg'd malitiously into the Light;
(Which makes her like the Hebrew Virgin mourn,
When from her face, her vaile was rudely torn.)   10
To you (my Lord) she now for succour calls,
And at your feet with Just confusion falls.
But she will thank the Wrong, deserv'd her Hate,
If it procure her that Auspicious Fate;
That the same wing may over her be cast,   15
Where the best Church of all the World is plac'd.
And under which when she is once retir'd,
She really may come to be inspir'd;
And by the Wonders which she there shall view,
May raise her self to such a Theam as You.   20
Who were preserv'd to Govern, & Restore
That Church, whose Confessour you were before.
And shew by your unweary'd present Care,
Your sufferings are not ended, though hers are.
For whilst your Crosier, her defence secures,   25
You purchase her Rest, with the Loss of Yours.
And Heav'n who first refin'd your worth, & then
Gave it so large, & eminent a scæne;
Hath paid you what was many wayes your due;
And done it self a greater right then You.   30
For after such a rough & tedious storm
Had torn the Church, & done her so much harm;
And (though at length rebuk'd, yet) left behind

Such angry reliques, in the Wave & Wind;
No Pilot could, whose skill or Faith were less,   35
Mannage the shatter'd Vessell with success.
The Piety of the Apostles Times,
And Courage to resist this Ages Crimes;
Majestick sweeteness, temper'd, & refin'd,
In a Polite, & Comprehensive Mind;   40
Were all requir'd Her Ruines to repair,
And all united in her Primate are.
In your aspect; so Candid, & Serene,
The Conscience of such Virtue may be seen;
As from the sullen scismatick gains consent   45
A Church-man may be Great, & Innocent.
This shall those Men reproach, if not Reduce;
And take away their fault, or their Excuse.
Whilst in your Life, & Government appear
All that the Pious wish, & Factious fear.   50
Since the prevailing Cross her Ensign's spread,
And Pagan Gods from Christian Bishops fled;
Time's curious Ey, till now, hath never spy'd
The Churches Helm so happily supply'd.
Merit & Providence so fitly mett,   55
The Worthiest Prelate, in the highest seat.
   If noble things, can Noble Thoughts infuse,
Your Life, (my Lord) may, ev'n in me, produce
Such Raptures, that of their Rich Fury Proud,
I may perhaps dare to repeat aloud.   60
Assur'd, the World that Ardour will excuse,
Applaud the Subject, and forgive the Muse.

                                        [pp. 347–9]

9–10. *Parentheses probably added later: they occur outside the text block*

In Memory of Mr Cartwright

Stay, Prince of Phancie, stay, we are not fit
To welcome, or admire thy Raptures yet;
Such horrid Ignorance benights the Times,
That Wit & Honour are become our Crimes.
But when those happy Pow'rs which guard thy dust,   5
To us, & to thy Memory shall be just,
And by a flame from thy blest Genius lent,
Rescuc us from our dull Imprisonment,
Unsequester our Fancies, & create

A Worth that may upon thy Glories wait: 10
We then shall understand thee, & descry
The splendour of restored Poetry.
Till when let no bold hand profane thy shrine,
'Tis high wit-Treason to debase thy coin.

[p. 351]

Rosania's private Marriage

It was a wise and kind designe of Fate,
That none should this day's glory celebrate;
For 'twere in vaine to keepe a time which is
Above the reach of all Solemnities.
The greatest Actions pass without a noise, 5
And Tumults but prophane diviner joys.
Silence with things transcendent nearest Suits,
The greatest Emperours are served by Mutes.
And as in ancient time the Deities
To their owne Preists reveal'd noe Misteries 10
Untill they were from all the World retir'd,
And in Some Cave made fit to bee inspir'd;
Soe when Rosania (who hath them outvi'd,
And with more justice might bee deifi'd;
Who if Shee had theere Rites & Alters, Wee 15
Should hardly think it were Idolatry,)
Had found a breast that did deserve to bee
Receptacle of her Divinity;
It was not fit the gazing world should know
When Shee convey'd her Selfe to him or how. 20
An Eagle Safely may behold the Sun,
When weake eyes are with too much light undone
Now as in Oracles were understood,
Not the Preists only but the common good:
So her great Soule would not imparted bee, 25
But in designe of generall Charity
She now is more diffusive then before,
And what men then admir'd, they now adore.
For this Exchang makes not her Power less,
But only fitter for the Worlds adress: 30
May then that mind, (Which if wee will admit
The Uneverse one Soule, must sure bee it)
Informe this all, (which till Shee Shin'd out, lay
As drowsy men doe in a cloudy day)
And Honoure, Vertue, Reason soe dispence 35
That all may owe them to her influence,
And while this age is thus imploy'd, may Shee,

Scatter new blessings for posterity.
I dare not any other wish preferr,
For only her bestowing adds to her   40
And to a Soule So in her Selfe compleat
As would bee wrong'd by any Epethete,
Whose Splendours fix'd unto her chosen Spheare,
And fill'd with love & Sattisfaction there
What can increase the Triumph but to see   45
The World her convert & her History.

            [pp. 358–9]

Transcribed in a different hand; see headnote
12. in] *inserted*
17. breast] s *inserted*
18. Receptacle] *altered from* Receptacall (*or vice versa*)

To the Right Honourable Alice Countess of Carbury, on her enriching Wales with her Presence.

1

As when the first day dawn'd Mans greedy Eye
Was apt to dwell on the bright Prodigy,
Till he might careless of his Organ grow,
And so his wonder prove his danger too:
So when your Country (which was deem'd to be   5
Close-mourner in its own obscurity,
And in neglected Chaos so long lay)
Was rescu'd by your beams into a Day,
Like men into a sudden Lustre brought,
We justly fear'd to gaze more then we ought.   10

2

From hence it is you loose most of your Right,
Since none can pay't, nor durst doe't if they might.
Perfection's misery 'tis that Art & Wit,
While they would honour, do but injure it.
But as the Deity slights our Expence,   15
And love's Devotion more then Eloquence:
So 'tis our Confidence you are Divine,
Make's us at distance thus approach your Shrine.
And thus secur'd, to you who need no Art,
I that speak least my Wit, may speak my Heart.   20

3

Then much above all zealous injury,
Receive this tribute of our shades, from me,
While your great Splendour, like eternal Spring,

To these sad Groves such a refreshment bring,
That the despised Countrey may be grown, 25
And justly too, the Envy of the Town.
That so when all Mankind at length have Lost
The Vertuous Grandeur which they once did boast,
Of you, like Pilgrims they may here obtain
Worth to recruit the dying world again. 30
                                          [pp. 369–70]

Title. Alice] *MS* Alce

[God]
Out of Mr More's Cup. Conf.

Thrice happy he whose Name is writ above,
   Who doeth good though gaining infamy,
Requiteth evill turns with hearty love,
   And cares not what befalls him outwardly;
Whose worth is in himself, & onely bliss [5]
In his pure Conscience, which doth nought amiss:

Who placeth pleasure in his purged soul,
   And vertuous Life his treasure does esteem;
Who can his Passions master & controul,
   And that true Lordly Manliness doth deem: [10]
Who from this World himself hath clearly quit,
Counts nought his own but what [lives in his spirit:]

So when his spirit from this vain World shall flit,
   It bears all with it whatso'ere was dear
Unto it self passing an easy Fit; [15]
   As kindly Corn ripened comes out of th'Ear.
Careless of what all idle men will say,
He takes his own & calmly goes his way.

   Eternall Reason, Glorious Majesty,
Compar'd to whome what can be said to be?
Whose Attributes are Thee, who art alone
Cause of all various things, & yet but One;
Whose Essence can no more be search'd by Man, 5
Then Heav'n thy Throne be grasped with a span.
Yet if this great Creation was design'd
To severall ends, fitted for every kind;
Sure Man (the Worlds Epitome) must be
Form'd to the best, that is to study thee. 10
And as our Dignity, 'tis Duty too,
Which is summ'd up in this, to know & doe.

These comely rowes of Creatures spell thy Name,
Whereby we grope to find from whence they came,
By thy own change of Causes brought to think   15
There must be one, then find that highest Link.
Thus all created Excellence we see
Is a resemblance faint & dark of thee.
Such shaddows are produc'd by the Moon-beams
Of Trees or Houses in the running streams.   20
Yet by Impressions born with us, we find
How Good, Great, Just thou art, how unconfin'd
Here we are swallow'd up, & daily dwell
Safely adoring what we cannot tell.
All we know is, thou art supremely good.   25
And dost delight to be so understood.
A spicy Mountain on the Universe,
On which thy richest Odours do disperse.
But as the Sea to fill a Vessel heaves
More greedily then any Cask receives,   30
Besieging round to find some gap in it,
Which will a new Infusion admit:
So dost thou covet that thou mayst dispence
Upon the empty World thy Influence;
Lov'st to disbourse thy self in kindness: Thus   35
The King of Kings waits to be gracious.
On this Account, O God enlarge my heart
To entertain what thou wouldst fain impart.
Nor let that soul, by several titles thine,
And most capacious form'd for things Divine,   40
(So nobly meant, that when it most doth miss,
'Tis in mistaken pantings after Bliss)
Degrade it self in sordid things delight,
Or by prophaner mixtures loose its right.
Oh! that with fixt unbroken thoughts it may   45
Admire the light which does obscure the day.
And since 'tis Angels work it hath to doe,
May its composure be like Angels too.
When shall these clogs of sense & Fancy break,
That I may hear the God within me speak?   50
When with a silent & retired Art
Shall I with all this empty hurry part?
To the still Voice above, my Soul, advance;
My light & Joy's plac'd in his countenance.
By whose dispence, my soul to such frame brought,   55
May tame each trech'rous, fix each scatt'ring thought;
With such distinctions all things here behold,
And so to separate each dross from gold,

That nothing my free soul may satisfie,
But t'imitate, enjoy, & study thee. 60

[pp. 382–5]

Title. [God]] *Dering MS; omitted in this MS*
Cup] *MS* Cop
[8]. And] *written after a false start* A, *presumably adjusted for indentation*
[12]. [lives in his spirit:]] *Dering MS; omitted in this MS*
2. whome what] *MS* whomewhat

Mary Roper?'s
'The Sacred Historie'

Leeds University Library, Brotherton Collection MS Lt q 2

'The Sacred Historie' is a verse paraphrase of the story of Genesis, in heroic couplets. As a clearly royalist enterprise by a woman, it provides an interesting parallel to Lucy Hutchinson's recently discovered poem on Genesis, *Order and Disorder* (Hutchinson 2001). Preliminary material, including devotional poems, a title page, a prose dedication and extracts from psalms, is followed by over 7700 lines of biblical narrative, divided into sections with titles. The story of Joseph is interrupted twice to include several poems on the Civil Wars, Protectorate and Restoration of the monarchy. The volume concludes with lengthy verse paraphrases of Psalms 107 and 8.

This manuscript is a neatly written presentation copy in a single rounded italic hand, with hardly any mistakes or corrections. It is dated ': March : 10 : 1669 : ' (fol. 2r) and 'June : 4 : 1670 :' (p. [232]) and seems from the dedicatory epistle to have been intended for Queen Catherine de Braganza, wife of Charles II. (The provenance of the manuscript, however, suggests that the volume never reached her; see the biographical note.) It is a large quarto in fours, of 119 leaves. The binding is a crimson morocco with gilt tooling including thistle and rose motifs. Pages are ruled in red. Pasted into the manuscript are more than forty engravings, mostly portraying the Genesis story and taken from the illustrated Bible published by Henry Hills in 1660, but also including a version of William Marshall's famous engraving of Charles I in prayer for the *Eikon Basilike*, and two unidentified engravings depicting Charles II (see plate 8).

All titles given in this edition reproduce those in the manuscript itself. Titles of extracts are prefaced by '*From*'. Biblical characters are often introduced by two or three letters in the margin of the manuscript; for example, in 'Mans Shamefull Fall' the serpent is denoted by 'Se' and the woman by 'Wo'. Biblical references are also provided in the margins. Punctuation in the manuscript is almost non-existent. Full stops are used only for two purposes: as an apostrophe mark, e.g. 'He.le,' '.gainst,' 't.Enjoy'; and as a pause or comma, e.g. 'Our King . Like Joseph . was in Greate Distresse'. In both cases they have been exchanged in this edition for the more modern punctuation marks.

BIOGRAPHICAL NOTE

The author of 'The Sacred Historie' deliberately remains anonymous, declaring in her dedication to the Queen, 'I dare not Presume to Present My Name into the

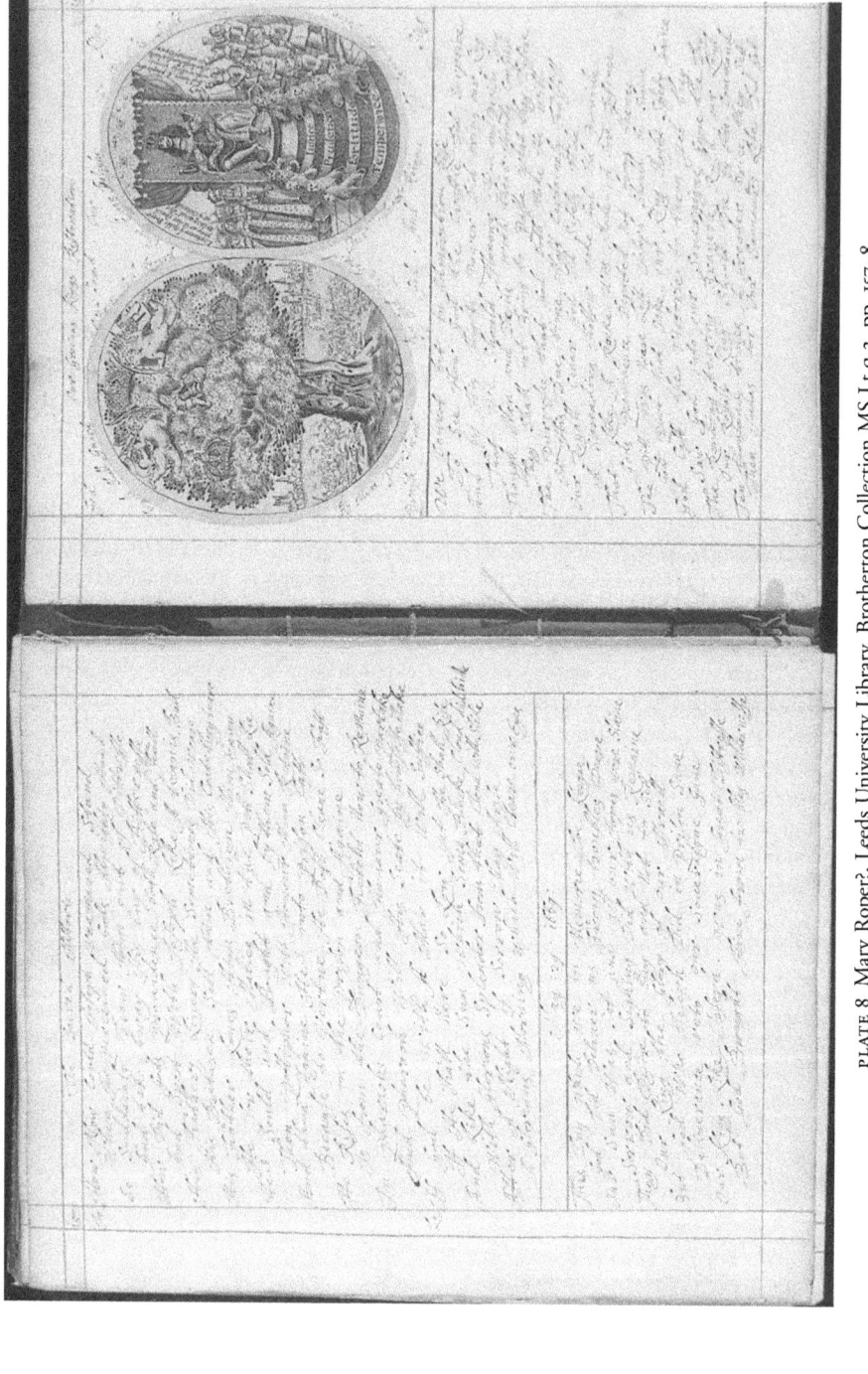

PLATE 8 Mary Roper?, Leeds University Library, Brotherton Collection MS Lt q 2, pp. 157–8

presence of your Royall Majestie' (fol. iiir). Nevertheless, in her prefatory poem there is a strong suggestion of the Christian name of Mary: 'Mary Her Magnificat to God Doth Raise / As thou Hast Given Me Her Name So I / Sing Praises to the Highest Majestie' ('A Prayer' (see below), lines 28–30). The provenance of the manuscript points to an association with the Roper family of Kent. The signatures of Elizabeth Rooper in 1692, Cholmeley Dering in 1807, and John Harrison in 1923, despite the differing surnames, plot a direct line of descent from the Ropers of Kent through the Henshaw, Dering and Harrison families. I have therefore tentatively ascribed to the anonymous author the name of 'Mary Roper?'.

The manuscript itself offers little in the way of biographical details, but there are clues to the poet's background. Her political affiliations are obviously royalist, as is clear not only from her verse but also from her choice of illustrations, pasted in from the *Eikon Basilike*, the 1660 illustrated Bible and the unidentified source of the engravings of Charles II. The Ropers were known as recusants, but the manuscript seems rather to focus on Church of England concerns.

Another biographical pointer is her consciousness of her relative lack of wealth and status. In her dedication to the Queen she says 'two great enemies Meanness and Povertie the one made me unfit the other unable to approach into your gracious presence', although she says she would 'account it the greatest Earthly Felicitie I Could Enjoy to See your Majesties Royall Face in Favour' (fol. iiir). She twice compares herself to the widow who puts two mites into the offering ('A Prayer' (see below), lines 31–2; prose dedication, fol. iiir). There is no specific reference to the death of a husband, however; instead, after her version of the death of Rachel, she inserts into the biblical text an eight-line poem on the death of her father, whom she calls God's 'Labourer' (*MS*, p. 201). It may well be that he died during the composition of the work. She is acutely aware of the injustices perpetrated during the Civil Wars, making many references to the evils of sequestration of church lands and the ill-treatment of those loyal to the monarchy, and it seems likely that something of this nature happened to her immediate family. So far, however, a conclusive identification of the author has not been possible.

Bibliography:
Eikon Basilike (1649), Holy Bible (1660), Hutchinson (2001) Hasted (1778: I), Rooper (1958)

JSM

A Prayer

Most Glorious God I Humbly Beg of thee
   Accept this Sacrifice Offred By Mee
Unto thy Majestie for Helpe I Flie
   To be Accepted off by the Most High
Oh Let My Soule for Ever Blesse the Lord 5
   While I Have Being and Can Speake A Word
Let Me on Earth Sing Praises to His Name
   The Glorious Saints in Heaven Doe the Same
Lord by thy Holy Spirit Show Me the Beauty
   Of Holinesse and that Praise is My Duty 10

Out of the Mouths of Babes and Sucklings Praise
    Thy Mighty Power Unto thy Selfe Doth Raise
O Lord thou Knowst it is My Souls Desire
    That She in thy High Praises May Mount Higher
Above these Transitorie Joyes Below   15
    Lord Let My Soule Some Heavenly Pleasures Know
Since From all Creatures thou Dost Praise Command
    That Gratefull Sacrifice Let Me Attend
My Mornings Excercise to thee I Give
    My Noones Repose to Him by whom I Live   20
My Evenings Pleasure Shall Attend on thee
    What Entertainement Like thy Word Can bee
Therefore On Holy Dayes I thought Upon
    The Wondrous Works thy Holy Arme Hath Done
Thus My Small Part of time to thee I Give   25
    Who Art My God in Whom My Hope Doth Live
Miriam Deborah and Hannah All Sing Praise
    Mary Her Magnificat to God Doth Raise
As thou Hast Given Me Her Name So I
    Sing Praises to the Highest Majestie   30
Thou Once the Widowes two Mites Didst Accept
    Doe not My Mite of Praises Now Reject
Lord Let My Soul thy Noble Praises Sound
    Till Death Doth Lay My Body in the Ground
So Shall My Soul Begin Before I Die   35
    To Sing the Anthenms of Eternitie

                              Amen

                                                      [fol. i verso]

The Royall Element of Fire

                What Mortall Eye Can See the Imperiall Seate
                    Of this fierce Element or Endure its heate
                The Sight of God is Like Devouring fire
                    His Throne a flame that Never Shall Expire
Reve   Christs Eyes were Like a flame of fier his feete   5
1 14   As if they burned in a furnace Greate
2 Thessa   In Flaming Fier I'th Judgement day Christ Comes
1 8   His fervent heate and Fire the Earth Consumes
2 Peter   The Heavens shall be Dissolved in this Fire
3 12   The Elements Melt the Suns bright Beames Expire   10
                Though Fire's the Element God Doth Enclose
                    And With his Breath burns up his Greatest foes
                Yet he that furious Element doth binde
                    To be Mans Servant in its Place Asign'd

To Comfort and to Warme him in his Neede 15
   And to Make ready Wherewith he should feede
But if Mans Wickednesse against God be high
   Fire will Revenge and be Mans Enemie
If God in Fiery Flames with Man Contend
   His Worldly Comforts Shall in Smoake asscend 20
And Who Can Stand before Devouring Fire
   Untoucht by harme or his breath not Expire
When the fierce flames with furie Mount on high
   And with their Gastly Lights Make Darknesse flie
And raise a Rednesse on the Sable Skie 25
   If God Rebuke they in a Moment Die
For God Commands the Fire to Praise his Name
   And his Commands will Curbe the furious flame
God doth this Element to Man Subdue
   That Men high Praises Might to God Renew 30

[p. 5]

---

20. Comforts] *inserted*

From Mans Shamefull Fall

[. . .]
Methinks I See upon the Knowledge tree
   A Subtill Serpent whose Discerning Eye 20
Saw this Rare Woman Walking all aloane
   In Paradice Viewing the Trees Each one
Whose Bending boughs did Stoope to her faire hand
   Laden with Curious Fruits at her Command
She tasts and Eates and Walks with Pleasure Great 25
   But Drawing Nigh that Tree oh Dismall Fate
She Saw a Serpent and She heard him Speake
   Wonder Methinks Should Make her turne her backe
But as for Wonders they were Every where
   And Sin's the Cause of a bace Servile feare 30
She's not afraid, but hearkens to his Call
Se   Then he begins but hath God Said at all
Of Every fruitfull tree ye shall not Eate
   That Grows in Eden Surely t'is your Meate
Wo   Then did the Woman Conferrence begin 35
   With the Serpent who did worke her Ruin
If when the Devill tempts to any Sin
   We turne our backs we never fall therein
Had Eve Not Listned to the Serpents Call
   She had not helped Adam to his fall 40

Se	The Serpent Seing the Woman Not afraid	
	Goes on to Speake to her Yea hath God said	
	Ye shall not Eate of Every tree that Grow	
	In Edens Garden and Goodly fruite doe Show	
Wo	The woman Said yes we May Eate of all	45
	The fruite of Edens trees both Greate and Small	
	But of this tree the Lord will not permitt	
	That wee Should take one Apple off from it	
	If we doe tast or Touch this fruite so Nigh	
	God hath it Said and we shall Surely die	50
Se	The Serpent then with the Woman did begin	
	To put her off the thoughts of fearing Sin	
	Ye Shall not Surely die for God doeth know	
	This Tree Will Make you Wise and will you Show	
	All things your Eyes then opened Shall bee	55
	You Shall Know Good and Evill you Shall See	
	If that Like God you doe desire to be	
	Eate of this Tree you Certainly will See	
	This Poisonous Venum that the Serpent Cast	
	Upon the Woman Made her Swell So fast	60
	With Pride, that Shee Should be like the Most High	
	That then She Casts away all feare to die	
Wo	And when the woman Saw the tree was Good	
	To Sight and Tast it was a Pleasant Food	
	And Such a Tree as Nothing Could Devise	65
	To Make her So quicke Sighted and So Wise	
	Then from the Serpents hand the Fruite she takes	
	First Eates her Selfe and then Much hast She Makes	
	To finde out Adam that he Might Partake	
	Of this her Sin and So his God Forsake	70
	[. . .]	
		[pp. 17–18]

---

21. aloane] *second* a *altered from* n

From Lott His Wife And Daughters

	Had Lott from Wicked Sodom Gone Away	
	When Abraham Rescued Him and all the Prey	
	He had Not Seene Such Wickednesse and Shame	
	And He had kept his Substance from the Flame	
	Though Righteous Men Amongst the wicked Gaine	5
	They are Not Watered (Well) with Such a Raine	
Lott	Now Lott in Zoar was Afraid to bee	
	Unto the Mountaines in Greate hast Goes He	

Wi	Lots Wife was troubled that She Left Behinde	
	Her Riches and Her Treasure thers her Minde	10
	She Did not thinke of Gods Exceeding Grace	
	Drawing Herselfe out of that Fiery Place	
	But She turns Backe to See that Dismall Fire	
	Which did Provoke the Lords Inkindled Ire	
Lo	Cause Shee His Strict Commands did Dissobey	15

        Lots Wife was troubled that She Left Behinde
           Her Riches and Her Treasure thers her Minde   10
Wi   She Did not thinke of Gods Exceeding Grace
           Drawing Herselfe out of that Fiery Place
        But She turns Backe to See that Dismall Fire
           Which did Provoke the Lords Inkindled Ire
Lo   Cause Shee His Strict Commands did Dissobey   15
           Turning to Sodom Not Going her Way
        Her Feete begin to Fix her Blood to Chill
           A Saltish Spirit Doth her Body Fill
        Her Eyes are Set Her hands Hang downe and all
           Her Breath Exspires but Downe She Cannot Fall   20
        Now She is turn'd into a Pillar of Salt
           That Men Might feare Before the Lord to Halt
        This Pillar Flavius Josephus see
           As He Reporteth in His Historie
        My wonders Great how they Could Goe Away,   25
           Whilst She Transform'd Behinde them there did Stay
Lott   But Feare and Griefe and Care Gave wings to Flie
           Unto a Mountaine in a Cave to Lie
        Where Lots owne Daughters Not Fearing Sodoms Fire
           To Incest have Inkindled their Desire   30
Dau   By this they will Keepe up their Fathers Name
           But this will Bring them to an Open Shame
        They thought all Mankinde had beene Dead but they
           To Fill the World they Made themselves A Prey
        To Sin and to Gods Wrath for So Great Sin   35
           Which they had Plung'd themselves and Father in
        They were in Sodom Bred and Sodoms Flame
           Might have them Frighted from this Sinfull Shame
        But we Should Feare to Live where Sin doth Dwell
           For our Corrupted Hearts Loves Sin too well   40
        After this time God did them Never Grace
           The Scripture for their Names doth finde No Place
        But from their Spurious Ofspring shall Proceede
           Nations Whose Curse Posteritie Shall Reade
Ab   Good Abraham Who Gods Vengeance Sought to Stay   45
           Goes out and Sees Gods Judments in Aray
        He Saw the Smoake of Sinfull Sodom High
           And with the Blacknesse of it Darke the Skie
        The Sulphurous Flames those Citties did Surround
           Yet Left the Shape of them upon the Ground   50
Josephus   The Signes and Reliques then of Sodoms Fire
689   By Gods Appointment in that Place Appeare
        Trees Spring up in the Ashes which doe Beare
           All Kinde of Fruits which to the Eye are Rare

But if you touch them they to Ashes Fall 55
   If tast they in your Mouth are turn'd to Gall
Here was a Land Most Rich and Fertile Made
   For Sin by God in Desolation Laid
[. . .]

[pp. 64–5]

51 *(marginal note).* Josephus] MS Josephu

From The Birth of Esau and Jacob

[. . .]

Re   Joy is not Alwayes Pure we often Finde
     Some Sharpnesse when we thinke we have Sweete Wine
   Even So Rebeckah Here Greate Joy Did See
     When She Perceiv'd Her Selfe with Childe to be 40
   But When the Little Infants Did So Strive
     And Wrastle in Her Wombe as Soone as Live
   And Did to Her Torture and Torment Bring
     In that Close Place by often Wrastelling
   She Was Sore Troubled and Amaz'd She Said 45
     For One Deare Childe to God I Often Praid
   But I too Earnest Was With God and He
     Hath Heard My Prayers that I Might Sorrow See
   Here is Some Vulture that will teare My Heart
     And Will Me from My Other Comforts Part 50
   For Sure No Little Infant Can Strive So
     And with its Striving So Increase My Woe
   At Last She Doth Resolve She will Enquire
     Of God, and to His Oracle Repaire
   Some thinke She Mount Moriah Did Asscend 55
     And With Her Sacrifices there Attend
   But Others thinke She to Melchizedek
     The Priest of God Her Journey Did Direct
   However She of God Did Counsaile take
Lo   And He this Answer unto Her Did Make 60
   Two Nations in thy Body thou Dost Beare
     And from thy Wombe two People Shall Appeare
   He that Seemes Least Shall Beare the Greatest Sway
     The Elder Shall the Younger then Obey
   Great God What a Darke Sentence here is Shown 65
     Methinks Her Wonders Now are More then One
   Was it Not Early to Begin Such Warrs
     Their Present Combates Promise Future Jarrs
   Her Present Pangs and troubles She Hath here
     Puts Her in Minde What After She Must Beare 70

	But Now Her time is Come with Bitter throes
Re	And in Her travaile She Hath Paines and woes
Esa	She Beares a Son with Red and Rugged Haire
	For Which the Name of Esau he Doth Beare
	The Second Son Did Pull Him by the Foot 75
	Because So Hastily He Issu'd out
Ja	He for the Birthright in His Birth Did Strive
	Therefore the Name of Jacob Doth Receive
	[. . .]

[pp. 84–5]

From Rebeckahs Subtilty

	Wisdom's Presented Like a Matron Grave
	Who Sage Advice and Wholsome Counsaile Gave
	Directing Mortals in So Good A Way
	That None Who follow Her Advice Can Stray
	When Wisdome Sees A Cloud of Evill Rise 5
	She Sends out Prudence who the Plott Descries
	Knowledge and Understanding then She Doth
	Employ to finde a Remidie for Both
	Wittie In-ventions they Bring to Her Minde
	Wisdome the Choisest out of them Doth Finde 10
	And then Gives Wholsome Counsaile Which if wee
	Receive we May be Counted Blest to bee
Re	Thus this Grave Matron Good Rebeckah Heere
	When She Did Esaus Rugged Nature Feare
	Wisdome Sujests Inventions to her Minde 15
	That She Might Safety for Her Jacob finde
	If She Can Bring't About that Isaac May
Ja	Be Pleas'd to Send Jacob His Son Away
	She'l Make't His Earant to Seeke Out A Wife
	And by that Subtilty to Save His Life 20
	But in this Exigent She Must Beware
	Wisdom and Prudence Must Her Words Prepare
	Passing From Jacob She Doth Isaac Finde
	Whose Soule Sees Heaven though His Eyes were blinde
	And Doth begin Her Passion to Reveale 25
	Yet the Designe thereof She will Conceale
Re	How is My Life a torment When I Feare
	Lest My Son Jacob Should A Wife take Heere
	Lett Esaus Mariage Make us Now Provide
	A fitting Person to Make Jacobs Bride 30
	Amongst My Brothers Daughters He May Wed
	And take Some of My Kindred to his Bed

Therefore Send Jacob Now and Let Him Chuse
   A Wife in time Lest Wee Our Son doe Loose
In Mariage With the Canaanitish Race   35
   Whose Idols Will Good Abrahams Seede Disgrace
What Pleasure Can I Ever Se in Life
   If off these Ladies Jacob take A Wife
Isaac though Blinde His Reason Saw it Cleare
   And for His Journey Quickly will Prepare   40
And though Feare Forct it to Rebeckahs Minde
   Isaac the Hand of God in it Doth Finde
[. . .]

[pp. 96–7]

May 29 1669

This Day which we in Memorie Doe Keepe
   God Did Deliver us From troubles Deepe
Our Sun Was Set and all our Hopes were Slaine
   Sorrow and Sighing Did With us Remaine
They Did Desire to buy and Not to Sell   5
   Our King the Glory of our Israell
But God Who Joseph Did in Prison Save
   Deliverance unto our Soveraigne Gave
Our King, Like Joseph, was in Great Distresse
   But God Brought Him from troubles Wildernesse   10
We Cannot but in Admiration Rise
   To See How God the Craftie Did Surprize
And by His Mighty Power Did bring our King
   That We Should Honour Him and Praises Sing
Though Men and Devils with their Heads Conspire   15
   They Shall not Bring to Passe what they Desire
The Purposes that God Doth Make He will
   In His Due time Most Certainely Fulfill
Our Royall Cedar God Did Safely Hide
   A Spreading Hollow oake God Did Provide   20
That Like A Rocke Was Made A Sure Defence
   Gods Providence Departed Not from thence
The Pitt Was Neare Lest Joseph Should be Slaine
   God Placed that Oake our King Might Safety Gaine
God Cast the Victorie to them yet they   25
   Saw God unto our Soveraigne Gave the Day
The Rending tearing Bramble Rul'd our Land
   Our Royall King Should Die by His Command
Ten thousand times A Greater Price they Sett
   Then Judas for Our Saviours Life Did Get   30

Which Made them Seeke and Search their Prize to Finde
   But Like Elishas Seekers they Were Blinde
(God Made them So) for He it Was Did Save
   Our Blessed Soveraigne He Deliverance Gave
This Bramble Cut our Glorious Cedar Downe   35
   The Roote and Royall Branch God Kept Unknown
(To Him) His Eagles Eyes Could Not Descry
   The Hiding Place Where Gods Anointed Lie
Though Search He Did and Usd His Utmost Power
   But it Was God, Was our Kings Saviour   40
T'was God Preserv'd Our Soveraigne Night and Day
   Secret Nor Open traitors Could Not Him, Slay
And When Gods time Was Come Brought him Againe
   A Glorious King Amongst Us to Remaine
Gods Mercies Alwayes Have A Fruitfull Wombe   45
   His Blessings then in A Great troope Did Come
The Wisest Man on Earth Could Not Devise
   A Way to Compasse Such an Enterprize
Without A Drop of Blood If God Had Not
   Guided His Hand and Chosen Him A Lott   50
God With our King Did Peace and Plenty Give
   Under Our Cedars Shadow Now We Live
The Bramble God Cut Downe Which tore up those
   Who for their Loyalty He Counted Foes
Our Hearts Were Ready With Despaire to Die   55
   We Did Not See God Hearkned to Our Crie
And When Gods Mercies Came Joy Seiz'd us So
   That Like A Dreame We Could it Hardly Know
And Now our Sun With Greater Glory Rise
   To Cheare our Hearts and to Delight our Eyes   60
For His Great Sorrows Lord Double Honour Give
   Lengthen His Daies that He Long time May Live
Now Like A Father He Cares for us all
   Forgiving our Rebellions and our Fall
And Immitating God He Did Extend   65
   Mercy to those that Highly Did Offend
Lord Let thy Mercyes Raise our Heavy Hearts
   And of thy Praises Let us Sing our Parts
Lord Let thy Holy Spirit our Soules Inspire
   And Let us Praise thee With our Whole Desire   70
Let Lives and Actions Praise thy Holy Name
   For thou art Great and Wondrous is thy Fame

                                                      [pp. 157–60]

Title. May 29 1669] *MS* May : 29 : 1669
24. Placed] *MS* Plact
31. Search] a *altered from* r
53. Bramble] e *altered from* s

Our Kings Sorrows and Suffrings

What Wonders were there in Our Iron Age
   Acted Upon the Irreligeous Stage
Such New Religeon Was in Fashion Grown
   As would Not the Apostles Doctrine Own
Those Men Religeon Did So Much Abuse   5
   That Sacriledge Against the Church they Use
They Rob'd Her Treasures tooke Away Her Lights
   And Did Bereave the Church of all her Rights
Religeon that Doth Sacriledge Maintaine
   It Hath No Other Godlinesse but Gaine   10
But Such Great Moths from thence Doe Often Come
   That Great Estates Doe Suddainly Consume
Josephs Religeon Did Keepe Him from Sin
   Theirs is A Cloake Made Up to wrapp it in
When People Doe Fault With Religeon Finde   15
   Then Loyaltie will Loiter Farr Behinde
Did they Deale Better With the Faiths Defender
   Whose Vertues in His troubles Cast Such Splendor
They Swore they Would A Glorious King Him Make
   But When they Have their Prey His Life they take   20
His Wisdome Vertue Piety Was So Great
   Goodnesse Might Well Seeke Shelter from His Seate
But they Ungratefully Cast Him Away
   His Clemency and Goodnesse Made Him their Prey
Like Christ they Spitt Upon Our King And Cry'd   25
   Let our Hands in His Purple Blood be Dy'd
But He Like Christ Forgave His Enemies
   Who triumpht Over Him With Tyranies
God Seemed Deafe to Him When He Did Pray
   Yet His Recourse Was Unto God Alway   30
God Seemed So to Forsake Christ When He
   Upon the Crosse by Wicked Men Did Die
Yet Were His Prayers Answer'd and His teares   *Heb 5:7*
   His Patience was an Antidote for's Feares
Wisdome Prudence and Patience our Kings Crown   35
   From Dreadfull Suffrings Rais'd A High Renowne
He Was His Peoples Martyre and His Blood
   He Did Not Vallew to His Peoples Good
T'was His Owne Subjects that Him Murthered
   Rebels and Traitors in His Kingdome Bred   40
The Best of Kings by 't Worst of Men is Dead
   They off this Famous Kingdome Cut the Head
Then Dismall Misery With us Did Dwell
   Confusions Made this Kingdome Like to Hell

(Not Hell) for there's A Head Here was A Stumpe 45
  And in Short time, that provd A Rotten Rumpe
Their Oaths their Covenants and all their Vows
  Doe but Binde Others and themselves Unloose
One Pawns His Soule for's Safety yet Doth thinke
  Which Way He May Deaths Bitter Cup then Drinke 50
They Studied all they Could Devise to Make
  Him Ignominious and His Glory Take
Our Sacred King Religeon Nourished
  And for Her Sake they Did Cut off his Head
They tooke His Life His Bodies in the Ground 55
  But's Fame and Glory through the World Doth Sound
And Now Our Joseph's Come Againe to Save
  Those Men Alive that Dig'd for Him A Grave
Those Men that Majestie So Sore Did Wound
  Their Names Doe Rott and Stinke Above the Ground 60
                                          [pp. 187–9]

---

25. Cry'd] y *altered from* i
57. Joseph's] p *altered from* s

Englands Sad Lamentation

Our King is Dead Laws and Religeons Gone
Tyrants Oppresse us Our Miserys Unknown

  Egyptian Darkenesse Hath us Over Spread
  Dying Religeon Hides Her Fainting Head
  To Liberty of Goodnesse wee were Dead 5

The Flower the Creame and Glory of Our Land
Our Cedar and His Stately trees Did Stand
In Feare of Felling by Rebellions Hand

  All our Foundations Now Unsetled Were
  Good Laws Abollisht and New Upstarts Dare 10
  Invent New Laws No Loyall Blood to Spare

Into an Annarchy our Kingdomes Grown
Our Princly Governours Slaine or Unknown
And Plebians A Princely State will Own

  Our King and Nobles Now All Banisht are 15
  For their Adversities they all Prepare
  But to their Native Place Dare Not Come Neare

Atheism and Prophainnesse us Disgrace
Liberty and Fanatick Rage takes Place
All sorts of Irreligions Makes us Bace 20

With Magistrates Meccanicks will be Bold
Our Ministers Dare not the Truth Unfold
Kings Lands are Gone Now Church Lands Shall be Sold

All Sorts of Learning Now they Doe Despise
Men Wise and Learned Cannot Hope to Rise
Once Glorious England Now She Gasping Lies

    When A Protector Put us all in Feare
    And Oligarchicall Government was Heere
    Then England for Rebellion Paid full Deare

Our Kingdomes Body no Place was Left Free
From the Effects of this our Miserie
Our Wound's so Desparate that Wee Must Die

    Unskilfull Chyrurgeons Gave us Hope to Finde
    Ease for our Paine, but they (Alasse) were Blinde
    And Did torment Our Body and our Minde.

This was the Miserie our Land was in
For our Most Impious Most Horrid Sin
The Murther of Our Gracious Soveraigne

    How Often Did Good Subjects Seeke in vaine
    To Bring Our King unto His Crown Againe
    But their Good Counsaile Blasts and they are Slaine

All the Kings Loyall Subjects Mourning Goe
They wish His Happinesse but Doe Not Know
Which way tis Possible Comfort Can Grow

    God Seemed Deafe unto our Soveraignes Cry
    Yet He Preserved was by the Most High
    And Covered as the Apple of His Eye

Wee with our Miseries to Heaven Flie
And Humbly Did Beseech of the Most High
To Ease us of our Dreadfull Miserie

    And Now all Hope of Helpe From Man is Lost
    For all Designes that were Contriv'd are Crost
    And Now Our Vineyard to wilde Beasts Lie Wast

[pp. 190–1]

---

4. Dying] i *altered from* e
22. not the Truth] *written on a slip of paper pasted over illegible words*

From Famines Miserie

[. . .]
   Now the Egyptians Sorely Doe Complaine   25
    For Famine Puts them to Such Extreame Paine
   That Without Food they'l Die yet Nothing Have
    To Buy them Meate for which their Stomacks Crave

Jo   With One Accord to Joseph now they Fall
    On Knees they Beg His Pitty on them all   30
   [. . .]

[Egy] Buy all our Land Our Bodies thou Shalt Gaine
    To be thy Slaves Doe but Our Lives Maintaine   40
   [. . .]

Jo   As you your Selves Have Said So will I Doe
    And Egypts King now all your Land Shall Owe
   As for the Corne you Shall Have What you Neede   45
    Also to Sow the Land I'le Give you Seede
   And When God Gives Increase you all Shall Bring
    The Fifth Part of Increase Unto the King
   And Now Four Parts Againe to you I Give
    That you With Comfort on the Same May Live   50
   This Law I Make the Fifth Part you Shall Give
    T'is all the Kings: Four Parts you Shall Receive
   This unexpected Favour Joy Restor'd
    And Now they Joseph for His Love Ador'd
   [. . .]

Jo   Thus Joseph Pharaohs Riches Did Increase
    And Bindes His Subjects Here to Live in Peace
   This Greate Revenue to the King He Gaines
    With His Sucsessors it Intire Remaines

Kin   Yet Heathen Pharaoh for His Priests takes Care   65
    And of their Sacred Lands will Have No Share
   He that all Egypts Land Did take Away
    On Consecrated Land No Hand will Lay
   But Such A Portion He to them Alows
    That they May Live and Neede Not Breake their vows   70
   How Shall that King Against us Christians Rise
    Though Unto Idols He Did Sacrifice
   Yet He thought Sacriledge So Great A Sin
    As would Him Ruin if He Lived in
   Our times Did Sacriledge So Much Conveigh   75
    Our Gods Priests Lands they would take Quite Away
   The Fifth Part of their Meanes t'was Hard to Gaine
    Though in Deepe Povertie they Did Remaine
   They thought their Lives Enough for them to Keepe
    And still in sorrow they would Make them Sleepe   80

> But God Did Pitty of His Servants take
> That Suffered so Sorely for His Sake
> And Forct from them the Sacred Lands Away
> He tooke Account Before the Judgement Day
> Let Men be warn'd by this and Have A Care   85
> Lest with the Sacred things they Bring A Snare
> Upon themselves Gods Blast Consumes them So
> Their Just Riches for their Sacriledge Goe

[pp. 202–3]

---

39. *(marginal note).* [Egy]] *MS* Egy *in marginal note at line 31*

II

Julia Palmer's 'Centuries' of devotional verse

William Andrews Clark Memorial Library
MS P1745 M1 P744 1671–3 Bound

The devotional verse of Julia Palmer exists in an autograph fair copy, bound in a plain octavo volume whose only ornamentation is ruling in blind and a zigzag roll on the edges of the boards. The 265-page manuscript contains authorial revisions and deletions but it is for the most part neatly produced. Palmer's peculiar usage of commas instead of apostrophes has been silently corrected in this edition (e.g. 'cov,nant' has become 'cov'nant'). The poems are arranged into two sections of one hundred poems, though the 'First Century' does not contain a poem 62, making the total number of poems 199. Palmer did not explicitly label her poems as 'Centuries'—these titles are editorial additions—but in arranging her poems in this manner she was following the genre popularised by the nonconformist writer William Barton, who had published four 'Centuries' of verse by 1668 and was to publish two more.

Many of the poems are dated between 28 September 1671 and 21 July 1673, evidently their dates of composition. Only once is the chronological arrangement broken: in the 'Second Century', poem 48 is dated 26 September 1672 and thus should follow poem 52, dated 25 September 1672. This disruption (and the few occasions when Palmer skips ahead in her transcription, needing to delete a word or an entire line) indicates that she transcribed this fair copy at a later date, following another manuscript copy of her work. The two-year period of composition suggests that she used her poems as a kind of spiritual journal, a genre in which the writer's self-examination typically involves dramatic shifts from confidence that one is saved to conviction that one is a reprobate (and back). Palmer's poetry of personal salvation, alternating between fear that she is unworthy of God's grace and thankfulness for his mercy, certainly fits this pattern. One of the prescribed headings for the material in a spiritual journal, according to Isaac Ambrose's *Media* of 1657, was 'Experience': Palmer has given four of her poems that heading.

Palmer's nonconformity is obvious from both her biography and her poetry, with its jargon such as 'free grace' and 'giving in', to describe the blessings of God. Her poetry displays Presbyterian leanings in particular with its emphasis on the necessity of 'duties' and 'ordinances' (set ceremonies ordained by authority, such as holy communion). More radical sects, such as the Baptists and Quakers, disapproved of such services, and of the use of poetry for spiritual matters. Palmer draws often on the erotic poetry of the Song of Songs, depicting a spiritual marriage with Christ in heaven as her passionate desire, a popular nonconformist trope. A longing for death thus pervades the manuscript.

The immediate audience for her work is indicated in her dedication on the first flyleaf (beneath her name, the date 1671, and some shorthand, used here and elsewhere in the manuscript to obscure personal details): 'I Leave this Book to Mr Joseph Bisco senior. if he out Live me otherwiss. I Leave itt to Mr James pitson Apothicary'. Biscoe was not only a prominent apothecary but also a committed nonconformist, becoming a parishioner of the Independent preacher John Nesbitt later in life. Each of Palmer's 'Centuries' begins with a short poem which indicates that she desired an audience for her poetry whom she could help to praise God. The first poem of the 'Second Century' ends with a strong statement of an expected readership: 'That I to others, still may be / A light, to lead them unto thee' (p. 162, lines 7–8). It is conceivable that a number of Palmer's poems were intended to be sung as hymns; many of them use iambic pentameter in combinations of four, three and two feet, standard hymn metres. Whether Palmer's poems circulated in her own or in Biscoe's London congregation is uncertain, but she certainly portrayed her poetic voice as authorised by God.

BIOGRAPHICAL NOTE

Nothing is known of Julia Palmer's parentage, but she was probably the Julia Hungerford who married Nicholas Palmer on 12 May 1664 at All Hallows, London Wall. The baptism of their child, Samuel, on 17 June 1667, took place at St Margaret's, Westminster, a church which Joseph Biscoe (the dedicatee of Palmer's manuscript) and his family also attended. Julia Palmer's absence from later Anglican records, and the sensibilities displayed in her poetry, suggest that she became a nonconformist. Her husband is probably the 'Mr Palmer of London' who preached at New Windsor in 1669 (Matthews 1934, 380). A licence to preach for 'Nicholas Palmer, Presbyterian, at Mrs. Jane Price's new house, Frogmore, New Windsor, Berkshire' was requested on 24 May 1672 and granted on 10 June (*CSPD* 1672, 55, 216). Nicholas Palmer was buried at New Windsor on 28 February 1681. Their son Samuel is listed in the Court Minutes of the Society of Apothecaries on 7 July 1682 as being the son of the deceased Nicholas Palmer of New Windsor, Berkshire, and as being bound to the apothecary Edward Baker for eight years. It appears that Samuel never finished his apprenticeship as he is not listed as having been freed. Julia Palmer's dedicatee, Joseph Biscoe, was both a nonconformist and an officer in the Society of Apothecaries: he became master in 1711–12. Perhaps Palmer's gift of her poems to him, some time after they were originally written, was intended to help her son's fledgling career, and to reach a wider audience of nonconformists.
Bibliography:
Ambrose (1657), Barton (1668, 1688), Palmer (2001)
CSPD (1672), Matthews (1934)

VB

From the '*First Century*'

63 experience march 3 71/2

I heard of one has got the start
And is to her dear Jesus gone

But ah this word, did break my hart
Fainting, for thy salvation

Shouldst thou fecth home, thine one by one   5
And leave me out, untill the last
Ther is no wrong, in what is done
Though I look on, as an outcast

I have so litle of thee here
Me-thinks I look, like none of thine   10
Thou givst to others, hea'vns Chear
Feasting them in thy house of wine

I have no reason, to complain
Because of my unworthynese
Yet till drench'd, in the ocean main   15
I shall, be always comfortlese

Unworthynese, shall never make
Mee leave off, after thee, to presse
For if that should. att all take place
I may not look, for more, or lesse   20

Oh that I could, by faith espy
ane hole to Look, in att thee still
Till thou removst me, up on high
to have of thee, my joyfull fill

[p. 100]

Title. 63] *replacing* 53 *deleted*
71/2] *replacing* 7 *deleted*

79   The Child in a strangers arms

Oh world, what means thy tempting charms
I'me like a litle Child
Infolded in, a strangers arms
whilst in thee, I am held

If the Child doe, its father spy   5
it then can take no rest
But will strecth out, its arms, and cry
in'ts fathers arms to nest

Whatever you. to it can give
it will not satisfie   10
Nothing can to it give releife
But still t'will moane, and cry

Untill its father, do it take
and then its crys, doe cease

> Its fathers arms can only make 15
> it still, & be at peace
>
> Oh pity Lord, my weary soull
> still reaching after thee
> And cannot rest, till thou condole
> and strecth thine arms, to me 20
>
> My soull cannot be quiet sung
> with this worlds luluby
> somthing There is that from thee sprung
> that makes mee restlesly
>
> Desire, and long, once for to be 25
> in thy sweet arms entwin'd
> I cannot come, to reach att thee
> whilst I am here confin'd
>
> Thou hast more pity in thee Lord
> then fathers, on the earth 30
> I shall not then, be long in word
> where is nought else, but dearth
>
> Thy meaning's hid, I know it not
> but surely thou wilt own
> Thy own desires thou'st in me wrought 35
> and fecth me, to thy throne

[pp. 129–30]

23. somthing There is] *replacing* There is somthing; *first* somthing *inserted, second* somthing *deleted*
36. thy] MS thy thy

86 The soull veiwing Christ in his humiliation, rejoyces att & longs for a sight of his now glorious exaltation, & his second apearence

> Come now my soull, behold thy king.
> both in his low estate
> And then by faith, to heaven spring
> and veiw his glory great
>
> Thou seest him born of parents poor 5
> and in a manger laid
> This world will scarce open its door
> to him that all things made
>
> When thou shalt see him come again
> atendants he will bring 10

The saints, shall be his blessed traine
and angels on the wing

His visage here, was marred more
then the sons of men.—yet
Thou'lt see heaven, and earth adore   15
when on the throne hees sett.

His beauty shall be as the sun
whose reflect beams shall dart
To warm, refresh, and overrun
Thy soull, & ev'ry part   20

Thou seest him in the garden now
sweating great drops of bloud.
The weight of sin, did make him bow
gods wrath, came as a floud.

Thou'lt see, him shortly triumphing   25
as having paid the dept
And fully satisfi'd for sin
b'ing o're all as head

Thou seest him now, at pilats bar
acus'd by enemies   30
Thou shalt see him exalted far
above the earth, and skys

Thou seest him crown'd with thornes, & led
unto the high preists hall
And ther unjustly condemned   35
and flouted att, by all

Thou'lt see him next with glory clad
Sitting in majesty
His glory shall thy hart, make glad
and still delight thine eye.   40

Thou seest him now, my soull by faith
upon mount Calvary
Crucified and in the height
of soull perplexety

Thou'lt shortly see him, set upon   45
the top of Zion hill
Mounted as king upon his throne
his foes, to crush, and kill

With sound of trumpet he will come
to Judg both quik, and dead   50

To fecth his own unto his home
and to ther dearest head

Oh hasten Lord, this blessed day
the joy of ev'ry saint
When thou, shalt fully bear the sway   55
and we with thee, shall haunt.

[pp. 140–1]

Title. 86 The soull] *surmounted by seven shorthand symbols*
1. behold thy king] *inserted, replacing* & tocch veiw thy king *deleted*
2. low] *replacing* glory *deleted*
7. its] *inserted, replacing* the *deleted*
16. when on the throne hees sett.] *added below, replacing* and bow down at his feet *deleted*
36. by] *replacing* all *deleted*
50. Judg] *replacing* rai *deleted*

88 more to the same purpose

He that hath said, it is but yet
A litle while. & then I come
He will not soe his word forget
As not to fecth his banish'd home

Although to thee, a thousand yeers   5
Ar in thy sight, but as a day
Yet thou dost know a day apears
To me a yeer, in the delay

Of that which I, doe still desire
The full enjoyment, of, thy self   10
The only, object, I admire
My god, my rock, and saving health

Oh that thou wouldest march apace
Over the ruged coasts of time
That I with joy, may see thy face   15
And bath in seas, of love devine

[pp. 142–3]

93 About spirituall discourse June 13 72

What means this sinfull. modesty
Which maketh me, most times, soe shy
To speak how good thou art
when soe I might
others envite   5
To come, and take a part

Who wilt thou speak for, oh my soull
If not for him, whose thou art whole

why then art thou so loth
for to begin 10
to speak of him
And set his glory forth

Canst thou another. object find
More sutable unto thy mind
That thou dost not delight 15
of him always
To speak the praise
Unto thine utmost might

Is this the reason. 'cause thine hart
Within, is the most baren part 20
If that with god weare fild
thou wouldst alway
from day, to day
To speak of him be skild

Canst thou pretend, to be the freind 25
Of Christ, and not still att one end
Of thy discourse find place
to speak somthing
of that sweet king
And of his love, and grace 30

Somtimes thou fearst hipocrisie
When cecreet prid, thou dost espy
And soe to speak art loth
resoulving wroung
to hold thy tounge 35
And silent, be hencforth

Wherby thou dost but gratifie
The devill thy grand enemy
Before thou art a ware
therfore goe on 40
through grace alone
And break thou, through this snare

Tis thou Lord, must open my lips.
That I may not, thy grace eclips
And make me readyly 45
to speak of thee.
As I shall see
Fitt opurtunity

[pp. 148–9]

---

3. speak] *followed by* w *deleted*
9. art thou] *replacing* art thou *deleted*
23. to day] *replacing* day t *deleted*

From the 'Second Century'

**25   our mistakes for want of skill in the methouds of the spirit
in the actings of grace from whence proceeds trouble**

We fill our selfs with fear
And restlese, soull perplexety
Because we do not wisly eye
considering what is
Gods dealings here, with his   5
We look for god, & find him nott
Our ignorance doth so besott
Though he to us draw neer

We would be drawing lines
And boldly choking out the way   10
In which he should himself display
we this way look, and pore
whilst att another door
He doth come in, & yet we flee
Away, & cry, it is not hee   15
'cept when the spirit shines

Somtimes in duty we
Do look for brokenese of hart
Litle of this he doth impart
In steed of this, he doth   20
faith, in high acts draw forth
Or else he doth desires extend
And make them strongly, to him bend
Hee's in his actings free

When we hope to find in   25
Duty, our harts with love, enflam'd
In steed of this, we ar asham'd
that we love him, no more
whom angels, do adore
And we ar brought in dust to lye   30
From sence of want, & poverty
and this from him, doth spring

Somtimes he sees it fit
To disapoint us in desire
That we his counsels, may admire   35
we look much joy, to find
and sorrow, fils our mind
In this, ther is as much of him
As when with joy, fil'd to the brim
Though we do, so slight it   40

When we doe cry, & call
And think streight to be answered
We'r only; with deniells fed
Tis fit, that thou shouldst carve
and to thy self, reserve   45
The liberty, to deall with thine
As thou seest good, who wilt refine
and do them good, by all

Doe as thou wilt, oh lord
but this one thing, I will desire   50
That I may dayly, grow up high'r
Untill I come to thee
Where I shall fully see
And veiw the products of thy love
In the Herusalem above   55
whilst I thy praise record

Oh give to me whilst here
So much, that through thy grace I may
Thy love, & bounty; still display
that others they may be   60
drawn, to run after thee
Oh let me always run apace
Untill I end my weary race
and see my saviour deer

[pp. 194–6]

Title. spirit] *followed by* s *deleted*
1. selfs] *followed by* s *deleted;* elfs *superimposed on illegible letters (original word possibly* soules *or* soulls*)*
8. to] *followed by* d *deleted*
16. spirit] *followed by* s *deleted*
50. but] *added on the left, replacing* Only *deleted*
one] *inserted*

42   The soull looking att, and longing for an eternall saboath. sep 8 72

When shall that blessed, saboath morning dawn
That saboath of eternall rest, upon
My soull, that it might sweetly once begin
Thy love, and praise, eternally to sing
That blessed saboath which shall know no night   5
The Sun of righteousnese, shall be itts light
No sleeping, dresing, eating, in it shall
Steall out a part, away from god, but all
Of it, shall be employ'd to sing his praise
Whillst we sit under his delighting rays   10

No Luring bait of sin, and vanity
Shall from a deity, draw off our eye
In it no deviating thought shall be
Once to estrange, or steall, the hart from thee
The body shall not be. a clog again   15
Unto the soull, to keep it down, when fain
It would upon the wing, sweetly ascend
But it shall freely, to its motions bend
Our hope, into enjoyment shall be led
Our faith, into fruition swalowed   20
Our pray'rs, shall into halalujahs, turn
Our harps of praise, shall never out be. worn
The church, that we shall Joyne with, in that day
Shall have no spot, no blemish, no decay.
No Jaring discord in our musick then   25
For want of love, but all shall say Amen
No diference in Judgment shall appear
For all things then, shall unto us, be clear
When I from this church. militent shall soar
I then shall Joyne, with that triumphant chore 30
Oh that I might but know. I quikly shall
gett to that vision, beautificall
In that eternall, sweet, saboath of rest
Where I shall in thy bosome make my nest
Looking down on this world of vanity   35
As one, that is set on a mountain high
Looks on the ship, that brought him safe to land
Liing, all broke, to shivers, on the sand
Rejoycing in this, that he is got safe
Out of the reach, of any bousterous wave   40
No depths of greif, shall swalow me again
But I shall ever with thee, live, and reign
Uninterupted communion, with thee
I shall enjoy, when I this day shall see
The world, and cretures, shall not call me off 45
From the enjoyment of him, whom I love.

              [pp. 210–11]

---

25. then] *replacing* then *deleted*
32. vision] *replacing* vits *deleted*

  45 The soull clouded. sep 12 72

Why turnest thou thy face away
On the inshutting of the day

Whilst all things doe in darknese shroud
Thou wrapst thy self, up in a cloud

Thou knowst I cannot be content
Whilst I'me out of thy presence pent

Except upon my soull thou shine
I must have leave, to moane, & pine

Oh shew thy self, to me with speed
Or take mee up that I may feed

My eyes, to satisfaction,
Upon thy well beloved son

When it is with me att the best
I cannot here take, up my rest

Much lesse, when thou art gone, can I
The Least true satisfaction spy

Yet Lord, I hope, that I am thine
And though the gates of hell combine

Thy cov'nant firm, they cannot break
Or make thy promises to leak

Oh let my faith, break through each throng
And in the dark, make thee, her song

I must not always, live by sence
Untill thou calst me up from hence

And then I know. thou'lt clear the sky
On me, to all, eternity.

[p. 213]

---

3. shroud] *MS* shourd

46 The soull by faith, triumphing over saten, & rejoycing in hopes of future freedome. through Christ alone

Oh what a reall comfort tis
To think, though Saten, doth here tempt
and seek to foyle
tis but a while
And I shall be, for e're exempt
From all thosse subtletys, of his

In duty here, he will not rest
But att mine elbow, he doth stand
my soull to vex

and it perplex 10
But when climb'd to the holy land
Hee shall me then, no more molest

He doth whilst here, still evermore
Throw in his fire brands ore the wall
for to enflame 15
and play his game
But thou shalt with him quite each score
When Christ shall set thee free, from thrall

[p. 213]

67 The souls desire, June 6 73

A burning beacon, of pure love
Still strongly, flaming up to thee
I'de be, untill thou doe remove
Mee up, where love. shall perfect be

This grace of love, is mine eye 5
The thing, I greatly doe desire
For itt the richest pearls, should lye
Under my feett, as durt, and mire

I will desire no greater pleasure
Then in thesse flames, of love to ly 10
I will seek for, noe richer tresure
Then. wings of love, wheron to fly

If thou'lt not fill me to the brim
Whilst here, oh hasten my remove,
Unto that place, where I shall swim 15
In seas, of pure, unmixed, love

[p. 235]

73 The devills picture, June 25

Why lookst thou, with a grudging eye
On those, that have atainments high
This weed, impure
god wont endure

Shall worthlese clay, att him repine 5
Who seeth fitt for to refine
thosse, hee intends
for higher ends

Why wouldst thou have, none better then
Thy self, among the sons, of men 10

Sure this doth smell
too strong of hell.

What wouldst thou shine, thy self alone
And in the world, wouldst thou have none
with thee to vie   15
for sanctity

Why fearest thou, others should be
More holy, then thy self, and see
more of the love
of god, above   20

Oh what art thou, thus to aspire
Who art far worse, then durt, and mire
unworthy of
a look of love

Oh Saten, I doe somtimes see   25
My self, by this, soe like to thee
that I doe hate.
my self, and state

And if I knew, which way to run,
From itt, away, I would be gone,   30
This dismall sight,
itt doth, soe fright.

[pp. 240–1]

Mary Astell's presentation manuscript for Archbishop Sancroft

Bodleian Library MS Rawlinson poet. 154

Bodleian MS Rawlinson poet. 154 is a composite volume, comprising several manuscripts written in the late seventeenth and early eighteenth centuries. Part Four of the volume is a presentation manuscript of poems on sacred subjects, dedicated on the title-leaf to William Sancroft, Archbishop of Canterbury, and dated 1689. A prefatory letter, addressed to 'your Grace', indicates that the writer is female (she refers to herself with female pronouns and entreats the archbishop to look favourably on 'the failures of a Womans pen'), but is subscribed only with the initials 'MA'.

The identification of 'MA' as Mary Astell was made in 1982 by Ruth Perry, citing the evidence of handwriting and the inclusion of certain phrases commonly used in Astell's prose work (Perry 1982, 1986). The composite manuscript probably derives at least in part from Sancroft's papers, some of which were inherited by Richard Rawlinson.

Astell's manuscript, a quarto, consists of forty-nine leaves, numbered 50°, 50^i–97 in the running foliation of the composite volume. There is evidence throughout the collection of careful preparation of the text. The manuscript is a fair copy, written in Astell's clear rounded italic, with very few cancellations. The dedication on the title page, 'A Collection of Poems... 1689', is enclosed within a frame of double-ruled red lines, while each subsequent page (i.e. fols 51–93) has a red double-ruled left margin. Where the end of a poem is not coterminous with the end of a page, it is separated from the next poem by a single red line. Catchwords are used on most pages. Careful planning is also evident in the order of the poems, which manifest a clear progression in subject: from the introductory invocations to God and the poet's muse in 'The Invitation', through meditations on the poet-speaker's life in the world, the last things of death, judgement, heaven and hell, and moral reflections on the Christian life, and concluding in prayers of thanksgiving and glorification. The chief poetic model acknowledged in the manuscript is Abraham Cowley; however, the influence of George Herbert's *The Temple* is also apparent.

According to dates in the margin of the manuscript, Astell's poems were composed over a period of several years, from at least 1683 until 1688. In her prefatory letter to Sancroft, Astell refers to having already received assistance from the archbishop at a time 'when even my Kinsfolk had failed, and my familiar Friends had forgotten me'. Astell moved from her native Newcastle to London at some time in the late 1680s, and it seems likely, as Perry suggests, that these allusions to personal distress refer to troubles she had experienced during her first months as a single woman in the capital. Her choice of patron, in 1689, is also significant. William Sancroft was a high-church Anglican who had been one of the seven bishops imprisoned in 1688 for refusing to endorse James II's Declaration of Indulgence. Subsequently, however, Sancroft was one of the 'non-juring' clergy who felt unable to accept the legitimacy of William of Orange's accession. As a result he was suspended as archbishop on 1 August 1689 and deprived of office on 1 February 1690. Although there is no clear evidence as to whether Astell's manuscript was presented to Sancroft before or after his suspension, his principled opposition to the new monarchy had been known from the end of 1688, and the likely consequences would not have been difficult to predict. (The reference in her dedicatory letter to 'real worth' rather than 'external Greatness' being 'the true motive to veneration and esteem' tends to suggest that she did know of the threat to Sancroft's position.) Astell, who was to be a consistent supporter of the non-juring cause for the rest of her life, thus begins her literary career with an expression of piety which is also an emphatic political statement.

A complete text of all Astell's poetry in the Rawlinson manuscript can be found in Perry (1986), Appendix D.

BIOGRAPHICAL NOTE

Mary Astell (1666–1731) was born in Newcastle in 1666, the daughter of a coal merchant, Peter Astell, and his wife, Mary Errington, an heiress from an old Catholic family. The Astell family was staunchly royalist and Anglican, and Mary and her brother Peter (born in 1668) were brought up in the Church of England. After the deaths of her parents, Astell moved to London in the late 1680s, and settled in Chelsea. She appears to have struggled financially during her first few years in London: hence her dedication of her manuscript poetry to William Sancroft, who had a reputation for benevolence. Little else is known about her early years in London, but in 1693 she began a philosophical correspondence with John Norris, a Platonist and one of the earliest English critics of John Locke. Norris encouraged her reading of French philosophy, and in 1695 arranged the publication of their correspondence as *Letters concerning the Love of God*. Meanwhile, Astell had already published (anonymously) her tract *A Serious Proposal to the Ladies, for the Advancement of Their True and Greatest Interest*, which advocated the foundation of an educational academy for women. In this and later publications, her energetic exposition of the injustices suffered by women in contemporary England is joined with a conservative respect for hierarchy and tradition. Thus in *Some Reflections upon Marriage* (1700), she deplores the low status of married women and defends a woman's right to abstain from matrimony, but concedes the necessity for women to defer to their husbands within marriage.

In a fiercely partisan age, Astell was a convinced Tory and determined controversialist. In *A Fair Way With The Dissenters* (1704), written in response to Defoe's satire *The Shortest Way with the Dissenters*, she calls for the destruction of Protestant Dissent as a political force. *Moderation truly Stated* (1704), written against the Presbyterian James Owen, denounces the practice of occasional conformity, whereby Dissenters qualified for public office by occasionally attending

Church of England services. In *An Impartial Enquiry into the Causes of Rebellion and Civil War in this Kingdom* (1704) she identifies Whigs and Dissenters as the main source of political instability in England, rejecting the threat allegedly presented by Catholicism. *The Christian Religion, as Profess'd by a Daughter of the Church of England* (1705) defends the established church against the religious heterodoxy (as she saw it) of Locke's *The Reasonableness of Christianity* (1695) and Damaris Masham's *A Discourse concerning the Love of God* (1696). Her last published book was *Bart'lemy Fair* (1709), a polemic addressed to the Whiggish Kit Cat Club, attacking the Earl of Shaftesbury's *Letter Concerning Enthusiasm*. She later wrote a manuscript preface for Lady Mary Wortley Montagu's *Turkish Embassy Letters*.

Astell's writings elicited responses from such distinguished contemporary writers as Defoe, Locke, Steele and Swift. However, she took no part in literary society in London, but lived quietly in Chelsea, where in 1709, supported by her patrons Lady Elizabeth Hastings and Lady Catherine Jones, she opened a charity school under the auspices of the Royal Hospital. From the mid-1720s she lived in Lady Catherine Jones's household. She died of breast cancer in 1731.

Bibliography:
Astell (1986, 1996)
Perry (1982, 1986)

GW

A
COLLECTION OF POEMS
humbly
presented and Dedicated
TO
the most Reverend Father in
GOD
W I L L I A M
By Divine Providence
Lord ARCHBISHOP of
CANTERBURY &c.
1689

May it please your Grace

Next to the committing of a Crime, the doing of that which stands in need of an Apology, has ever been most disagreeable to me. But since we cannot command our own circumstances, and are therefore sometimes inforced to do, not as we would but as we can; this, tho it will not excuse us in the commission of an evil, may be allowed to Apologize for a less proper and less becoming Action. Of which sort your Grace may justly reckon, this my repeated boldness and importunity, as I must needs confess it in a person of my sex, and meaness, to intrude into so venerable a presence, with nothing else to recommend me but a few trifles, which even themselves stand in need of an excuse. It is not without pain and reluctancy, that I break from my beloved obscurity, (which is so agreeable to my temper and proper for my sex,) to expose to so judicious a Censure, those mean productions which a little reading, a small experience, and smaller fancy, has made shift to bring forth; and yet I may say as David did in another case, is there not a Cause? Not to mention what your Grace dos not love to hear, but what I must always remember with Honour and Veneration, that real worth (and not only external Greatness) which is the true motive to veneration and esteem: Permit me to say, that the Condiscention and Candor, with which your Grace was pleased to receive a poor unknown, who hath no place to fly unto and none that careth for her Soul, when even my Kinsfolk had failed, and my familiar Friends had forgotten me; this my Lord, hath emboldened me to make an humble tender of another offering, which tho but of Goats hair and Badger skins, is the best I have to give, and therefore I hope may not be altogather unacceptable.

May your Grace be pleased to receive it with your wonted Charity and Goodness, and pass a favourable censure upon the failures of a Womans pen, who would very thankfully be informed of her errours and amend them; and permit me with all Humility to profess my self

   My Lord,
    Your Graces
     Most humble, thankfull,
     and obedient Servant;
      MA.

[fols. 50ⁱr–51v]

---

6. repeated] *Perry* repented

The Invitation

made June 28
1683

I

Come Muse, and leave those wings that soar
 No further than an Earthly flight,
Let us the GOD of Heav'n implore,
 And tune our Notes Ætherial height;
Heav'n thy Parnassus be, thence learn thy Song,
Thy Saviour's side shall be thy Helicon.

II

Hark how he calls, come unto me
 All that are laden and opprest,
My service is true Libertie,
 My bosom an Eternal Rest,
With open arms he begs of thee to come,
Make hast my Soul, leave all & thither run.

III

Wipe thy blind eyes dark'ned with tears,
 From all but Penitentiall ones,

   Harbour only Religious Fears,   15
    And for thy Sins keep all thy Groans;
  Then he who never lets us sigh in vain,
  Will turn to brightest Joy thy Greif & pain.

      IV
   Teach ev'ry word to chant his Praise,
    And ev'ry verse to sing his Love,   20
   His Crown of thorns shall be thy bays,
    His Cross shall be thy shady Grove,
  Which will at last be to a Kingdom blown,
  And thy sharp bays will sprout into a Crown.

             [fol. 52r–v]

Jan 7. 1687/8   **In emulation of Mr Cowleys Poem**
      call'd the Motto page 1

      I
What shall I do? not to be Rich or Great,
  Not to be courted and admir'd,
  With Beauty blest, or Wit inspir'd,
Alas! these merit not my care and sweat,
  These cannot my Ambition please,   5
My high born Soul shall never stoop to these;
But something I would be thats truly great
In'ts self, and not by vulgar estimate.

      II
If this low World were always to remain,
If th'old Philosophers were in the right,   10
  Who wou'd not then, with all their might
Study and strive to get themselves a name?
  Who wou'd in soft repose lie down,
Or value ease like being ever known?
But since Fames trumpet has so short a breath, 15
Shall we be fond of that which must submit to Death?

      III
Nature permits not me the common way,
  By serving Court, or State, to gain
  That so much valu'd trifle, Fame;
Nor do I covet in Wits Realm to sway: 20
  But O ye bright illustrious few,
What shall I do to be like some of you?
Whom this misjudging World dos underprize,
Yet are most dear in Heav'ns all-righteous eyes!

IV

How shall I be a Peter or a Paul? 25
   That to the Turk and Infidel,
     I might the joyfull tydings tell,
And spare no labour to convert them all:
   But ah my Sex denies me this,
And Marys Priviledge I cannot wish; 30
Yet hark I hear my dearest Saviour say,
They are more blessed who his Word obey.

V

Up then my sluggard Soul, Labour and Pray,
   For if with Love enflam'd thou be,
     Thy JESUS will be born in thee, 35
And by thy ardent Prayers, thou can'st make way,
   For their Conversion whom thou may'st not teach,
Yet by a good Example always Preach:
And tho I want a Persecuting Fire,
I'le be at lest a Martyr in desire. 40

[fols 52v–53r]

Enemies

Mar 18. 1683

I

I Love you whom the World calls Enemies,
   You are my Vertues exercise,
     The usefull Furnace to refine
My dross, the Oil that maks my Armour shine.

II

Nay you're the best of men because you are 5
   The truest Friends, tho this appear
     A Paradox to them who seem,
The only men of Wit & of esteem;

III

Who measure Friendship by the Rule of Pow'er,
   And love him best who has most store; 10
     Who prostitute that sacred Name,
Unto the partn'ers of their sin and shame.

IV

Yet if the merits of a Friend be weigh'd,
   His worth in a just balance laid,
     Light Flattery will blow away, 15
And just reproof will all the rest out-weigh.

V

But a Friend's loving eyes are sometimes blind,
    And will not any blemish find,
    Or if a secret ulcer they espie,
They'l sooner Balsom than sharp Wine apply.   20

VI

Kind Monitors you tell me of my faults,
    Your spurs correct & mend my halts,
    With cleansing Physick purge my mind,
That no crude humours may remain behind.

VII

Meekness wou'd lose her vast inheritance   25
    If you were not the evidence;
    You bring to light our Charitie,
Without you we shou'd but half Christians be.

VIII

Best Benefactors! let Earth's Children pray
    For those who give them loads of Clay,   30
    Who puff their bubbles, I'le for you
Implore, & think it God-like so to do.

    [fols 53v–54r]

Mar 30.1684   **Ambition**

I

What's this that with such vigour fills my brest?
    Like the first mover finds no rest,
    And with it's force dos all things draw,
Makes all submit to its imperial Law!
Sure 'tis a spark 'bove what Prometheus stole,   5
    Kindled by a heav'nly coal,
    Their sophistry I can controul,
Who falsely say that women have no Soul.

II

Vile Greatness! I disdain to bow to thee,
    Thou art below ev'n lowly me,   10
    I wou'd no Fame, no Titles have,
And no more Land than what will make a grave.
I scorn to weep for Worlds, may I but reign
    And Empire o're my self obtain,
    In Caesars throne I'de not sit down,   15
Nor wou'd I stoop for Alexanders Crown.

III

Let me obscured be, & never known
  Or pointed at about the Town,
  Short winded Fame shall not transmit
My name, that the next Age may censure it: 20
If I write Sense no matter what they say,
  Whither they call it dull, or pay
  A rev'rence such as Virgil claims,
Their breath's infectious, I have higher aims.

IV

Mean spir'ited men! that bait at Honour, Praise,   25
  A Wreath of Laurel or of Baies;
  How short's their Immortality!
But Oh a Crown of Glory ne're will die!
This I'me Ambitious of, no pains will spare
  To have a higher Mansion there,   30
  Where all are Kings, here let me be,
Great O my GOD, Great in Humilitie.

[fols 54v–55r]

Ap. 8. 1684

Solitude

I

*the wish p. 22

Now I with gen'rous *Cowley see,
This trifling World & I shall ne're agree.
Nature in busi'ness me no share affords,
And I no bus'iness find in empty words:
  I dare not all the morning spend   5
  To dress my body, & not lend
A minuit to my Soul, nor can think fit,
To sell the Jewel for the Cabinet.

II

  My' unpolish'd converse Ladies fly
'Twill make you dull, I have no railery,   10
I cannot learn the fashionable art,
To laugh at Sin, and censure true desert.
  Alas I no experience have,
  With my weak eyes to make a slave,
Nor am I practis'd in that am'rous flame,   15
Which has so long usurpt Loves sacred name.

III

No satisfaction can I find
In balls and revelling, my thinking mind,

Can't reconcile 'em with a mournfull Spirit,
Nor with the solid comfort they'l inherit 20
  Who here love sorrow; Complement
  I am as guiltless of as paint,
No fucus for my mind or face I use,
Nor am acquainted with the modern Muse.

IV

  O happy Solitude, may I 25
My time with thee, & some good books employ!
No idle visits rob me of an hour,
No 'impertinents those precious drops devour.
  Thus blest, I shall while here below
  Antedate Heav'n; did Monarchs know 30
What 'tis with GOD, & Cherubims to dwell,
With Charles they'd leave their Empires for a Cell.

                              [fols 55v–56r]

Vertue

1

Go dispicable Vertue go,
  And seek some other World,
Go live with them whom we have rob'd of Gold,
  Since thou art far too mean and low,
For this refined age, perhaps the dull 5
The sottish Indian, may admit of thee,
    But we are full
Of sparkling wits, who know thy poverty,
And see thro thy home-spun simplicity.
  Some sixteen hundred years ago, 10
When men did only practick notions know,
And infant Christianity began
With its mirac'lous force t'impose on man:
Vertue perhaps, like some new thing might be
Admir'd and follow'd, for it's noveltie. 15
But we by their dear bought experience find,
  That Vertue's nothing but a name,
Which neither can protect from loss nor pain,
  A name by cunning men design'd,
To lay restraints on the best part of Humane-kind. 20

2

Go, Vertuous fop and leave the World to us,
  'Twas never sure design'd for thee;
  A mind so nice and scrupulous,
Can never rise to wealth or dignity.

Alas poor man! he cannot one thing say, 25
    And act a quite contrary way!
No gain goes down with him, but what must be
First measur'd in the scales of equity.
He cannot swallow Oaths, and Perjury,
His squeamish stomach hardly can digest a lie. 30
Nor can with evil means good ends persue,
Nor lawfull things with ill intention do.
Religion that unfashionable thing,
    Too firm and closely sets on him,
He thinks it still the same, and knows not how 35
Wisely to make it to his int'rest bow.
Dull Soul that never our great secret hit,
    Who for a Cloak make use of it,
    (None better villanies to hide)
    And then 'tis quickly thrown aside, 40
When our designs it can no longer fit.

3

Why do I thus idly my time employ?
Since others seek preferment why shou'd I,
For some weak scruples slip the oppertunity?
He that will nothing do but what is best, 45
May properly be said to live in jest.
    He that will for Preferment stay,
Till he come to it by a reg'lar way,
    May with the blinded Jews,
Vainly himself for evermore amuse, 50
With expectation of the ever absent day.
    But he that never boggles at a vice,
    Obtains his purpose in a trice;
    And what great hurt is done?
Only a Verteous simpleton out-run. 55
    If he to Heav'n has been a debter,
    He hopes hereafter to do better;
Tho much of his too-morrows may be past,
Yet this hereafter sure will come at last;
    And when it comes O then, 60
A little matter sets all right again,
A Lord forgive me wipes away the shame and sin.

4

But one thought more before I venture out,
    Let me but solve one little doubt:
Will Vertue always under hatches lie? 65
And Vice for ever have impunity?
See which bids fairest for Eternity.

Ah now I find Vertue's the only good;
They who forsake her never understood
   Her safety and felicity,   70
Let me with Vertue live, and with her die,
I cou'd have richer bargains offer'd me,
As the World thinks, but now I plainly see,
There's nothing glorious or rich but thee!
    Enough thou hast to charm us here,   75
    Enough to bear our charges on the way,
But ah what hast thou at the great rewarding day!
And I'me content to have all laid up there.
Content said I, nay rather let me say,
    For this I'le study, strive and pray;   80
And to the World this last farewell I give,
Henceforth my only bus'ness shall be how to live.
                                      [fols 84v–86r]

The Complaint

1

What dost thou mean my GOD, (said I,
Once in a sad and melancholy fit,)
   Why dost thou so severely try
      Thy Servant, as if yet
I had not been explor'd sufficiently.   5
   So much to stretch will break the wire,
What Gold can always strugle with the fire?
And Lord what mortal in thy sight can stand,
If all his ways be too exactly scan'd?

2

   If I ask wealth, it is to be   10
Thy Steward only, not to make it mine.
   And when I wou'd have dignitie,
      'Tis that it might be thine,
And Vertues light to more advantage shine.
      'Tis my design when Wit I crave,   15
That thou both use and principal shou'd have.
For well I know that these no blessings be,
If as from thee they came, so they ascend not up to thee.

3

   Yet without these I can be pleas'd,
When thou remember's me how oft they are,   20
    A spur to Vice, and Vertues snare,
      Strong Souls have been diseas'd,

By coming fresh into infected air.
    Who wou'd a cup of Poyson take,
That of his Ant'idote he might trial make?
All are not fit the Ordeal to endure,
Conquest is brave, but Peace is most secure.

4

    But yet methinks 'tis somewhat hard,
My mind be'ing to the lowest measure fit,
      Content with wages, begs not a reward,
        Thou shou'dst contract it yet,
And I of necessaries be debar'd.
      Long have I liv'd on hope, but will
A Hope that's always baulk'd continue still?
Is't not a sign the flood dos still remain,
When my poor Dove comes empty home again?

5

    Lord thou didst give thy only Son
To die for me, and can I doubt thy Love?
      In his dear name thou bids me come,
        And yet no Prayers will move!
Friendless and helpless, I'me exposed here,
      As if thou took'st of me no care.
My equitable suit canst thou deny,
Since all I ask is oppertunity,
To serve my GOD and trafick for Eternity?

6

    Fondly I thus complain'd, when lo
A beamling shot from Heav'n upon me shin'd;
      In a right medium did the objects show,
        And my dull thoughts refin'd.
Then I remembred who did undergo
      Far worse for me, why shou'd I mone,
Since 'tis my daily Prayer, GODs will be done?
Ah simple Soul cou'dst thou his Wisdom see,
Thou wou'dst not sad, but pleas'd and joyfull be,
Dos not thy GOD know best what's good for thee?

[fols 86r–87r]

13

Marie Burghope's country house poem, 'The Vision'

Huntington Library MS EL 35/B/62

The manuscript of Marie Burghope's 'The Vision. Or A Poeticall View of Ashridge in the County of Bucks' was a presentation copy for its dedicatee Mary Egerton which is still preserved in the library of the Egertons' descendants today. A facsimile copy is held at the Huntington Library.

Following three blank leaves, the first item in the manuscript is an elaborate title page which indicates the topic of the poem: a description of Ashridge—the country estate of the Earls of Bridgewater—and a history of members of the Bridgewater family, 'Written by one of the Female Sex' in 1699 (cf. *VCH Hertford* 2: 210–14). It is written in what is probably Burghope's autograph throughout, a clear and non-cursive italic script, with running heads and marginal notes. The poem itself is twenty-five pages long, prefaced by a four-page prose epistle dedicated to Lady Mary Egerton, eldest daughter of the third Earl of Bridgewater. The Bridgewaters had a distinguished tradition of literary interests; their history of artistic patronage included Milton's 'Comus', written for the family and performed before the first Earl in 1634.

In the prose dedication (not reproduced here) Burghope heaps scorn on those men who see no value in female education, arguing that a learned woman makes the best housewife and the best Christian. She explains that the writing of poetry is usually considered the worst manifestation of learning in a woman, but insists that she herself only entertains the muses during periods of leisure, and that surely that can be no worse than women's ordinary chat. The Muse in this work implores Lady Mary's protection, and Burghope hopes she will pardon all defects in it since it is only for the diversion of Lady Mary and the Bridgewater family.

In the poem itself the speaker, Burghope, sits in contemplation, whereupon she sees a chariot carrying her Muse. The Muse takes Burghope to Ashridge ('The promis'd Earthly Paradice'), where the poet describes the exterior and interior of the estate in detail. When the Muse takes her to the library, Burghope asks if her own poem might lodge there, and the Muse gives her consent. When they enter the walk Burghope meets the Genius of the estate who tells her the history of the family and the house from 1260, ending with a description of the current inhabitants, including Mary Egerton. Burghope's forty-five marginal notes gloss references in the text to people, places or events, and are keyed to various symbols in the poem. Two of these marginal notes, on the third Earl's career, are in a different hand; this hand has also emended a line in the text which refers to the Duke of Gloucester. Perhaps these notes were written by a member of the Bridgewater family.

As a country-house poem, 'The Vision' may be compared with earlier poems such as Aemilia Lanyer's 'To Cooke-ham', Jonson's 'To Penshurst', Marvell's 'Upon Appleton House', and Charles Cotton's description of Chatsworth in *The Wonders of the Peak* (1681; cf. Fowler 1994). Katherine Austen's country house poem 'On the Situation of Highbury' survives in her manuscript of poetry and religious meditations written between 1664 and 1668 (British Library Additional MS 4454, fol. 104r). Other elements of this tradition can be found in two Margaret Cavendish poems, 'A Dialogue between a Bountiful Knight and a Castle Ruined in War' (i.e. Bolsover Castle) and 'Nature's House', and two Anne Finch poems, 'Upon My Lord Winchilsea's Converting the Mount in His Garden to a Terrace' and 'To the Honourable the Lady Worsley at Long-leate' (both c.1702). William McClung notes that by the end of the seventeenth century the country-house poem no longer displayed Jonson's irony or contrasted the well-run estate with its opposite; instead poems such as the anonymous 'Belvoir: Being a Pindarick Ode upon Belvoir Castle, the Seat of the Earls of Rutland, made in the Year 1679' simply survey the estate, the buildings, their interiors, and the history of the family (McClung 1977, 174).

'The Vision' has been edited in full by Betty Travitsky (Egerton 1999).

BIOGRAPHICAL NOTE

Marie Burghope (dates unknown) was probably the daughter of the third Earl of Bridgewater's chaplain, the Reverend George Burghope (Senar 1983, 6, 38). He preached the first sermon at Ashridge's new chapel, completed in 1699, which is described in the poem. George Burghope was also rector of the nearby church of St Peter and St Paul at Little Gaddesden from 1691 to 1713. His wife's name was Margaret (Bell 1949, 142, 69). Marie had at least one sibling: a brother named Musidorus, a minister like their father, who died in 1701. The burial register of Little Gaddesden indicates that Musidorus was born in Edlesborough, Buckinghamshire in 1677 (Bell 1949, 153–4; cf. *VCH Buckingham* 3: 360); perhaps Marie was born there too. If Marie was born around this date she would have been close in age to Mary Egerton, the dedicatee of her poem, who was twenty-three in 1699.

NOTES ON TRANSCRIPTION

Triplets (three lines with the same end rhyme) are marked in the facsimile with one} at the right of the lines; this notation has not been reproduced. Marginal note markers have been recorded as either $^{(+)}$, $^+$, ^{x}, $^{\parallel}$ or $^:$ though several of the markers are actually three dots in various configurations, or five dots in the shape of a cross. Quotation marks that appear on the lower left of the beginning of a line in the facsimile have been recorded as normal quotation marks to the upper left ("). All inserted words have a caret (^) beneath them; this has not been recorded in the notes. Solid and broken lines and dashes of various lengths in the manuscript have been standardised to the following: __, ---, _____, -, —. It is difficult to distinguish upper case from lower case letters, particularly with s, w, and l when they appear at the beginning of a word. The few substantive differences between this edition and Travitsky's are recorded in the notes; however, differences in capitalisation are not noted. There is a large number of minor corrections in the manuscript. Where these corrections make no difference in sense or metre, or the previous reading is illegible, they have not been noted.

References:

Egerton (1999), Fowler (1994)

Bell (1949), McClung (1977), Senar (1983), *VCH Buckingham* (3), *VCH Hertford* (2)

VB

The Vision.
Or
A Poeticall View of Ashridge in
the County of Bucks.
The ancient Seat of the Right Honorable
John Earle of Bridgewater.
Together with the History & Characters
Of the most considerable Members
Of that Noble Family.
Written by one of the Female Sex
in the year
1699

[fol. [i] recto]

The Vision.
A Poeticall Description
Of Ashridge Com Bucks.

Cool was the western Air, serene the Day,
And Phoebus did his radiant Beames display.
When I ore-shaddow'd in an Arbour sate,
Contemplating the wond'rous Turnes of Fate.
My wand'ring Thoughts such Objects brought in veiw   5
That Poets scarce could feigne, & yet were true.
The Palaces adorn'd with riseing Towers,
Attended round with humble Walks & Bowers,
And Gardens deck'd with the most fragrant Flowers.
Strong & delightfull Mansions, which might prove   10
The best for War, the best for Peace & Love.
Man too imploy'd my Thoughts, their Rise & Fall,
What glorious deeds they've done, & what they shall.
Where are the Hero's of the former Age,
And what are those that now are on the Stage.   15
How these do domineer upon the Ball,
Till Death stops their Tumultuous Breath, & all

Are carried to the common Funerall.
The World's an Island where we act & do
And is surrounded with a Sea of woe.   20
A Land of sorrows, & a Vale of Teares,
And Man a Machine mov'd with hopes & feares.
Short is his time, yet long his works remaine,
And Monumentally his Name retaine.
And thus (well pleas'd) I past from Things to Men,   25
And then as pleas'd from Men to Things agen.
__ When lo! there did a Sight appear
Which rais'd my wonder equall to my fear.
An open Chariot, fild with radiant Light,
Drawn by two winged Horses snowey White;   30
Within a Nymph with grave but lovely Face
In awefull Posture, & Magestic Grace,
Sate; with one Hand supporting of her Head,
The other held a Wand; These words she said.

    "'Behold thy Muse appears, — perciveing well   35
"Thou might'st in our Celestiall Art excell,
"Had'st thou a Subject great enough; & be
"My Oracle, as I shall be to Thee.
"Then know, an Object soon thou shalt descry
"Not only with thy Intellect, but Eye;   40
"An Object, & be sure no Aid I'l spare
"Worthy thy song, & my Poetic Care.

    This said, She lift me up whilst all amaz'd
Much on the Earth, much more on Her I gaz'd.
Swifter then Winds, or quicker far then Thought,   45
We thro the yeilding trackless Air were brought;
And then descending down, --- Tis here said She
The promis'd Earthly Paradice you'l see.

(+) cald Princes Rideing before the House

    T'was in a Walk⁽⁺⁾ where Art & Nature strove
To shew their utmost skill, & truest Love.   50
The Prospect did at once please & Surprize,
Delightfull Wonder danc'd before my Eyes.

    The stately Beech exactly in a Row
On both the sides in full proportion grow.
Their lofty Tops so ev'n & verdent are,   55
You'd think 'em spacious Pastures in the Air.
So thick that even the Suns all peircing Eye
Can scarce the Beauty of the Walk descry.
Th'o to adorn, & make it please the sight
He checkers it with Gems of purest Light.   60
The winds all thro the Place came whispering forth

                    To pleasure more, or more to tell its worth
                    Tis all with natures Colours fully spread,
                    The growndwork green, richly enamelled
                    With native Flowers, neither sown nor sett.   65
                    The Dazy & the blew ey'd violett.
                    Their notes the little Winged Chorus raise,
                    And chant with Sweet melodious Strains its Praise.
                    And Eccho too is there, & so will be
                    To make an Everlasting Harmony.   70
                    Here sure the Favourites of the Muses came
                    (Att lest they sho'd) to Eternize their Name,
                    And toak (so great variety it yeilds)
                    All they have said of the Elisium Feilds.

(+)   The Object next that cald away my Eye   75
The House   Was a Magestic Palace⁽⁺⁾ standing by.
 its selfe   Tis seated on a Rise adorned round
                    With Trees, by Art & Natures favours Crownd.
                    Erected too with such aspireing hight,
(+)   That tho it pleas'd, it dazl'd soon the sight.   80
The Park   From whence the Woods⁽⁺⁾ & Plains are all descry'd,
                    Where numerous Traines of well fed Deer reside;
                    So swift, so grown, that one may well declare
                    Their Lives scarce in their Masters Power are,
                    And yet they pay them to reward his Care.   85
                    So that a Monarch's Palace this might prove,
                    Or else as Poets sing the Seat of Jove.

(+)
The Lodge   The very Anti-Palace⁽⁺⁾ seem'd to be
                    Sufficient Subject for my Muse & me.
                    Tis fairly wrought thr'o out & so compact;   90
                    And every frosted Stone laid so exact
                    With such a Symmetry, It may be sworn
                    All the whole Mass is but made up of One.
                    Here my Surprize was great, The Blind & Lame
                    And other Poor o'rejoy'd togather came.   95
                    They were not surer of th'approaching Day
                    Then to be sent with full Supplys away.
                    It still increas'd, in this hard Age to see
                    All other marks of Hospitality.
                    Here Friends & Strangers too with equall Care   100
                    And bounty unconfin'd, refreshed are.
                    And had there not been Nobler Objects nigh
                    To entertaine my Sight, even so had I.

                        A large & spacious Square then — next was seen,
                    Bigirt about with never fadeing Green.   105

So high so thick, & so compacted grown,
You'd think it did supply the Place of Stone.
Apollo here sure keeps his sacred Court,
Whether his sons for Lawrels doe resort:
Or rather even a short and transcient veiw   110
Inspires Poets, & can crown them too.
And it had been Pernassus Top to me,
If the Indulgent Muse had left me free.
But instantly She wav'd Her powerfull Wand

(+)
The Library

And so we past into the Vatican⁽⁺⁾.   115

   Here sacred Learneing do's tryumphant sitt,
Accompaned with Eloquence & Witt.
Others for knowledge Travell, cutt the Line,
Hazard those Seas that on the Poles confine.
From hence the greater World we have in veiw,   120
And learne to understand the Lesser too.
Rome may her numbers boast; this do's excell
In better Books & being chosen well.
What 'ere the Ancients or the Moderns write,
The Brittan, or the Athen — Stagerite   125
Is here recorded. Science do's appear
In full Meridian & Declention here.
"'Haile mighty Founder of these sacred Piles!
"On the great Owner now extend your smiles.
"'Tis He alone's design'd, He only can   130
"And will Compleat what you so well began.
"And thou my Muse my willing Soul inspire
"With such Magestic sense, & such Poetic Fire;
"That I may something say, worthy to be
"By Him transmitted to Posterity   135
"Among those numerous all delightfull store.
"Grant but this small Request I'l ask no more.

   The Goddess smil'd in Token of consent;
And so into the stately Hall we went,
Plac'd in the Front, whose lofty Top do's show   140
Above the other Building all below.
Hung round with Draughts, so well perform'd, you'd call
The very Copys The Originall.
Here Horse & Hound in full Proportion stand,
And wonder now, as when alive command.   145

(+)
Some new
alterations

There's added⁽⁺⁾ too what ere suppos'd to be
Worthy this Age, or of Posterity.
The finest Ornaments, to let us know
How great it is, & will be ever so.

+ The great Staires	A large⁺ Ascent was next adorn'd all ore With Loves, & Cupids, or what pleased more.	150
x The Picture of the Battle betwixt the Giants and the Gods, which the Muse describes & passes by the rest	The ancientˣ Battle t'wixt the Gods & Men, Gigantic Warrs, Pelion on Ossa; When The mighty Typheus Heaven to conquer strove, And was transfix'd by Thunder-bolts of Jove. Painters & Poets too have both the skill Truth in the Guise of Fables to instill. The Warr in Heaven; the Dragons fallen Powers Hissing thro Air hott Inferus devours. This Warr continues still, Sin Heaven wou'd claime, And right t'Immortall Pleasures doth maintaine. Rebellious Man! Remember well the Odds, Th'unequall combate between Men & Gods. Condemn'd to Flames like Typheus thou must lie, And dieing still must live & never die.	155 160 165
‖ The great dineing Room	Proceed, sweet Muse, into the‖ Room of State Where other Objects thy Attendance waite. High was the Place, magnificently great, Where Kings or Gods might well accept a Treat. Each Part thereof did wonderfull appear, And Each deserv'd the strictest notice here. The Hangings keep those Storys fresh in veiw, That scarce the Pen or Presse cou'd ever doe. The very Windows in this glorious Sphere Are so prodigious Big, so wond'rous clear, That by the Touch alone, not by the Eye. They are distinguish'd from the crystall Skie.	 170 175
+ The Pictures above both sides which the Muse describes & reflects upon as She goes on	But above all, those full proportion'd⁺ Draughts Most pleas'd, & most employ'd my serious Thoughts. What did I see? My old admir'd Friends Drawn out to all th' Advantage Art pretends. Homer's fam'd Hero's One Side doth display, The other Virgil's full as fam'd as They.	 180
	Patroclus here with Teares for License seeks To bring Assistance to the sinking Greeks. Angry Achilles weeps, Briseis Lost, And leaves in Rage the hated Greecian Host. O had He nere return'd! Then Troy had stood, And Xanthus Waves had nere been stain'd with Blood.	185
	Hector was always my dear favorite Care, And therefore fear'd to see Him pass to War. But while He's drag'd att fierce Achilles Wheel	190

A strange remorse I cannot chuse but feel.
    This base unmanly Action lost Him more,
Then all He got with th'Aid of Gods before.   195

    Aeneas was secure from Deaths allarmes
By Gods, & by impenetrable Armes.
But Turnus had not One to save his Life,
But a Week Goddesse, & Joves envious Wife.
And these, in vaine, too late did interpose.   200
The very Fates were listed with his Foes.
Lavinia was engraven in His Heart.
Love & unwearied Courage took his part.
Aided by these, He fires the Trojan Fleet,
Which chang'd to Naides their Master meet.   205
His Prowess next you see young Pallas felt,
Whilst He with joy seiz'd on the fatall Belt.
When there I saw Him fall before his Foe,
Methought t'was pitty that it sho'd be so.
That He had done what ever Man cou'd doe   210
And was the greater Hero of the Two.

+ The withdrawing   The⁺ rest (noe doubt) had rais'd some sweet debate,
Room & Bed Cham-   And all the adjacent Sumptious Rooms of State.
ber adjoyning   Their Hangings wrought with Skillfull Ladys Hands
                    The stately Bed, which wonder too commands;   215
                    Whole Walls of Crystall Mirrors, where you'l find
                    New Rooms, & other company behind.
                    These had been veiw'd with far more curious Eyes,
+ The Ceder &   Had not my Guid pass'd to both⁺ Galleries.
the other Gallery
hang'd full of   Scenes most delightfull, fitt for Recreation   220
the Pictures of   And what's more Manly far, for Contemplation.
their Ancesters   They are thro-out with finest Peices fill'd.
                    Drawn by some Angell, or by one as skill'd.
                    Or else they'd not such admiration give,
                    Nor seem (as Artists own) to think & live.   225
                    "O Sacred Power of the Painters Art!
                    "That can both Colour Air & Shape impart.
                    "That can raise former Hero's from the Grave,
                    "And their Externall Part from sickness save.
                    "Keep & perpetuate their Looks & Meen,   230
                    "And reproduce Them on this Mortall Scene.
                    "Painters to Poets by the Learn'd are joyn'd.
                    "Those draw the Face of Man, but these his mind.
                    "Each of them doth the Power of Death controul,
                    "Those represent the Body, These the Soul.   235
                    Thus all their Ancestors in state appear,

And seem Immortall when once placed here.
Here the fam'd Line their former charmes pertake.
And still a glorious Constellation make.
And when our Starrs are added to this Sphere,   240
T'will surely then the milkey way appear.

Urg'd on with ardent Zeal I had said more
But that my Eyes, & Feet pursu'd the Door.
Which led me down the Stairs, & let me see
+ The Cloysters   +The old remaines of ancient Piety.   245

A Fountaine do's the middle part containe
And Art it's Rivall Nature truely feigne
I had the Idea of the Muses Seat,
And of an Academic sweet retreat.
Of that Religion too, that is profest.   250
The very Walls themselves will speak the rest
Tho not in letter, yet in equall worth,
Painters as Books can History sett forth.
In apt Ideas never could there be
ll The Muse   ‖A livelier Draught of sacred History.   255
referrs to the
History of our   "'Divine, Immence unimitable Love!
Saviours Life &   "Thou dost (cry'd I) my Zeal & pitty move.
Passion painted   "How lively Art presents thee to my veiw!
on the walls of   "Thy Life & Suff'rings seem perform'd anew.
the Cloysters   "Lo here thy great Humilitys display'd,   260
                   "And here the God of nature's mortall made.
                   "How Innocent & charmeing do'st thou rest
                   "An Infant att thy holy Mothers Breast!
                   "So lively by the Skillfull Artist done,
                   "I'm ready to adore with Simeon.   265
                   "Wonder Surrounds me still! Here I behold
                   "Thy Selfe imploy'd with wonders manifold.
                   "To thee the Poor, To thee the Lame & Blind
                   "Adoreing come, & quick Assistance find.
                   "And here againe I cast my weeping Eye,   270
                   "And see thee in thy bitter Agony!
                   "Oh how thy dear, Thy precious purple Gore
                   "Falls down like Tears from every weeping Pore!
                   "And here my tortur'd Soul is rack'd to see
                   "The craggy steep Ascent of Calverye,   275
                   "And thou expanded on the Cursed Tree.
                   "Att this amazeing Prospect I begin
                   "To dread the fatall dire effects of Sin.
                   "But here my fears are past, Thou mounts to Bliss;
                   "Hence Greif is turn'd to Joy, & Sorrow banish'd is.   280

	When thus these sacred Paintings had posses'd	
	The uttmost Limits of my Thoughtfull Breast;	
+ The Chapel	I heard a+ Choire with grave Composure sing	
	Celestiall Anthems to our heavenly King.	
	Att first I thought it Paradice had been,	285
	And instantly its Glorys sho'd have seen.	
	Nor was I much deceiv'd. The Type it prov'd	
	Of Heaven, & shou'd as Heaven be us'd & lov'd.	
	The noble Owner, & his numerous Traine	
	By Prayers were rendering Tribute back againe	290
	To Him that all bestows; By Prayers too	
	Such is his Sense of God, & Such He thought his due.	
	The Service ended as I reach'd the Dore	
	And I my thoughts imployed as before.	

    The Cloysters leads you to the House of Prayer,   295
Fills you with Hevenly thoughts, with Love & Fear,
Fitt Introduction sure, A proper way,
We ought to meditate before we pray.
No gaudy Pagentry of Rome is there,
Pictures to steal our Eyes, & spoile our Prayer.   300
But all compleatly decent, fitt to be
An House, not made for Pomp, but Piety.
But what my utmost Admiration rais'd,
Can't be enough by Men or Angells prais'd,
T'was Now __ In these Vile times, erected new.   305
But what won't Greatness joyn'd with vertue doe.
T'will stem the vicious Torrent of the Age;
And in the Cause of God without restraint engage.
T'will dare be good, & good Example show,
To Kings, If they will Learn, & subjects too below.   310
Tis this the noble Founder here has done
His Acts all shine, but this outshines the Sun.
This seeming Flight & Hyperbolic strain
I did or was prepareing to maintaine. ---

	When lo my Guide directed on, whilst I	315
	Suppos'd no other Objects cou'd be nigh —	
	That might deserve a Thought or please my Eye.	
	But soon the supposition prov'd untrue,	
+ The Garden	When the delightfull+ Garden past my veiw.	
	Surely it might with Eden's well compare,	320
	And Eve in Innocence be Mistress There.	
	She'd want no walks nor solitary Bowers,	
	But live as pleas'd as then, besett with Flowers.	
	Yes, & more pleas'd by far (If it can be)	
	No Serpents there, nor yet forbidden Tree.	325

The very Maze it selfe These Truths might prove,
Since it inspires with Poetry & Love,
A Bliss not much unlike the Joys above. . . .
So much inspires you'd think the Tunefull nine
Had set each Branch, whilst Cupid drew the line.   330
T'was there I wish'd to stay, but wish'd in vaine
For instantly the Scene was chang'd againe.
T'was chang'd to that delightfull Walk, where We
At first this Glorious Edifice did see.

    T'was there the Muse her long keept silence broke,   335
But words so full of Mystery She spoke,
I cou'd not comprehend; but stood to see
With expectation what th' Event wou'd be.

+ The Genius of   When straite appear'd a⁺ venerable Sire,
the Place   Who rais'd my thoughts with admiration higher.   340
Upon his ancient hoary Head was sett
A glittering enamell'd Coronett.
A rich imbroder'd velvett Robe He wore,
Imbossed well with Gold, & wrought all ore
With stately Ash, all green, that seem'd to grow   345
With Beach, & Oak, & humble Shrubs below.
Beneath the horned Herd in numbers lay
To shun (as (Nature taught) the Scorching Day.
Whilst others fedd void of the usuall fears,
Of Dogs pursuits, or of the Hunters snares.   350
So nat'rally that as He nearer drew
I thought they were not figur'd out, but true.
But ere my thoughts had ended this dispute
The Reverend Form did thus the Muse salute.

"Harmonious Goddess, see at thy desire   355
"I from my secret dwelling Place retire.
"I heard thee powerfully invoke my Name,
"To know whats thy commands I hither came.

    To whom the Muse (after Obeisance made)
In Tunefull Words, & well adapted said.   360

    "Charm'd with the Beautys of this Lovely Seat,
"And all thats rich, Majesticall, & Great,
"I aske the favour fully to relate
("For long Thou hast within these Mansions sate)
"Who rais'd this famous Structure, First possest,   365
"And why so often Chang'd? Thou know'st the rest.

    Att which He thus began. This House you see
Was rais'd & given for Works of Piety.

A. Dom. 1260.	When Love divine ran thro the noblest Blood,	
	Nor yet Religion so corrupted stood.	370
	Ambition had not yet possest the Gown,	
	Nor rais'd, so high as now, the Triple Crown.	
: Edmund Earle of Cornwall Son to Richard king of the Romans	Great ᛭ Cornwells Gift — whose pure transcendent Mind The viler Part of Greatness still declin'd. Not for himselfe a Coronett He wore, But for well plac'd Devotion, & the Poor.	375
:The Bonehomes of Ashridge — Brothers of the Order of St Austin	He made devoted ᛭ Brotherhood his Heir; Thus did he dye & thus to Heaven repair.	
	These in true sanctity & holy Love,	
	Were one below, as Saints are one above.	380
	Long did They live to God & vice disown,	
	And pray'd for others Good, as for their own.	
	But when corrupted grew the Fountaine Head,	
	The Poyson its Contagion quickly Spread,	
	Thro all the Parts of this fam'd Rivolett.	385
	And then its Purity declin'd, & after Sett.	
	The Great Jehovah to revenge the wrong	
	These fall'n degenerate Brothers had so long,	
	And bassely done to Him, & Piety,	
+ The dissolution of Abbys in King H. 8 Reigne &c	Gave out a just, but ruinous Decree. + Then did their Lands & Houses pass away To those who'd use Them better far then They. Tho (like a Stream when Winds contrary blow, Which in its nat'rall Course serenely flow)	390
	T'was restless, & disturb'd, impatient still	395
	Under each Masters various Powerfull will,	
+ Tho: Egerton Lord Chancellor of England	Till⁺ Egerton arose. __ But then became Calme as before, & as before the same.	
	This mighty Man (who quickley rose so high	
	By Learneing, Goodness, Justice, Equity)	400
	Purchas'd this Seat; nor was it more then due,	
	And had possession, & just Title too.	
: John Earle of Bridgwater the first Earle of that name	His ᛭ Son as Heir of his great Fathers worth, Had Honour added too Illustrious Birth. Still did He in a Sphere exalted move, A Monarchs Dareling, & the Peoples Love.	405
+ He was Lord president of Wales	And as a signe of both He had a⁺ Trust Wherein He shew'd himselfe both great & Just. But t'was not long ere Clouds did first Arise	
	Then with thick darkness overspread the Skies.	410
	Schism in Church, & faction in the state	

	Did ruine bring, & Sorrows cumulate.	
	The best of Men & Kings laid down his sacred Head.	
	The truest Church on Earth was bleeding left for dead.	
x He died 1649	Englands Rebellion did his joys abate,	415
1649 in the	He,ˣ old, gave up his willing life to fate.	
70th' year of		
his Age	But not before his⁺ Son so well had known	
+ John Earle of	To raise his Country Honours, & his own.	
Bridgwater the	For by Paternall care He first was taught,	
2d Earle of that	Ev'n all that StatesMen knew, or Nobles ought.	420
name	He soon the depth of Learneing did attaine,	
	And seem'd to have (nor is't a Poets Strain)	
	The universall system in his Brain.	
	He rose all Loyall, & all Loyall Sett.	
	Both Piety & Prudence in Him mett.	425
	And for's Devotion. cou'd I but aspire	
	To sett it forth with such Seraphic Fire	
	As He perform'd it. I shou'd never fade,	
	But as Immortall as himselfe be made.	
	Methinks I see Him, makeing no account	430
: To the Church of	Of Humane Splendour, pass to Horebs Mount.	
Little Gaddesden	As Moses did, & garded still by none,	
every 14th day of	But Innocence, & by Himselfe alone.	
the Month on	See how with Lift up Hands & Heart, He bows	
which his Lady died	Confesses all his Sins, renews his vows.	435
	With Job He pleads for his whole family.	
	Thus here He did begin Eternity.	
‖ Elizabeth his Lady	Near in that Church doth His lov'd ‖Consort rest.	
Late Countess of	Her Soul in Heaven, Her Immage in his Breast.	
Bridgewater	In Natures gifts She did all far excell,	
	And in all Graces had no Parrallell.	440
: The Inscription on	Tho Her Memorialls great, yet words by far	
her Tombe over	Too Scanty are to speak Her Character.	
the Vault in	So when the Objects raised out of Sight	
that Church	We are not able to describe the flight.	445
	So when the Sun shines bright, we quickly find	
	That the bold Gazers Eyes are soon struck blind.	
	She was His Life, No Joys He had beside.	
	To live with Her He liv'd, to follow Her He dy'd.	
	He dy'd _____	
	_____ But yet (sweet Goddess) now forbeare	450
	To shed for His Retreat one pittieing Tear.	
+ John the 3d	Since He's not gone, but still Surviveing Here	
Earle of—	He's still surviveing in his Noble⁺ Son,	
Bridgwater at	Who well sett out ere th' others Race was run.	

present alive	And now so strictly do's His Steps pursue,	455
	He must oretake, & even surpass Him too.	
	He knows both Things & Men as well as Books:	
	And casts the noblest Rays where e're He Looks.	
	All that the wise of truest worth esteem	
	Without the lest Alloy, appears in Him.	460
	Nay! Oft I've thought the vertues of the whole	
	Transcendent Line, were Centre'd in His Soul.	
	His former Patience, & submissive will	
	(Which rais'd Men's wonder, & do's Angells still)	
	Under the worst Ecclips that Heaven 'ere knew,	465
	Or Man withstood, this Character makes true.	
	So doth his noble Deeds, & well plac'd good,	
	Er'e since his Sun in its meridian stood.	
	Exactest Justice is his cheifest care;	
	Each Subjects property in Peace & War.	470
	Divine Astrea, banished from hence,	
	Recal'd by Him doth Equity dispence.	
	The public Good employs his thoughtfull Head,	
	Nor can He be by Bus'ness wearied.	
: He is the first Comissioner of the Admiralty	Integrity has made Him rule the Seas,	475
	Govern the watry Realms, & as He please	
	The Ships direct, & Mariners appease	
	Nay more __ Integrity has made Him stand	
: He is also one of the Lords Justices of England during his Majesty aboad beyond seas &c.	Amongst the Petty Kings, who now command	
	And manage Regall Power, in this Land.	480
	Till Conquer'ing William doth in triumph come,	
	Haveing secur'd the Peace of Christendom.	
: The present Countess of Bridgewater Daughter to the Late Duke of Boulton	Indeed tis fitt He thus adorn'd sho'd be,	
	None less (tho yet more noble born) then He	
	Cou'd have obtain'd (what Monarchs might admire	485
	And wish in vaine) The sacred nuptiall Fire,	
	And wond'rous Love of that all conquering Dame	
	Who from the loyns of mighty Boulton came.	
	This noble Pair are so much one in Love,	
	And all the Married Graces from above,	490
	That for their union (One may say indeed)	
	When Heaven made One the other was decreed.	
	That Time its selfe the Charmes sho'd never end,	
	That did her youthfull bloomeing years attend.	
	T'was surely so decreed! __ for still appears	495
	(The riseing Sun The glory of the Spheres)	
	Her virgin-matchless Beauty, tho she be	
	The Mother of a glorious Progenie;	
	And all for nobler ends then Sight's design'd.	

	It figures out the Beautys of the Mind.	500
	From whence (If skill were not extreemly faint)	
	I cou'd draw out a most accomplish'd Saint.	
	Shes pious, not precise, no Bigott, yet unfeign'd.	
	She dayly merits, tho her Faith's unstain'd.	
	And here I own I sho'd have Angells Sight	505
	Rightly to view this pure transcendent Light.	
	Then Pardon If too near Approach I shun.	
	Tis by its Rays we best describe the Sun.	
+ My Lord Brackley the Eldest : probably — the Muse — foretells that he will be Lord Justice of the Forests.	And among these the auspicious riseing+ Peer Deserves my first Address, & knowledg here. Tis He, Tis He, that is design'd to Reigne Ore ev'ry Stately Wood & ev'ry Plain Within this Spacious Realm; & will become The Potent Earle in his great Fathers Room. When He in triumph do's ascend the Skyes, His Son (as high as Mortall can) will rise. And ti's but fitt He sho'd; If merit be Rewarded as He ought, it must be He. For this a basis is so firmly laid, Ti's even Impossible to be betray'd By any basse Ignoble Act; The Sun May sooner from its well fixt Center run; Then He goe back that has so well begun. His Modesty (a Gift divinely good, Now little known, less throly understood) And humble Speech, hereafter will dispence Discourse most fluent, & profoundest sense. His sweet ingageing temper do's foretell He'l conquer, & all Conquests soon excell. Those may Mens Bodys possibly subdue; He will their Hearts, & yet preserve them too. For this with native Knowledge tis design'd, And forreigne too, to cultivate his Mind. For this to furthi'st Countrys He doth roam, And with their Spoils att last He will come home. Thus will His highten'd Virtues quickly show How great He'l be Above, as well as here below.	510 515 520 525 530 535
+ Mr William.	The+ second Son deserves the same esteems; He'l be no otherwise then what He seems. Serious as Age, Active as youth we find; And more to things of Men, then those of Boys inclin'd. In time He'l be a Patriot, & pursue What e're true Principles invite Him to.	540

: Mr Henry	Then for the third; I wou'd have Eaton say	
	How pregnant are his Parts, how quick & Gay.	545
	What mighty Hopes we may Conceive of Him	
	Who drinks so soon of Learneings Sacred Stream.	
: Mr John	The fourth, Tho young, already is thought fitt	
	To be Companion (& do's meritt it)	
: His Highnesse	To the Apparent Heir of Brittans Crown.	550
the Duke of	A Prince by birth, more by acquir'd renown.	
Glocester	Whose Sense in Humane Things, & Things divine,	
	Do's even beyond the reach of Manhood shine.	
	And is indeed to such Perfections come,	
	He's fitt to leade abroad, & rule att Home.	555
	What then to our young Hero's due, or shall,	
	Who Copys from this great Originall.	
	What will He be e're halfe his Race is run?	
	Att lest the primar Star to this Resplendent Sun.	
: Mr Charles	: The youngest last, in Age th'o but a Child,	560
the youngest	May yet a perfect Man in sense be Stil'd.	
Son	He knows, & speaks so well, it do's appear	
	That without objects his Idea's are.	
	Nor that his knowledge comes by slow degrees,	
	Or just as He reflects, or as He Sees.	565
	But has it all innate, & wants alone	
	Corporeall Pow'r to make it fully known.	
+ about	"Haile wonderous Childe! Thou dost att once confute,	
knowledge -	"And silence too, our Sages warme+ dispute.	
whether	"Those Tenents that before seem'd all untrue,	570
naturall &	"Att lest disputed were, are clear'd by you.	
innate or by	"It must be so. — you else nere cou'd have been	
reflection &c	"So knowing, yet so little tought, or seen.	
	"Go on — & be our English Stagirite,	
	"Men's false Conceptions change, maintain the right.	575
	"By Study prove what Nature do's declare,	
	"And be our wonder still, as now you are!	
+ the Lady	+ A charmeing Nymph is next. __ At which the Muse	
Mary the	Some unknown words, that silenc'd Him, did use.	
Eldest	But yet to me such Pow'r They did Impart,	580
Daughter	Methought She shott Herselfe into my Heart.	
& Patronesse	Whilst I all rapture, & Inspir'd said —	
of this Poem	"This mighty Task be mine. __ Haile lovely Maid!	
	"Haile! You whom Blushes doe as much adorn,	
	"As Art do's Nature, or the Sun the Morn.	585
	"Whose Carriage sweet, & Disposition's so;	
	"And do's command all Eyes, all Hearts below!	
	Att which I fail'd, or durst not higher Sore.	

The Goddess thus _____
"Admir'd Maria, I your Aid Implore,   590
"Or else this pleasing visionary Scene
"Will vanish soon like some abortive Dream.
"Your Patronage will animate much more
"Then all the Heliconion Nymphs before.
"Their aid preserves no Works from Destinie;   595
"But this by yours, Immortal, as your selfe wille be.
   Flush'd with these Hopes, This kind Auspicious Fate,
I'l try the mystic sequell to relate.
   After a soft, but short melodious straine
Of Music heard, the Sage went on againe.   600
   I well commend your Care, & Zeal to raise
A Trophy to the fam'd Marias Prayse.
And yet my Off'rings due. __ Oft have I seen
How blest the Sight! How ravishing t'has been!
Her pass along like some triumphing Queen,   605
Thro these fam'd Woods, as well to Hunt the Deer,
As take her Solitary foot walks Here.
Att whose Approach the Birds in Consort sing,
And Woods expect an Everlasting Spring.
The horned Beasts o'rejoy'd forsake their shade, 610
And Gaze, as if she was to be obey'd.
Oft have I heard the Sylvan Goddess prays'd;
How Men admir'd, & Temples to her rais'd,
The Beast admire here, but Men adore,
Diana much deserv'd, Maria more.   615

+ The Lady   The fair⁺ Eliza last my thoughts employ,
Elizabeth   And fills me with unknown Extatic Joy.
the youngest It must be so — When e're such Witt & Sense
Daughter   Appears, adorn'd with so much Innocence!
Her pretty Modest Looks, & sweet address,   620
Is much beyond an Artist's Skill t'express.
In ev'ry Thing She has her years surpast.
She's now admir'd, but will b' ador'd att last.
Maria's fam'd Perfections reigne alone,
The world has yet no equall ever known;   625
Eliza's but in Bloom, yet do's surprize;
But when she do's to Her Meridian rise,
T'will surely then be said within one Sphere
Two Suns without a Paradox appear. ---

   Thus ends my Taske __ But say who can exell, 630
Say (bright Celestiall Nymph For thou canst tell)
If there be any such, say who can be
More pleas'd (or has more reason for 't) then me!

Indeed if there's a Paradise below,
Tis here, & I it's uttmost Pleasures know. 635
Long have I been its true Domestic Gard,
And liv'd in full Content as a Reward;
And wou'd till this Expanded Frame dissolves,
And Nature to its ancient Heap devolves.
Thus long I'd live under this Noble Race; 640
Others may higher mount, none find so blest a Place.

   Thus ceas'd the Sage __ And then my sacred Guide
Smiling in this Prophetic Strain reply'd.
   Yes now I see! Heaven has the mystic State
Of things to come reveal'd, reveal'd the Fate, 645
The prosperous Fate, of this delightfull Pile!
I see ten thousand Blessings on it Smile,
Ten thousand thousand years (If time Commands
So long duration to the whole) it stands.
I see from hence a Race of Hero's come, 650
A numerous Race! Behold how Christendome
Dreads, & admires their brave diffusive Soul!
How Fame transmitts their Acts from Pole to Pole!
I see great Brittan free from all Alarm's
Its Monarchs Great, still Conqu'ring by their Armes, 655
The Church & state in lasting union Joyne;
Religion by their Care from Ages shine.

ll. The Muse takes her leave of the Genius

‖ Then as for you thrice Happy Reverend Sire,
Alls given to you, you have, or can desire.
Here Crown'd with Joy, you'l live Just as before, 660
Till Heavenly Blessings cease, & Times no more,
These secrets are by Inspiration made,
Retire in Peace, retire into thy Shade.
   He laught, & then harmonious Strains were heard,
Just like to those Above, so dissapeard. 665

   Then did, we in the shineing Chariot mount,
And of the Earth below make no account.
Ascending upwards instantly we were,
Quicker then Thought, hirl'd thro the yeilding Air,
And soon in wond'rous Pomp we did orelight, 670
Where first I had this visionary Sight.
She sett me down __ But whilst I did prepare
Some gratefull Speech. — She vanish'd into Air.
Where full of wonder & content I sate,
And on the vision thus did ruminate. 675

   What mean the Fates? & why all this to me
A worthless Thing? Tis strange that Destiny

       Sho'd not assigne some of Apollo's Heirs,
       Sublime in Thought, & vacant too from Cares
       To see as I & sing this glorious Seat!   680
       T'woulde be in verse, as in it selfe compleat!
       And yet the Honours greater still I own;
       I felt the Power to me before unknown.

+ Samuell   So the devoted⁺ Youth by Heaven was chose.
the Prophet   Before the learn'd, & aged, to disclose   685
       Things past, & Things to come! — And may my Theme,
       Dear Ashridge, flowrish like Jerusalem.
       May it like that ascend, like that be great,
       And share in all Things, But its sinking state.

           The End

           [pp. 1–25]

 Title. The Vision ... Com Bucks] The Vision *is separated from* A Poeticall ... Com Bucks *by the top marginal rule.* The Vision *subsequently appears as the running head in the top margin on pp. 2–25*
 19. Island] *inserted*
 32. Magestic] *Travitsky* Majestic
 33. Hand] *inserted*
 35. perciveing] *Travitsky* perceiveing
 64. growndwork] *Travitsky* grownd work
 81 *(marginal note).* The] *conjectural reading;* Th *not visible in the facsimile*
 82. fed] *MS* feed
 85. his] *superimposed on* their
 90. compact] *superimposed on illegible word, possibly* exact
 110. even] *inserted*
 119. confine] *first* n *inserted*
 138. Goddess] *MS* Goddest
 178 *(marginal note).* above] *inserted, replacing* above *deleted*
 179. most] *inserted*
 193. strange] *MS* strang
 194. Action] *MS* Ation
 205. Master] *abbreviated* Mʳ
 207. Whilst] *Travitsky* Whilest
 208. When] *replacing* Then; W *superimposed on* T
his] *inserted*
 219 *(marginal note).* Ceder] *Travitsky* Cedar
 221. And] *superimposed on* But
 244. Stairs] *MS* Star's
 247. Nature] *inserted*
 258. lively] *replacing* lovely; i *superimposed on* o
 273. weeping] *inserted*
 288. as Heaven,] *inserted*
 290. were] *superimposed on* was
 311. this] *superimposed on* the
 321. Mistress] *The symbol* ⸬ *is written before* Mistress *but there is no corresponding marginal note*

332. Scene] *replacing* Scent; *final* e *superimposed on* t
was] *inserted*
338. th'] ' *superimposed on* e
Event] E *superimposed on* e
348. the] *inserted*
349. fedd] *superimposed on* feeding
void] *inserted*
361. this] *Travitsky* thy
365. Structure,] *comma after* Structure *superimposed on* ?
369. ran] *MS* run
373. Cornwells] *Travitsky* Cornwalls
410. Then] *replacing* That; en *superimposed on* at
420. Ev'n] ' *superimposed on* e
448. Life,] *inserted*
471. Astrea] *replacing* Astra; e *superimposed on* a
475–7 *(marginal note)*. He is the . . . Admiralty] *written in a second hand*
476. Realms, & as] *Travitsky* Realms as
479–82 *(marginal note)*. He is also . . . seas &c.] *written in a second hand*
during] *MS* dure-
481. triumph] *Travitsky* ttriumph
493. sho'd] *replacing* who'd; s *superimposed on* w
501. extreemly] *first* e *underlined in MS*
505. Angells] *superimposed on* Sight
506. this] *MS* this this
526. And] *MS* An
532. tis] *Travitsky* 'tis
534. furthi'st] *replacing* furthiest; e *deleted. Travitsky* farthi'st
538. second] *inserted*
550. Apparent] *inserted in second hand, replacing* presumptious *deleted*
558. Race is run] ce, s, *and* u *underlined in MS*
559. Resplendent] *final* e *underlined in MS*
567. Pow'r] ' *superimposed on* e
573. tought] *Travitsky* taught
580. Pow'r] ' *superimposed on* e
589. thus] *four or five horizontal lines after* thus
595. Works] W *superimposed on* D
603. Off'rings] ' *superimposed on* e
655. Conqu'ring] ' *superimposed on* e
664. were] *MS* we're; *Travitsky* W'ere
668. instantly] *MS* instanly
677. strange] *MS* strang
680. Seat!] ! *superimposed on* ?; *Travitsky* Seat?
681. T'woulde] *Travitsky* T'would
684. Youth] replacing Yourth; th *superimposed on* rth
690. The End] *replacing* The End. *deleted; followed by flourish with flower*

The following Copy Burlesq'd

Can
~~Coulde~~ Sacharissa ~~can~~ then forsake
Her Coffee Tea and Chocolate
And leave us here to sigh and grone
And Puffe and frett for her return
Come Cherry brandy ease the smart
That gripes and treuges thus my heart

How cou'd she now at this time leave us
To read and study Epictetus
When good Bartholmee so near was
Sure she forgot sweet Punchenello
That prity little dapper fellow
Thate us'd to court and kiss a c'eek
And breath his Passion in a squeek
Or else she takes all ways to vex it
That now unkind she makes her exit
confines her self to countrey village
Where nothing's seen but Plow and Tillage
Yet see her there at Wakes advancing
The Fiddles play and straight to dancing
And in a Morriss numbly figing
Till constable with face forbiding
Quite ends the sport then home they flye
Like frighten'd Rats when catt is coye

PLATE 9 Octavia Walsh, Bodleian Library MS Eng. poet. e. 31, fol. 161v

14

Octavia Walsh's verse miscellany

Bodleian Library MS Eng. poet. e. 31

Octavia Walsh's verse miscellany is a small vellum-bound volume, 165 leaves in length. Despite some variations in the handwriting, it is likely that all the poetic contents of the manuscript are in her own hand (see plate 9). The volume has been reversed and written in from both ends, with fols 33–121 left blank. The lower cover bears an inscription which the Bodleian *Summary Catalogue* suggests may read 'Octavia Walsh her book 1694' (II: 711). The only other date in the volume occurs in an enigmatic note on fol. 1v: 'Monday January the 22 1705. The children were sent to school.' There is a pen-and-wash portrait of the poet herself—identified in a later hand as 'Mrs Octavia Walsh sister to William Walsh Esq. of Abberley Lodge in the County of Worcester'—on fol. 3r; this whole leaf is a later addition to the manuscript.

Apart from preliminaries (including three recipes, transcribed in another later hand), Octavia Walsh's manuscript consists entirely of poetry. Most of her poems are on spiritual or moral subjects, including several pastorals. However, the collection also includes several philosophical and satirical items, as well as an unfinished narrative poem set in Persia, based on a story from Xenophon's *Cyropaedia*. All but one of the poems in the front section of the manuscript are on religious subjects, while, at the back, spiritual poetry is interspersed with lighter and more secular verse. Most of the poems are fair copies with a few corrections, but a few, notably the Persian narrative poem, have been extensively reworked and corrected. It seems likely that Octavia Walsh's literary practice was influenced by her brother, William, who favoured similar poetic genres. There are numerous, if minor, verbal similarities between the Walshes' poems, and the possibility that at least some of the poems in Octavia's manuscript may in fact have been William's composition cannot be altogether discounted. However, all the poems included here were accepted as Octavia's work in a second extant manuscript of her poetry, copied after her death at the instigation of her nephew, William Bromley. The present location of this second manuscript is unknown, but a microfilm copy is held at the British Library (RP 343).

None of Octavia Walsh's poems was published in her lifetime. However, in 1719 a few of her religious lyrics were published in the collection *Poems upon divine and moral subjects. by Dr. Patrick . . . and other . . . hands.* No connection between any of the Walsh family and Simon Patrick, Bishop of Ely, is known, although William Walsh had political links with the dedicatee of the Patrick volume, William Talbot, Bishop of Salisbury. One of Octavia Walsh's poems, 'At length my soul the fatal union finds', is reproduced in Lonsdale (1989).

BIOGRAPHICAL NOTE

Octavia Walsh (1676–1706) was the daughter of Joseph and Elizabeth Walsh of Abberley House, Worcestershire. Her father, Joseph Walsh, fought on the royalist side in the Civil Wars, and, though deprived of his estate in the early 1650s, successfully petitioned for its return after the Restoration. Her mother, born Elizabeth Palmes, belonged to a distinguished Yorkshire family. Octavia was probably the youngest of eight children known to have been born to Joseph and Elizabeth in the 1660s and 1670s. Her elder siblings included William, a distinguished poet, critic and politician, and Anne, who married Francis Bromley, and inherited Abberley after William's death in 1708 (Nash 1781–82, I: 2–3, *VCH Worcester*, 4: 220–1).

Little is known about Octavia Walsh's life. Her poetry testifies to a thoughtful interest in religion, with a distinct preference for moderation. Her funeral elegy on an unnamed clergyman praises his ability to reconcile the 'jarring Partys' of faith and reason, and to avoid the rival extremes of atheism and superstition (fols 12v–13r). Several poems praise the virtues of country retirement over the snares of city life. Less solemn interests are evinced by her satirical poems, including the mildly scatological 'To Urania', and 'To Mrs T', in which she mocks the 'Eternall nonsense' of the Sternhold and Hopkins psalter. It is not known whether she ever travelled outside Worcestershire; her references to city life, fashions and institutions may depend on information received from her brother. She died of smallpox in 1706, unmarried, and was buried on 12 October in Worcester Cathedral. Since the last poem in the reversed section of her manuscript, 'The Princely Persian lead his warlike Host' (fols 131–122 rev.)—by far the longest poem in the collection—is evidently unfinished, it is likely that death interrupted her work on the miscellany.

Through her brother, Octavia Walsh had connections with many of the most important politicians and literary men of the late seventeenth and early eighteenth centuries. William Walsh, as MP for Worcestershire between 1698 and 1705, and for Richmond, Yorkshire, in 1705, had close political links with two of the leading statesmen of the 1690s and early 1700s: John Lord Somers and the Duke of Shrewsbury (Freeman 1934, 1948). He also belonged to the prestigious Whig society the Kit Cat Club, whose members included leading writers such as Addison, Steele, Prior, Congreve and Vanburgh. His literary correspondents, meanwhile, included Dryden, Wycherley and Pope. While there is no evidence that Octavia Walsh met any of her brother's literary friends, it is plausible to suppose that she would have known of their work through him. Her own poetry testifies to an admiration of Waller, Cowley and Horace, and a familiarity with Stoic thinkers such as Epictetus.

Bibliography:
Lonsdale (1989), Patrick *et al.* (1719)
Freeman (1934, 1948), Nash (1781–82: I), *Summary Catalogue*, *VCH Worcester* (3)

GW

'O let our Praise ascend the Skyes'

    O let our Praise ascend the Skyes
    from Heav'n and Earth its accents rise
In Glory to Heav'ns mighty King
    O let our Praise his courts ascend
    The vaulted Skyes in sunder rend   5
And fall before that never failing spring

    That Pow're that being did bestow
    On Heav'n above and earth below
And what the ocean hydes
    That fix'd the Stars in yeilding Air   10
    And told the raging Sea how far
It might advance its Tydes

    Whose word alone mankind did frame
    Whose word alone destroys the same
And turns again to Clay   15
    Whose word disjoyns the trembling Earth
    And gives mankind a second Birth
To endles pain or Joy

    In mee his Glory he display'd
    The creature that his hand has made   20
He's pleas'd his might to show
    In making me feirce terrors tast
    In Earthly Happines first plac't
To make my fall more lowe

    When Sunk in Anguish and dispair   25
    He Show'd a Tender fathers care
Who erring Sons correct
    And tho somtimes he hid his face
    Deny'd his never failling grace
He did me not reject   30

    But Show'd me plain when life he lent
    It was not to be Idely spent
In Sublunery Joyes
    But that towards Heav'n I bend my mind
    There never failing pleasures find   35
That know of no alloyes

    What Lover show'd such gentle Art
    In gaining of an equal Heart
As this great King for mine
    His Rival first he did remove   40
    Then to revive my Deaden'd love
Hee tryes by ways Devine

    O Sacred Lord tho Earth denyes
    To my poor life its due supplyes
And Heav'n in anger lowers   45
    Tho o'er my Head its thunder breaks
    The ground convulsive terrorrs shakes
And raging flame devours

    Tho mountains to high Heav'n aspire
    In furious flames of Liquid fire   50
And Hell displayes its woes
    Tho the wyde ocean feels its Pow'rs
    And Raging flames its waves devours
And all its depths disclose

    Yet in thy mercy still secure   55
    These stormes with patience I'll endure
And with its fury cope
    Its Dreadfull force may move my fear
    But ne'er shall make me once dispair
Or loose in thee my hope   60

    One look of thine can these dispell
    Enchain the furies that rebell
The blessed from 'em save
    Or else thou can'st their Souls remove
    To thy eternal Realms above   65
And Tryumph o'er the Grave

                                              [fols 8r–9r]

---

10. fix'd] *inserted, replacing* Set *deleted*
yeilding] *inserted, replacing* liquid *deleted*
13. word alone] *replacing* only word; alone *inserted,* only *deleted*
18. endles] *inserted, replacing* Anxious *deleted*
22. feirce terrors] *inserted, replacing* vain pleasure *deleted*
38. equal] *inserted, replacing* Earthly *deleted*
46–7. *Deleted text* Convention fears the *between these lines*
55. thy] *inserted, replacing* his *deleted*
57. And with . . . cope] *inserted in pencil, replacing* And in my maker hope *deleted*
60. Or loose . . . hope] *added below in pencil, replacing* In thee my Stay and prop *deleted*

'Fond flattring world thou ne'er shalt boast'

    Fond flattring world thou ne'er shalt boast
        a conquest o'er me more
    Since what in thy persuit I lost
        kind solitudes restore

    Foll'wing those Joyes that folly bring   5
        and thy alluring Charms

I from the Viper drew his sting
  and hug'd him in my arms

My reason long in chains was led
  like an imprison'd slave   10
Or as a wreach that long was dead
  no liberty cou'd have

without my reason I enjoy'd
  all thy weak Pow'r cou'd bring
which show'd thy own was not destroy'd   15
  but knew the useles thing

(for with those slaves that follow thee
  & thy enjoyments charm
Strong reasons force can ne'er agree
  but thy weak Power disarm)   20

Kind Solitude brought in its Power
  & show'd thy gilded bait
I like a wreach got safe to shore
  see what misfortunes wait

Upon the sea where once I saild   25
  & as I thought from harme
my captiv'd reason ne'er bewaild
  nor saw the coming storm

but now within this little Creek
  where I at anchor ride   30
I view the Rocks that others split
  & scorn the wind & tide

Resolving ne'er again to trust
  the treacherous ocean more
but here will mix my humble Dust   35
  with thine o happy shore

                    [fols 164r-163v (rev.)]

---

5. bring] *altered from* brings; s *deleted*
7. sting] *altered from* stings; s *deleted*
13. enjoy'd] *followed by* all thy *deleted*

The following Copy Burlesq'd

Can Sacharissa then forsake
Her Coffee Tea and Chocolate
And leave us here to sigh and Grone
And Puffe and frett for her return

Come Cherry brandy ease the smart 5
That Gripes and twinges thus my heart
   How cou'd she now at this time leave us
To read and study Epictetus
When good Bartholemee so near was
Sure she's forgot sweet Punchenello 10
That prity little dapper fellow
Thats us'd to court and kiss a cheek
And breath his Passion in a squeek
Or else she takes all ways to vex it
That now unkind she makes her exit 15
Confines her self to country village
Where nothing's seen but Plow and Tillage
Yet see her there at Wakes advancing
The Fiddles play and straight to dancing
And in a Morriss nymbly Jiging 20
Till constable with face forbidding
Quite ends the sport then home they flye
Like frighten'd Ratts when Catt dos crye

[fol. 161v (rev.)]

---

1. Can] *inserted, replacing* Since *deleted*
then] *inserted, replacing* can *deleted*

'Could Sacharissa leave the Town'

Could Sacharissa leave the Town
   That daily conquests made
Were not al our hearts her own
   by gentle Love betrayd
Cou'd she chief fav'rite of the Sacred Nine 5
Their Tuneful seat so easily decline

2

Cou'd she the stiff neck'd youths of court
   That Daily homage paid
With all the numerous resort
   Of Witts that sought her aid 10
So calmly quit and bid the world Adieu
Dull Epictetus Morrals to persue

3

But see amongst the Rurall Swains
   Cheif Nymph she dos advance
The Musick ecchos throw the Plains 15
   And Order frames the dance

While Pan and all his Court spectaters are
Pleas'd with a Nymph so Good so Wise so fair
[fol. 161r (rev.)]

---

5. Sacred] *inserted, replacing* tuneful *deleted*

An enquiry into the cause of the miserys of Mankind an Essay

Is it not strange yee Powers that Mortals shoud
Persue their Misery & flye their good
While each for Happiness their Voyage take
To gain that point a teadious Journy make
No pains nor time to compas it they spare   5
And towards one Port they all courses steer
But when put out they diff'rent ways persue
While each dos think he has it in his View
Some fancy it must lye towards Mammons Court
Those to that place with wondrous hast resort   10
This makes the Merchant plow the troubled sea
And Danger court to be from Danger free
For Happiness a wreached life he gains
Instead of Health insufferable pains
His mind the seat where Happiness shou'd rest   15
Is with loud care & weighty grief opprest
The fear of what in time may come to pass
Makes him not tast the present Joy he has
A whisling wind or Rusling in the Trees
Invades his quiet & destroyes his peace   20
A troubled Sea or Pirate will undoe
His present Joy & all his future too.
His fancy that had guided him the way
And made him think there pleasure only lay
Then wracks his mind with what he once might be   25
Wou'd cruel Heaven be but as kind as shee
  For this the Miser hoards up all his store
Makes himself Rich by making others Poore
Hee fancys Happiness consists in wealth
In heaping up his evill gotten pelth   30
But never tasts what Joy from wealth proceeds
Tis closer lock't from his than others needs
How can those trifles e'er delight thy mind
That's more from thee than all the world confin'd
To overreach or gain anothers Land   35
Hee may thy god and thee alike command
Thy Darling Mony then has liberty

And Pluto's may from thee securely flye
Wherein's thy pleasure in what lyes thy Joy
What is the thing that dos thy mind employ   40
If 'tis in using of thy wealth why then
The borrowers are much the Happiest Men
They spend with pleasure what with care & pain
And nightly watching thou dost strive to gain
If in the sight of Gold thy pleasure lyes   45
And all thy Joys thou tak'st in at thy Eyes
Thy Neighbours Gold wou'd yeild as much content
As those vast Sums that in thy Chest are pent
If Joy dos in full bags alone reside
And only from the Poor her graces hide   50
How comes it then that since thou'st gaind thy store
Thou'rt more unhappy than thou wer't before
Pale Meager Care dos in thy Bosom keep
Sworn enemie unto the God of Sleep
Suspicious Jealousy false optick shows   55
And makes thou fancy all thou seest thy foes
Thy foes encreas as thou encreasest store
Thy maners some have made thy fancy more
Since thou hast gaind this mighty wealth thou art
Ten times more wreached than before thou wert   60
Thy Bliss was to one object then confin'd
Which to attain thou strongly bent thy mind
But now thou hast this mighty bliss atain'd
Too well thou seest how little thou hast gaind
Missing it there each thing pretends to have   65
The mighty blessing that thy fancy craves
So that thy want which was in one thing plac't
Is now removed to ev'ry thing thou seest
   Some do at Greatness catch and think to be
Above their neighbours true felicity   70
That wreaches Bliss is to a blast confin'd
It's Self it's Maker and upholder Wind
Men's voices are his Empire and his Rule
The Envious Admiration of a fool
Confine him to a desert there his State   75
Won't bee sufficient to sustain it's weight.
But in the crowd where Malice bears the Sway
And some with Envious Eyes his state Survey
There 'tis it pleases all this mighty Bliss
Is only made by others wreachedness   80
Were there not fools to envy and admire
There wou'd be none that Greatness did desire
'Tis plain his Enemies create his Joy

Those make his Bliss that others bliss destroy
To them alone he dos his pleasure owe 85
No Joy he tasts but what his foes bestowe
Let 'em but calme their envious desires
Then all his mighty Happiness expires
Unhappy wreach who e'er he be that does
In gilded Titles all his Joy repose 90
   Think on Sejanus none more blest than hee
In gaudy titles and a high degree
Greatness and Wealth Submitted to his will
And Trains of Flatterers persued him still
Think on him now of all those Joyes bereft 95
With nothing but remorse of Conscience left
His wealth and friends his dire misfortune flyes
And by his own Ignoble hand he dyes
This mighty man that a few days before
Was happy call'd and awfull terror bore 100
One little Spot of Earth must now contain
And all his Glory in the Grave remain
   Distress and misery the great attend
And in their clutches oft their glorys end
The Man's most wreached that is plac't on high 105
His faults are Obvious to the meanest Eye
Some blame his Pride some his desire of wealth
And all men know him better than himself
While Servile flatterers abuse his Eares
So much that to himself he ne'er appears 110
Before his Vices they a Curtain draw
And only what he pleases is the Law
The wreach grows Proud in hopes h'as conquer'd fate
And on a Pinacle he Struts in State
Till turning giddy fall alas he must 115
And like Tarpeia with his booty crush'd
The wreach that dos from off a hillock fall
Will feel no bruise because the step was small
But he that tumbles from a mountains height
O'erwhelms himself with his own Pondrous weight 120
   The sensual wreach that happiness dos place
In such delights that dos his make debase
That in Leud sports mispends his pretious time
And pleasure meets swimming in Bowles of Wine
(for that alone can bribe his Judg within 125
And make him relish and digest his Sin)
Meets with more care in pleasing his desires
Than virtue in her strictest sense requires
All she dos ask is that wee blest will bee

And hope for better things than here wee see 130
But Vice dos ten times harder lawes impose
And unto dangers all her train expose
Some times to love his tender Soul enclines
And spends whole days and nights in senseless whines
The fear of disopointment's then the Curse 135
Lett him obtain he find's h'as gain'd a worse
A Jealouse Husband then disturbs his Joyes
And infamy and Scorne his bliss destroyes
Or what's as bad he in his brest dos bear
Deep rooted Jealousy the Husbands care 140
Too well he know's that women if they Sin
Will stick at nothing when their hands are in:
Then soon they loath what was so highly priz'd
For Women once enjoy'd are still despis'd.
  To Wine he next retires for with a friend 145
What matter's it tho he his living spend
In foul excess the loathsome wreaches roule
Yet still my friend must press the other Bowle
Un to his mouth the luscious bowle he heaves
Nauciating ev'ry drop yet none he leaves 150
He scornes to flinch let none so meanly think
He'll baulk no health when 'tis his turn to drink
But little thinks that the next rising Sun
Will find his body Sick Estate undone.
For fear of Dun's he dares not show his Head 155
And in short time is forc't to beg his bread
Yet think him blest think he no sorrow has
But young and Rich as ever Creasus was
His wicked appetite can relish nought
But what by vices hand is to him brought 160
His Happiness he always near him Sees
And when he thinks he's surest then it flyes
It courts his Hand as Birds young childerns do
While still their near but flye if they persue
Ah! wreached State before he dos posses 165
'tis Happiness but afterwards distress
Like hungry Midas when tis but in Sight
'tis wholsome food to please the appetite
But if his mouth it e'er approaches nyer
He finds he's curst in gaining his desire 170
Without it famish'd but in eating burst
Eagar to have it but by having curst
After he's thus to vice a prosolite
Under her banners still resolved to fight
From Bliss Eternall finds himself debard 175

Know's vertues God won't vices friends reward
He therefore charges the almightyes thrown
And with Blasphemoase words wou'd pull it down
Ungratefull wreach to use that breath which he
Did so indulgently bestow on thee   180
against the Doner as thy enemy
Small Joy methinks it sure shou'd yeild to thee
That thou e'er long must barely nothing bee
That that same thing that now makes so much stir
And thus dares call the Almighty out to War   185
Must one day dye and into nothing turne
And only live in infamy and scorne
'tis very strange but yet too true alas
Without this thought thou tasts no Happiness
   Leave wreaches thus in vain to court the Air   190
And guide your cources by their proper Star
Seek out a Mercury to point the way
And let him show you what will lead astray
   The Merchant after all his care and toyle
Returnes a Bankrupt to his native Soil   195
Or think him Rich with gold and Jewils blest
And laden with the Glorys of the East
Where lys his happiness he's old himself
And cannot tast the mighty Joy of wealth
His friends are throw long absense dead and worn   200
And he a Wife or Son is left to mourn
Throw his great toil and labour and the Clime
So often shifting in so short a time
He has the Gout Catharrs and Palsies gaind
In ev'ry Joynt and lym the wreach is paind   205
And yet with fear expect's the hand of Death
Hourly to stop the current of his Breath
   The Miser that has Rak'd such heaps of Gold
Is at that pass before he's Rich he's old
The fear of Death then rack's the wreaches mind   210
With grife to leave those mighty Sums behind
That his Dear Mony which from sin was pent
Shou'd by his Heir in Luxury be spent
But far from Happiness he finds he's plac'd
Too late he sees it in the mind must rest   215
While his is quite o'er-whelm'd with black affrights
Of cous'ners by day and theeves by night
His nightly watching's how to gain his wealth
Made him neglect that better thing his health
His body that's with pain and Hungar worn   220
For recompence consumptions then return

Too late he finds that Death no bribes will take
Nor all his store can't Times swift running slack
Wrong'd Orphans tears and Widows grife he sees
And in his face his tortur'd Conscience flyes 225
He'd freely then resign his mighty Store
For a small thing but one dayes respite more
But all in vain fond wreach thy glas is run
Before the buis'ness of thy life's begun

   Those that have long enjoy'd the mighty Name 230
Of honors Riches and of Publick fame
And with contempt look down on them below
Must Happiness in full perfection know
But know Sejanus always must be poor
While his unbounded Will desires more 235
Who can't contract his will to sute his Fate
Within the compass of a Narrow State
His Empire can't enlarge nor ever bee
Seated in what he thinks a high degree

   The sensual wreach that always has persu'd 240
And follow'd Pleasure as his only good
Finds Epicurious has a blunder made
Unless in vertue he the pleasure laid
Grown old in Sin at Deaths approach he flyes
In hopes to find a shelter from his Eyes 245
But ah in vain Alas where e'er he runs
He always carryes with him what he shuns
Take Courage man and look him in the face
What dost thou fear after Death nothing is
Can't thy Old notions now their comfort bring 250
Dos conscience wound thee with her Scorpion sting
Call wine and friends and banish conscience quite
How dares she thus to hinder thy delight
Thy friends and Wine small comfort yeild thee now
Their very sight encreases more thy woe 255
No Gen'rous Rock the wreach too late dos find
Can hide him from a self revenging mind
Conscience which he once thought an airy name
Invented by a Superstitious Brain
He plainly feels to be a Hell within 260
That knaw's his Heart like vultures for his Sin
   Leave thus in vain to court the fleeting Wind
And think not Joy in such delights to find
Seek not without in hopes to find that thing
Which only keepes a residence within 265

Nothing is happiness that can't be known
As well in Deserts as upon a Throne
Indulgent Heav'n that gave us the desire
Never design'd to gratifie it here
But has reserv'd it till wee all shall come   270
At the last Day to hear our Gen'ral Doom
 To Heav'n submit and always think that he
Knows better what is for our good than wee
What e'er your fortune be no more require
But to his Sacred will sute thy desire   275
Loos not thy time which flyes away too fast
But live as thou e'er long will wish thou had'st
 May wee so ever live that when cold Death
Shall come to claim the tribute of our Breath
Wee may with Joy the fatel Sentence hear   280
Without the least regret or anxious fear
        [fols 158v-153v (rev.)]

Title. an Essay] *later addition*
39. Wherein's] *MS* Where in's
43. spend] *preceded by deleted letter*
55. Jealousy] *probably altered from* Jealousys; *followed by deleted letter*
optick] *probably corrected from* opticks; *followed by deleted letter*
103. attend] *altered from* attend's; *'s deleted*
104. end] *altered from* end's; *'s deleted*
133. his] *altered from* their; *t and* r *deleted, is superimposed on* ei
Soul] *altered from* Souls; s *deleted*
157. Yet] *inserted, replacing* But *deleted*
160. hand] *altered from* hands; s *deleted*
212. sin] *conjectural reading; MS unclear*
228, 246, 262. in vain] *MS* invain
237. Within] *altered from* Withing; g *deleted*
Narrow] *replacing* little *deleted*
242. Epicurious] *replacing unclear deletion, possibly* Epictetus *or* Epicurious *miswritten*
248. look] *inserted, replacing* meet *deleted*
258. once] *inserted*
265. within] *altered from* withing; g *deleted*

In imitation of Horace

 In vain the angry billows roar
  In vain the winds employ their rage
 A ship that's in her self secure
  Without concern their pow'rs engage

 Tho the bright God his Beams denys   5
  And rolling waves to Heav'n aspire
 Whose Languid light the suns supplys
  With Just enough to show its ire

  Yet still she bears against the Wind
   And boldly grapples with her fate   10
  Till Leaky grown she's forc'd to bend
   And sink beneath her watry weight

  Ev'n so no storms without can wound
   A man that keeps his mind serene
  They may his depth of courage sound   15
   But ne'er o'ercome while safe within

  But if at fortunes frowns he mourn
   Or from her Malice basely shrink
  His Vessell Leaks, his ruders torn
   And soon beneath its weight will sink   20
         [fol. 143 v–r (rev.)]

 Title. imitation] *MS* imitaletion
 8. show its ire] *replacing* give dispair; give dispair *deleted,* show *inserted,* its ire *added at end of line*
 17. mourn] *possibly superimposed on* moan
 18. from] *inserted, replacing* at *deleted*
 19. Leaks, his ruders torn] *replacing illegible deleted word,* Leaky grown; Leaks *superimposed on* Leaky, grown *deleted,* his ruders torn *added at end of line*

SELECT BIBLIOGRAPHY

Manuscript sources

Parentheses following a MS shelfmark denote the section in this volume in which the manuscript is cited.

British Library, London
Additional MSS 4454 (Burghope), 6409 (Seager), 10037 (Seager), 12047 (Sidney), 19333 (Hutchinson), 25901 (Hutchinson), 39779 (Hutchinson), 46172N (Hutchinson), 46372 (Sidney)
Egerton MS 3789 (Sidney)
Harleian MS 4955 (Cavendish)
Lansdowne MS 740 (Southwell)

Centre for Kentish Studies, Maidstone, Kent
Penshurst MS (Sidney; privately owned)

Leeds University Library, Brotherton Collection
MSS Lt q 2 (Roper), Lt q 32 (Pulter)

Inner Temple Library, London
MS Petyt 538, vol. 43 (Sidney)

Northamptonshire Record Office, Northampton
Fitzwilliam Collection Misc. vol. 793 (Hutchinson), MS IC 3415 (Introduction), Montagu of Boughton Correspondence vol. 3 (Introduction)

Nottinghamshire Archives, Nottingham
DD/HU1–4 (Hutchinson)

Hallward Library, University of Nottingham
Portland MSS PwI 69, 86–90, 118–20, 367–8 (Cavendish), PwV 19, 25 (Cavendish)

Bodleian Library, Oxford
Bodleian MSS Douce 361 (Sidney), Eng. misc. c. 19 (Seager), Eng. poet. e. 31 (Walsh), Rawlinson poet. 16 (Cavendish), Rawlinson poet. 154 (Astell)

National Library of Wales, Aberystwyth
MSS 775B, 776B (Philips)

Worcester College, Oxford
MS 6. 13 (Philips)

William Andrews Clark Memorial Library, Los Angeles
MSS L6815 M3 C734 (Ley), P1745 M1 P744 1671–3 Bound (Palmer)

Folger Shakespeare Library, Washington
MSS V.a.104 (Wroth), V.b.198 (Southwell)

Huntington Library, San Marino, California
MSS HM 743 (Seager), EL 35/B/62 (Burghope)

Ohio State University Library, Columbus, Ohio
MS Eng. 16 (Sidney)

University of Texas at Austin, Humanities Research Center
Misc* HRC 151 Philips MS 14,937 (Philips)

Beinecke Library, Yale University, New Haven
Osborn Collection, MSS b. 233 (Cavendish), fb. 100 (Hutchinson)

Printed sources

Place of publication, where not otherwise stated, is London.

Primary texts

Allestree, Richard (?) (1673), *The Ladies Calling*, octavo.
Ambrose, Isaac (1657), *Media: the middle things*.
An Answer to The most Envious, Scandalous, and Libellous Pamphlet, Entituled MERCURIES MESSAGE (1641).
Ashmole, Elias (1652), *Theatrum Chemicum Britannicum*.
Astell, Mary (1986), *The First English Feminist*, ed. Bridget Hill (Aldershot: Gower Publishing).
Astell, Mary (1996), *Political Writings*, ed. Patricia Springborg (Cambridge: Cambridge University Press).
Babrius and Phaedrus (1965), ed. Ben Edwin Perry, Loeb Classical Library (Cambridge, MA: Harvard University Press).
Barton, William (1668), *Four Centuries of Select Hymns*.
Barton, William (1688), *Six Centuries of Select Hymns*.
Bright, Timothy (1588), *Characterie: An Arte of shorte, swifte, and secrete writing*.
Butler, Samuel (1837), *Sidneiana* (William Nicol for the Roxburghe Club).
Calendar of State Papers Domestic (1672).
Cavanaugh, Jean Carmel (1984), 'Lady Southwell's Defense of Poetry', *English Literary Renaissance*, 14 [4 pp., following p. 284].
Cerasano, S. P., and Marion Wynne-Davies, eds (1996), *Renaissance Drama by Women: Texts and Documents* (Routledge).
Chauncy, Henry (1700), *The Historical Antiquities of Hertfordshire*, 2 vols.
Crawford, Patricia, and Laura Gowing, eds (2000), *Women's Worlds in Seventeenth-Century England* (Routledge).
Donne, John (1640), *LXXX Sermons Preached by that Learned and Reverend Divine John Donne*.
Egerton, Elizabeth (1999), *Subordination and Authorship in Early Modern England: The Case of Elizabeth Cavendish Egerton and Her 'Loose Papers'*, ed. Betty S. Travitsky (Tempe: Arizona Centre for Medieval and Renaissance Studies).
Eikon Basilike (1649).
Featley, Daniel (1629), *Cygnea cantio: or, Learned decisions, and most prudent and pious directions for students in divinitie; delivered by our late soveraigne of happie memorie, King James, at White Hall a few weekes before his death*.
Fletcher, Giles (1610), *Christs Victorie, and Triumph in Heaven, and Earth, over, and after Death* (Cambridge).
Fowler, Alastair (1994), *The Country House Poem: A Cabinet of Seventeenth-Century Estate Poems and Related Items* (Edinburgh: Edinburgh University Press).
French, John (1651), *The Art of Distillation*.
Goulart, Simon (1621), *A Learned Summarie upon the Famous Poeme of William of Salust, Lord of Bartas*.
Greer, Germaine, Susan Hastings, Jeslyn Medoff, and Melinda Sansone, eds (1988), *Kissing the Rod: An Anthology of Seventeenth-Century Women's Verse* (New York: Farrar Straus Giroux).
Herbert, George (1945), *The Works of George Herbert*, ed. F. E. Hutchinson (Oxford: Oxford University Press).
Herbert, Mary Sidney (1998), *The Collected Works of Mary Sidney Herbert, Countess of Pembroke*, ed. M. P. Hannay, N. Kinnamon and M. Brennan, Vol. II: *The Psalmes of David* (Oxford: Clarendon Press).

Herodotus (1920–25), *Herodotus*, trans. A. D. Godley, Loeb Classical Library, 4 vols (Heinemann).
Hester, John (1596), *The First Part of the Key of Philosophy*.
The Holy Bible containing the Old Testament and the New (1660).
Howell, James (1645), *Epistolae Ho-Elianae: Familiar Letters Domestic and Forren*.
Hutchinson, Lucy (1973), *Memoirs of the Life of Colonel Hutchinson*, ed. James Sutherland (Oxford University Press).
Hutchinson, Lucy (1996), *Lucretius: De rerum natura*, ed. Hugh de Quehen (Duckworth).
Hutchinson, Lucy (2000), *Memoirs of the Life of Colonel Hutchinson*, ed. N. H. Keeble (Phoenix Press).
Hutchinson, Lucy (2001), *Order and Disorder*, ed. David Norbrook (Oxford: Blackwell).
Josephus, Flavius (1928), *Jewish Antiquities, Books I–IV*, trans. H. St. J. Thackeray, Loeb Classical Library (Heinemann).
Josephus, Flavius (1930), *The Jewish War, Books IV–VII*, trans. H. St. J. Thackeray, Loeb Classical Library (Heinemann).
Littleton, Adam (1669), *A Sermon at the Funeral of . . . the Lady Jane, Eldest Daughter to his Grace William, Duke of Newcastle, and Wife to the Honourable Charles Cheyne*.
Lonsdale, Roger, ed. (1989), *Eighteenth Century Women Poets: An Oxford Anthology* (Oxford: Oxford University Press).
Maier, Michael (1617), *Atalanta Fugiens* (Oppenheim).
Maier, Michael (1625), *De Lapide Philosophico* (Frankfurt).
Mercuries message, or The coppy of a letter sent to William Laud late Archbishop of Canterbury, now prisoner in the Tower (1641).
More, Henry (1642), *Psychodia platonica: or A platonicall song of the soul* (Cambridge).
More, Henry (1646), *Democritus Platonissans* (Cambridge).
Osborne, Dorothy (1987), *Letters to Sir William Temple*, ed. Kenneth Parker (Penguin).
Overbury, Thomas, et al. (2003), *Characters, together with Poems, News, Edicts, and Paradoxes based on the eleventh edition of* A Wife now the Widow of Sir Thomas Overbury, ed. Donald Beecher (Ottawa: Dovehouse Editions).
Palmer, Julia (2001), *The 'Centuries' of Julia Palmer*, ed. Victoria E. Burke and Elizabeth Clarke (Nottingham: Trent Editions).
Patrick, Simon (1669), *A Friendly Debate Between a Conformist and a Non-Conformist*, 3rd edition.
Patrick, Simon *et al.* (1719), *Poems upon divine and moral subjects. Originals and Translations. By Dr. Patrick . . . and other eminent hands*.
Philips, Katherine (1664), *Poems by the incomparable Mrs. K. P.*
Philips, Katherine (1667), *Poems by the incomparable Mrs. K. P.*
Philips, Katherine (1990–93), *The Collected Works of Katherine Philips, the Matchless Orinda*, ed. Patrick Thomas, Germaine Greer and Roger Little, 3 vols (Stump Cross: Stump Cross Books).
Pliny the Elder (1601), *The Historie of the World*, trans. Philemon Holland.
Rathmell, J. C. A., ed. (1963), *The Psalms of Sir Philip Sidney and the Countess of Pembroke* (New York: New York University Press).
Ripley, George (1591), *The Compound of Alchymy*, trans. Ralph Rabbards.
Sedley, Charles (1668), *The Mulberry-Garden*.
Segar, William (1587), *The Blazon of Papistes*.
Shakespeare, William (1986), *The Complete Works*, ed. Stanley Wells and Gary Taylor (Oxford: Oxford University Press).
Sidney, Philip (1962), *The Poems of Sir Philip Sidney*, ed. William A. Ringler (Oxford: Oxford University Press).
Siebmacher, Johann Ambrosius (1619), *Wasserstein der Weysen* (Frankfurt).
Southwell, Anne (1997), *The Southwell–Sibthorpe Commonplace Book, Folger MS. V.b.198*, ed. Jean Klene (Tempe: Medieval and Renaissance Texts and Studies).

Stevenson, Jane, and Peter Davidson, eds (2001), *Early Modern Women Poets (1520–1700): An Anthology*, with contributions from Meg Bateman, Kate Chedgzoy and Julie Saunders (Oxford: Oxford University Press).

Suetonius (1997), *Lives of the Caesars*, trans. J. C. Rolfe, Loeb Classical Library, 2 vols (Cambridge, MA: Harvard University Press).

Trill, Suzanne, Kate Chedgzoy, and Melanie Osborne, eds (1997), *Lay By Your Needles Ladies, Take the Pen: Writing Women in England, 1500–1700* (Arnold).

Vaughan, Henry (1650), *Silex Scintillans*.

Verstegan, Richard (1605), *A restitution of decayed intelligence: in antiquities concerning the most noble and renowmed English nation* (Antwerp).

Watts, Isaac (1728), *Hymns and Spiritual Songs in Three Books*.

Whately, William (1640), *Prototypes, or The Primarie Precedent Presidents out of the Booke of Genesis*.

Whitney, Geoffrey (1586), *A Choice of Emblemes* (Leiden).

Wilkinson, Robert (1607), *Lots Wife, A Sermon Preached at Paules Crosse*.

Willet, Andrew (1605), *Hexapla in Genesin, That is, A Sixfold Commentary upon Genesis* (Cambridge).

Wroth, Lady Mary (1621), *The Countess of Montgomery's Urania*.

Wroth, Lady Mary (1992), *The Poems of Lady Mary Wroth*, ed. Josephine A. Roberts, 2nd edition (Baton Rouge: Louisiana State University Press).

Wroth, Lady Mary (1995), *The First Part of the Countess of Montgomery's Urania*, ed. Josephine A. Roberts (Binghamton, NY: Medieval and Renaissance Texts and Studies).

Wroth, Lady Mary (1996a), *Poems: A Modernised Edition*, ed. R. E. Pritchard (Keele University: Keele University Press).

Wroth, Lady Mary (1996b), *The Early Modern Englishwoman 1.10: Mary Wroth*, ed. Josephine A. Roberts (Aldershot: Scolar Press).

Wroth, Lady Mary (1999), *The Second Part of the Countess of Montgomery's Urania*, ed. Josephine A. Roberts, Suzanne Gossett and Janel Mueller (Tempe: Renaissance English Text Society in conjunction with Arizona Center for Medieval and Renaissance Studies).

Wynne-Davies, Marion, ed. (1998), *Women Poets of the Renaissance* (Dent).

Secondary texts

Abraham, Lyndy (1990), *Marvell and Alchemy* (Aldershot: Scolar Press).

Alexander, Gavin (1996–97), 'Constant Works: A Framework for Reading Mary Wroth', *Sidney Newsletter and Journal* 14.2, 5–32.

Alexander, Gavin (2000), 'A New Manuscript of the Sidney Psalms', *Sidney Journal* 18.1, 43–56.

Applegate, Joan (1993), 'Katherine Philips's "Orinda upon Little Hector": An Unrecorded Musical Setting by Henry Lawes', *English Manuscript Studies 1100–1700* 4, 272–80.

Barash, Carol (1996), *English Women's Poetry, 1649–1714: Politics, Community, and Linguistic Authority* (Oxford: Clarendon Press).

Beal, Peter (1980), *Index of English Literary Manuscripts. 1. 1450–1625* (Mansell).

Beal, Peter (1998), *In Praise of Scribes: Manuscripts and their Makers in Seventeenth-Century England* (Oxford: Clarendon Press).

Beal, Peter, and Margaret Ezell, eds (2000), *Writings by Early Modern Women. English Manuscript Studies 1100–1700* 9.

Bell, Vicars (1949), *Little Gaddesden: The Story of an English Parish* (Faber and Faber).

Bennett, Martyn (2000), *Historical Dictionary of the British and Irish Civil Wars 1637–1660* (Chicago: Fitzroy Dearborn).

Berry, William (1830), *Pedigrees of the Families in the County of Kent* (Sherwood, Gilbert and Piper).

Brennan, Michael G. (1988), *Literary Patronage in the English Renaissance: The Pembroke Family* (Routledge).

Brewerton, Patricia (2002), '"Several keys to ope' the character": The Political and Cultural Significance of Timothy Bright's "characterie"', *Sixteenth Century Journal* 33, 945–61.

Brown, Sylvia, ed. (1999), *Women's Writing in Stuart England: The Mothers' Legacies of Dorothy Leigh, Elizabeth Joscelin, and Elizabeth Richardson* (Stroud: Sutton).

Burke, Victoria E. (2002), 'Medium and Meaning in the Manuscripts of Anne, Lady Southwell', in George L. Justice and Nathan Tinker, eds, *Women's Writing and the Circulation of Ideas: Manuscript Publication in England, 1550–1800* (Cambridge: Cambridge University Press), 94–120.

Burke, Victoria E., and Jonathan Gibson, eds (2004), *Early Modern Women's Manuscript Writing: Selected Papers from the Trinity/Trent Colloquium* (Aldershot: Ashgate).

Burke, Victoria E., and Sarah Ross (2001), 'Elizabeth Middleton, John Bourchier, and the Compilation of Seventeenth-Century Religious Manuscripts', *The Library* 7th ser, 2, 131–60.

Cavanaugh, Jean Carmel (1967), 'The Library of Lady Southwell and Captain Sibthorpe', *Studies in Bibliography* 20, 243–54.

Clarke, Elizabeth (2002), 'Anne Southwell and the Pamphlet Debate: The Politics of Gender, Class, and Manuscript' in Cristina Malcolmson and Mihoto Suzuki, eds *Debating Gender in Early Modern England, 1500–1700* (Basingstoke: Palgrave), 37–53.

Coolahan, Marie-Louise (2003), '"We live by chance, and slip into Events": Occasionality and the Manuscript Verse of Katherine Philips', *Eighteenth-Century Ireland* 18, 9–23.

Considine, John (2000), 'The Invention of the Literary Circle of Sir Thomas Overbury', in Claude J. Summers and Ted-Larry Pebworth, eds *Literary Circles and Cultural Communities in Renaissance England* (Columbia: University of Missouri Press), 59–74.

Crawford, Patricia (1993), *Women and Religion in England 1500–1720* (Routledge).

Davidson, Peter (1999), 'Marvell's Gardens: Clues to Two Curious Puzzles', *Times Literary Supplement*, 3 December, 14–15.

de Clercq, Carlo (1978–79), 'Quelques séries italiennes de Sibylles', *Bulletin de l'Institut Historique Belge de Rome* 48–9, 105–27.

de Clercq, Carlo (1981), 'Quelques séries de Sibylles hors d'Italie', *Bulletin de l'Institut Historique Belge de Rome* 51, 87–116.

Dove, Linda L. (1998), 'Composing (to) a Man of Letters: Lady Anne Southwell's Acrostic to Francis Quarles', *American Notes and Queries* 11.1, 12–17.

Ezell, Margaret (1987), *The Patriarch's Wife: Literary Evidence and the History of the Family* (Chapel Hill: University of North Carolina Press).

Ezell, Margaret (1988), '"To Be Your Daughter in Your Pen": The Social Functions of Literature in the Writings of Lady Elizabeth Brackley and Lady Jane Cavendish', *Huntington Library Quarterly* 51, 281–96.

Ezell, Margaret (1993), *Writing Women's Literary History* (Baltimore: Johns Hopkins University Press).

Ezell, Margaret (1999), *Social Authorship and the Advent of Print* (Baltimore: Johns Hopkins University Press).

Ezell, Margaret (2002), 'The Posthumous Publication of Women's Manuscripts and the History of Authorship', in George L. Justice and Nathan Tinker, eds, *Women's Writing and the Circulation of Ideas: Manuscript Publication in England, 1550–1800* (Cambridge: Cambridge University Press), 121–36.

Freeman, Phyllis (1934), 'William Walsh's Letters and Poems in MS Malone 9', *Bodleian Quarterly Record* 7, 503–7.

Freeman, Phyllis (1948), 'Walsh and Dryden: Recently Discovered Letters', *The Review of English Studies* 24, 195–202.

Gibson, Jonathan (2004), 'Cherchez la femme—Mary Wroth and Shakespeare's *Sonnets*', *Times Literary Supplement*, 13 August, 12–13.

Greaves, Richard (1986), *Deliver Us From Evil: The Radical Underground in Britain, 1660–1663* (Oxford: Oxford University Press).

Greer, Germaine (1996), *Slip-Shod Sibyls: Recognition, Rejection and the Woman Poet* (Penguin).

Grossmann, F. (1950), 'Holbein, Torrigiano and Some Portraits of Dean Colet: A Study of Holbein's Work in Relation to Sculpture', *Journal of the Warburg and Courtauld Institutes* 13, 202–36.

Hageman, Elizabeth, and Andrea Sununu (1994), '"More Copies of it Abroad than I could have Imagin'd": Further Manuscript Texts of Katherine Philips, "the Matchless Orinda"', *English Manuscript Studies 1100–1700* 5, 174–216.

Hannay, Margaret P. (1990), *Philip's Phoenix, Mary Sidney, Countess of Pembroke* (Oxford: Oxford University Press).

Hannay, Margaret P. (2002), 'The Countess of Pembroke's Agency in Print and Scribal Culture', in George L. Justice and Nathan Tinker, eds, *Women's Writing and the Circulation of Ideas: Manuscript Publication in England, 1550–1800* (Cambridge: Cambridge University Press), 17–49.

Hasted, Edward (1778), *History and Topological Survey of the County of Kent*, 4 vols.

Hobbs, Mary (1992), *Early Seventeenth-Century Verse Miscellany Manuscripts* (Aldershot: Scolar).

Justice, George L., and Nathan Tinker, eds (2002), *Women's Writing and the Circulation of Ideas: Manuscript Publication in England, 1550–1800* (Cambridge: Cambridge University Press).

Klene, Jean (2000), '"Monument of an Endless affection": Folger MS V.b.198 and Lady Anne Southwell', *English Manuscript Studies 1100–1700* 9, 165–86.

Kraner, Werner (1931), 'Zur englischen Kurzschrift im Zeitalter Shakespeares. Das Jane-Seager-Manusckript. (The Divine Prophecies of the Ten Sibyls.)', *Shakespeare-Jahrbuch* 67, 26–61.

Lake, Peter (1988), *Anglicans and Puritans? Presbyterian and English Conformist Thought from Whitgift to Hooker* (Unwin Hyman).

Longfellow, Erica (2004), 'Lady Anne Southwell's Indictment of Adam', in Victoria E. Burke and Jonathan Gibson, eds, *Early Moden Women's Manuscript Writing: Selected Papers from the Trinity/Trent Colloquium* (Aldershot: Ashgate), 111–33.

Love, Harold (1993), *Scribal Publication in Seventeenth-Century England* (Oxford: Clarendon Press).

McClung, William A. (1977), *The Country House in English Renaissance Poetry* (Berkeley: University of California Press).

Madan, Francis (1950), *A New Bibliography of the Eikon Basilike of King Charles the First* (Oxford: Oxford Bibliographical Society Publications).

Marotti, Arthur F. (1995), *Manuscript, Print, and the English Renaissance Lyric* (Ithaca: Cornell University Press).

Masson, David (1871–94), *The Life of Mr John Milton*, 7 vols (Macmillan).

Masten, Jeff (1991), '"Shall I turne blabb?": Circulation, Gender, and Subjectivity in Mary Wroth's Sonnets', in Naomi J. Miller and Gary Waller, eds, *Reading Mary Wroth* (Knoxville: University of Tennessee Press).

Matthews, A. G. (1934), *Calamy Revised: Being a Revision of Edmund Calamy's Account of the Ministers and Others Ejected and Silenced 1660–2* (Oxford: Clarendon Press).

May, Steven W. (1991), *The Elizabethan Courtier Poets: The Poems and their Context* (Columbia: University of Missouri Press).

Medoff, Jeslyn (1992), 'The Daughters of Behn and the Problem of Reputation', in Isobel Grundy and Susan Wiseman, eds, *Women, Writing, History 1640–1740* (Batsford), 33–54.

Morley, Henry (1973), *Memoirs of Bartholomew Fair*, ed. David Braithwaite (Hugh Evelyn).

Nash, Treadway (1781–82), *Collections for the History of Worcestershire*, 2 vols.

Norbrook, David (1997), 'Lucy Hutchinson's "Elegies" and the Situation of the Republican Woman Writer (with text)', *English Literary Renaissance* 27, 468–521.

Parker, Tom W. N. (1998), *Proportional Form in the Sonnets of the Sidney Circle: Loving in Truth* (Oxford: Clarendon Press).

Perry, Ruth (1982), 'A Seventeenth-Century Feminist Poet', *Times Literary Supplement*, 20 August, 911.

Perry, Ruth (1986), *The Celebrated Mary Astell* (Chicago: Chicago University Press).

Piper, David (1957), 'The 1590 Lumley Inventory: Hilliard, Segar and the Earl of Essex—II', *Burlington Magazine* 99, 299–303.

Race, Sidney [S. R.] (1938), 'Colonel Hutchinson, Governor of Nottingham Castle, and Regicide', *Notes and Queries* 174, 39.

Rienstra, Debra, and Noel Kinnamon (2002), 'Circulating the Sidney–Pembroke Psalter', in George L. Justice and Nathan Tinker, eds, *Women's Writing and the Circulation of Ideas: Manuscript Publication in England, 1550–1800* (Cambridge: Cambridge University Press), 50–72.

Rooper, John Royden (1958), *The Rooper Story* (S. Straker & Sons).

Ross, Sarah, (2000), 'Women and Religious Verse in English Manuscript Culture, c.1600–1668' (unpublished doctoral thesis, University of Oxford).

Schleiner, Louise (1994), *Tudor and Stuart Women Writers* (Bloomington: Indiana University Press).

Scott-Warren, Jason (2000), 'Reconstructing Manuscript Networks: The Textual Transactions of Sir Stephen Powle', in Alexandra Shepard and Phil Withington, eds, *Communities in Early Modern England: Networks, Place, Rhetoric* (Manchester: Manchester University Press), 18–37.

Seal, Jill [Jill Seal Millman] (1997), 'Psalms, Sonnets, and Spiritual Songs: Some Traditions and Innovations in English Religious Poetry, c.1560–1611' (unpublished doctoral thesis, University of Nottingham).

Senar, Howard (1983), *Little Gaddesden and Ashridge* (Chichester: Phillimore).

Shrewsbury, J. F. D. (1971), *A History of Bubonic Plague in the British Isles* (Cambridge: Cambridge University Press).

Smith, Rosalind (2000), 'Lady Mary Wroth's *Pamphilia to Amphilanthus*: The Politics of Withdrawal', *English Literary Renaissance* 30, 408–31.

Souers, Philip W. (1931), *The Matchless Orinda* (Cambridge, MA: Harvard University Press).

Speaight, George (1990), *The History of the English Puppet Theatre* (Robert Hale).

Spurr, John (1998), *English Puritanism, 1603–1689* (Basingstoke: Macmillan).

Starr, Nathan Comfort (1931), '*The Concealed Fansyes*: A Play by Lady Jane Cavendish and Lady Elizabeth Brackley', *Publications of the Modern Language Association of America* 46, 802–38.

A Summary Catalogue of Post-Medieval Western Manuscripts in the Bodleian Library, Oxford: Acquisitions 1916–1975 (1991), ed. Mary Clapinson and T. D. Rogers (Oxford: Clarendon Press).

Tilley, Morris Palmer (1950), *A Dictionary of the Proverbs in England in the Sixteenth and Seventeenth Centuries* (Ann Arbor: University of Michigan Press).

Tyacke, Nicholas (1987), *Anti-Calvinists: The Rise of English Arminianism, c.1590–1640* (Oxford: Clarendon Press).

Victoria History of the County of Buckingham (1905–28), ed. William Page, 4 vols (The St Catherine Press).

Victoria History of the County of Hertford (1902–23), ed. William Page, 4 vols (The St Catherine Press).

Victoria History of the County of Worcester (1901–26), ed. William Page, J. W. Willis-Bund and H. Arthur Doubleday, 4 vols (The St Catherine Press).

Waller, Gary F. (1979), *Mary Sidney, Countess of Pembroke: A Critical Study of Her Writings and Literary Milieu* (Salzburg: University of Salzburg).

Wheale, Nigel (1999), *Writing and Society: Literacy, Print and Politics in Britain 1590–1660* (Routledge).

Westby-Gibson, John (1888), 'A Monograph on Timothy Bright, the Father of Modern Shorthand, 1586–88', in *Transactions of the First International Shorthand Congress Held in London From September 26th to October 1st, 1887* (Isaac Pitman), 75–83.

Williams, Arnold (1948), *The Common Expositor, An Account of the Commentaries on Genesis 1527–1633* (Chapel Hill: University of North Carolina Press).

Woudhuysen, H. R. (1996), *Sir Philip Sidney and the Circulation of Manuscripts 1558–1640* (Oxford: Clarendon Press).

INTERPRETATIVE NOTES

Jane Seager: British Library Additional MS 10037

To the Queenes most Excellent Majesty
1. eyen] eyes.
4. Renomed] renowned.
6. Defendress] refers to Elizabeth's title, as English sovereign, of 'defender of the faith' (*Fidei defensor*).
7. preordeyned] decided in advance—a word often associated with Calvinist theology.
9. pencell] paintbrush.
10–11. accompting] accounting.

Samia
Title. Samia] the Samian sibyl, from the island of Samos in Greece. Sibyls' names derive from their supposed places of origin. Seager has numbered each of the sibylline prophecies in pink ink. 'Samia' is the second prophecy in the manuscript.
2. the worldes obscurity] all things in the world which are mysterious, or all things which the people of the world do not understand.
4. knotty . . . race] the Old Testament.
6. this great King] Christ.
of] by.
9. divines] discloses.
Anno Mundi. 2720] in year 2720 after the foundation of the world. The supposed date of the sibyl's prophecy.

Cimmeria
Title. Cimmeria] the Cimmerian sibyl, who lived at Lake Avernus in the Campania region of Italy. In classical mythology, the Cimmerians were a people thought to live in perpetual darkness. The fourth prophecy.
1. a sacred virgine myld] the Virgin Mary.
4. Lord of hosts . . . King] Jesus.
6. clap their hands] Isaiah 55:12.
7–10. A wondrous starr . . . gold] Matthew 2:1–12.
Anno Mundi. 3380] see concluding note to 'Samia', above.

Tyburtina
Title. Tyburtina] the Tiburtine sibyl, from Tibur, the old name for Tivoli, near Rome. The ninth prophecy.
3–4. a mayden shall conceave . . . Nazareth] Luke 1:26–38.
5. Bethlem] Bethlehem: see Matthew 2:1 and Luke 2:1–16.
6. habytt . . . flesh] a human body.
7. by an Angell] the Angel Gabriel: Luke 1:26.
8. blest of women all] cf. Luke 1:48.
Anno Mundi. 3890] see concluding note to 'Samia', above.

'Lo thus in breife'
7. Characteres] i.e. 'characteress', a female 'characterer' portraying or depicting something. With a nod towards Bright's 'charactery', the shorthand system used in the manuscript.
10. to] too.

Mary Sidney: British Library Additional MS 12047

For notes on the Countess's use of her sources see *Works*. Obscure passages may be clarified by reference to the biblical text.

Psalm 75 Confitebimur

This psalm is interpreted as spoken by a royal figure, before he takes the throne.

Title. Confitebimur] 'Unto thee, O God, do we give thanks'. The Latin titles for Sidney's psalm translations reproduce (sometimes in abbreviated form) the headings used in the Book of Common Prayer, which are straightforward translations of the first line of each of the Psalms. Translations of Latin titles provided here (and in subsequent notes) follow the Book of Common Prayer, which uses Coverdale's version of the Psalter.

3. thy name] God's name is here used to mean God himself.

10. sawcy horne] the horn is a symbol of strength; to lift up one's horn was to boast about one's own power.

19–24. A troubled cup ... floweth] The cup of God's wrath is a conventional biblical figure.

20. weare] where.

Psalm 89 Miserecordias

This psalm's setting is a defeat in battle; the psalmist evokes the covenant between God and Davidic royalty, and then mourns its apparent failure, before appealing to God to honour it.

Title. Miserecordias] mercy, or loving-kindness: 'My song shall be always of the loving-kindness of the Lord'.

1–2 (marginal note). Eveninge prayer 17 Day] Rubrics for morning and evening prayer are given, despite the haphazard ordering of psalms in the manuscript (making the text useless for liturgical purposes).

9–12. Lo ... scorn] The speaker here is God.

9. leagud] made a covenant.

13. running ... unworn] This refers to the sun, often depicted as a chariot, moving across the sky.

16. holy troops] angels.

21. redoubt] 'to dread, fear, stand in awe or apprehension of' (*OED* v.).

24. armor like] This image, not in the original psalm, probably comes from Ephesians 6:10–17, where the armour of God is described, and faith is described as a shield.

27. *Pharao*] the ruler of the Egyptians. The Israelites' escape from slavery in Egypt is described in the early chapters of Exodus. The Coverdale Psalter translates this line as 'Thou hast subdued Egypt, and destroyed it'. (Many other translations, including the King James or Authorised Version, refer not to Egypt but to Rahab, a sea monster.)

35. *Thabor* and *Hermon*] mountains in northern Israel. Mount Tabor, near the sea of Galilee, overlooked the valley of Jezreel. Mount Hermon marked the northern boundary of Israel with Lebanon.

42. poste] 'to ride, run, or travel with speed or haste; to make haste, hasten, hurry' (*OED* v.^{1}, 2)

52–96. ayd ... assuring] The speaker here is God, through his prophet.

56. annoynted] i.e. as king.

59. closlie] secretly.

65–6. twixt ... desine] between the sea and the river, i.e. in the whole country.

69–70. thow ... salvation] God here directs what the king will say to him.

71. first born roome] God will give his anointed king the room reserved for his first-born child. This image is not in the original psalm.

75. lining] i.e. linning. To lin is 'to cease, leave off; desist' (*OED* v. 1).

78. like] equal, similar.

83. randon] random.

84. froward] unreasonable, ungovernable (cf. *OED* A.1).

105. rebatest] beat down.
126. Christ] This anachronistic reference to Christ is substituted for the 'anointed one' of the psalm. 'Christ' also means 'anointed'.

Psalm 89 Miserecordias *[ii]*
This variant version is unique to this manuscript. It is written in quantitative hexameters. Quantitative metres, intended to emulate classical forms of metre, enjoyed a brief phase of popularity in the late sixteenth century. The Countess later rewrote all of her quantitative psalms in more traditional English metres. It would thus appear that this is copied from an earlier working draft.

Title. Miserecordias] See note to previous version.
1 (marginal note). idem] Latin, meaning 'the same', i.e. the same date.
5–7. soaner ... then] sooner ... than.
23. Phæroa] see note to '*Pharao*', previous version, line 27.
27. Thabor and hermon] see note to previous version, line 35. In the following line, Sidney pictures Tabor and Hermon as mountains to the east and west.
30. puisance] power.
33. hy] hie, or hurry.
41–68. one exalted ... in heaven] God is pictured as the speaker here.
45. prickt on] driven, goaded.
49. Eufrates] The Euphrates was intended as the eastern border of the land promised to Abraham (Genesis 15:18).
71. raisest] i.e. raze, destroy.
72. passengers] 'a passer by or through' (*OED* 1a).
74. feld] field.

Psalm 122 Letatus sum
A psalm of praise for the rebuilding of Jerusalem, and a prayer for peace. There are three extant versions of this psalm. Two are recorded in this manuscript, both in quantitative metres. The other variant version has rhymed stanzas. This version is written in unrhymed hexameters.

Title. Letatus sum] 'I was glad'.
4. Salem] meaning 'peace', another name for Jerusalem; also at line 12.
8. seat] in biblical times, a position of authority, judgement and instruction; cf. Exodus 18:13; Proverbs 31:23; Matthew 5:1–2.

Psalm 122 Letatus sum *[ii]*
This version is written in asclepiadic metre (see *OED*).
Title. Idem] Latin, meaning 'the same', i.e. the same psalm.
13. seat] see previous version, note to line 8.

Psalm 75 Confitebimur *[ii]*
Title. Confitebimur] See note to previous version (p. 230).
17. horne] see previous version, note to line 10.
19. born] borne.
28. caitife] a poor wretched person (cf. *OED* 2)—at the opposite of the social scale from a king.

Psalm 113 Laudate dominum
This variant version is unique to this manuscript. The psalm urges praise from those in lowly positions, emphasising God's concern for them.

Title. Laudate dominum] 'Praise the Lord'.
16. to sway the state] This involvement in affairs of state may be implied but is certainly not stated in the biblical text. On seating and authority see the note on Psalm 122, line 8.
17. barren] Barrenness was considered a curse in biblical times.
19–20. To ... exceeding] This is a version of the 'Gloria', which is said at the end of every psalm in church services, according to the liturgy in the Book of Common Prayer.

Lady Mary Wroth: Folger Shakespeare Library MS V.a.104

From Section 1 of the Folger manuscript

Masten (1991) and Alexander (1996–97) argue that the title *Pamphilia to Amphilanthus* (present in both *MS* and *1621*) applies only to this first section of 55 poems. The 1621 revisions leave the numerical structure of this section unaltered, unlike all the other sections of the manuscript: seven groups of six sonnets each followed by a song, followed by a concluding group of seven sonnets. As Parker (1998) and Alexander have shown, this section—in both print and manuscript—features elaborate numerological patterning comparable to that used in sequences by Philip Sidney and Robert Sidney.

1

The sequence's opening poem.
1. prove] prove to be.
2. hiere] hire, i.e. remove.
4. swifter then . . . require] swifter than those thoughts (or things more generally) that need most swiftness.
5. wing'd desire] not Cupid, the winged god of love, who is inside the chariot (line 7). Venus's chariot is usually said to be drawn by doves.
11. shute] Roberts's misreading of 'shute' (Folger manuscript) as 'shutt' has led to unwarranted critical observations.
12. martir'd] killed.
13. itt] the wound made by Cupid's arrow?
14. binn] been.

16

2. passage] a way out.
5. Goodwines] the notorious Goodwin Sands, off Kent, cause of many shipwrecks.
7. in this kind] in this manner.
10. save . . . scope] except that my thoughts remain free.
13. crost] undermined.
14. falsefy] prove to be false.

19

1. beecoming] suiting.
2. lightsome] happy, punning on 'light'.
4. absence power] absence's power?
doth . . . controle] does not allow to be happy; 'The power of sorrow at the beloved's absence prevents happiness' (Pritchard, in Wroth 1996a).
5–7. The very . . . griefe-full role] 'The trees act out their sorrow for the parting of summer in costumes of dying leaves' (Pritchard, in Wroth 1996a), perhaps punning on 'roll' (parchment record).
5. condole] express sympathy with.
8. prest] forced.
9. her] Summer's.
11. huese] hues (colours).
vade] decay, fade.
13. for] as a result of.
14. who . . . see] who also experience absence.

23

2. hunt] Wroth's husband, Sir Robert Wroth, was a hunting enthusiast.
hauke] hawk.
play] gamble.
4. prise] prize (value).
5. eyes] observation.

6. this daylike night] a cryptic phrase describing the other people whose activities have been listed earlier in the sonnet and who spend their time on 'poore vanities' rather than 'true pleasure' (line 8).
7. dispose] behave.
them-selves] referring to the people mentioned in lines 1–3.
as voyd of right] as though compulsorily? (Pritchard, in Wroth 1996a).
9. my . . . chase] I hunt my thoughts.
10. my . . . fly] my mind immediately imagines its desired state of affairs with as much swiftness as a hawk flies down on its prey.
11. tauke] talk.
13. move] have an effect on people.

31
1. tædious] tedious, i.e. wearisome.
way] path, road.
2. lay'd downe] having lain down.
5. blinded] Fortune is traditionally blind.
14. move] attempt to affect.

36
1. Juno . . . Jove] In classical mythology, Jove (Jupiter) was notorious for his infidelity to Juno.
6. chafeing] vexed.
7–8. to / hy one] someone hurrying.
8. never ground did prove] never took root.

48
2–3. the stronger . . . brighter] the stronger, greater, purer and brighter it gets.
4–5. then . . . brest] an address to Pamphilia's hopes.
6. that part] i.e. 'my brest' (line 5).
6, 14. will] thought by Roberts (Wroth 1992) to pun on the name of William Herbert, Wroth's lover.
10. impart] communicate.
13. fuell . . . smart] love?
smart] pains.
14. prove] am.
Pamphilia's signature, surrounded by slashed 'S's or '*s fermé*', marks the end of the first section of the manuscript. It is followed by a blank leaf.

From Section 3 of the manuscript

Alexander (1996–97) argues that the poems in Section 2 of the manuscript (one unnumbered sonnet, eight unnumbered songs and a verse dialogue) do not form a unified sequence, unlike the numbered poems in Section 3. In 1621 five sonnets, including 'Like to the Indians', from *MS* Section 3 swapped places with sonnets in Section 1.

10
Usually linked by critics to Wroth's involvement in Ben Jonson's and Inigo Jones's *Masque of Blackness* (1605) and *Masque of Beauty* (1608) in which James I's wife Anne of Denmark and court ladies including Wroth were made up as Ethiopian nymphs.
3–4. ever . . . him] the more I've worshipped him.
5. to blacknes runn] are black.
6. whitenes] whiteness's.
7. then] than.
griefs store] a full supply of grief.

8. undunn] undone, with a possible pun on 'dun' (brown) (Wynne-Davies 1998).
10. worthles rite] 'double pun on *worth/Wroth* and *rite/write*' (Wynne-Davies 1998).
13. Phœbus] Phoebus's (the sun's).
$ . . . $] the $ marks register the conclusion of a sequence of ten numbered sonnets within section 3.

From Section 4 of the manuscript

The order of poems in the 'crown' is identical in both *MS* and *1621*. The crown is the only section of the manuscript in which sonnets are not limited one to a page but run on in a continuous sequence across page-breaks.

Several critics have seen the crown's spiritualised conception of love (abandoned in its final sonnet) as a major turning-point in the sequence as a whole, forming a crucial staging-post in Pamphilia's emotional development. Sonnet crowns were written by both Wroth's father Robert Sidney and her uncle Philip Sidney.

[1]
1. labourinth] In classical mythology, Theseus rescued Ariadne from the Minotaur's labyrinth guided by a thread (cf. line 14).
2. sids] i.e. sides.
4. lett mee] if I.
goe forward] i.e. be too bold?
7. nor fainte] not faint.
crosses] troubles, and perhaps 'confusing intersections in the maze' (Pritchard, in Wroth 1996a).
8. stand still] to stand still.
mourne] end in tears.
11. doubts] uncertainties.
allay] modification, tempering.
12. traveile] hard work.
hire] efforts.
13. move] influence.

2
4. phant'sie] fancy.
never roome had lent] was absent.
6. ills from us remove] remove ills from us.
7. light] the light.
brings] which brings.
8. prove] experience.
9–12. Love is . . . joyes increase] Wynne-Davies (1998) finds a succession of New Testament images in these lines, which she links to Mary Sidney's psalm translations.
11. oyle] lamp oil.
12. increase] production of offspring (joy might be mother and/or child or children).
14. bands] bonds.

8
2. nott admires] does not recognise and appreciate.
4. raines] reigns.
6. worth] punning on 'Wroth'.
12. intise] entice.
13. phant'sies] fancies (whims).

13
3. holly] holy.
4. will] possible pun on William Herbert.
5. thes titles] the 'titles' that follow in lines 6–8 ('happy lyfe maintainer', etc.).

have theyr fill] are fulfilled.
6. meere] mere (pure and/or sole).
7. skill] deviousness.
8. directnes] i.e. the opposite of 'skill and fraude'; a marginally clearer reading than *1621*'s 'directions' (instructions to be good).
10. kinde, and just] modifying 'ruller' rather than 'affections'.
11. fained] desired, with pun on 'feigned'.
13. This crowne] this crown of sonnets.
all that . . . more] everything else I have.
14. beestow'd] gave away.

14
3. choyse] special.
4. one] i.e. heart.
5. tribute] payment to a conqueror.
6. faith untouch'd is] is untouched (pure) faith.
6–7. discharge . . . mee] pay off my debts.
8. envyes sore] the wound of envy.
9. attend] stand by.
11–12. bend / to] focus on.
14. In this . . . I turne] repeating the first line of the first poem of the crown.

From Section 5 of the manuscript

In *1621* three sonnets in MS Section 5 (including 'Faulce hope') swapped places with sonnets in Section 1.

1
1. spill] kill.
2–3. unaturall . . . wombe] hostile to your own child.
4. plenty gives . . . dearth] and provides bounty which (paradoxically) leads to greater shortage.
6. them] the same people as 'those who appointed are to death' (line 7). The tyrants reward the people they condemn to death.
profitts fill] fill of profits.
8. the greater falle] the fall of the people appointed by the tyrants.
theyr will] the tyrants' will, with a possible pun on William Herbert.
9. shadow] hide.

'My muse now hapy'
This sonnet, the final poem in the printed text, seems to celebrate a nobler form of constancy than the agonised love described hitherto, though its exact nature (spiritual? worldly?) is uncertain. In the manuscript it is followed, and thus undercut, by further poems of a clearly worldly nature.
3. phant'sies] imaginative feelings.
6. prove] turn out to be.
9. sun] son, i.e. Cupid.
13. of] off.
14. your honor prove] be honourable.

From Section 7 of the manuscript

Three of the poems in section 7, including both given here, were moved in 1621 into the text of the *Urania*.

'A sheapherd who noe care did take'
In the *Urania* this poem is recited by the Duke of Wertenberg, who says that it was composed by his lady Lycencia as a means of covering her ill fortune.

2. aught] anything.
7. theyr sport his fare] their games his meat and drink.
8. theyr sight] seeing them.
11. which ne're miss] which always involve.
12. incombrances] burdens, problems.
17, 147, 151, 217, 306. chang] change.
23–4. wheras . . . lay] where a fair young maiden lay behind a willow tree.
28. band] bond.
30. love borne] born of love and/or supported ('borne') by love.
31–2. heavnly drops . . . disgrace] The tears (drops) were called forth by sorrow as proud witnesses of her disgrace.
34. furder] further.
46. scrip] shepherd's bag.
51. grownd] basis.
52. crost] thwarted.
54. Cupids service] serving Cupid, god of love.
54–5. ties . . . respects] only cares about his infatuation.
56. wavelike] fleeting?
63–4. unfolde . . . reliefe] speak about her unresolved sorrows.
65. His new sun] the lady.
67. triumph] victory celebration; she implies that the willow glories in her desolate condition ('state decayd').
68. the fruit . . . mee] The plant which most aptly symbolises my situation (as the next two lines explain).
71. vade] fade, decay.
72. move] decay?
73. My songs shall . . . still] like the well-known 'willow song' quoted by Shakespeare (*Othello* 4.3.38–55).
86. hy] hurry.
88. try] experience.
99. your keepe] keeping you.
108. suteth] suit each other.
109. faire] fair lady.
115. tow] two.
117. hy] hurry.
119. byding] resting.
125. must bee] were.
126. pearlike] pearl-like.
127. limd] limned (drawn).
138. othes] oaths.
140. couler] colour (gloss over).
143. ar us bereav'd] are taken away from us (by faithless people we fall in love with).
144. sought to . . . delay'd] fobbed off when we approach the beloved?
149. as] that.
151. brought] brought home.
152. abroad bee blowne] be made public.
159. sallow] willow.
160. Aradeame] 'plougher of home ground' (Roberts (Wroth 1995)).
163. inthralld] enchanted.
166, 173. hether] hither.
175. whose absence martirs mee] the absence of whom kills me.
176. whose sight . . . tyes] the sight of whom incapacitates me.
186. cace] case (predicament).
187–8. who thus . . . in disgrace] who will experience grief and disgrace like me (as we're both unrequitedly in love).

187. partaker] sharer.
needs] necessarily.
191. payd] given to you.
195–6. your freedome . . . my care] you'll be just as free as before, and you won't be able to accuse me of causing you pain.
202. counsell] advice.
203. humour fond] foolish whim.
207. prov'd] turned out to be.
217. chance] bad luck.
218. my affection turne] love someone else.
219. disdaine, which . . . rang] being rejected, which makes others seek a new lover.
move] moves.
219, 308. rang] range (go off to someone else).
231. and liberty . . . prove] and wish everyone to be free.
240. plaine] lament.
244. both] both of us.
246. els butt] anything else except.
247. procure my grave] kill me.
251. my only] only my.
255. then pitty . . . receave] have pity on my pain.
258. coming] future.
259. care] trouble.
271. your . . . mov'd] the same thing (declaring your love) has led to your predicament.
276. fold] a sheep-fold.
278. fortune blind] Fortune was traditionally said to be blind.
280. a state . . . binds] a situation circumscribed by bad luck.
286. biding] home.
287. his liberty did win] that deprived him of his liberty.
289. And pleasingly . . . fall] and accepts with pleasure his fall into bad fortune.
290. his griefe accounts delight] thinks his grief delight.
295. haples] unlucky.
297. dide] died.
300. were turn'd . . . streame] similar to the fate of Arethusa (Ovid, *Metamorphoses*, book 5).
306. ficle] fickle.

'I, who doe feele'
The final poem in the manuscript, ending the Folger sequence on an unequivocally worldly and despairing note. In the *Urania* this poem is composed by the despairing Antissia, suspecting that Amphilanthus loves Pamphilia and not her. Its narrative situation is thus roughly parallel to that of the previous poem, Antissia being in Aradeame's position.
9. try] undergo.
14. gett] beget, engender something.
17. hy] hasten away.
21. fained] feigned.
23. wrack] ruin.
25. My state I see] I am aware of my predicament.
29. Salimanders] i.e. Salamanders, mythical reptiles thought to be able to live in fire.

Anne Southwell: Folger Shakespeare Library MS V.b.198

Sonnett ('Beauty, Honor, yeouth, and fortune')
Title. Sonnett] used in the seventeenth century to refer to any short piece of verse.
4. Gambols] playful things.

9. noysome] disagreeable.
10. noughts] nought.
11–14. O happy . . . lost Gayning] i.e. sacrifice of worldly things—a form of 'dying'—leads to spiritual rewards (or life), paradoxically resulting in gain through loss. Cf. John 12:24 (Southwell 1997, 191).
13. accompt] account.

Sonnett ('O how happy were I dearest')
6. might . . . the] perhaps a question.
6. the] thee.
7. deme] judge.
10. are thy Addition] 'are added gratuitously by you'?

'All.maried.men.desire.to.have good wifes'
3. They are owr head] cf. 1 Corinthians 11:3: 'the head of the woman is the man'.
6. the text] Genesis 2:21–5.
taene] taken.
7–8. A. simbole . . . savinge good] Adam's side, from which the rib which made Eve was taken, symbolises the wound made in Christ's side by the spear after the crucifixion (see John 19:34).
8. spowse] The Church was traditionally figured as the bride of Christ.
10. Adam . . . a sleepe] Adam slept while Eve was taken from his side (Genesis 2:21).

Anne Southwell: British Library Lansdowne MS 740

To the kinges most excellent Majestye
Title. To . . . Majestye] Charles I or James I (see headnote).
1. Battlike] hidden away like a bat.
5. Cherubins] i.e. Cherubim: angels.
did tender] gave.
8. to bigg] too full up with emotion.
12. these sparckles] these lines, the products of her mind.
14. states abilitye] skill in governing.
15. attractive goodnes] quality of drawing me towards you by your virtue.
20. Epitome] representation in miniature.
21. nursing father] Isaiah 49:23.

extra stanza
1. feet of clay] Daniel 2:33–4.
2. watrye balles] earthly eyes.
5. off] of.
court] In *Folger*, the 'court' is unequivocally God's; in Lansdowne reference to the royal court may be intended.
6. councell] counsel (political advice).

Precept 4
Title. Precept] commandment.
Remember . . . hallowed it] Exodus 20:10–11, quoted in the Geneva translation.
sabaoth] Hebrew for 'armies'—as in the phrase 'Lord of Sabaoth' (Lord of Hosts)—frequently confused with 'Sabbath', i.e. day of religious rest, Sunday for Christians. See also line 30, below.
1. admired ball] the earth.
3–6. engrayl'd it . . . living wights] In pre-Copernican cosmology, the earth, at the centre of the spherical cosmos, was surrounded by concentric spheres of water, air and fire; the moon, the planets and the stars ('starrye lights', line 5) were located on further concentric spheres.

3. engrayl'd] adorned.
4. vallence] curtain.
7. this . . . prince] Adam.
10. to . . . call] God calls to man, his 'type', created in God's image (Genesis 1:27).
12. hee] God.
14. acquittance] release from debt.
16. ingrave . . . engrave] punning on two senses: 'consign to the grave' and 'imprint deeply on oneself'.
22. yoaked bandes] the yoke coupling together oxen.
23–4. tis six . . . that's gods] As only one day out of seven is God's, it is unreasonable to 'steal' it by working on it.
33. thy . . . affoord] your labours will bring you plenty.
48. thy future rests appeare] salvation is prefigured.
63. facultyes] capabilities.
68. Cherubines & Thrones] orders of angels.
76. noe . . . assumes] is completely spiritual (unearthly).
79–83. Only thy . . . in order] Before the six days of creation, 'the earth was without form, and void; and darkness was upon the deep. And the Spirit of God moved upon the waters' (Genesis 1:2, Geneva Bible).
84. & made . . . fruitfull border] referring to the sphere of water (see note on lines 3–6).
85. & from . . . seperat] the work of the first day of creation (Genesis 1:3–5).
86–90. dividing cold . . . livery weares] Renaissance cosmology believed the world was made out of four elements: earth (cold and dry), water (cold and wet), air (hot and wet) and fire (hot and dry). Before creation, the qualities of cold, hot, dry and wet were jumbled up together and not yet sorted into elements.
88. simpathye] mutual attraction.
90. livery] servants' uniform.
93. milliarious yeeres] periods of one thousand years.
94. longitude] timespan.
reckoning] computation, with a pun on 'reckoning' in the sense of 'rendering an account of one's life or conduct to God at death or judgement' (*OED* 4c).
cast] estimated.
95. A thousand . . . Lord] 2 Peter 3:8.
97–132. The first . . . Sabbath day] In these six stanzas, Southwell shows how the six days of creation prefigure six thousand-year segments of human history from the fall of Adam to the last judgement.
97. voyd & emptye] See Genesis 1:2.
98. Adams apostasye] the fall of mankind, the result of Adam's failure to obey God's command not to eat the fruit of the tree of knowledge (Genesis 3).
99–102. raigning a thousand . . . are night] God's separation of light from darkness, the work of the first day of creation, foreshadows the division between good people, figured as the descendants of Seth (Adam and Eve's third son) and bad people, descendants of Cain (Adam and Eve's eldest son and the murderer of Abel, their second son).
103–8. The second day . . . channell take] On the second day, God created 'the firmament' (understood in the Renaissance to be the sphere of the fixed stars), dividing the waters above the firmament from the waters below it. Southwell seems to follow the view that the waters above the firmament formed a higher, 'crystalline' sphere.
104. counsells] schemes.
107. christaline] clear water.
108. sulpharous channell] hellish (fiery) stream.
109–14. The third day . . . giddye waves] On the third day, God divided the land from the sea. Southwell compares the virtuous figures of Moses and Abraham to 'fruitfull solid ground' (line 113), directed by God. Moses received the ten commandments from God (Exodus 20).
112. Satrapick] associated with eastern tyrants (satraps).

113. graves] engraves.
114. drad] dread (to be feared).
the . . . waves] the other people are light-headed and foolish.
119. Alpha & omega] beginning and end (from the first and last letters of the Greek alphabet), i.e. Christ, addressed in these two lines. See Revelation 22:13.
122. Hydraes] many-headed snakes.
124. childing] pregnant.
gall] bitterness, poison.
131–2. when all . . . Sabbath day] the last judgement.
133. his Image] Adam and Eve (see note on line 10).
to the barre] to undergo trial.
135–6. a fierye . . . of life] See Genesis 3:24.
139. wizzard] wise man (sarcastic).
139 (textual note). gazeling] gosling, i.e. foolish, inexperienced person (*OED* 3).
gallant] fashionable gentleman.
141–2. Jahells nayle . . . Judiths sword] biblical heroines. Jael killed the Israelites' enemy Sisera by hammering a tent-peg into his skull (Judges 4–5); Judith cut off the head of the Assyrian general Holofernes, who lusted after her (apocryphal Book of Judith).
143. enabled] strengthened.
146. finite dust] earthly mankind; cf. Genesis 2:7.
147. keepe] look after.
[153] (textual note). adornes] beautify.
156. impe] graft, implant.
161. expired] breathed out.
164. attiring] trivial self-adornment.
169–70. Seven hundred . . . capacityes] in the Jewish Torah.
174. mold] earthly flesh ('mold' is the dust of Genesis 2:7).
201. all creators] belonging to the creator of everything
203. ape] figuratively, a foolish person.
204. bedlame] madman (literally, inhabitant of Bedlam, a London asylum).
205. cobwebbes] fanciful and flimsy reasoning.
279. be . . . turpified] let him be made dirty by doing these things (the things mentioned in lines 277–8).
280. Chima'raes] unreal fancies, i.e. the muses.
281. Heliconian hill] Helicon, in classical mythology the home of the muses; part of Parnassus (see next note).
282. Pernassus] Mount Parnassus in Greece, used here to refer to one of the fountains on the mountain.
285. pelf] worldly riches. In Protestant theology, God's grace is freely given—it cannot be 'bought' by good works, as Catholics assume.
286. base] mean.
291. because it . . . time] because it takes longer.
292. measures quantitye] poetic metre.
294. Ingott] a piece of metal.
curious] delicate, elaborate.
295. it] rhyme.
296. packhorse] i.e. a clumsy vehicle.
299. carryed] carried out.
300. proportions] punning on poetic metre.
301. rugged] rough, unpolished.
twine] piece of writing.
302. quickening] enlivening.
308. corrivalls] joint rivals.
my love] Jesus.

309–12. hee is fresh ... doth adorne] The language of these lines is reminiscent of the Song of Songs.

312. hayres reflex] hair's reflection.

319. triple sence] perhaps a reference to the three senses in which the Bible could be read: literal, moral and spiritual. This stanza refers to Old Testament prophets who foresaw the birth of Christ.

320. harolds] heralds.

321. point] quality.

322. Coles ... theyr tongues] symbolises the divine inspiration of the Old Testament prophets: see Isaiah 6:6–7.

323. Davids ofspring] the Jews.

338. dunghill] the world.

340. Halcion day] particularly calm day.

357. & passive ... fee] can cultivated earth bring forth no plants?

359. full] i.e., complete?

361. ground baytes] baits thrown down to the bottom of a river.

362. fussome] fussy, or fulsome?

368. her] the world's.

369–72. lightening & thunder ... choke] the lightning, thunder and 'dunghill smoke' (line 371) of these lines are all images for worldly distraction or corruption.

372. pudder] poke about, dabble.

374. currall] coral (red, like lips).

376. that love] i.e. divine love.

377. accident] an inessential feature of something.

378. superficies] outer appearance.

clay] mortal human flesh.

380. to whome ... bene] to whom Nature has been a true mother (i.e. I am physically attractive).

381. rue] be sorry.

382. leprous] corrupt.

384. basest] most depraved, with a pun on 'base metal' (non-valuable metal).

386. not to ... glasses] i.e. the dames should not pay heed to their flattering servants, the appearance of their own bodies or their mirrors.

387. place or trappings] high status or its adornments.

388. approve] prove.

389. soe layed] given in this way.

390. fayre soft ... soules] The belief that women had no souls seems to have been current in the seventeenth century, though it had no doctrinal backing. See also Astell, 'Ambition', line 8 and note.

391. you ... men] addressing women.

393. contemne] treat with contempt.

394. only formall clay] just earthly material, with no immaterial soul.

401–2. Adam did sleepe ... lame] Genesis 2:21; cf. Southwell's 'All.maried.men.desire. to.have good wifes', p. 62 above).

401. frame] form.

402. lame] weakened.

433. superciliums] eyebrows.

435. they] male love poets.

437. dowrye] gift.

sett] deliberately placed.

439–40. Minervaes ... owle] the owl was associated with Minerva, Roman goddess of wisdom.

440. these battes & crowes] the critical men.

442. this wanteth ... gender] listing men's criticisms of women's grammar.

443–4. then must . . . a thistle] Elizabeth Clarke suggests that these lines refer to Stuart imagery of roses and thistles associated with James I, and thus imply criticism of the King (Longfellow 2004, 120, n. 16).
443. frame] write.
445. Sybells] pre-Christian prophetesses. See Seager headnote.
450. least] lest.
455. bedesman] i.e. beadsman, someone who prays for someone else (perhaps with Catholic connotations).
minion] lover.
456. scape] escape.
458. that admired virgin Queene] Elizabeth I.
459. stellifyed] glorified (literally, transformed into a star).
460. Debora] Israelite leader (Judges 4–5).
teene] damage.
461. Romes proud bulles] papal edicts. Elizabeth I was excommunicated by the Pope in 1570.
whose] i.e. Elizabeth's
462. church and state . . . fortifie] Southwell celebrates Elizabeth for re-establishing the Church of England, and for bringing security and order to her country after the disruptions of the reign of the Catholic Mary I.
463. sanguine] cheerful: i.e. a woman in whom the humour of blood predominates (see *OED* 3a). The 'sanguine' was one of the four 'complexions', or temperaments, recognised by pre-modern physiological theory. Melancholy (line 469) was another.
of all] by everyone.
466. spanniells] nosy people, suspicious that a merry woman must be unchaste.
467. on drye foot] relying only on the scent of a dry foot (i.e. on little evidence).
it cannott bee] i.e. people assume it cannot be.
468. hold . . . simpathye] co-exist in the same person.
469. melancholly] See note to line 463. Melancholy was thought to be caused by the predominance of black bile.
471. beare . . . bee] put up with the criticism that she is.
473. great in place] of high social status.
gravitye] seriousness.
475. complexion] see note to line 463.
476. sophist] specious reasoner.
dotes] foolish thoughts.
477. landskip] superficial?
detection] explanation.
478. coates] coverings?
480. tender] value.
485. stay] support.
487. Bee wise . . . Doves] as Jesus advised his disciples: see Matthew 10:16.
488. borne subjects . . . obey] cf. Ephesians 5:22; Colossians 3:18.
489. clogges] earthly encumbrances.
490. them] the critical men of lines 399–402, 441–2.
491. bountyes] gifts.
492. naked they . . . returne] paraphrases Job 1:21.
499. keepe . . . burning] be prepared (cf. Matthew 25:1–13).
500. head] husband.
501. him] Christ.
504. Queene Sabaes] the Queen of Sheba's (1 Kings 10).
disgraces] outshines.
505. hold this state] enjoy this condition.
507. count] estimate.
toyes] trivial things.

571. angle] corner.
574. gleane] pick up wheat left behind by reapers, like the biblical Ruth (Ruth 2).
tares] weeds. Separating wheat from tares is a biblical injunction: see Matthew 13:25–30.
575. sectes & schismes] splits in the Church.
577. bread of life] Jesus: see John 6:35.
want] lack.
578. living water] Jesus: see John 4:10–11.
581. In thee . . . & be] paraphrases Acts 17:28.
654. busye] overactive.

Anna Ley: Clark Library MS L6815 M3 C734

A Christmasse Caroll
10. Angles] angels.
15. Ishais] Jesse's.

Upon a sermon preached in S Paules Church
This is an acrostic poem, the first letters of each line spelling the name of the preacher. John Squire was the minister at St Leonard's, Shoreditch, where Roger Ley was curate. His sermon was published as *A Sermon on the Second Commandement* (1624). Squire was accused by Parliament of papistry and defended himself at parliamentary committee on 18 February 1640. The accusations were published as *Articles Exhibited in Parliament, Against Master John Squire, Viccar of Saint Leonard Shoreditch, August 7th. 1641* (1641). In response, Squire apparently caused his defence to be published the same year (*An Answer To a printed Paper Entituled Articles Exhibited in Parliament Against Mr. John Squier*, 1641). Roger Ley includes an account of these events, taken from Squire's own notes, on which he based his defence at parliamentary committee (Clark MS, fols 185r–191r). Squire preached Anna Ley's funeral sermon in 1641. He was ejected from St Leonard's after the battle of Edgehill in October 1642, and died at Richmond in November 1653.
Title. the Second Commandement] Exodus 20:4. Protestants believed that the statues and images of Catholic churches transgressed this commandment's prohibition of graven images, and were idolatrous (line 2).
2. Roomes] Rome's.
3. with . . . hide] i.e. as attempted by Adam and Eve after eating the forbidden fruit (Genesis 3:7)—and just as ineffectually.
5–7. this fountaine . . . this Antidote] i.e. the commandment.

Upon the death of King James
King James VI and I died in 1625. Throughout this poem, the king of England (formerly James, now his son Charles) is figured as the sun.
2. urania] Muse of Astronomy.
3. Aonian grove] in classical mythology, inhabited by the Muses.
4. Pheebus] Phoebus, the sun god.
6. Charles his waine] Charles's wain is the constellation of the Plough. Ley's allusion may also pun on 'waine' as Scots for child (i.e. Charles his [James's] son).
7–9. ride on . . . thy steeds] In classical mythology, the passage of the sun from dawn to dusk was explained as the sun-god driving his carriage ('Carre', line 11) across the sky.

Upon the great plague
Title. the great plague . . . James] James's death in March 1625 was closely followed by one of the worst outbreaks of plague in the seventeenth century, described by a modern historian as 'a national calamity', which, in occurring 'at the beginning of the reign of ill-starred Charles I may well have been regarded as an evil portent' (Shrewsbury 1971, 346).
6. thy cheifest seat] London.

12. king of peace] James was renowned for his love of peace; his personal motto was the biblical tag 'Beati pacifici'—blessed are the peace-makers. His efforts to keep his kingdoms out of European wars (lines 13–14) were not appreciated by all of his subjects.

17–20. His pen . . . deadly sting] James's anti-papal publications included the anonymous *Apology for the Oath of Allegiance* (1607), and the acknowledged *Premonition to all most Mighty Monarchies, Kings, Free Princes, and States of Christendom* (1609).

An answer to Mercuries message anno 1641

This poem is a refutation of the anonymous pamphlet *Mercuries Message, or The Coppy of a Letter sent to* William Laud *late Archbishop of Canterbury, now prisoner in the Tower* (1641). Laud, who had been appointed Archbishop of Canterbury in 1633, was impeached and imprisoned in 1640, committed to the Tower of London in March 1641 and executed in 1645. During his period as Archbishop, Laud had introduced numerous reforms which outraged radical (and many moderate) Protestants in the Church of England, who felt that these innovations were steering the Church too close to Roman Catholicism (see notes to lines 11–12, 19–22, 64–6, 68, 71–4, below). He was also known for his uncompromising support for episcopacy (government of the church by bishops). His attempt, with Charles I, to tighten the grip of episcopacy on the traditionally Presbyterian Church of Scotland led to the Bishops' Wars in the late 1630s. *Mercuries Message*, published after Laud's imprisonment in the Tower, condemned Laudian reforms and sparked off a brief pamphlet war, four subsequent titles in support, variously, of Laud and 'Mercury' appearing over the next few months. Ley seems to have been aware of at least one of these later publications (see note to line 1, below). She also develops the contemporary argument by conflating 'Mercury' with Martin Marprelate, pseudonymous author of a series of notorious anti-episcopal tracts published in 1588–89.

It should also be noted that Anna Ley's authorship of 'An answer to Mercuries message' must be considered conjectural. Given that—according to Squire's sermon—Ley died in October 1641 after a long illness, there must be some doubt as to her ability to have responded to this topical pamphlet war. Furthermore, the poem is textually unstable, subject to a number of corrections by both Hands A and B, and its final thirteen lines are transcribed by Hand B later in the manuscript, after a gap of 15 folios, at the end of the section concerned with Anna Ley's death. Lines 126–9 are echoed in Roger Ley's elegy cycle, 'Albion in blacke', which commemorates and defends ten conformist divines against nonconformist criticism.

Title. him that did delight . . . accuser of the Brethren] Satan.

Conventicle] a private religious meeting, chiefly associated with radical Protestants.

Martines] Martin Marprelate, also in lines 1 and 45.

1. Whie how now] echoes the opening of *An Answer to The most Envious, Scandalous, and Libellous Pamphlet, Entituled MERCURIES MESSAGE* (1641), ('How now! what ist which I doe vainly read').

3. Mercury is heathenish] Mercury was the messenger of the gods in Roman mythology.

4. Amsterdam] home of several well-known English Protestant congregations. Many radical English Protestants who got into trouble with the authorities at home took refuge in Amsterdam.

11–12. Furies come . . . namles booke] Whereas *Mercuries Message* had argued that Laud's reforms brought the Church of England too close to popery, Ley, like many conformists, argues that the criticisms of radicals such as 'Mercury' inadvertently give comfort to the Catholic Church by dividing and undermining Protestantism.

12. this mad namles booke] the anonymous *Mercuries Message*.

14. delinquent] one who fails in his duty. The term was specifically used by the parliamentary side during the Civil Wars to denote a supporter of Charles I.

17. mauger] variant of maugre: in spite of.

19–22. Clearely produce . . . justly claime] rejects the claim of radical Protestants that the name and office of bishops are unscriptural.

37–40. Our Churches... downe laid] alludes to early reformers of the Church of England, such as Cranmer and Ridley (see note to line 100), later martyred for their beliefs.

39. for... Strong] a biblical image: see 1 Timothy 3:15.

41. sectaries] radical Protestants who wanted to separate from the Church of England: usually (as here) an abusive term.

49. Whitgift] John Whitgift (1530?–1604), Archbishop of Canterbury from 1583–1604, was a defender of the episcopal form of church government, and the prime target of the Marprelate tracts. See Lake (1988).

51. To... began] i.e. the crackdown against radical Protestants instigated by Whitgift after the publication of the Marprelate tracts.

64. garments] Radical Protestants opposed the wearing of elaborate vestments by the clergy.

65–6. the railes... boarde] One of Laud's controversial reforms was to have the communion table moved to the east end of churches and enclosed by rails.

68. the Zelots... kneele] Laud's insistence that communicants should kneel to receive the bread and wine was opposed by many in the church. 'Zelots' (i.e. Zealots) is a disparaging conformist term for radical Protestants.

71–4. Who though... halfe way] Many Protestants who approved of the use of ceremony in the church none the less felt that some of Laud's reforms (such as bowing at the name of Jesus) had gone too far. See Spurr (1998, 88).

82. the droopeing hierarchie] quotes *Mercuries Message*, line 3.

85–6. Downe went... then preaching] paraphrases *Mercuries Message*, lines 11–12.

90. lecturers] Ley's stress on the Church of England's support for lectures (extra sermons) counters *Mercuries Message*'s claim that the Laudian church had tried to suppress them (lines 19–20).

91. some two houres... weeke] *Mercuries Message* had complained that Laud wanted congregations to hear only 'one Sermon... but one houre long' (lines 39–40).

99. our service booke] the Book of Common Prayer, or Prayer Book, which prescribed the liturgy for use in Church of England services. Its use was opposed by many radical Protestants (cf. *Mercuries Message*, line 12).

100. martyrs were and holy men] The first and second editions of the Prayer Book (1549, 1552) were overseen by Thomas Cranmer (1489–1556), Archbishop of Canterbury, with the help of Thomas Goodrich (d. 1554), Bishop of Ely, Nicholas Ridley (1500?–55), Bishop of London, and others. Cranmer and Ridley were both imprisoned upon the accession of the Catholic Queen Mary, and executed for heresy.

104. The prince of darkenes] Satan.

107–8. he doth rave... Jesus bow] pejoratively paraphrases *Mercuries Message*, lines 151–7.

109. Church commands] To *Mercuries Message*, the fact that the Church rules, or Canons, prescribe bowing at the name of Jesus is part of the problem (line 57). The *Constitutions and Canons Ecclesiasticall* of the Church of England, published in 1640, formalised and defended Laud's liturgical innovations, and were strongly opposed by his enemies in the Church (see Tyacke 1987, 238–42).

we the scripture have] cites scriptural authority: 'at the name of Jesus every knee should bow' (Philippians 2:10).

121. impostumed] infected.

121–4. Breathd from... foule blast] refers to the diatribe against Laud's fellow-bishops in *Mercuries Message* (lines 159–66). Ley's lines 123–4 are a direct quotation from *Mercuries Message* (lines 165–6).

Jane Cavendish: Yale University, Beinecke Library Osborn MS b. 233

Passions Contemplation

William Cavendish, Jane Cavendish's father, went into exile in continental Europe as a result of his defeat at the battle of Marston Moor in July 1644. Many of her poems express her grief at the loss of her father. This is the first of two poems by Cavendish entitled 'Passions Contemplation'; the second follows on p. 6 [fol. 3v]; *Rawl.*, p. 4.

4. Centryes] sentries.
13. Devines] theologians.

On her Sacred Majestie
The subject of this poem is Queen Henrietta Maria, wife of King Charles I.
5. quinticence] quintessence, the purest form of any substance.

The Quinticens of Cordiall
Elizabeth Cavendish Brackley, Jane Cavendish's sister, is the subject of this poem.
Title. Quinticens] see note to previous poem, line 5.
Cordiall] of or belonging to the heart; also, restorative medicine.
6–7.] unclear. A possible interpretation is that if Elizabeth says her Lord (William Cavendish) is returned and adds that she will remain, then all is well. Alternatively, if Elizabeth names Gilbert's water, then her Lord is returned, and Cavendish asks her to remain.
6. Gilberts water] a medical beverage.

An answeare to the Verses Mr Carey made
Thomas Carew (1595?–1639?), royalist poet and dramatist, addressed two New Year's poems to Lucy Percy Hay, Countess of Carlisle (1599–1660): 'Give Lucinda pearl, or stone' and 'Those that can give, open their hands this day'. The former poem is the more likely provocateur to Cavendish's answer poem, as it is copied in the Newcastle Manuscript (see headnote). However, Cavendish's wholesale departure from the premises of either poem renders its critique equally applicable to both. The Countess of Carlisle wielded significant power and influence at court; most famously, her pre-emptive warning to John Pym of the King's plan to arrest five Members of Parliament ensured their absence on the appointed day in 1642. William Cavendish, the poet's father, had been appointed a Knight of the Bath with Lord Carlisle in 1610, and remained on friendly terms with both Carlisles through the 1620s and 1430s.

9–10.] It is of no benefit to disregard female honour when engaging in flirtatious conversation.
20. Mee, for to stile] to call me.

On my honourable Grandmother
Elizabeth Hardwick Talbot, Countess of Shrewsbury (1520–1608), known as Bess of Hardwick, was Jane Cavendish's paternal great-grandmother. An extremely influential Elizabethan courtier, who married four times and acquired great wealth, Elizabeth was ambitious on behalf of her offspring. She and her fourth husband, George Talbot (1528?–90), were custodians to Mary, Queen of Scots, and Elizabeth's grand-daughter, Arbella Stuart, was for many years a threat to the thrones of England and Scotland. The Countess died fourteen years prior to Jane Cavendish's birth. The poem, therefore, is addressed to the matriarch of the author's paternal line, in order to negotiate competing lines of descent with the aim of claiming the upper genealogical hand for Jane Cavendish's own branch of the family. Thus, Elizabeth's three sons—Henry, William and Charles—are considered in turn. The eldest, Henry Cavendish (1550–1616), was married to his stepsister, Grace Talbot, and died without legitimate issue, having been disinherited by his mother. The second son, William Cavendish (1551–1626), was favoured by his mother in her will. He became first Earl of Devonshire in 1618, thus establishing a formidable line of prominent Cavendishes (his great-grandson William became the first Duke of Devonshire in 1694). The Countess of Shrewsbury's third son, Charles, is the author's paternal grandfather; hence, his son William, the poet's father, emerges triumphant. Cavendish appropriates the parliamentarian sobriquet for William Waller—William the Conqueror—for her own father, highlighting both his victories as royalist commander and his pre-eminence in the family line.

1. the very Magazine of rich] storehouse, commercial or military; here used as metaphor for Talbot's wealth.

3–4. your wealth . . . durst not peach] possibly a reference to Talbot's marriage settlements with her third and fourth husbands, William St Loe and George Talbot. St Loe's estate was settled on Elizabeth and her heirs, excluding his former issue, while her marriage to Talbot was conditional on two further marriages between their offspring, thereby uniting the families' wealth.

4. peach] impeach, i.e. bring to trial.

To heaven, or a confession to God

10. To receave thee] to take communion.

11. Thy table] the communion table.

12. thy passions] Jesus' sufferings on the cross.

14–15. crucefie . . . sacred selfe] commit more sins, thus rendering necessary (afresh) the sacrifice of Jesus (cf. Hebrews 6:6).

On the .30.th of June, to God

This poem commemorates the royalist victory, led by the author's father, over the parliamentary army at the battle of Adwalton Moor on 30 June 1643.

9. Fairfax] Thomas Fairfax, commander of the parliamentary army.

13. Rebells] the parliamentary side, viewed as rebels both to the King and to the Church of England.

16. votery] i.e. votary, a devoted worshipper.

Hopes preparation

This poem anticipates the author's acceptance of the sacrament of communion. Having received the sacrament, however, the speaker transforms the poem into a plea on behalf of her father in exile.

3. vizard] a mask.

6. Leaven . . . Cake] obscure. The 'Cake' is probably the communion bread, which was traditionally unleavened.

8. Lre] This abbreviation is used for 'letter' elsewhere in the manuscript; however, its meaning here is not entirely clear.

12, 22, 23. holly] holy.

44. my Bywords pray] my frequent prayer.

'My lord it is your absence makes each see'; 'My lord your absence makes I cannot owne'

Both poems occur at the end of the pastoral co-authored by Jane Cavendish and her sister Elizabeth Brackley. The initials 'J.C.' and 'E.B.' denote authorship. Both function to dedicate the pastoral (signalled by the references to 'sheppardesses') to their father in exile.

Lucy Hutchinson: Nottinghamshire Archives DD/HU2

'Leave of yee pittying freinds'

1, 67. of] off.

30. enchants] enchantments.

35. vizards] masks.

44. guilt] gilded.

54. *Bloody Tower*] a part of the Tower of London where Richard III was said to have murdered his brother and nephews, and where John Hutchinson was imprisoned in 1663 (Hutchinson 2000, 306).

Another on the Sun Shine

Title. Sun] The sun was traditionally associated with the king. As Norbrook points out (Norbrook 1997, 475), Hutchinson rewrites the image to produce an oblique attack on the court and the monarchy, instead imagining a future where there will only be one king, Jesus.

4. guilt] gilded.

20. disgorgd] vomited.

27–33. Thou sawst . . . exile Led] probably refers to the failure of the interregnum settlements, and the suffering of former parliamentary leaders (such as John Hutchinson) after the Restoration. A more specific allusion may also be intended.

36. Reuines] Ruins.

38–54. By thyne . . . everquenched Light] Hutchinson refers to biblical prophecies in Revelation 6:12–14 and 7:16, Joel 2:10, 31 and 3:15, and Isaiah 60:19, about the 'day of the Lord' – God's judgement on his enemies, and blessing for the godly. The sun will be darkened, the moon will turn to blood, the stars will fall and the godly will see by the light of God. See also 2 Peter 3:10–12.

Upon two pictures
This poem is followed in the manuscript by two related poems, 'On the Picture in Armour' and 'On the Picture of the Prisoner'.

Title. Upon two pictures] Norbrook suggests the portrait by Robert Walker reproduced by Sutherland (Norbrook 1997, 474 (n. 14), 494 (n. to title); Hutchinson 1973, opposite 66).
  Greate] Grate.

14–15. Those whome . . . abandond him] 'Those' may be the English people, whom John Hutchinson and his political allies wanted to save from the tyranny of monarchical rule, but who proved treacherous in welcoming back the Stuarts at the Restoration.

24. false aydes] former parliamentarians who had betrayed the cause. Traitors named in the *Life* include Anthony Ashley Cooper and Richard Ingoldsby (Hutchinson 2000, 273–4, 279).

27. Chrusht . . . fall] Hutchinson compares her husband to Christ conquering his foes in his death: see Genesis 3:15, Luke 20:17–18.

To the Gardin att O:
Title. O:] Owthorpe.

9. Just] See textual note. I follow Norbrook in correcting 'Jus' to 'Just', but the word may also refer to 'Jus' as in law: the law of gratitude forbids etc. On the other hand the scribe occasionally leaves off the final 't' – see textual notes to 'Another on the Sun Shine', line 21, and 'The Recovery', line 38.

11. empaled] enclosed.

26. Culture] nurture.

The Night
7. Orenas] i.e., Orena's rooms. 'Orena' is Hutchinson's literary persona, possibly echoing Katherine Philips's 'Orinda' (Norbrook 1997, 480), used only in this poem and the poem following it in the manuscript, 'Another Night'. Her husband is given the persona 'Philocles' in another poem, 'On my Visitt to W S' (*MS*, p. xxx).

45–6. What is Assended . . . amoung the dead] See Luke 24:5, the angels' words at the empty tomb.

56. centure] girdle, compass.

The Recovery
16–18. By its . . . refines] Hutchinson uses alchemical vocabulary to figure the transforming power of Christ through his cross, which alongside the image of Christ as rock is described in terms of the philosopher's stone. (For Hutchinson's links with alchemy, and the use of alchemical ideas in religious thought, see Abraham 1990, 2–3, 25–6.)

19. In this rocke . . . Spring] Moses drew water from the rock (Numbers 20:10); in the New Testament, this was seen as prefiguring Christ (1 Corinthians 10:4).

43. viued] viewed.

48. Guilt] gilded.

50. erected on the Sands] See Matthew 7:24–7, the parable of the wise and foolish builders. Here 'Loves Rocke' (line 8) is contrasted with the sand of the mortal world.

59. horred] horrid.

70. Cousenage] deception, trickery.

On The Spring 1668
27. hiew] hue.

'Here a greate Patriot lies'
This is the second in a series of eight epitaph poems towards the end of the manuscript. Hutchinson reworks several of the same ideas through these poems.

3. Of noble ... parentage] The Hutchinsons were an established Nottinghamshire family, although Hutchinson states (Hutchinson 2000, 31) that none of them before her father-in-law (Sir Thomas Hutchinson) had held a rank above esquire.

13. Greate Kings] God's.

'Ye Sons of England'
This is the seventh in Hutchinson's series of eight epitaph poems (see 'Here a greate Patriot lies').

3. Marble] John Hutchinson's grave.

Hester Pulter: Leeds University Library, Brotherton Collection MS Lt q 32

On the Same
Title. On the Same] The previous poem in the manuscript is entitled 'Upon the Death of my deare and lovely Daughter J.P.' (fol. 16v). A later annotating hand has identified 'J.P.' as 'Jane Pulter, baptized May 1. 1625. buried oct 8. 1645 aet. 20'.

4. Cinthia] the moon.
7. Phebus] Phoebus Apollo, god of the sun.
11. Aurora] the dawn.
12. he'd] head.
18. Thams] the River Thames.
19. Diana] the virgin goddess of hunting.
27. Poe] the River Po, Italy.

The Circle (notes supplied by Jayne Archer)
Title. The Circle] i.e. life as an ongoing cycle of birth and death, here compared to the alchemical opus, the experimental process embarked on in order to try to produce the philosopher's stone. The opus and the philosopher's stone (the product of the opus) are traditionally represented as a circle, in which all contraries are finally united: see, for example, Ripley (1591). In alchemical emblems, this often takes the form of the *ouroboros*, a serpent biting its own tail: see, for example, Maier (1617, 1625).

1. Chimick Art] i e. alchemy, the transmutation (or refinement) of matter and spirit. 'Chymistry' was used increasingly during the seventeenth century to encompass both the technical/experimental and the religio-spiritual aspects of alchemy.

2. vizet] visit.
Nature in her Morning dress] a popular topos for scientific investigation in the early modern period, also used by alchemists. See Hester (1596, sig. A7), Ashmole (1652, sig. B4) and French (1651, sig. A3v).

3. Mercurie and sulpher] In ancient alchemy, mercury ('the white', identified with the feminine principle) and sulphur ('the red', identified with the masculine principle) are the basic principles in all matter. In the alchemical opus, these two opposing principles are united in the so-called 'chymical wedding' which results in the philosopher's stone. In the early modern period, under the influence of Paracelsus, a third principle, 'Salt', was also identified.

filterys] filters.

7. Silver and in Gold] referring both to metallic elements used in alchemical work, and also to the two opposing principles of Luna (the feminine principle) and Sol (the masculine principle), which are united in the philosopher's stone. Perhaps an allusion to those alchemists who wrongly concentrate on riches rather than spiritual transformation.

8. Fretting vermill poyson] i.e. vermilion (or 'cinnabar'): mercuric sulphide, a reddish poison. Perhaps an allusion to the tradition that the philosopher's stone is highly poisonous just prior to its accomplishment.

9. refin'd] i.e. spiritual as well as physical transmutation.

10. Calcind] calcination, the oxidation of a metal. A stage in the alchemical opus where the prima materia ('first matter') is subjected to intense and rapid heating, creating a black calx. The calcination to dust described in lines 10–11 refers to death.

11. Urn] perhaps an allusion to the alchemical vessel (limbeck), in which the alchemist transforms not simply the prima materia but himself or herself.

13. Man . . . Glory] man the microcosm, in which all aspects of the macrocosm (i.e. the universe) are reflected. A central topos in ancient alchemy, and in the Emerald Tablet, the 'bible' of alchemy, in which it is written: 'The structure of the microcosm is in accordance with the structure of the macrocosm.'

14. primitive's Dust] an allusion to Genesis 2:7 ('And the Lord God formed man of the dust of the ground'), often cited by alchemical writers, who compared the biblical creation to the alchemical opus. Cf. Vaughan (1650, 28).

The perfection of Patience and knowledg

16. infranchised] released.

25. the Trump doth Sound] at the Day of Judgement, when souls will be summoned from their graves by the last trumpet.

30–1. sublim'd . . . Calcin'd] Sublimation is the extraction of spirit from matter, and the transformation of the spirit into the quintessence (the fifth essence or element of which all heavenly bodies are composed). Calcination is an early stage in the alchemical opus in which matter is heated very rapidly, leaving burnt, charred remains. Sublimed states and calcined states are opposites: the former is stable, immaterial and immortal; the latter is death-like, impure and mortal (note provided by Jayne Archer).

34–5. Sad Saturns . . . Malignancie] In astrological terms, the aspect of Saturn is gloomy and sad. For Pulter, the planet's influence was particularly malignant because Saturn was said to have eaten his children, and thus the planet was thought to preside over the death of children.

36. Conjunctions] an astrological term referring to conjunctions of the planets, which were thought to have particularly dramatic consequences for a nation.

39. Sol] the sun.

43–5. Venus . . . Occident] See *Paradise Lost*, V: 166. On certain occasions the same planet, Venus, which is Vesperus, the evening-star, appears as Hesperus, the morning-star, the following morning. Donne's Paradox XI is on this subject. 'Occident'—west—is the opposite of 'orient'.

46. Etheriall Fier] According to medieval cosmology, the space beyond the moon was filled with an element called 'ether', sometimes imagined as a purer form of fire.

47–8. this Terren . . . Unto all] whether the earth ('Terren', earthly) revolves around the sun.

58–9. wee shall know . . . known] adapts 1 Corinthians 13:12.

This was written 1648, when I Lay Inn

7. Nights Pale Queen] the moon.

16. Love sick EnDimion] In classical legend, Endymion was in love with the moon.

22. Empres of their Night] 'Empress of the Night' was a common poetic term for the moon.

23. Venus, Usher . . . Day] See note on 'The perfection of patience and knowledg', lines 43–5.

26. or . . . or] either . . . or.

33–6. And now . . . the rest] Pulter is considering whether the Copernican model for the cosmos is more accurate than the Ptolemaic. Even in 1667 Milton did not feel able to commit himself to either system. Cf. *Paradise Lost*, IV: 592–7.

43. Four bright Attendents] The four moons of Jupiter had only recently been discovered. It is possible that Pulter read about them in Henry More's *Psychodia platonica: or A platonicall song of the soul* (1642, 96). (I owe this reference to Sarah Hutton.)
44. Flagrant] red.
47. Fixed stars] the Milky Way.
51. Uglie Wife of Accharon] Orphne, or Gorgyra (meaning Darkness), was the wife of the river-god Acheron.
54. Eumenedes] the Furies, whose task was to punish human fugitives from justice.
66. As her pain started again, so did the comforts of daylight.

The Larke

The similarity of the action in this poem to the Mower episode in Marvell's poem 'Upon Appleton House' (lines 390–430) supports Peter Davidson's claim (Davidson 1999) that Pulter had read Marvell's poetry in manuscript. Both poems depict a 'Massacker' (line 65): but the episode in which the mower kills the bird in the nest by accident is turned by Pulter into an indictment of the careless 'Rurall Clown' who rather than mourn his mistake (as does Marvell's mower) takes the one surviving bird home with him for his child to play with. (In Marvell the bird is a rail, which, like the lark, nests on the ground.) The sweaty mower in Marvell's poem smells like Alexander; Pulter's 'clown' is sweaty in an unpleasant way. Pulter's poem may have been suggested by Marvell's 'orphan parent's call' (line 413): she clearly identifies strongly with the bereaved lark, and turns this episode into a bitter depiction of her consistent preoccupation, the loss of her children. Alternatively, both poets could have been drawing on a stanza in Giles Fletcher's *Christs victorie, and triumph* (1610, 66), which depicts the same situation. Here, the bird is a lark, and the parent's mourning song is a simile for the Virgin Mary's lament at the death of Christ. Pulter clearly finds an affinity between the lark's song and the female poetic voice.

1. Arachne] Arachne was turned into a spider by Minerva.
2. Tincile] tinsel: the spider's web.
26. Flora] goddess of flowers.
29. Rurall Clown] country bumpkin.
31. Unbracet] with his clothing undone.
32. Temp'] The Vale of Tempe in Thessaly, Greece, was proverbially beautiful.
33. stew'd in sweet] soaked in sweat.
Gripple hide bound] tenacious, narrow-minded.
35. sweltring him] sweating profusely.
35. high'd] hurried.
37. Purling] rippling, murmuring.
40. stradling] straddling: probably refers to the bandy-legged way he is walking.
57. Syth] scythe.
61. squale] a squalling child.
62. Who in a thred ... Hale] The child puts a thread around the lark's neck and pulls it tight.

To Sir Wm. D.

Title. Sir Wm. D.] Sir William Davenant, royalist poet and playwright.
Frontispiece] nose (see headnote).
2. Cheapside ... Cross] the market cross at Cheapside, London, was a famous landmark. One of the 'Eleanor Crosses', it was removed in 1643.
3. Diall ... Gnoman] the gnomon is the upright post of the sundial, which casts the shadow on the dial.
8. one Flesh] i.e. having given a graft of flesh to Davenant's face, with a pun on the sexual intimacy of marriage. There is a series of jokes in the poem drawing attention to the fact that Davenant had lost his nose through contracting a sexually transmitted disease.
14. Blur my Fame] compromise my reputation.

15. Gallant Dame] fine-looking woman.
20. my Leg] a curtsey.
27. blind Boy] Cupid.
28. Toy] Cupid is using his bow and arrow to have fun at Davenant's expense.
29. Chit] child.
31–4. Some Coy ... a Knight] The 'Coy young Lass' is Angelica, the heroine of Ariosto's epic poem *Orlando Furioso* (English translation by John Harington published 1591). After spurning all the heroes of the Christian army, including Orlando, she chooses the pagan page Medoro as her lover (canto 19).
36. Astolpho like] In *Orlando Furioso*, Astolfo goes to the Moon to seek his friend Orlando's lost wits (canto 34).
44. or ... or ... or] either ... or ... or.
45–50. A bold ordinance ... in grain] Pulter thinks that Davenant has lost his title as well as his nose—in which case the 'bold ordinance' is 'An Ordinance concerning the Peers of of Parliament, and other Honours and Titles' of 1646 (*Acts and Ordinances of the Interregnum 1642–1660*, 1911, I: 885). It declares void any title conferred since 20 May 1642 which was not confirmed by both houses of Parliament, and Davenant was knighted by Charles I in 1643. She seems to say that royal favour has replaced the title and that the knighthood is now engrained and bonded (line 50)—despite the fact that Davenant still has no nose.
46. Parces] the Fates.

'Dear God from thy high Throne look down'
Note Pulter's imagery of various alchemical processes in this religious lyric (notes provided by Jayne Archer).
4. calcine] see above, note to 'The perfection of Patience and knowledg', lines 30–1.
7. Should I to Tears dissolved be] This literary commonplace often appears in alchemical literature: the human body is compared to the alchemical vessel, with tears the distillate of experience and emotion.
11. Rarify'd] rarification: another alchemical term meaning the extraction of spirit from matter, here using spirit as spiritus (air).
13–14. Atoms ... dances] according to the Greek philosopher Democritus, the visual world is produced by the dance of tiny particles, or atoms. Democritan theory was best known in the Renaissance through the summary in Lucretius' *De rerum natura*.

Emblemes

'When God (who is to Mercie most inclin'd)'
The story of the Pied Piper, later made famous by Browning, first came to England in Richard Verstegan's *A restitution of decayed intelligence* (1605, 85). It was popularised in James Howell's *Familiar Letters* (1645). Pulter however cites Verstegan as her source in the marginal note to lines 21–2. There were several editions of Verstegan printed during the seventeenth century.
7–11. Spain ... Gyaros Rats] These plagues are listed in Pliny's *Natural History*; see Philemon Holland's translation, I, 8, 29 (Pliny 1601, 212).
13. Hamell] Hamelin.
21. Weasers brim] the edge of the River Weser (named by Verstegan).
27. Telesma] seventeenth century version of 'talisman', a consecrated object endowed with a magic power to avert evil.
28. Five such ... make] In 1 Samuel 6, a plague of haemorrhoids and mice smote the country of the Philistines when they stole the Ark of God from the Jews. They had to make

five golden haemorrhoids and five golden mice and give back the Ark before the plagues were remitted.

31. Burgers] i.e. burghers, townspeople.
44. Saxons] Hamelin is in Saxony.

'Who can but pitty this poor Turtle Dove'
1–4. Turtle Dove . . . more] According to myth, the turtle-dove is so faithful to its mate that after its death it does not seek another. Many Renaissance poems had taken the turtle-dove as their theme, including, most famously, Shakespeare's *The Phoenix and the Turtle*.

10–13. Who loosing . . . have] See textual note. Arthur Pulter had a paternal uncle, Edward, who may be 'My Unckle Edw. P.'. Alternatively, Hester Pulter's mother, Mary Petty, may have had a brother named Edward.

14–20. Who beeing . . . are Seen] See textual note. St Jerome's story of the much-married bride and groom is retold by Donne in a sermon preached on Easter Day 1627. Pulter's page reference accurately cites the 1640 folio of Donne's sermons. ('Damascus' is an error for 'Damasus'.)

17. Alcestis] daughter of Peleus, king of Thessaly, she gave her own life to save her husband, Admetas. See Goulart (1621, 149).

Artimitius] Probably Artemesia, wife of King Mausolus, ruler of Halicarnassus. When he died in 353 BC Artemesia was broken-hearted and built for him a tomb which became one of the seven wonders of the ancient world, and which ensured that his name is now associated with all stately tombs.

19. Deboras, and Annas] Deborah, wife of Lapidoth, was a prophetess and judge of the children of Israel (Judges 4:4). Anna was a prophetess who recognised the baby Jesus as the Messiah (Luke 2:36). Deborah and Anna are often listed in catalogues of virtuous biblical women, but Pulter seems particularly interested in their status as faithful married women. Anna, whose husband had been dead for 84 years, exemplifies the virtuous widow, as Deborah does the virtuous wife.

23. Game] gamely, i.e. vigorously.
25–6. Hide Park, Hanes . . . Mulbery Garden] I have not been able to trace Hanes, but the others—Hyde Park, St John's College, Oxford, St Catherine's Hall, Oxford, Spring Garden, and Mulbery Garden—are all places where women could go for walks, and ensure that they would be noticed by the opposite sex. Pulter is particularly concerned about their reputation for sexual assignations.

31. a scurvey . . . Tart] delicacies on sale at some of these locations. See Sedley (1668).
40. Anchorites] hermits: women who retire from the world for religious reasons.
41. Halcions] Alcyone, according to Greek mythology, was the daughter of Aeolus, the wind god. Her husband, Ceyx, drowned in a shipwreck during a trip to consult an oracle. Alcyone followed her husband and jumped into the sea. The gods took pity on the couple and transformed them into sea birds, Alcyone becoming a kingfisher or halcyon.

48. Infine] in conclusion.
49. ahe'd] ahead.

'When royall Fergus Line did rule this Realm'
The story of the mouse and the oyster was used by Geoffrey Whitney in *A Choice of Emblemes* (1586, 128), but with an entirely different moral in which the mouse is punished for his greed. Note also that Pulter has set this emblematic occurrence in her personal history.

1. Fergus Line] the Stuart dynasty, in this case James I, to whom Pulter's father was High Treasurer.
13. Mecian Tongues] mouse languages.
15–16. hee that writ . . . Mecian Knights] The poet is Homer. The *Batrachomyomathia* was included in George Chapman's *The Crowne of All Homers Works* (1624), and had been translated most recently by William Fowldes as *The Wonderful and Bloudy Battell Between Frogs and Mice* (1634). The poem is now known not to have been by Homer.

26. Deliane Twins] Apollo and Diana (who between them control the tides), born on the island of Delos.

31. A vulgar] the common people. Hester Pulter is particularly hostile to Cromwell, who seems to be the 'dul Fish' (line 29; i.e. the oyster). As often in her poems, she is thinking sympathetically of royalist prisoners.

Katherine Philips, National Library of Wales MS 776B

To the Excellent Rosania
'Rosania' is the sobriquet given to Mary Aubrey Montagu by Philips. Mary Aubrey and Philips became friends while attending Mrs Salmon's school in Hackney as children. The friendship continued after Philips's departure for Wales with her mother in 1646, though it cooled slightly after Aubrey's marriage to Sir William Montagu (see 'Rosania's private Marriage'). The pair remained on good terms, however, and Montagu nursed Philips during her fatal illness in 1664. The scribe of the manuscript, Polexander (unidentified), here dedicates the volume to Montagu.

4. Lethe] classical river of forgetfulness.
Elisium] Elysium is the mythical location for the enjoyment of a pleasant afterlife.

23. devoirs] duties; refers to the care she took nursing the dying Philips.

28. Jacobs-Staff] Jacob's ladder, Genesis 28:12. Jacob dreams of a ladder linking earth and heaven, 'the angels of God ascending and descending on it'.

To Antenor On a Paper of mine
Antenor is Philips's sobriquet for her husband James Philips, a prominent Cromwellian. This poem defends the author's royalist stance in the poem 'On the double murther of the King' (see below). The 'Adversary' of James Philips mentioned in the title—identified in the Dering Manuscript as a certain 'J. Jones'—had threatened to publish Katherine Philips's 'On the double murther of the King' in order to damage her husband's reputation. Thomas (*Works*, I: 346) proposes that 'J. Jones' may have been Jenkin Jones of Llandetty (b. 1623), a parliamentarian who was appointed an approver of ministers under the Act for the Better Propagation and Preaching of the Gospel in Wales in 1650. James Philips was appointed a Commissioner by the same Act.

7–8. Eves rebellion ... tast] Genesis 3:6, 17.

15. Mint] i.e. the place where slanders are devised.

On the double murther of the King
A rare instance of chronological presentation in the Rosania Manuscript, this poem, which immediately follows 'To Antenor On a Paper of mine', supplies the text of the 'Paper' which J. Jones had threatened to publish. 'On the double murther of the King' is an answer to a poem by the leading Fifth Monarchist, Vavasour Powell. Powell, like Jenkin Jones, was appointed an approver of ministers by the 1650 Propagation Act, and was preaching in Cardiganshire in February of 1653/4. Intriguingly, the manuscript's title suggests that Powell wrote his verse at Philips's house (although Thomas (*Works*, I: 261) interprets this as indicating that the compiler of the manuscript copied his version of the poem from one made by Philips herself). Powell's poem 'On the late K. Charles of Blessed Memory' has recently been discovered by Hageman and Sununu (1994, 128–31).

3. that Son] In Herodotus, King Croesus has a mute son, and the Delphic oracle has prophesied that if he should ever speak, it would be the sign of doom for his father. When Croesus is in danger from Persian forces, the son cries out a warning, and the Persians capture Croesus. See Herodotus (1920–5, I: 109).

10. The dying ... Ass] In the fable by Phaedrus, the dying lion can endure attacks by a boar and a bull, but 'seem[s] to die a second death' when attacked by an ass (*Babrius and Phaedrus* 1965, 217).

26. sequester] to set aside, to confiscate, to remove from the possession of the owner temporarily (*OED*, 1, 2, 3a). There is a topical resonance: during and after the English Civil Wars, many lands were sequestered from parties on both sides.

To Palæmon on his discourse of friendship
'Palæmon' is Francis Finch, whose prose treatise *Friendship* circulated in manuscript from October 1653, and was privately printed in March 1653/4. Finch's treatise was addressed to the twinned friends 'Lucasia-Orinda' (Anne Owen and Katherine Philips) and dedicated to Owen.

24. Fairy Knights . . . Cambina's wand] cf. Spenser's *Faerie Queene*, Book IV, canto iii, stanza 48: Cambina's wand of peace heals the strife between Triamond and Cambel, and transforms them from deadly enemies to close friends.

To the Queen's Majesty
The occasion for this poem is the illness of Queen Catherine of Braganza, consort to King Charles II, in late 1663.

18. great Charles's] Charles II.

20. He lost . . . once] England, Scotland and Ireland, in the Civil Wars (also known as the War of the Three Kingdoms).

25. Thracian Heroe] Orpheus, a legendary Greek poet from Thrace. Upon the death of his wife Eurydice, Orpheus persuaded the gods to release her from the Underworld. They agreed on condition that he should not look back at her while she followed him; he did, and she vanished for ever.

Arion on a Dolphin
Written on the anticipated return of King Charles II to England in 1660.

Title. Arion] Greek lyric poet, seventh century BC. During a sea-journey from Italy he was thrown overboard by sailors, but a dolphin, hearing his song, bore him safely to land.

28. Defender of the Faith] title held by the monarch as head of the Church of England.

30. writt] Henry VIII was granted the title of Defender of the Faith by the Pope, in recognition of his anti-Lutheran writings.

34. Athanasius] St Athanasius (c.296–373), bishop of Alexandria, opponent of Arianism (which denied the true divinity of Jesus Christ). He was exiled from his see five times, between 336 and 366.

54. Lawrell's] laurels.

68. As Shebah's . . . Court] See 1 Kings 10:1–13. The Queen of Sheba visits King Solomon to witness for herself the glories of the kingdom of Israel.

To the Queen-Mother
Queen Henrietta Maria, wife to King Charles I, left England for France with her daughter, Henrietta Anne, for the latter's marriage to the Duke of Orleans.

10. the Royall Martyr] Henrietta Maria's husband, Charles I.

18. Immortall Father] Henri IV, King of France (reigned 1589–1610), victor in many battles during the French Wars of Religion.

27. our Great Charles] Charles II.

28. Illustrious Gloucester] Henry, Duke of Gloucester, King Charles II's younger brother, died of smallpox on 13 September 1660, aged twenty-one. Philips wrote an elegy on his death.

29. Princess] Mary, Princess Royal of England and Princess of Orange, eldest daughter of Charles I and Henrietta Maria, died of smallpox on 24 December 1660, aged twenty-nine.

31. colder parts] Holland, where Princess Mary had lived ('shin'd') following her marriage to William of Orange in 1641. Her death occurred just two months after her return to England in October 1660.

In memory of my Deare F:P:
'F:P:' is Katherine Philips's stepdaughter, Frances.

21. hast] hasten.

32. Spring head] i.e. God.
35. it] Frances's soul.
38. it might know . . . known] paraphrases 1 Corinthians 13:12.
45. Masques] court entertainments.
80. cradle] Frances, probably born in 1647, would have been less than a year old when Katherine Fowler married James Philips.

Ode upon Retirement

The Dering Manuscript provides the subtitle 'made upon occasion of Mr. Cowley's on that subject'. Abraham Cowley (1618–67), the royalist poet, moved to Barn Elms in London in 1663. Philips's visit to Cowley at home provides the occasion for her poem 'Upon the engraving K:P: on a Tree in the short walke at Barn-Elms' (*Works*, I: 208). Cowley was the author of a Pindaric ode on Philips and her poetry, published in 1663 (*Works*, III: 191–5).

64. officiously] attentively.
73. the Man] Cowley.
77. Parthian Conquest] The Parthians were famed for their ability to shoot backwards when retreating.

A Retird friendship

This poem is dated 23 August 1651 in the Tutin Manuscript. Ardelia is unidentified.

5. Here is . . . Crowns] The Battle of Worcester, at which Charles II tried and failed to win his father's kingdoms, was fought on 3 September 1651.

Inconstancy in Friendship

Addressee unidentified.

9–10. Nero . . . fire] According to Suetonius, the Emperor Nero set Rome on fire for the pleasure of watching it burn (Suetonius 1997, II: 149–51).
21. frantick] mad.

To my Excellent Lucasia

'Lucasia' is Anne Owen, a member of the Welsh gentry. She was adopted into Philips's self-proclaimed Society of Friendship in 1651. The warmth of Orinda's declarations to Lucasia is sometimes linked by critics to Philips's supposed estrangement from Mary Aubrey following the latter's marriage (see 'Rosania's private Marriage', and notes). Philips later tried to arrange a marriage between Owen and her own friend Sir Charles Cotterell ('Poliarchus'). However, Owen married Colonel Marcus Trevor, later Viscount Dungannon, in 1662. The sources differ as to the dating of this poem: the Dering Manuscript gives 17 July 1652, while the Tutin Manuscript is unclear, reading either 1651 or 1653. Moreover, the bestowing of the sobriquet 'Lucasia' and her adoption into the Society of Friendship is commemorated in another poem, dated December 1651 in all three manuscripts.

Wiston Vault

Wiston, Pembrokeshire, was the home of the Wogan family, relatives of Philips's husband. The poem is not written about a specific death; rather, it imagines Orinda's immortality through Lucasia.

EPITAPH ON HECTOR PHILLIPS

Philips's son, Hector, died on 2 May 1655. This poem was set to music by Henry Lawes; see Applegate (1993).

Title. St. Sith's Church] the London church where Philips herself was later buried. It was burnt down in the Great Fire of London, and never rebuilt.

16. Hermes-seal] alchemical term for a hermetic seal. Hermes Trismegistus was said to be the founder of alchemy.

To my Lord Arch-Bishop of Canterbury

The Rosania Manuscript is the sole manuscript source for this poem, addressed to Gilbert Sheldon (1598–1677), Archbishop of Canterbury. Sheldon was Warden of All Souls College, Oxford, from March 1626 until he was ejected by the parliamentarians in March

1648. He was also chaplain to King Charles I. At the Restoration, Sheldon was made Dean of the Royal Chapel and Bishop of London. He was an adviser to Charles II, and presided over the Restoration settlement of the Church of England. He was appointed Archbishop of Canterbury in August 1663.

8. dragg'd malitiously ... Light] refers to (and disclaims responsibility for) Marriott's publication of Philips's poetry in January 1664.

9. the Hebrew Virgin] See 2 Samuel 13:1–20. Tamar, the daughter of King David, is raped by her brother Amnon, and rends her garment (signifier of virginity) in grief.

16. the best Church ... World] the Church of England.

22. Confessour] Sheldon remained loyal to the Church of England even when it was suppressed in the 1640s and 1650s.

25. Crosier] the pastoral staff or crook of a bishop.

42. Primate] the head of a province of the Church. The Archbishop of Canterbury is the Primate of All England.

45. scismatick] someone who did not acknowledge the authority of the Church of England: here, a Catholic or, more probably, a nonconformist.

46. Church-man] a priest of the Church of England.

47. Reduce] bring back (into the true Church).

51–2. Since the prevailing ... fled] since Christianity became established.

In Memory of Mr Cartwright
William Cartwright (1611–43), royalist and prolific poet, playwright and theologian, died of camp fever in Oxford during the Civil Wars. Philips could not have known him personally. This elegy was printed as the first of fifty-four commendatory poems in Cartwright's posthumous *Comedies, Tragi-comedies, With other Poems*, published by Humphrey Moseley in 1651. It is, therefore, the first of Philips's poems to have appeared in print.

9. Unsequester] free from solitude; probably also an allusion to the parliamentary sequestration of royalist property.

Rosania's private Marriage
This poem commemorates the marriage of Mary Aubrey (Rosania) to Sir William Montagu sometime prior to September 1652—an event to which Philips was not invited.

21. Eagle ... Sun] a proverbial expression (Tilley E3).

31–2. if wee will ... Soule] as some contemporary neoplatonists believed.

To the Right Honourable Alice Countess of Carbury
Alice Egerton Vaughan (1619–89) was an important figure in some of the most distinguished royalist literary and musical circles of the seventeenth century. By birth she was a member of the Egerton family later celebrated by Marie Burghope in 'The Vision'. Her younger brother John married Elizabeth Cavendish, Jane's sister, in 1641. Alice appeared as the Lady in Milton's 'Comus', and was a pupil of the Cavalier and court musician Henry Lawes. She was the recipient of an answer poem authored by Jane Cavendish. In 1652 she married Richard Vaughan, Earl of Carbery. The Earl was a patron of the churchman Jeremy Taylor, an ally of Philips's. The 'Water-poet', John Taylor, whose verse attack on Philips has recently been discovered (Beal 1998, 282–4), visited the Vaughans in Wales in August 1652.

3. his Organ] his 'greedy Eye' (line 1).

[God]
[1–18]. Thrice happy ... goes his way] These eighteen lines are not by Philips but are extracted (with minor variants) from a poem by her contemporary, Henry More: 'Cupid's Conflict' (lines 265–83), printed in *Democritus Platonissans* (1646). More (1614–87) was an academic philosopher and theologian, one of the so-called 'Cambridge Platonists'. (His work also seems to have been admired by Hester Pulter.) 'Cupid's Conflict' describes an argument between Cupid and the poet 'Mela', who writes not for earthly love, nor for money, but for love of God. Philips uses the extract from More's poem as the inspiration for her own meditation on the same subject ('Eternal Reason, Glorious Majesty'), which follows. For a variant version of Philips's lines see the Tutin MS, edited in *Works* (I: 138–41), and the Dering MS.

6. Heav'n thy ... span] a biblical image: see Isaiah 40:12.
27. spicy Mountain] a biblical image: see Song of Songs 8:14.
53. still Voice] Cf. 1 Kings 19:11–12. Elijah seeks the Lord, but finds him neither in wind, nor earthquake, nor fire, but in a 'still small voice'.

Mary Roper?: Leeds University Library, Brotherton Collection MS Lt q 2

A Prayer
This poem dedicates the manuscript volume to God.
9–10. Beauty / Of Holinesse] This biblical expression is associated with the doctrines of Archbishop Laud during the reign of Charles I. Puritans objected strongly to his perceived Catholic leanings in terms of rites and images. See notes on Ley, 'An answer to Mercuries message', p. 244.
11. Babes and Sucklings] Matthew 21:16, Psalm 8:2.
24. thy Holy Arme] Psalm 98:1.
27. Miriam Deborah and Hannah] Old Testament women recorded as singing praises to God in the Bible. See Exodus 15:1–21; Judges 5; 1 Samuel 2:1–10.
28. Magnificat] the song of praise sung by Mary, the mother of Jesus; see Luke 1:46–55.
29. Her Name] an apparent indication of the identity of the author of this manuscript; see biographical note.
31. Widowes two Mites] Luke 21:1–4.

The Royall Element of Fire
This poem is the first of four poems on the elements of fire, air, water and earth created by God. Although the creation of the elements is not specifically described in the Genesis account, it was included in literary treatments of the creation such as Du Bartas' 'La Sepmaine' of 1578. Roper alters the traditional hierarchy to place fire before air. The poem is full of biblical imagery.
3. Devouring fire] Exodus 24:17.
4. His Throne a flame] Daniel 7:9.
5–6 (marginal note). Reve 1 14] Revelation 1:14.
7–8 (marginal note). 2 Thessa 1 8] 2 Thessalonians 1:8.
11–12. Fire's ... foes] Psalm 97:3.
21. Who Can Stand ... Fire] Nahum 1:6, Malachi 3:2.
27. God Commands the Fire] This may mean that God demands sacrifice by fire as part of man's worship to him.

From Mans Shamefull Fall
See the biblical account in Genesis 3:1–6.
19. the Knowledge tree] cf. Genesis 2:17.
28–30. Wonder ... feare] Roper here seems to be answering the charge often levelled at Eve, that she displayed sinful curiosity and boldness (see Williams 1948, 119–21).
31. not afraid] (see also lines 41 and 62). Lack of fear is represented ambiguously both as a sign of purity and later as a result of pride.

From Lott His Wife And Daughters
See the biblical account in Genesis 19:30a, 26, 30b–38, 27–8. Roper changes the chronology slightly.
2. Abraham Rescued Him] See Genesis 14.
10. Treasure] Matthew 6:21. Wilkinson (1607, 22) makes this connection: 'as where the treasure is, there will the heart be also, so where the heart is, there will the eye be also'.
17–21. Her Feete ... Salt] Cf. Hutchinson (2001, 174; canto 13, lines 155–66).
23–4. Flavius Josephus ... Historie] *Jewish Antiquities* Book I, 203–4 (Josephus 1928, 101). Wilkinson (1607, 45) also mentions this.
23. see] saw.

34. To Fill the World] This was a divine command first given to Adam and Eve, and given again to Noah's family after the Flood; Genesis 1:28 and 9:1.

44. Nations] According to Genesis 19:37–8, Lot's descendants became the Moabites and the Ammonites, enemies of Israel who worshipped idols.

51–6. Signes . . . Gall] *Jewish War* Book IV, 484–5 (Josephus 1930, 143–5). Wilkinson (1607, 44) also mentions this. Cf. *Paradise Lost*, IX: 564–6.

51–2 (marginal note). Josephus 689] This page number is correct for most editions of Thomas Lodge's popular translation of the works of Josephus, first published 1609.

From The Birth of Esau and Jacob
See the biblical account in Genesis 25:21–6.

55–8. Some thinke . . . Direct] These possibilities are considered but rejected by Willet (1605, 275).

60 (marginal note). Lo] Lord.

73–4. She Beares . . . Esau] 'Esau' means 'hairy'. Another name for Esau was 'Edom', meaning 'red'.

75–8. The Second . . . Jacob] 'Jacob' means 'grasps the heel', or 'deceives'.

From Rebeckahs Subtilty
See the biblical account in Genesis 27:41–28:1. The narrative here is unusual and goes further than Hutchinson's in presenting Rebeckah's strategems in a positive light (see Hutchinson 2001, l–li, 235, Norbrook's introduction, and canto 18, lines 209–24). Male commentators on Genesis often rebuked Rebeckah for her use of deceit, while admitting that it had been used by God for good ends (e.g. Whately 1640, 8–12 [second pagination]).

Title. Subtilty] Usually a trait associated with Satan (Genesis 3:1).

1. Matron Grave] See also line 13. Rebeckah is compared to the figure of Wisdom (Proverbs 1:20–33, 8:1–9:6).

19. Earant] errand.

21. Exigent] emergency, extremity.

29. Esaus Mariage] Esau had married Judith and Bashemath, both Hittites (Genesis 26:34).

May 29 1669
This follows the account of Joseph's interpretation of Pharaoh's dreams, leading to his release from prison and his new status as an adviser to Pharaoh. The dating marks this poem as written for the anniversary of King Charles II's entrance into London on 29 May 1660 (his thirtieth birthday). The poem is accompanied by two oval woodcuts (see plate 8).

5. to buy] a reference to the price on Charles II's head (see note to lines 29–30).

5–8. to Sell . . . Gave] Charles II is compared with Joseph (Genesis 37:12–36, Genesis 39).

19. Royall Cedar] Ezekiel 17:22–4.

20. oake] Charles hid from his enemies in an oak tree after the battle of Worcester (see plate 8). In fact the oak was not at Worcester but in a wood near Boscobel House in Shropshire.

23. Pitt] Genesis 37:22–4.

27. Bramble] Judges 9:7–15 (Jotham's parable). The bramble here signifies Cromwell.

29–30. Ten thousand . . . Get] Matthew 26:15 states that the price for Judas's betrayal of Jesus was thirty silver coins. The reward for the King's capture was £1000, or 20,000 shillings, or 240,000 pence. The latter may have been what Roper had in mind, although the silver coins probably equate more nearly to a shilling.

32. Elishas Seekers] 2 Kings 6:18.

36. Roote and Royall Branch] A biblical image (Isaiah 11:1), also a reference to the Root and Branch Petition of 1640. This petition, presented by Londoners to Parliament, demanded that episcopacy (government by bishops) should be extirpated from the Church of England. See Bennett (2000, 202).

58. Like A Dreame] This echoes Psalm 126, when the captives return to Zion.

62. Lengthen His Daies] God's promise to King Solomon (1 Kings 3:14).

Our Kings Sorrows and Suffrings

This poem is the first of five royalist poems on the Civil War, interregnum and Restoration. It follows the account of Joseph's self-revelation to his brothers in Egypt. It is accompanied by a version of William Marshall's famous engraving from the *Eikon Basilike* (1649), of Charles I in prayer, pasted into the manuscript.

1. Iron Age] the period of the English Civil Wars.

2. Irreligeous Stage] This may refer ironically to the parliamentarian ban on plays.

6. Sacriledge] A common accusation levelled by royalists at republicans was that the sale of church lands—which the latter advocated—was an act of sacrilege. Simon Patrick includes the issue of church property in his discussion of sacrilege (Patrick 1669, 58–62).

7. Lights] windows; presumably stained-glass, many of which were destroyed during the Civil Wars.

11–12. Moths . . . Consume] Matthew 6:19–20. Here the image is used ironically to accuse the parliamentarians of stealing and storing treasures on earth.

13–14. Josephs . . . Cloake] Genesis 39:12. Roper contrasts Joseph's flight from sin, leaving his garment, with the parliamentarians' concealment of sin.

17. the Faiths Defender] title held by Charles I as head of the Church of England.

19–20. They Swore . . . Life they take] condemns the treachery against Charles I of subjects who had sworn oaths of allegiance to him. A more specific allusion may be intended.

25–6. Like Christ . . . be Dy'd] Matthew 26:67; 27:24–5, 30.

33–4 (marginal note). Heb 5:7] Hebrews 5:7.

45. Head . . . Stumpe] Even Hell has a head, i.e. Satan. Roper pictures England as a body without a head. The image of a kingdom as a body is common in the Renaissance: see Shakespeare, *King John*, 4.2.112, *2 Henry IV*, 3.1.37, and especially *Coriolanus*, 1.1.94–144.

46. Rumpe] The so-called Rump Parliament was formed from 'purging' the Long Parliament of its more conservative element in December 1648. It was this Parliament that arranged the trial of Charles I. It was eventually ejected by Cromwell in April 1653.

47. Oaths . . . Covenants . . . Vows] The many oaths, covenants and vows sworn by Charles's enemies included the Solemn League and Covenant (1643) and the Self-Denying Ordinance (1645).

49–50. One Pawns . . . Drinke] obscure.

57–8. Our Joseph's . . . Grave] the return of Charles II, drawing on images of Christ's resurrection and second coming.

59–60. Those Men . . . the Ground] probably a reference to the exhumation of parliamentary leaders such as Cromwell and Ireton after the Restoration, as well as to their ignominious reputations.

Englands Sad Lamentation

This poem is the third in the royalist sequence. It is written in an unusual form for Roper, in stanzas of rhyming triplets. It immediately precedes a partner poem in the same form entitled 'Gods Gracious Deliverance Restoring Our Mercyfull King'.

3. Egyptian Darkenesse] The ninth plague on Egypt was complete darkness (Exodus 10:21–3).

7. Our Cedar] the king; see note to line 19 in 'May 29 1669', p. 259.

14. Plebians] commoners.

19. Fanatick] denotes a religious mania, applied at this time to nonconformity.

21. Meccanicks] manual workers (*OED* 2a).

23. Sold] refers to the sale of Church of England lands during the interregnum. See note to 'Our Kings Sorrows and Suffrings', line 6 (above).

24. All Sorts . . . Despise] a frequent anti-parliamentarian accusation. Royalists liked to identify all parliamentarians with the radical sects, some of which privileged individual inspiration above conventional learning and were led by men with little or no formal education.

27. Protector] Oliver Cromwell became Lord Protector in December 1653.

28. Oligarchall Government] government by a small number of people; also possibly a pun on Oliver Cromwell's name.

33. Chyrurgeons] surgeons.
41. Slaine] possibly a reference to the failure of the pro-monarchical Love's Plot of 1651, and the subsequent execution of the principal plotters.
47. Apple] pupil (see Psalm 17:8).
53. Vineyard] biblical symbol of Israel, here applied to England.

From Famines Miserie
See the biblical account in Genesis 47:13–26.
71. Against us Christians Rise] See Matthew 12:41–2, Luke 11:31–2.
73. Sacriledge] (also line 88) See note to 'Our Kings Sorrows and Suffrings', line 6 (above). Patrick (1669, 62) uses this example specifically: 'if *Pharaoh* had such a respect to the *Ægyptian* Priesthood as not to sell their Land; Christian Princes & Governours should not be more unkind (if not unjust) in these days, nor expose to sale those Lands which have been settled upon the Priests of the most High God'.

Julia Palmer: Clark Library MS P1745 M1 P744 1671-3 Bound

From the 'First Century'

63 experience
5. fecth] fetch.
thine] the elect.
12. house of wine] Song of Songs 2:4: 'banqueting-house' in the King James (Authorised) Version. Palmer is using a translation of the original Hebrew idiom. It is unlikely that she knew Hebrew herself, but she probably heard these translations in a sermon.
22. ane] probably 'one'.

86 The soull veiwing Christ in his humiliation
This poem is a meditation on Christ's life and death.
13. His visage . . . more] Isaiah 52:14.
21–2. Thou seest . . . bloud] Luke 22:44.
28. b'ing] being.
29. pilats] Pilate, the Roman governor who judged Jesus.
46. Zion hill] not a metaphor for heaven, but the Mount of Olives, on which it was thought Jesus would descend at his Second Coming, since it was the place from which he ascended into heaven (Acts 1:12).
56. haunt] dwell.

88 more to the same purpose
Title. more to the same purpose] The title of the previous poem, number 87, is 'The soull encouraging it self with the hopes of the speedy satisfaction of its desires in the full enjoyment of god'.
1–2. He that . . . I come] John 16:16, Hebrews 10:37.
5–6. Although to . . . a day] Psalm 90:4.

93 About spirituall discourse
32. cecreet] secret.
43. open my lips] Psalm 51:15.

From the 'Second Century'

25 our mistakes for want of skill in the methods of the spirit
10. choking] probably 'chalking'.
44. carve] serve up.
61. drawn, to . . . thee] Song of Songs 1:4.
63. weary race] 1 Corinthians 9:24, Hebrews 12:1–2.

42 The soull looking att, and longing for an eternall saboath
The 'sabbath rest' which is the subject of this poem is treated in Hebrews 4:1–11. For Palmer, this 'rest' promised to believers is to be expected after death, in heaven.
6. The Sun . . . itts light] Malachi 4:2; Revelation 21:23.
15. clog] 'a block attached to the leg or neck of a man or beast, to prevent escape or impede motion' (*OED* 2).
29. church. militent] the church after the ascension of Christ and before his Second Coming, in a state of continual militancy against Satan.
30. chore] choir.

45 The soull clouded
2. inshutting] shutting is the close of a day or nightfall: 'in' perhaps functions as an intensifier.
18. And though . . . combine] Matthew 16:18.
23. live by sence] 2 Corinthians 5:7.

46 The soull by faith, triumphing over saten
6. subtletys] Genesis 3:1.
7. duty] 'homage, submission, due respect, reverence' (*OED* 1a).
14. fire brands] Ephesians 6:16.
17. quite] require.

73 The devills picture
This poem purports to sketch 'The devills picture' but it becomes clear by stanza 7 that in fact Palmer is describing herself. This is why, in the final stanza, she tries to flee the sight she has conjured up, but is unable to do so (lines 29–30). The sin that she has in common with Satan is spiritual pride.
5–8. Shall worthlese clay . . . higher ends] Romans 9:20–1.

Mary Astell: Bodleian Library MS Rawlinson poet. 154

[Dedicatory letter]
WILLIAM . . . CANTERBURY] William Sancroft (1617–93). See headnote. Astell's identification of Sancroft as holding his title 'By Divine Providence' may indicate her conviction that human authorities had no right to deprive a consecrated archbishop of office.
14. as David . . . not a Cause] 1 Samuel 17:29.
22. Goats hair . . . skins] often associated in the Bible, e.g. Exodus 35:23.

The Invitation
5–6. Parnassus . . . Helicon] in Greek mythology, mountains favoured by the Muses, and therefore the source of poetic inspiration.
6. Thy Saviour's side] pierced by a Roman soldier after Jesus' death on the cross (John 19:34). See George Herbert's poem 'The Bag' for an earlier innovative use of this conceit.
7–8. Hark how . . . opprest] See Matthew 11:28.
21. bays] the traditional reward for poetic merit.

In emulation of Mr Cowleys Poem
Title. Mr Cowleys Poem] Abraham Cowley (1618–67) was a royalist poet much admired in the seventeenth century (see notes on Katherine Philips, 'Ode upon Retirement'). The page reference provided by Astell for his poem 'The Motto' is correct for any of the imprints of Cowley's collected poems between 1668 and 1688. Astell's eschewing of worldly success, however, contrasts with the overt ambition of Cowley's poem, which begins: 'What shall I do to be for ever known, / And make the age to come my own?'.
9–10. If this . . . the right] Astell implicitly contrasts the belief, ascribed to the philosophers of the ancient world, that the world will exist indefinitely with the Christian teaching that human life and the existence of the world are brief and finite.

25. a Peter or a Paul] the greatest missionary apostles.
30. Marys Priviledge] i.e. in physically giving birth to Jesus.

Enemies
25. Meekness wou'd . . . inheritance] According to the Sermon on the Mount, the meek shall inherit the earth. See Matthew 5:5.
31. Who puff their bubbles] who swell their vanity.

Ambition
2. the first mover] the primum mobile (literally, the first moving thing): in medieval astronomy, the outermost of the spheres believed to revolve constantly round the earth; also, God the creator.
5. what Prometheus stole] according to Greek mythology, Prometheus stole fire from heaven and gave it to humankind.
8. Who falsely . . . Soul] belief often attributed (erroneously) to Greek philosophers such as Aristotle. Astell's source may have been the preface to *The Ladies Calling*, which refers to 'that Philosophers Paradox, who said, Women had no souls' (Allestree? 1673, sig. b6r).
13. to weep for Worlds] i.e. as Alexander (line 16) is said to have done.
23. Virgil] the most admired of classical poets.
25. bait at] are tempted by.
26. A Wreath . . . Baies] the traditional reward for poetic achievement.
28. a Crown . . . die] See the apocalyptic promise of 1 Peter 5:4: 'when the chief Shepherd shall appear, ye shall receive a crown of glory that fadeth not away'.
30. a higher Mansion there] In John 14:2 Jesus tells the disciples 'In my Father's house are many mansions', where the faithful will be received.

Solitude
1. gen'rous Cowley] On Cowley, see note on 'In emulation of Mr Cowleys Poem', above. The page reference for 'The Wish' is correct for any of the imprints of Cowley's collected poems between 1668 and 1688. As with her previous imitation of Cowley, Astell echoes the opening of her poetic model: 'The Wish' begins 'Well then; I now do plainly see, / This busy world and I shall ne'er agree'. Cowley, however, concludes his poem not with the religious retirement favoured by Astell but with the desire to be alone with his mistress.
8. Cabinet] jewellery case.
14. my weak . . . a slave] the enslavement of the lover by a mere look from his lady was a convention of Petrarchan poetry.
22. paint] cosmetics.
23. fucus] rouge.
30. Antedate] anticipate.
32. Charles] Charles V, Holy Roman Emperor, who in 1557 abdicated his titles and retired to a monastery.

Vertue
11. practick] i.e. practical.
49–51. the blinded Jews . . . day] The Jews' continuing expectation of their Messiah was regarded as redundant by Christians such as Astell, who believed in Jesus as the Messiah.
78. all laid up there] Jesus advises his disciples 'lay up for yourselves treasures in heaven' (Matthew 6:20).

The Complaint
The spiritual narrative of this poem, from aggrieved self-righteousness to humble devotion following a revelatory recollection of God's love, resembles George Herbert's 'The Collar'.
8–9. Lord what mortal . . . scan'd] echoing the Psalmist: 'If thou, Lord, shouldest mark iniquities, O Lord, who shall stand?' (Psalm 130:3).
16. use and principal] banking vocabulary (following 'wealth', line 10): both the interest and the capital.

35–6. the flood . . . Dove] The end of the biblical flood was signalled when a dove Noah had sent out from the Ark returned with an olive branch in her beak. See Genesis 8:11.

48. a right medium] their true context.

52. my daily Prayer] the Lord's Prayer. See Matthew 6:10 and Luke 11:2.

Marie Burghope: Huntington Library MS EL 35/B/62

'The Vision'

Title. Ashridge Com Bucks] i.e. Ashridge in the county of Buckinghamshire. The country estate Ashridge was owned by the Egerton family between 1604 and 1927. Following boundary changes, it is now in the county of Hertfordshire. The estate is currently owned by the National Trust.

2. Phoebus] the Greek sun god.

16. Ball] earth.

69. Eccho] As told by Ovid, Echo was a nymph who fell in love with the beautiful youth Narcissus. She faded into just a voice when her love was not returned.

71. Favourites of the Muses] poets.

74. Elisium Feilds] in classical mythology, good and great souls passed after death to Elysium, or the Elysian Fields, to enjoy a happy afterlife.

87. Jove] Jupiter, king of the gods in Roman mythology. See also lines 155 and 199.

108. Apollo] the Greek and Roman god of poetry. His sons (line 109) are poets.

109. Whether] whither.

112. Pernassus Top] Mount Parnassus was sacred to Apollo and the Muses.

115. Vatican] used figuratively with reference to the literary treasures preserved in the Vatican library in Rome.

118. Line] probably referring to the rope used to tie a ship to a pier or dock.

122. Rome may . . . boast] more books may have been written on the Roman Catholic faith, but the library contains better and well-chosen Protestant works of 'sacred Learneing' (line 116).

125. The Brittan . . . Athen—Stagerite] probably British or Greek philosophers generally. 'Athen—Stagerite' refers specifically to Aristotle, born in Stagira, Macedonia, but long resident in Athens. See also line 574.

127. full Meridian] full splendour, like the sun at mid-day. See also lines 468 and 627. Declention] sunken or fallen condition.

134–5. "That I may . . . to Posterity] Marie Burghope's wish was granted: her manuscript remains in the library of a descendant of the Earls of Bridgewater. See headnote.

142. Draughts] drawings, pictures.

152–5. The ancient . . . of Jove] These lines refer to the war between the giants and the gods in Greek mythology. The gods were attacked by the giants, but triumphed with the help of a mortal, Hercules. Pelion and Ossa were mountains the giants piled on each other in an attempt to storm heaven. Typheus was one of the most vicious monsters who opposed Zeus, and who was destroyed by Zeus's lightning bolts.

158–9. The Warr . . . Inferus devours] In Christian tradition, the war in heaven occurred when Lucifer and other angels rebelled against God and were cast into hell. See Isaiah 14: 12–15 and *Paradise Lost*.

159. Inferus] hell.

182. Homer's fam'd Hero's] i.e. the heroes of Homer's epic poem, the *Iliad* (described below, lines 184–95).

183. Virgil's] i.e. the heroes of Virgil's epic poem, the *Aeneid* (described below, lines 196–211).

265. Simeon] In the Bible, Simeon was a devout man who recognised the infant Jesus as the messiah when Mary and Joseph presented him at the temple. See Luke 2: 25–35.

299. gaudy Pagentry of Rome] Protestants frequently depicted the Roman Catholic religion as concerned more with excessive display and riches than with true spirituality.

329. the Tunefull nine] the nine Muses of classical legend.

339–40 (marginal note). Genius] the local deity presiding over Ashridge (a classical term).

371. Gown] the clergy.

372. the Triple Crown] the Papal crown.

377–9 (marginal note). The Bonehomes... St Austin] Edmund Earl of Cornwall (1250–1300; see marginal note to line 373) founded the monastery of the order of Bonshommes at Ashridge in 1283. The Bonshommes followed the rule of St Augustine.

390–2 (marginal note). The dissolution... Reigne &c] Henry VIII ordered the dissolution of all Roman Catholic monasteries in England in 1536. Ashridge was dissolved in 1539.

397–8 (marginal note). Tho: Egerton... England] Thomas Egerton (c.1540–1617), Lord Ellesmere, was an eminent lawyer who ended his career as Lord Chancellor.

403–5 (marginal note). John Earle... that name] John Egerton, first Earl of Bridgewater (1579–1649) was the son of Thomas Egerton and his first wife Elizabeth Ravenscroft. He became President of the Council of Wales and Lord Lieutenant of Wales and the counties on the Welsh border in 1631. Milton's masque 'Comus' was written for performance at the Earl's castle at Ludlow in 1634; the child performers in the masque included the future second Earl of Bridgewater and his brother and sister.

409–15. But t'was... joys abate] These lines allude to the events of the Civil Wars, which culminated in the beheading of Charles I on 30 January 1649 (line 413).

414. The truest Church] the Church of England, radically disrupted by the upheavals of the Civil Wars.

416. He] i.e. the first Earl of Bridgewater.

418–21 (marginal note). John Earle... that name] John Egerton, second Earl of Bridgewater (1622–86) was the son of the first Earl and his wife Frances Stanley. He became a Privy Councillor in 1666.

431. Horebs Mount] where God spoke to Moses (line 432) out of a burning bush. See Exodus 3–4: 17.

432 (marginal note). Little Gaddesden] a village close to Ashridge. The second Earl of Bridgewater and his Countess were buried at the parish church at Gaddesden.

438–40 (marginal note). Elizabeth his Lady... Bridgewater] Elizabeth Cavendish (c.1626–63) was the second daughter of William Cavendish, later Duke of Newcastle, and his wife Elizabeth Basset Howard. Her manuscript prayers and meditations have been published (Egerton 1999); see also headnote and biographical note to Jane Cavendish, Elizabeth's elder sister, elsewhere in this volume. Elizabeth died in childbirth in 1663.

452–6 (marginal note). John the 3d Earle... alive] John Egerton, third Earl of Bridgewater (1646–1701) was the son of the second Earl and his wife Elizabeth Cavendish.

468. meridian] see line 127.

469. Exactest Justice] For Egerton's legal responsibilities see lines 479–80 and marginal note.

471. Astrea] in classical mythology, the virgin Astraea was the patron of justice (or 'Equity', line 472). She was believed to have lived on earth during the Golden Age, dispensing justice to humanity. Later, in despair at human wickedness, she fled the earth and returned to heaven.

481–2 (marginal note). during his Majesty... seas] i.e. during King William's military campaigns in continental Europe in the 1690s.

481. Conquer'ing William] William of Orange (1650–1702) who had become William III of England in the Glorious Revolution of 1688–89, alongside his wife Mary II (1662–94). The adjective 'Conquer'ing' refers both to his victory over James II in the Revolution and to his military successes against the French in the Nine Years War of 1689–97.

482. the Peace of Christendom] possibly a reference to the controversial Treaty of Ryswick (1697), which temporarily brought peace to western Europe after the Nine Years War.

483–8 (marginal note). The present Countess . . . Boulton] Jane Powlett (d. 1716), eldest daughter of Charles, first Duke of Boulton, and his wife Mary, became the second wife of the third Earl in 1673.

509–11 (marginal note). My Lord Brackley the Eldest] Scroop Egerton (1681–1745) was the eldest surviving son of the third Earl and his wife. He later held several important court appointments in the households of George, Prince of Denmark, Caroline Princess of Wales, and George I, and was created first Duke of Bridgewater in 1720.

538 (marginal note). Mr William] William Egerton (1684–1732).

544 (marginal note). Mr Henry] Henry Egerton (d. 1746), appointed Bishop of Hereford in 1724.

544. Eaton] Eton, the prestigious boys' school.

548 (marginal note). Mr John] John Egerton, page to Henry Duke of Gloucester (see below, marginal note to lines 550–2).

550–2 (marginal note). His Highness the Duke of Glocester] William, Duke of Gloucester (1689–1700) was the only surviving son of Princess (later Queen) Anne. As Anne was heir to her childless brother-in-law, King William, the Duke was second in line to the throne. The correction of 'presumptious' (i.e. presumptive) to 'Apparent' in line 550 (see textual notes) testifies to the complex and unprecedented constitutional arrangements which had been devised to settle the royal succession after the Glorious Revolution. By law, Princess Anne and her heirs had priority in the succession over the heirs of any second marriage of William III. Duke William was therefore more properly heir apparent (i.e. certain to succeed, should he survive William III and his mother) than heir presumptive (liable to be displaced in the succession by the birth of a nearer heir).

559. primar] first. This predates the first usage of the term listed in the *OED* (1721).

560–2 (marginal note). Mr Charles the youngest Son] Charles Egerton (d. 1725).

568–73 (marginal note). about knowledge . . . by reflection] the issue addressed in Book I of John Locke's *An Essay on Human Understanding* (1690).

570. Tenents] tenets, i.e. philosophical opinions.

574. Stagirite] Aristotle. See also line 125.

578–83 (marginal note). the Lady Mary . . . Poem] Mary Egerton, Burghope's dedicatee. She married William, Lord Byron, in 1703, but died of smallpox shortly afterwards, on 12 April 1703. See headnote.

594. Heliconion Nymphs] the Muses, believed to live on Mount Helicon.

616–19 (marginal note). The Lady Elizabeth . . . Daughter] Elizabeth Egerton, who married Thomas Catesby, Lord Paget, in 1718.

627. Meridian] see line 127.

652. diffusive] 'dispensing or shedding widely or bountifully' (*OED* 1).

678. Apollo's Heirs] i.e. poets (see note to line 108).

684–5 (marginal note). Samuell the Prophet] In 1 Samuel 3, God chooses the child Samuel, rather than the elderly priest Eli, to prophesy of 'Things past, & Things to come' (line 686) concerning Israel.

689. its sinking state] the defeat of Israel by the Philistines (1 Samuel 4). Burghope's anxieties for contemporary England may include worry over the alleged moral decline of the nation (the reason given by God for Israel's downfall in 1 Samuel 3, and a charge frequently directed at late seventeenth-century England), or fears over the constitutional future should the exiled James II and his Catholic heirs attempt to reassert their claim to the throne.

Octavia Walsh: Bodleian Library MS Eng. poet. e. 31

'O let our Praise ascend the Skyes'

This poem, although not an imitation of any one psalm, is in the style of many of the biblical psalms of praise, and is dense with biblical language and imagery. Cf. also Proverbs 8:24–9.

4. O let . . . ascend] alludes to Psalm 100:4: 'Enter into his gates with thanksgiving, and into his courts with praise'.
7–12. That Pow're . . . Tydes] glosses the creation story, Genesis 1.
10. fix'd the Stars] Genesis 1:12.
11–12. told the raging Sea . . . its Tydes] Genesis 1:9–10; see also Proverbs 8:29.
13. Whose word alone] Genesis 1:26; see also John 1:3.
15–16. turns again . . . trembling Earth] See Psalm 104:29–30.
15. Clay] Genesis 2:7 describes the creation of man 'of the dust of the ground'; elsewhere in the Bible this creating substance is referred to as clay (e.g. Job 33:6).
17. a second Birth] i.e. life after death. See also John 3:3, where Jesus explains that a man cannot see the kingdom of God unless he is born again.
25. When] i.e. when I was.
26–7. Tender fathers . . . Sons correct] Proverbs 3:11 and Hebrews 12:5–11.
28. hid his face] withdrew his (apparent) favour: see Psalms 22:24 and 30:7.
33. Sublunery] earthly; literally, under the moon.
36. alloyes] admixtures (which would inevitably have lessened the 'pleasures' of line 35).

The following Copy Burlesq'd
Title. The following Copy] refers to the next poem, 'Could Sacharissa leave the Town'.
1. Sacharissa] so far unidentified. It is unlikely that Walsh is specifically referring to the most famous literary Sacharissa, the addressee of several poems by Edmund Waller (1606–87). The use of the name may, however, be a homage to Waller, whom Walsh admired.
2. Coffee Tea and Chocolate] sophisticated consumer luxuries only to be found in London (or other major cities).
8. Epictetus] first-century Stoic philosopher, popular in the late seventeenth and early eighteenth centuries, much read by women.
9–10. Bartholomee . . . Punchenello] probably an allusion to Bartholomew Fair, held annually from 1133 to 1855 at West Smithfield, London, on 24 August (feast-day of St Bartholomew). Punchinello was a character in the puppet plays held at the fair. See Morley (1973, 336) and Speaight (1990, 148–75).
18. Wakes] rural church festivals (*OED* 4b).
20. Morriss] morris-dancing.

'Could Sacharissa leave the Town'
5. the Sacred Nine] the muses.
12. Epictetus] see note to previous poem, line 8. His *Discourses* and *Manual* are both concerned with morals.
17. Pan] Greek god of shepherds and flocks, also associated with music and dancing.

An enquiry into the cause of the miserys of Mankind
Verse essays on moral or philosophical subjects were popular in Walsh's time: famous examples include Rochester's 'Satire against Reason and Mankind' and Pope's *Essay on Man*.
5. compas] accomplish.
9. Mammons Court] Mammon was the god of money or covetousness: see Matthew 6:24, Luke 16:9–13, and Spenser, *The Faerie Queene*, Book II, canto vii.
26. shee] the 'fancy' of line 23.
30. pelth] ie. pelf: money, almost always 'evill gotten'.
38. Pluto's] In Greek mythology, Pluto was the god of wealth (and also of the underworld).
91–8. Sejanus . . . he dyes] As favourite of the emperor Tiberius, Sejanus became the chief administrator of the Roman Empire. He later lost the Emperor's favour and fell from power. Most ancient sources, however, say that Sejanus was executed on Tiberius's orders and dismembered by the Roman crowd.
116. Tarpeia] the daughter of the Roman commander of the Capitol during the Sabine War. Tarpeia is said to have offered to betray the city to the enemy if they would give her

what they bore on their left arms, i.e. their bracelets. The Sabines, however, threw their shields at her and crushed her to death.

125. his Judg within] conscience.

155. Dun's] demands for the payment of his debts.

158. Creasus] Croesus, ancient king of Lydia, whose immense riches were legendary.

167. hungry Midas] In Greek legend Midas gained the power to turn all he touched to gold, and then found he could get nothing to eat.

173. prosolite] i.e. proselyte: a convert.

177. thrown] throne.

192. Mercury] In Roman mythology, Mercury was messenger of the gods, and often acted as intermediary to point mortals in the right direction.

204. Catharrs] catarrh.

217. cous'ners] tricksters.

242. Epicurious] Epicurus, a Greek philosopher who taught that pleasure is the highest good. Epicurus did, in fact, also teach that the greatest pleasure is to be found in virtue (line 243), but this was not always recognised by his later followers.

271. the last Day . . . Gen'ral Doom] the Last Judgement.

In imitation of Horace

A free (and much reduced) imitation of Horace's Ode III.29.

5. the bright God] the sun.

19. ruders] rudders.

INDEX OF POETRY TITLES AND FIRST LINES

Note: square brackets denote the section in which each poem appears.

About spirituall discourse [Palmer]	*page* 174
'Afflicted England how thine ills increase,' [Ley]	82
'After long trouble in a tædious way' [Wroth]	40
'All.maried.men.desire.to.have good wifes' [Southwell]	62
Ambition [Astell]	188
'And why this vault & Tomb? alike we must' [Philips]	144
Another on the Sun Shine [Hutchinson]	100
Answeare to the Verses Mr Carey made, An [Cavendish]	91
Answer to Mercuries message anno 1641, An [Ley]	83
Arion on a Dolphin [Philips]	135
'As the Triumphant Sounds & Shewes' [Hutchinson]	107
'As when the first day dawn'd Man's greedy Eye' [Philips]	149
'Beauty, Honor, yeouth, and fortune' [Southwell]	61
'Behold the cheerfull daye shall shortly come,' [Seager]	18
Birth of Esau and Jacob, The, from [Roper?]	160
'Burning beacon, of pure love, A' [Palmer]	180
'Can Sacharissa then forsake' [Walsh]	219
Child in a strangers arms, The [Palmer]	171
Christmasse Caroll, A [Ley]	80
Cimmeria [Seager]	18
Circle, The [Pulter]	115
'Come darkest night, beecoming sorrow best;' [Wroth]	39
'Come Muse, and leave those wings that soar' [Astell]	185
'Come my Ardelia to this Bowre,' [Philips]	142
'Come now my soull, behold thy king.' [Palmer]	172
Complaint, The [Astell]	192
'Constant promises, the loving graces, The' [Sidney]	24
'Cool was the western Air, serene the Day,' [Burghope]	196
'Could Sacharissa leave the Town' [Walsh]	220
Crowne of Sonetts dedicated to Love, A [Wroth]	42
'Darest thou my muse present thy Battlike winge,' [Southwell]	62
'Dear God from thy high Throne look down' [Pulter]	122
Devills picture, The [Palmer]	180
Enemies [Astell]	187
Englands Sad Lamentation [Roper?]	165
Enquiry into the cause of the miserys of Mankind, An [Walsh]	221

EPITAPH ON HECTOR PHILLIPS [Philips]   145
'Eternall Reason, Glorious Majesty,' [Philips]   150
'Except my hart which you beestow'd before,' [Wroth]   44
experience [Palmer]   170
'Extreamly I deplore your loss' [Pulter]   121

Famines Miserie, from [Roper?]   167
'Faulce hope which feeds butt to destroy, and spill' [Wroth]   45
Following Copy Burlesq'd, The [Walsh]   219
'Fond flattring world thou ne'er shalt boast' [Walsh]   218
'Fowre brothers and a sister such I had' [Cavendish]   91
'Free from all fogs butt shining faire, and cleere' [Wroth]   44

'Go dispicable Vertue go,' [Astell]   190
[God] [Philips]   150
'Gods boundles bownties gods promise ever abyding' [Sidney]   28

'Had Lott from Wicked Sodom Gone Away' [Roper?]   158
'He that hath said, it is but yet' [Palmer]   174
'Heavens Glorie was wrapt up in Shrowds' [Hutchinson]   104
'Heavens glorious Eie which all the world surveyes' [Hutchinson]   100
'Hee that shunns love doth love him self the less' [Wroth]   43
'Here a greate Patriot lies if what the Grave' [Hutchinson]   109
Hopes preparation [Cavendish]   93
'How like a fire doth love increase in mee,' [Wroth]   41

'I did not live, untill this time' [Philips]   144
'I doe confesse great God my sinns are great' [Cavendish]   92
'I heard of one has got the start' [Palmer]   170
'I Love you whom the World calls Enemies,' [Astell]   187
'I think not on the State, nor am concern'd,' [Philips]   132
'I, who doe feele the highest part of griefe' [Wroth]   55
'If I could ever write a lasting verse' [Philips]   138
In emulation of Mr Cowleys Poem [Astell]   186
In imitation of Horace [Walsh]   227
In Memory of Mr Cartwright [Philips]   147
In memory of my Deare F:P: [Philips]   138
'In six dayes God made this admired ball,' [Southwell]   64
'In tender yeares a sacred virgine myld,' [Seager]   18
'In this blest labour may each papist see' [Ley]   81
'In this strang labourinth how shall I turne?' [Wroth]   42
'In vain the angry billows roar' [Walsh]   227
Inconstancy in Friendship [Philips]   143
Invitation, The [Astell]   185
'Is it not strange yee Powers that Mortals shoud' [Walsh]   221
'Is to leave all, and take the thread of love' [Wroth]   43
'It was a wise and kind designe of Fate,' [Philips]   148

'Joy is not Always Pure we often Finde' [Roper?]   160
'Juno still jealouse of her husband Jove' [Wroth]   41

Larke, The [Pulter]   119
'Leave of yee pittying freinds; leave of in vaine' [Hutchinson]   99
'Like to the Indians, scorched with the sunne,' [Wroth]   42
'Lo thus in breife (most sacred Majestye)' [Seager]   19
Lott His Wife and Daughters, from [Roper?]   158
'Lovely Apostate! what was my offence?' [Philips]   143

Mans Shamefull Fall, from [Roper?]   157
May 29 1669 [Roper?]   162
'Methinks I See upon the Knowledge tree' [Roper?]   157
more to the same purpose [Palmer]   174
'Most blessed time wherein we celebrate,' [Ley]   80
'Most Glorious God I Humbly Beg of thee' [Roper?]   155
'Most true god hath gyven mee the power, The' [Seager]   18
'Must then my folly's, be thy scandall too?' [Philips]   131
'My lord it is your absence makes each see' [Cavendish]   95
'My lord your absence makes I cannot owne' [Cavendish]   95
'My love life Crowne peace treasure Joys were lost' [Hutchinson]   105
'My muse now hapy, lay thy self to rest' [Wroth]   45
'My paine, still smother'd in my grieved brest,' [Wroth]   39
'My soul, in strugling thou dost Ill,' [Pulter]   115

Night, The [Hutchinson]   104
'No, No, unfaithfull World, thou hast' [Philips]   140
'Now I with gen'rous Cowley see,' [Astell]   189
'Now I'm prepared against my Lord doth come' [Cavendish]   93
'Now the Egyptians Sorely Doe Complaine' [Roper?]   167

'O fame most joyfull, o joy most lively Delightfull' [Sidney]   31
'O how happy were I dearest' [Southwell]   61
'O let our Praise ascend the Skyes' [Walsh]   217
'O what livelie delight o what a jollitie' [Sidney]   32
Ode upon Retirement [Philips]   140
'Oh what a reall comfort tis' [Palmer]   179
'Oh world, what means thy tempting charms' [Palmer]   171
On a Chamber-mayde [Cavendish]   91
On her Sacred Majestie [Cavendish]   90
On my deare Brothers and Sister. [Cavendish]   91
On my honourable Grandmother [Cavendish]   92
On the .30.th* of June, to God* [Cavendish]   93
On the double murther of the King [Philips]   132
On the Same [Pulter]   114
On the Spring 1668 [Hutchinson]   107
'Our King is Dead Laws and Religeons Gone' [Roper?]   165
Our Kings Sorrows and Suffrings [Roper?]   164

our mistakes for want of skill in the methouds of the spirit [Palmer]   176
'Our Sunne departed yet no night appeard,' [Ley]   81
Out of Mr More's Cup. Conf. [Philips]   150

Pamphilia to Amphilanthus, from [Wroth]   38
Passions Contemplation [Cavendish]   89
Perfection of Patience and knowledg, The [Pulter]   115
'Poore desolate Gardin Smile no more on me' [Hutchinson]   102
Prayer, A [Roper?]   155
Precept 4 [Southwell]   64
Psalm 75 Confitebimur [Sidney]   23
Psalm 75 Confitebimur [ii] [Sidney]   33
Psalm 89 Miserecordias [Sidney]   24
Psalm 89 Miserecordias [ii] [Sidney]   28
Psalm 113 Laudate dominum [Sidney]   34
Psalm 122 Letatus sum [Sidney]   31
Psalm 122 Letatus sum [ii] [Sidney]   32
'Publicke gladness is to us restor'd, The' [Philips]   134

Quinticens of Cordiall, The [Cavendish]   90

Rebeckahs Subtilty, from [Roper?]   161
Recovery, The [Hutchinson]   105
Retird friendship, A [Philips]   142
Rosania's private Marriage [Philips]   148
Royall Element of Fire, The [Roper?]   156

'Sad, Sick, and Lame, as in my Bed I lay' [Pulter]   117
Samia [Seager]   18
'See how Arachne doth her Howres Pass' [Pulter]   119
'Sheaphard who noe care did take, A' [Wroth]   46
Solitude [Astell]   189
Sonnett ('Beauty, Honor, yeouth, and fortune') [Southwell]   61
Sonnett ('O how happy were I dearest') [Southwell]   61
Soull by faith, triumphing over saten, The [Palmer]   179
Soull clouded, The [Palmer]   178
Soull looking att, and longing for an eternall saboath, The [Palmer]   177
Soull veiwing Christ in his humiliation, The [Palmer]   172
Souls desire, The [Palmer]   180
'Stay, Prince of Phancie, stay, we are not fit' [Philips]   147

'Table you here See presents, The' [Hutchinson]   102
'Tell mee noe more, her haire was lovly brown' [Pulter]   114
'That private shade, wherein my Muse was bred,' [Philips]   146
'Thee god, o thee, we sing we celebrate' [Sidney]   23
'Ther's nothinge more afflicts my greived soule' [Cavendish]   89
'This day I will my thankes sure now declare' [Cavendish]   93
'This Day which we in Memorie Doe Keepe' [Roper?]   162

This was written 1648, when I Lay Inn [Pulter]	117
'Those that the hidden Chimick Art profess' [Pulter]	115
'Thou lovely Bess, that art soe plumpe and young,' [Cavendish]	91
'Thrice happy he whose Name is writ above,' [Philips]	150
To Antenor On a Paper of mine [Philips]	131
To heaven, or a confession to God [Cavendish]	92
To my Excellent Lucasia [Philips]	144
To my Lord Arch-Bishop of Canterbury [Philips]	146
To Palæmon on his discourse of friendship [Philips]	133
To Sir Wm. D. [Pulter]	121
To the Gardin att O: [Hutchinson]	102
To the kinges most excellent Majestye [Southwell]	62
To the Queen's Majesty [Philips]	134
To the Queen-Mother [Philips]	136
To the Right Honourable Alice Countess of Carbury [Philips]	149
Tyburtina [Seager]	18
Upon a sermon preached in S Paules Church [Ley]	81
Upon the death of King James [Ley]	81
Upon the great plague [Ley]	82
Upon two pictures [Hutchinson]	102
Vertue [Astell]	190
Vision, The [Burghope]	196
'We fill our selfs with fear' [Palmer]	176
'We had been still undone, wrapt in disguise,' [Philips]	133
'wee o god to thee doe sing' [Sidney]	33
'Wer't not for you, I knew not how to live,' [Cavendish]	90
'What doe your thoughts begin in love to stray' [Cavendish]	91
'What dost thou mean my GOD, (said I,' [Astell]	192
'What means this sinfull. modesty' [Palmer]	174
'What Mortall Eye Can See the Imperiall Seate' [Roper?]	156
'What on Earth deserves our Trust?' [Philips]	145
'What shall I do? not to be Rich or Great,' [Astell]	186
'What Wonders were there in Our Iron Age' [Roper?]	164
'What's this that with such vigour fills my brest?' [Astell]	188
'When every one to pleasing pastime hies' [Wroth]	40
'When God (who is to Mercie most inclin'd)' [Pulter]	123
'When nights black mantle could most darknes prove,' [Wroth]	38
'When royall Fergus Line did rule this Realm' [Pulter]	126
'When shall that blessed, saboath morning dawn' [Palmer]	177
'Whie how now Martin what's the newes from hell,' [Ley]	83
'Who can but pitty this poor Turtle Dove' [Pulter]	125
'Whom does this stately Navy bring?' [Philips]	135
'Why lookst thou, with a grudging eye' [Palmer]	180
'Why turnest thou thy face away' [Palmer]	178
'Wisdom's Presented Like a Matron Grave' [Roper?]	161
Wiston Vault [Philips]	144

'Ye Sons of England whose unquenched flame' [Hutchinson] 109
'You justly may forsake a land which you' [Philips] 136
'You weare the very Magazine of rich' [Cavendish] 92
'Your lookes are Courage, mixt with such sweetenes,' [Cavendish] 90
'Yow that the life of servants doe professe' [Sidney] 34

EU authorised representative for GPSR:
Easy Access System Europe, Mustamäe tee 50,
10621 Tallinn, Estonia
gpsr.requests@easproject.com

www.ingramcontent.com/pod-product-compliance
Ingram Content Group UK Ltd.
Pitfield, Milton Keynes, MK11 3LW, UK
UKHW021836140426
5217IPUK00021B/1486